Jan Luba QC is a barrister in the housing team at Garden Court Chambers in London. He was called to the Bar in 1980 and was made Queen's Counsel in 2000. He is one of the leading authorities on housing law and practice. Jan is co-author of a number of housing law titles including *Defending Possession Proceedings* (LAG) and *Housing Allocation and Homelessness* (Jordans), and writes, with Nic Madge, the monthly series 'Recent developments in housing law' in *Legal Action*. He sits as a Recorder in the civil and criminal courts and at the Employment Appeal Tribunal.

Deirdre Forster is a solicitor and partner at Powell Forster Solicitors in London. She gained her experience of housing disrepair at Southwark Law Centre and now specialises in litigation involving disrepair, leasehold disputes and personal injury. Deirdre teaches housing law and civil litigation procedure to post-graduate university students and provides the housing disrepair training, with Beatrice Prevatt, for Legal Action Group.

Beatrice Prevatt is a barrister in the housing team at Garden Court Chambers in London. She practises in all areas of housing including disrepair. Beatrice has contributed to various housing law publications including *Landlord and Tenant Review* and *Current Law*. She writes the annual housing disrepair update for *Legal Action* and together with Deirdre Forster provides the housing disrepair training for Legal Action Group. Beatrice has also provided training for the Independent Housing Ombudsman, the Housing Law Practitioners Association and the Legal Services Commission. She is a trained mediator.

The purpose of the Legal Action Group is to promote equal access to justice for all members of society who are socially, economically or otherwise disadvantaged. To this end, it seeks to improve law and practice, the administration of justice and legal services.

Repairs
tenants' rights

FOURTH EDITION

Jan Luba QC, Deirdre Forster and
Beatrice Prevatt

Legal Action Group
2010

This edition published in Great Britain 2010
by LAG Education and Service Trust Limited
242 Pentonville Road, London N1 9UN
www.lag.org.uk

© Jan Luba QC, Deirdre Forster and Beatrice Prevatt 2010

Third edition © Stephen Knafler and Jan Luba 1999
Second edition © Jan Luba 1991
First edition © Jan Luba 1986

British Library Cataloguing in Publication Data
a CIP catalogue record for this book is available from the British Library.

Crown copyright material is produced with the permission of the
Controller of HMSO and the Queen's Printer for Scotland.

ISBN   978 1 903307 67 0

Typeset by Regent Typesetting, London.
Printed in Great Britain by Hobbs the Printer, Totton, Hampshire

Authors' note

The writing team for this fourth edition owe a great debt of thanks to Stephen Knafler who wrote much of the third edition and who has kindly allowed us to build on his material.

We would also like to thank the following family, friends and colleagues, for their invaluable support and advice: Jacqueline Everett, Tim Powell, Jane Grant, Pam Griffiths, Mel Cairns, Shaffiq Amin, Nina Tempia, Gary Monks, Sandie Dunne and Sula Dunne-Prevatt.

We very much welcome feedback from readers which can be directed to us care of the Legal Action Group where the excellent publishing team has done so much to bring this work to fruition.

The text reflects our understanding of the law of England and Wales as at the end of November 2009.

Jan Luba QC
Deirdre Forster
Beatrice Prevatt

November 2009

Contents

Authors' note   v
Table of cases   xi
Table of statutes   xxix
Table of statutory instruments   xxxiii
Table of European and international legislation   xxxvii
Abbreviations   xxxix
Introduction   xli

1   **Contractual rights   1**
Introduction   3
The contract of letting   3
Express terms   3
Meaning of 'repair' and 'disrepair'   7
Non-statutory implied terms for the benefit of tenants   13
Statutory implied terms for the benefit of tenants   18
Implied terms for the benefit of the landlord   30

2   **Rights beyond the contract   37**
Introduction   38
Common law rights   38
Statutory rights   42

3   **Civil remedies for disrepair   51**
Introduction   53
Direct action   53
Court proceedings   59

4   **Funding   95**
Legal aid   96
Before-the-event insurance   110
Conditional fee agreements   111

5   **Proceedings under the Environmental Protection Act 1990   121**
Introduction   123
Statutory nuisance   123

Action by local authorities   128
Action by tenants and other occupiers   131
Overview of procedure   134
Preparatory work   134
Procedure   135
Nuisance orders   142
Penalties   144
Compensation   145
Appeals   147
Costs   148
Environmental Protection Act 1990 and the Housing Acts   150
Note of warning   150

6   Bad housing and the Housing Act 2004   153
Introduction   154
Getting prepared to take action   155
Forms of action and their enforcement   167
Rehousing and compensation for displaced tenants   172
Council tenants   173
Conclusion   174

7   Housing conditions   175
Introduction   177
Area action   177
Asbestos   180
Asthma   182
Condensation dampness   183
Dampness (other than condensation)   188
Dangerous buildings   189
Dilapidated buildings   189
Drains and sewers   190
Fire precautions   191
Gas safety   191
Improvements   193
Multi-occupied property   194
Neighbouring property   195
Noise   195
Overcrowding   196
Refuse   197
Sanitary installations   198
Services (gas, water and electricity)   198
Vandalism   199
Vermin   199

8 Damages 201
General principles of damages awarded in contract and tort 202
Damages in disrepair cases 203
The purpose of damages 204
The approach to assessment 204
General damages 205
Special damages 210
Using the ombudsmen 214
Damages cases 214

APPENDICES

A **Legislation 229**

B **Technical information: understanding experts' reports 255**

C **Early Notification Letter (ENL) flowchart 263**

D **Precedents 265**

E *Kemp & Kemp* inflation table 291

Index 293

Table of cases

References in the right-hand column are to paragraph numbers.

Abdullah and Others v South Tyneside Borough
 Council, September 1987 *Legal Action* 12, South
 Shields County Court 7.31
Adami v Lincoln Grange Management Ltd (1997) 30
 HLR 982; [1998] 1 EGLR 58, CA 1.55
Adams v Rhymer Valley District Council (2001) 33 HLR
 446, CA 2.7
AG Securities Limited v Vaughan [1990] 1 AC 417; [1988]
 3 WLR 1205; [1988] 3 All ER 1058; (1989) 21 HLR 79;
 (1989) 57 P&CR 17; [1988] 2 EGLR 78; [1988] 47 EG
 193, HL 1.2
Al Hassani v Merrigan (1988) 20 HLR 238; [1988] 1
 EGLR 93; [1988] 03 EG 88, CA 1.105, 3.12, 3.122
Alderson v Beetham Organisation [2003] EWCA Civ 408 2.27
Alienus v Tower Hamlets LBC [1998] CLY 2987 8.85
Alexander v Mercouris [1979] 1 WLR 1270; [1979] 3 All
 ER 305; (1979) 252 EG 911, CA 2.27
Alker v Collingwood Housing Association [2007] EWCA
 Civ 343; (2007) 29 HLR 430, December 2007 *Legal*
 Action 29 1.12, 2.23, 2.34,
 2.46
American Cyanamid v Ethicon [1975] AC 396; [1975] 1
 WLR 316; [1975] 1 All ER 504, HL 3.98, 3.107
Andrews v Schooling [1991] WLR 783, CA 2.24
Anstruther-Gough-Calthorpe v McOscar [1924] 1 KB 716 1.28
Arabhalvaei v Rezaeipoor, December 2007 *Legal Action*
 30, Central London County Court 8.77
Arnold v Greenwich London Borough Council [1998]
 CLY 3518; [1998] 1 CL 383; May 1998 *Legal Action* 21,
 QBD 7.27, 8.62
Asco Developments & Newman v Lowes, Lewis and
 Gordon (1978) 248 EG 683, ChD 3.7
Aslam v Ali, December 2009 *Legal Action* 23,
 Birmingham County Court 8.80
Attica v British Gas [1988] QB 304 8.30

Ball v Plummer (1879) 23 SJ 656; (1879) *Times* 17 June,
   CA   1.83
Ball and Another v Plymouth City Council [2004] EWHC
   134 (QB); [2004] All ER (D) 38 (Feb), QBD   3.65, 7.43
Banco de Portugal v Waterlow & Sons Ltd [1932] AC 452;
   [1932] All ER Rep 181, HL, *On appeal from* (1931) 100
   LJKB 465; 47 TLR 359, CA, *On appeal from* (1930) 47
   TLR 214, KBD   8.44
Barclays Bank plc v Fairclough Building Ltd (No 2) 44
   Con LR 35; 76 BLR 1; [1995] IRLR 605; [1995] EGCS
   10; (1997) *Times* 15 February, CA   7.16
Barrett v Lounova (1982) Ltd [1990] 1 QB 348; [1989] 1
   All ER 351; [1988] 2 EGLR 54, CA   1.54, 1.55, 2.47,
                                                            3.161, 3.171

Bayoumi v Protim Services Ltd (1996) 30 HLR 785   2.26
Bell v Mazehead Ltd, March 1996 *Legal Action* 14,
   Shoreditch County Court   8.65
Berg v Trafford Borough Council (1988) 20 HLR 47, CA   7.63
Berryman v Houndslow LBC (1996) 30 HLR 567, CA   8.8
Billings (AC) & Sons v Riden [1958] AC 240; [1957] 3
   WLR 496; [1957] 3 All ER 1; HL   2.8
Bird v Greville (1884) Cab & El 317, QBD   1.40
Birmingham CC v Lee, *see* Lee v Birmingham City
   Council
Birmingham City Council v Oakley [2001] 1 AC 617;
   [2001] 1 All ER 385; [2000] UKHL 59, HL, *Reversing*
   (1998) 31 HLR 1070; [1999] Env LR D17, DC   5.3, 5.7, 5.11
Birmingham District Council v Kelly and Others (1985)
   17 HLR 572; [1986] 2 EGLR 239, QBD   5.82, 5.84–5.86,
                                                            7.37

Birmingham District Council v McMahon and Others
   (1987) 19 HLR 452; (1988) 86 LGR 63, QBD   5.8
Bishop Auckland Local Board v Bishop Auckland Iron
   and Steel Co Ltd (1883) 10 QBD 138   5.20
Bishop v Consolidated London Properties (1933) 102
   LJKB 257   1.36, 1.108
Boldack v East Lindsay District Council (1988) 31 HLR
   41, CA   2.37, 2.44
Bond v Chief Constable of Kent [1983] 1 WLR 40; [1983]
   1 All ER 456, DC   5.93
Booth v Thomas [1926] Ch 397   1.48
Boswell v Crucible Steel Co of America [1925] 1 KB 119;
   94 LJKB 383; [1924] All ER Rep 298, CA   1.83
Botross v Hammersmith and Fulham London Borough
   Council (1994) 27 HLR 179; (1995) 93 LGR 269;
   [1995] COD 169; [1994] NPC 134, DC   5.49, 5.93
Bowen v Bridgend [2004] EWHC 9010 (Costs) 25 March
   2004   4.76

Bradley v Chorley Borough Council (1985) 17 HLR 305;
[1985] 2 EGLR 49; (1985) 275 EG 801; (1985) 83 LGR
628, CA   1.29
Brent London Borough Council v Carmel (sued as
Murphy) (1995) 28 HLR 203, CA   8.24, 8.56
Brew Bros Ltd v Snax (Ross) [1970] 1 QB 612; [1969] 3
WLR 657; [1970] 1 All ER 587; (1970) 20 P&CR 829,
CA   1.19
Brikom Investments v Seaford [1981] 1 WLR 863; [1981]
2 All ER 783; (1982) 1 HLR 21; (1981) 42 P&CR 190;
(1981) 258 EG 750, CA   1.99
British Anzani (Felixstowe) Ltd v International Marine
Management (UK) Ltd [1980] QB 637; [1979] 3 WLR
451; [1979] 2 All ER 1063; (1978) 39 P&CR 189;
(1978) 250 EG 1183, QBD   3.13
British Telecommunications plc v Sun Life Assurance
Society plc [1996] Ch 69; [1995] 3 WLR 622; [1995] 4
All ER 44; (1997) 73 P&CR 475; [1995] 2 EGLR 44;
[1995] 45 EG 133; [1995] NPC 140, CA   1.105, 1.108
Brongard Ltd v Sowerby, December 2007 *Legal Action* 29,
Manchester County Court   8.75
Brown v Biggleswade Union (1879) 43 JP 554   5.87
Brown v Liverpool Corporation [1969] 3 All ER 1345;
(1984) 13 HLR 1, CA   1.83
Brunskill v Mulcahy [2009] EWCA Civ 686   1.77
Budd v Colchester Borough Council [1999] LGR 601;
[1999] JPL 717; [1999] All ER (D) 218; (1999) *Times* 14
April, CA   5.26
Buswell v Goodwin [1971] 1 WLR 92; [1971] 1 All ER 418;
(1971) 22 P&CR 162; (1971) 69 LGR 201, CA   1.67
Bygraves v Southwark LBC (1990) Kemp & Kemp, para
F2-035/2   8.82

C (a minor) v Hackney London Borough Council [1996]
1 All ER 973, CA   8.35
Calabar Properties Ltd v Stitcher [1984] 1 WLR 287;
[1983] 3 All ER 759; (1984)11 HLR 20; (1983) 268 EG
697, CA   1.106, 8.12, 8.15,
                                                                 8.33, 8.34, 8.38,
                                                                 8.40
Camden Nominees v Forcey [1940] Ch 352   3.11
Camden London Borough Council v Gunby [1999] 4 All
ER 602; [2000] 1 WLR 465; 32 HLR 572, QBD   5.28
Campden Hill Towers v Gardner [1977] QB 823; [1977] 2
WLR 159; [1977] 1 All ER 739; (1976) 13 HLR 64;
(1976) 34 P&CR 175; (1976) 242 EG 375, CA   1.84, 1.90, 1.91
Canterbury City Council v Ferris [1997] Env LR 14;
[1997] JPL B45, DC   5.91

Cardiff City Council v Cross, *see* R v Cardiff City Council
    ex p Cross
Carmel Southend Ltd v Strachen and Henshaw [2007]
    EWHC 1289 (TCC)   1.35
Carr v Hackney London Borough Council Positive
    treatment indicated(1995) 93 LGR 606; 160 JP 402;
    28 HLR 749, QBD   5.81
Carr v Leeds City Council, Wells and Coles v Barnsley
    Metropolitan BC (1999) 32 HLR 753; [2000] COD 10;
    [1999] All ER (D) 1117; (2000) 32 HLR 753, DC   5.105
Cavalier v Pope [1906] AC 428, HL   1.37, 2.3
Charalambous v Earle (Addendum to Judgment) [2006]
    EWCA Civ 1338; (2006) *Times* 15 November; [2006]
    All ER (D) 147 (Oct); [2007] HLR 8, CA   1.108–1.110
Chester v Powell (1885) 52 LT 722   1.40
Chin v Hackney London Borough Council [1996] 1 FCR
    653; 28 HLR 423; [1996] All ER 973, CA   3.47
Chiodi *see* Personal Representatives of Chiodi v De
    Marney
Churchill v Nottingham County Council, January 2001
    Legal Action 25, Nottingham County Court   1.119
City and Metropolitan Properties v Greycroft [1987] 1
    WLR 1085; [1987] 3 All ER 839; (1987) 19 HLR 458;
    (1987) 54 P&CR 266; [1987] 2 EGLR 47; (1987) 283
    EG 199, Ch D   8.34
Clark v Wandsworth LBC, June 1994 *Legal Action* 15   8.91
Clarke (Kathleen) v Taff Ely Borough Council (1980) 10
    HLR 44, QBD   2.40
Cockburn v Smith [1924] 2 KB 119   1.46, 2.10
Cocker v Cardwell (1869) LR 5 QB 15   5.24, 5.44
Cody v Philps, December 2005 *Legal Action* 28; *Housing
    Law Casebook*, para P12.11, West London County   1.9, 3.8, 3.118,
    Court   8.72
Collins v Hopkins [1923] 2 KB 617   1.40
Collins v Northern Ireland Housing Executive [1987] 2
    NIJB 27 CA(NI)   1.52
Conroy v Hire Token Ltd, February 2002 *Legal Action* 22   8.86
Cook v Southend Borough Council [1990] 2 QB 1; [1990]
    2 WLR 61; [1990] 1 All ER 243; (1990) 88 LGR 408;
    [1990] COD 120; (1989) 11 CL 323, CA   5.99
Coventry City Council v Cartwright [1975] 1 WLR 845;
    [1975] 2 All ER 99; (1975) 73 LGR 218, DC   5.14, 5.20
Coventry City Council v Doyle [1981] 1 WLR 1325; [1981]
    2 All ER 184, DC   5.7, 5.64, 5.82
Crawford v Newton (1886) 2 TLR 877, CA   5.82
Credit Suisse v Beegas Nominees Ltd [1994] 4 All ER
    804; [1995] 69 P&CR 177; [1994] 1 EGLR 76; [1994]
    11 EG 151; [1993] NPC 123, Ch D   8.19, 8.34

Crook v Birmingham City Council [2007] EWHC 1415
(Admin); [2007] NLJR 939; [2007] All ER (D) 191
(Jun)   4.76
Cunningham v Birmingham City Council [1997] EWHC
Admin 44; (1997) 96 LGR 231; 30 HLR 158; [1998]
Env LR 1   5.13

D & F Estates Ltd v Church Commissioners for England
[1989] AC 177; [1988] 3 WLR 368; [1988] 2 All ER
992; [1988] 2 EGLR 263, HL   2.11, 2.12
Dadd v Christian Action (Enfield) Housing Association,
December 1994 *Legal Action* 18, Central London
County Court   8.93
Dame Margaret Hungerford Charity Trustees v Beazeley
(1994) 26 HLR 269; [1993] 2 EGLR 143; [1993] EG
100; [1993] NPC 71, CA   1.35, 1.96
Dashwood v Dashwood [1927] WN 276; 64 LJNC 431,
ChD   3.129
Davenport v Walsall Metropolitan Borough Council
(1995) 28 HLR 754; [1996] Env LR D33, DC   5.95, 5.103
Davies v Peterson (1989) 21 HLR 63; [1989] 06 EG 130,
CA   8.19, 8.55
Dear v Newham London Borough Council (1988) 20
HLR 348, CA, *On appeal from* (1987) 19 HLR 391,
QBD   2.21, 7.90
Dear v Thames Water plc (1994) 33 Con LR 43   7.54, 7.55
Demetriou v Poolaction Ltd [1991] 1 EGLR 100; [1991] 25
EG 113; (1990) 63 P&CR 536, CA   1.55
Dent v Haringey LBC, December 1999 *Legal Action* 18;
Housing Law Casebook, para P16.38, Wood Green
Crown Court   5.15
Department of Environment v Thomas Bates & Son
[1991] 1 AC 499; [1990] 3 WLR 457; [1990] 2 All ER
943, HL, *On appeal from* [1989] 1 All ER 1075, CA,
Affirming (1987) 13 ConLR 1, QBD   2.11
Department of Transport v Egoroff (1986) 18 HLR 326,
CA   1.98
Designer Guild Ltd v Russel Williams (Textiles) Ltd
(trading as Washington DC), (2) [2003] EWHC 9024
(Costs), 20 February 2003, SCCO   4.85
Dinefwr Borough Council v Jones (1987) 19 HLR 445;
[1987] 2 EGLR 88; (1987) 284 EG 58, CA   1.103, 1.104
Director General of Fair Trading v First National Bank
plc [2001] UKHL 52; [2002] 1 All ER 97   1.8
Director of Public Prosecutions v Carrick (1985) 31
Housing Aid 5   7.88
Dobson v Thames Water Utilities [2009] EWCA Civ 28;
[2009] 3 All ER 319, CA   2.18, 2.56

Dodd Properties (Kent) Ltd v Canterbury City Council
[1980] 1 WLR 433; [1980] 1 All ER 928; (1979) 253 EG
1335, CA   8.11, 8.13, 8.44
Douglas-Scott v Scorgie [1984] 1 WLR 716; [1984] 1 All
ER 1086; (1984) 13 HLR 97; (1984) 48 P&CR 109;
(1984) 269 EG 1164, CA   1.84
Dover District Council v Farrar (1982) 2 HLR 32, DC   5.81, 7.33–7.36
Duke of Westminster v Guild [1985] QB 688; [1984] 3
WLR 630; [1984] 3 All ER 144; (1984) P&CR 42;
(1983) 267 EG 763, CA   1.45, 1.46, 1.50,
                                                        1.51, 2.10
Dunn v Bradford Metropolitan District Council [2002]
EWCA Civ 1137; [2003] HLR 154   2.45, 7.72
Dunster v Hollis [1918] 2 KB 795   1.46, 1.65

Earl v Charalambous [2006] EWCA Civ 1090; [2007]
HLR 8, CA   8.27, 8.29, 8.60
East Staffordshire Borough Council v Fairless (1998) 31
HLR 677; [1998] EGCS 140; [1998] All ER (D) 456;
EWHC 954 (Admin), DC   5.56, 5.57
Edlington Properties Ltd v JH Fenner & Co Ltd [2006]
EWCA Civ 403; [2006] 3 All ER 1200, CA *Affirming*
[2005] EWHC 2158 (QB); [2006] 1 All ER 98, QBD   3.16, 3.118
Edmonton Corporation v Knowles [1962] 60 LGR 124,
QBD   1.52
Edwards v Etherington (1825) Ry & M 268   1.40
Elmcroft Development v Tankersley-Sawyer (1984) 15
HLR 63; [1984] 1 EGLR 47; (1984) 270 EG 140, CA   1.23, 1.26, 1.32
Empson v Forde [1990] 1 EGLR 131; [1990] 18 EG 99, CA   8.45
English Churches Housing Group v Shine [2004] EWCA
Civ 434; [2004] HLR 42   8.21, 8.45, 8.46,
                                                        8.57, 8.59, 8.69
Evans v Clayhope Properties [1988] 1 WLR 358; [1988] 1
All ER 444; (1988) 20 HLR 176; [1988] 1 EGLR 33;
[1988] 03 EG 95, CA   3.19
Eyre v McCracken (2001) 33 HLR 169, CA   1.24, 1.26

Fadeyeva v Russia, October 2005 *Legal Action* 18, ECHR 2.55
Ferguson v Jones, December 2008 *Legal Action* 32,
Birmingham County Court   8.79
Fincar SRL v 109/113 Mount Street Management Co Ltd
[1998] EGCS 173; [1998] All ER (D) 636, CA   1.83
Fisher v Walters [1926] 2 KB 315   1.64
Forde v Birmingham City Council [2009] EWHC 12
(QB); [2009] All ER (D) 64 (Jan), QBD   4.74, 4.84
Francis v Cowliffe Ltd (1976) 239 EG 977; 33 P&CR 368,
DC   3.164

Goldmile Properties Ltd v Speiro Lechouritis [2003]
EWCA Civ 49; [2003] All ER (D) 278 (Jan), CA   1.50

Gordon and Texeira v Selico Ltd and Select
    Managements Ltd (1986) 18 HLR 219; [1986] 1 EGLR
    71; (1986) 278 EG 53, CA   1.47, 1.48, 2.14,
                                                        8.34
Gorman and Lane v Lambeth LBC, December 2009
    Legal Action 23, Lambeth County Court   8.81
Governors of the Peabody Trust v Reeve [2008] EWHC
    1432 (Ch); [2008] 43 EG 196, Ch D   1.8
Granada Theatres Ltd v Freehold Investment
    (Leytonstone) [1959] Ch 592; [1959] 1 WLR 570;
    [1959] 2 All ER 176, CA   1.83, 1.113, 8.45
Great Western Rly v Bishop (1872) LR 7 QB 550   5.20
Greater London Council v Tower Hamlets, *see* Tower
    Hamlets London Borough Council v Greater London
    Council
Green v Eales [1841] 2 QB 225   1.83
Greene v Chelsea Borough Council [1954] 2 QB 127;
    [1954] 3 WLR 12; [1954] 2 All ER 318; (1954) 52 LGR
    352, CA   1.44
Greg v Planque [1936] 1 KB 669   1.36
Griffen v Pillet [1926] 1 KB 117   1.105
Guerra v Italy (Application 14967/89) (1998) 26 EHRR
    357; 4 BHRC 63, ECtHR   2.51
Guinan v Enfield London Borough Council, June 1990
    Legal Action 16, Westminster County Court   7.83
Guppys (Bridport) Ltd v Brookling (1983) 14 HLR 1;
    [1984] 1 EGLR 29; 269 *Estates Gazette* 846, 942, CA 2.14

Habinteg Housing Association v James (1994) 27 HLR
    299, CA   2.15
Hadley v Baxendale (1854) 9 Exch 341   8.7
Hall v Howard (1988) 20 HLR 566; [1988] 2 EGLR 75,
    CA   1.104
Hallet v Camden LBC, August 1994 *Legal Action* 17,
    Central London County Court   8.64
Hammersmith London Borough Council v Magnum
    Automated Forecourts [1978] 1 WLR 50; [1977] 1 All
    ER 401; (1977) 76 LGR 159, CA   5.99
Harbutt's Plasticine Ltd v Wayne Tank and Pump Co Ltd
    [1970] 1 QB 447; [1970] 1 All ER 225; [1970] 2 WLR
    198, CA   8.39
Haringey London Borough Council v Jowett [1999] LGR
    667; 78 P & CR D24; (2000) 32 HLR 308; [1999] All
    ER (D) 420, DC   5.20
Harrison v Malet [1886] 3 TLR 58   1.39, 1.40
Hart v Windsor (1844) 12 M & W 68   1.38
Hatfield v Moss [1988] 40 EG 112; [1988] 2 EGLR 58, CA 1.84
Heffernan v Hackney Borough Council [2009] EWCA
    Civ 665; [2009] All ER (D) 75 (Jul), CA   3.38

Herbert v Lambeth London Borough Council (1992) 13
    Cr App R(S) 489; (1991) 24 HLR 299; (1994) 90 LGR
    310, DC   5.93
Hewitt v Rowlands (1924) 93 LJKB 729   8.14
Hillbank Properties v Hackney London Borough Council
    [1978] QB 998; [1978] 3 WLR 260; [1978] 3 All ER
    343; (1982) 3 HLR 73; (1978) 37 P&CR 218; (1978)
    247 EG 807; (1978) 76 LGR 677, CA   6.7
Hilton v Hopwood (1899) 44 SJ 96   5.62
Holding & Barnes plc v Hill House Hammond [2001]
    EWCA Civ 1334; [2002] L&TR 7   1.13
Holding & Management Ltd v Property Holding &
    Investment Trust Ltd [1989] 1 WLR 1313; [1990] 1 All
    ER 938; (1989) 21 HLR 596; [1990] 1 EGLR 65; [1990]
    05 EG 75, CA   1.24, 1.30
Holiday Fellowship Ltd v Viscount Hereford [1959] 1
    WLR 211; [1959] 1 All ER 433, CA   1.83
Hollins v Russell, *see* Sharratt v London Central Bus Co
    Ltd
Hopwood v Cannock Chase District Council (formerly
    Rugeley Urban District Council) [1975] 1 WLR 373;
    [1975] 1 All ER 796; (1974) 13 HLR 31; (1974) 29
    P&CR 1256, CA   1.83
Horrex v Pidwell [1958] CLY 1461   1.64
Hudson v Royal London Borough Council of Kensington
    and Chelsea (1986) (unreported); noted in December
    1985 *Legal Action* 171, Bloomsbury and Marylebone
    County Court   7.99
Hughes v Kingston upon Hull City Council [1999] QB
    1193; [1999] 2 All ER 49; [1998] All ER (D) 563, QBD   5.104
Hunter v Canary Wharf Ltd [1997] AC 655; [1997] 2 WLR
    684; [1997] 2 All ER 526, HL   2.18
Hussein v Mehlman [1992] 2 EGLR 87; [1992] 32 EG 59,
    Wood Green Trial Centre   1.80, 8.19
Hyde Southbank Homes v Oronkaye and Obadaria,
    December 2005 *Legal Action* 28, Bow County Court   1.81

Ibrahim v Dovecorn Reversions Ltd (2001) 82 P & CR 362;
    [2001] 2 EGLR 46; [2001] All ER (D) 106 (Mar), Ch D   1.84
Irvine v Moran [1991] 24 HLR 1; [1991] 1 EGLR 261, QBD   1.29, 1.73, 1.79,
                                                                    1.80, 1.83
Islington LBC v Keane December 2005 *Legal Action* 28,
    Clerkenwell County Court   1.7, 1.73, 1.118
Issa v Hackney London Borough Council, *sub nom*
    Hackney London Borough Council v Issa [1997] 1 All
    ER 999, [1997] 1 WLR 956, 95 LGR 671, CA   5.98

Jackson v Horizon Holidays Ltd [1975] 1 WLR 1468;
    [1975] 3 All ER 92, CA   3.45, 3.48, 8.35

Jackson v JH Watson Property Investment Ltd [2008]
EWHC 14 (Ch); [2008] 1 P & CR D45, Ch D;
December 2008 *Legal Action* 31 — 2.16
Jarvis v Swans Tours Ltd [1973] QB 233; [1973] 1 All ER
71; [1972] 3 WLR 954, CA — 3.45, 8.35
Jeune v Queens Cross Properties Ltd [1974] Ch 97; [1973] 3
WLR 378; [1973] 3 All ER 97; (1973) 26 P&CR 98, Ch D — 3.161
Johnson v Sheffield CC, August 1994 *Legal Action* 16;
[1994] CLY 1445, Sheffield County Court — 1.15, 7.27
Johnstone v Charlton and Taylor, May 1998 *Legal Action*
21, Sunderland County Court — 1.99
Jones v Public Trustee, September 1988 *Legal Action* 21,
Hastings Magistrates' Court — 5.58
Jordan v Achara (1988) 20 HLR 607, CA — 2.21

Ketteman v Hansel Properties Ltd [1987] AC 189; [1988]
1 All ER 38, HL, *On appeal from* [1985] 1 All ER 352;
[1984] 1 WLR 1274, CA, *On appeal from* (1983) 12
Con LR 16, HL — 3.42
Khadija Ali v Bristol CC [2007] 15 May, Bristol RPT (ref:
CH1/00HB/HPO/2007/005) — 6.65
King v South Northamptonshire District Council (1992)
24 HLR 284; (1991) 64 P&CR 35; [1992] 1 EGLR 53;
[1992] 06 EG 152, CA — 1.45, 2.43

L (a child) v Empire Estates (2002) 6 QR 13 — 8.87, 8.89
Lagden v O'Connor [2003] UKHL 64; [2004] 1 AC 1067 — 8.39
Lambeth London Borough Council v Stubbs [1980] JPL
517; (1980) 255 EG 789; (1980)78 LGR 650, DC — 5.64
Larkos v Cyprus (1999) 7 BHRC 244; [1998] EHRLR 653 — 1.98
Law v Hillingdon London Borough Council, December
1989 *Legal Action* 16, Isleworth Crown Court — 7.36
Lawton v East Devon District Council (1982)
(unreported); noted at *Roof* July/August 1982 p28 — 7.35
Lee v Birmingham City Council [2008] EWCA Civ 891;
[2008] NLJR 1180; [2008] All ER (D) 423 (Jul), CA — 3.52
Lee v Leeds CC [2002] EWCA Civ 6; [2002] 1 WLR 1488 — 1.43, 1.55, 2.46,
2.52–2.54, 3.48
Lee-Parker v Izzet [1971] 1 WLR 1688; [1971] 3 All ER
1099; (1971) P&CR 1098, ChD — 3.4
Lips v Older [2004] EWHC 1686 (QB); [2004] All ER (D)
168 (Jun), QBD — 2.10, 8.30, 8.47
Lister v Lane [1893] 2 QB 212, CA — 1.12, 1.24
Liverpool CC v Irwin [1977] AC 239; [1976] 2 All ER 39;
(1976) 13 HLR 38, HL — 1.45, 1.53, 1.87,
7.91
Lloyd v Rees [1996] CLY 3725, Pontypridd County Court — 7.29
Long v Southwark LBC [2002] EWCA Civ 403; [2002]
HLR 56 — 1.16, 7.91, 8.58

Lopez Ostra v Spain (Application 16798/90) (1994) 20
    EHRR 277, ECtHR   2.51
Loria v Hammer [1989] EGCS 126; [1989] 2 EGLR 249,
    ChD   1.108
Lubren v LB Lambeth (1988) 20 HLR 165, CA   8.29, 8.54
Lurcott v Wakeley and Wheeler [1911] 1 KB 905; [1911-13]
    All ER Rep 41, CA   1.18

McAuley v Bristol City Council [1992] QB 134; [1992] 1
    All ER 749; (1991) 23 HLR 586; [1991] 2 EGLR 64;
    [1991] 46 EG 155; (1991) 89 LGR 931; (1991) NPC 81,
    CA   1.115, 2.46, 7.72
McCaffrey v Lambeth LBC, August 1994 *Legal Action* 18;
    Kemp & Kemp para F2-0245/3, Wandsworth County
    Court   8.83
McCall v Abelesz [1976] QB 585, CA   8.35
McClean v Liverpool City Council (1988) 20 HLR 25;
    [1987] 2 EGLR 56; (1987) 283 EG 1395, CA   1.96
McCoy v Clarke (1982) 13 HLR 89, CA   8.18, 8.30
McDougall v Easington District Council (1989) 21 HLR
    310; (1989) 58 P&CR 201; [1989] 1 EGLR 93; (1989)
    87 LGR 527, CA   1.25, 1.26, 1.29,
                                                             1.30, 1.111, 7.72
McGourlick v Renfrew District Council (1982)
    (unreported); noted at [1982] *Scolag* 182; [1986]
    Scolag 83 Paisley Sheriff Court   7.35
McGreal v Wake (1984) 13 HLR 107; (1984) 269 EG 1254,
    CA   1.29, 1.104, 1.114,
                                                             7.72, 8.38
McGuigan v Southwark LBC, March 1996 *Legal Action*
    14, Central London County Court   8.92
McMinn v Bole & Van den Haak v Huntsbuild Ltd &
    Money [2009] EWCA Civ 1149   1.41, 2.23
McNerney v LB Lambeth (1989) 21 HLR 188; [1989] 1
    EGLR 81; [1989] 19 EG 77, CA   1.37, 2.3, 2.37
McPhail v Islington London Borough Council [1970] 2
    WLR 583; [1970] 1 ALL ER 1004, CA   5.44
Makin v Watkinson (1870) LR 6 Ex 25   1.100
Marcic v Thames Water Utilities Ltd [2003] UKHL 66;
    [2004] 2 AC 42, *Reversing* [2002] EWCA Civ 64;
    [2002] QB 929, CA, *Reversing in part* [2001] 3 All ER
    698, Tech & Constr Ct   2.56
Margereson v JW Roberts Ltd; Hancock v JW Roberts
    Ltd; Hancock v T&N Plc [1996] PIQR P358; [1996]
    Env LR 304; (1996) *Times*, 17 April, CA   7.16
Marlborough Park Services Ltd v Rowe and Another
    [2006] EWCA Civ 436; [2006] HLR 30; [2006] All ER
    (D) 91 (Mar), CA   1.83

Marshall v Rubypoint (1997) 29 HLR 850, CA   8.4, 8.8
Melles & Co v Holme [1918] 2 KB 100   1.36, 1.108
Middlemast v Hammersmith and Fulham LBC, *Housing
    Law Casebook*, para P16.48, West London County
    Court   3.43, 5.97
Millard v Wastall [1898] 1 QB 342   5.26
Miller v Emcer Products [1956] Ch 304; [1956] 2 WLR
    267; [1956] 1 All ER 237, CA   1.45
Miller-Mead v Minister of Housing and Local
    Government [1963] 2 QB 196; [1962] 2 WLR 284;
    [1963] 1 All ER 459; (1963) 14 P&CR 266; (1963) 61
    LGR 152, CA   5.35
Millington v Islington BC, August 1999 *Legal Action* 25;
    Housing Law Casebook, para P1.6, Clerkenwell
    County Court   3.43
Minchburn Ltd v Peck (1988) 20 HLR 392; [1988] 1
    EGLR 53, CA   1.109, 8.42, 8.52
Mira v Aylmer Square Investments Ltd (1990) 22 HLR
    182; [1990] 1 EGLR 45; [1990] 22 EG 61, CA, *On
    appeal from* (1989) 21 HLR 284, QBD   1.48, 8.8, 8.33
Montoya v Hackney London Borough Council,
    December 2005 *Legal Action* 28   1.95
Morcom v Campbell-Johnson [1956] 1 QB 106; [1955] 3
    WLR 497; [1955] 3 All ER 264, CA   1.19
Morgan v Liverpool Corporation [1927] 2 KB 131, CA   1.66
Morgan and Daniels v Birmingham County Council,
    December 2007 *Legal Action* 29, Birmingham
    County Court   1.81
Morley v Knowsley BC, May 1988, *Legal Action* 22, CA   2.39
Morris v Liverpool City Council (1988) 20 HLR 498;
    [1988] 1 EGLR 47; (1988) 14 EG 59, CA   1.100, 1.107, 7.98
Morris-Thomas v Petticoat Lane Rentals Ltd (1987) 53
    P&CR 238, CA   1.44
MSA v Croydon LBC [2009] EWHC 2474 (Admin)   3.165, 3.171
Murphy v Brentwood District Council [1991] 1 AC 398;
    [1990] 3 WLR 414; [1990] 2 All ER 908; (1990) 22
    HLR 502; (1990) 89 LGR 24, HL   2.5, 2.11, 2.26
Murphy and Peers v Stockport, August 2002 *Legal Action*
    27, Stockport County Court   2.18, 3.48
Murray v Birmingham City Council (1988) 20 HLR 39;
    [1987] 2 EGLR 53; (1987) 283 EG 962, CA   1.35
Murray v Kelly, December 2008 *Legal Action* 31   8.78
Muscat v Smith [2003] EWCA Civ 962; [2003] 1 WLR
    2853; [2004] HLR 65, CA   3.16
Mzae v Abigo, November 2004 *Legal Action* 29   8.69

National Coal Board v Neath Borough Council [1976] 1
    WLR 543; [1976] 2 All ER 478, DC   5.16

National Coal Board v Thorne [1976] 1 WLR 543; (1976)
74 LGR 429, DC   5.19
Nelson v Liverpool Brewery Co (1877) 2 CPD 311   2.17
Network Housing Association v Westminster CC (1995)
27 HLR 189; (1995) LGR 280; [1994] EGCS 173, DC   5.26, 5.84
New Haverford Partnership v Stroot [2001] 772 Atl Rep
(2nd) 792 Del; November 2003 *Legal Action* 13,
Supreme Court of Delaware   1.22
Newham London Borough Council v Patel (1978) 13
HLR 77, CA   1.96, 8.26
Niazi Services Ltd v Van der Loo [2004] EWCA Civ 53;
[2004] 1 WLR 1254; [2004] All ER (D) 139 (Feb), CA   1.81, 1.91
North British Housing Association Ltd v Matthews;
London and Quadrant Housing Ltd v Morgan [2004]
EWCA Civ 1736; [2005] 2 All ER 667; [2005] HLR 17;
[2004] All ER (D) 344 (Dec)   3.17
Northern Ireland Trailers v Preston County Borough
[1972] 1 WLR 203; [1972] 1 All ER 260, DC   5.99
Nottingham Corporation v Newton [1974] 2 All ER 760,
QBD   5.85

O'Brien v Robinson [1973] AC 912; [1973] 2 WLR 393;
[1973] 1 All ER 583; (1973) 13 HLR 7; (1973) 25
P&CR 239, HL   1.100, 1.101, 1.105
O'Connor v Old Etonian Housing Association Ltd [2002]
EWCA Civ 150; [2002] Ch 295; [2002] 2 All ER 101,
CA, *Reversing* (2001) 82 P & CR 378; [2001] All ER
(D) 118 (Feb, Ch D)   1.88
Ogunlowo v Southwark LBC, December 2005 *Legal
Action* 29; *Housing Law Casebook*, para P16.44,
Camberwell Magistrates' Court   5.15, 5.101
O'Toole v Knowsley Metropolitan Borough Council
(2000) 32 HLR 420; (1999) *Times*, 21 May, QBD   5.53

Palmer v Sandwell Metropolitan Borough Council (1988)
20 HLR 74; [1987] 2 EGLR 79; (1987) 284 EG 1487, CA   1.11, 1.80
Pamplin v Express Newspapers Ltd [1985] 2 All ER 185;
[1985] 1 WLR 689, QBD   4.98
Parker v Camden London Borough Council [1986] Ch
162; [1985] 3 WLR 47; [1985] 2 All ER 141; (1985) 17   3.19, 3.99, 3.101,
HLR 380; (1985) 84 LGR 16, CA   3.102, 3.171
Passley v Wandsworth LBC (1998) 30 HLR 165, CA   1.36, 1.108, 1.109
Patel v Mehtab (1982) 5 HLR 78, QBD   5.55, 7.33
Pearlman v Keepers and Governors of Harrow School
[1979] QB 56; [1978] 3 WLR 736; [1979] 1 All ER 365;
(1978) 38 P&CR 136; (1978) 247 EG 1173, CA   1.79
Pembery v Lamdin [1940] 2 All ER 434, CA   1.12
Perestrello e Companhia Limitada v United Paint Co
[1969] 3 All ER 479, CA   8.35

Personal Representatives of Chiodi v De Marney (1988)
  21 HLR 6; [1988] 41 EG 80, CA   8.19, 8.20, 8.53
Petersson v Pitt Place (Epsom) Ltd [2001] EWCA Civ 86;
  [2002] HLR 52   1.13
Phillips v Symes; Symes v Phillips [2004] EWHC 2330
  (Ch); [2005] 4 All ER 519; [2004] All ER (D) 270
  (Oct), Ch D   3.147
Pierce v Westminster CC, July 2001 *Legal Action* 27   8.67
Pirachia v Mavadia, December 2007 *Legal Action 30*,
  Lambeth County Court   8.26, 8.76
Pirelli General Cable Works Ltd v Oscar Faber &
  Partners [1983] 2 AC 1; [1983] 1 All ER 65, HL,
  Reversing (1982) 262 *Estates Gazette* 879, CA   3.42
Plough Investments Ltd v Manchester City Council;
  Same v Eclipse Radio & Television Services [1989] 1
  EGLR 244; [1989] EGCS 1   1.24
Post Office v Aquarius Properties Ltd [1987] 1 All ER
  1055; (1987) 54 P&CR 61; [1987] 1 EGLR 40; (1987)
  281 EG 798, CA   1.20, 1.21
Proudfoot v Hart (1890) 25 QBD 42   1.12, 1.76

Quick v Taff Ely Borough Council [1986] 1 QB 809;
  [1985] 3 WLR 981; [1985] 3 All ER 321; (1986) 18
  HLR 66; [1985] 2 EGLR 50; (1985) 276 EG 152, CA   1.20, 1.23, 1.34,
                                                                1.60, 1.78, 1.80,
                                                                2.52, 7.30
Quigley v Liverpool Housing Trust [1999] EWHC 593
  (Admin), QBD   5.70

R v Amey; R v Meah [1983] 1 WLR 346; [1983] 1 All ER
  865, CA   5.93
R v Birmingham City District Council ex p Sale (1983) 9
  HLR 33; (1984) 48 P&CR 270; (1983) 82 LGR 69,
  QBD   6.67
R v Birmingham City Council ex p Ireland [1999] 2 All
  ER 609; 31 HLR 1078; [1999] EGCS 4, QBD   5.56
R v Brent London Borough Council ex p Blatt (1991) 24
  HLR 319; [1991] NPC 134, DC   1.11
R v Bristol City Council ex p Everett [1999] 2 All ER 193;
  [1999] 1 WLR 1170, CA, *Affirming* [1998] 3 All ER
  603; [1999] 1 WLR 92, QBD   5.11
R v Bristol Corp ex p Hendy [1974] 1 WLR 498; [1974] 1
  All ER 1047; (1973) 27 P&CR 180; (1973) 72 LGR
  405, CA   6.75
R v Cardiff City Council ex p Cross (1982) 81 LGR 105, 6
  HLR 1; [1982] RVR 270; [1983] JPL 245, CA,
  Affirming (1981) 45 P & CR 156; 1 HLR 54; [1981]
  RVR 155; [1981] JPL 748, QBD   5.45, 6.77
R v Chappell [1984] Crim LR 574, CA   5.93

R v Cooper [1982] Crim LR 308, CA   5.93
R v Dorton [1988] Crim LR 254, CA   5.93
R v Dudley Magistrates' Court ex p Hollis [1998] 1 All
    ER 759; [1999] 1 WLR 642; 30 HLR 902; [1998] 18 EG
    133, QBD   5.59, 5.68, 5.99
R v East Hertfordshire District Council ex p Smith
    (1991) 23 HLR 26; (1991) 155 LG Rev 67, CA, *On
    appeal From* (1990) 22 HLR 176, QBD   6.75
R v Enfield Justices ex p Whittle, June 1993 *Legal Action*
    15; *Housing Law Casebook*, para P16.30, DC   5.107
R v Epping (Waltham Abbey) JJ ex p Burlinson [1948] 1
    KB 79; [1947] 2 All ER 537, KBD   5.47
R v Epsom and Ewell Corp ex p R B Property
    Investments (Eastern) [1964] 1 WLR 1060; [1964] 2
    All ER 832; (1964) 62 LGR 498, DC   6.58
R v Highbury Corner Magistrates' Court ex p Edwards
    (1994) 26 HLR 682, DC   5.61
R v Horsham Justices ex p Richards [1985] 1 WLR 986;
    [1985] 2 All ER 1114, DC   5.93
R v Inner London Crown Court ex p Bentham [1989] 1
    WLR 408; (1988) 21 HLR 171; [1989] COD 293, DC   5.102
R v Kerrier District Council ex p Guppys (Bridport) Ltd
    (1976) 32 P&CR 411; (1975) 74 LGR 55, CA   5.108
R v Liverpool Crown Court ex p Cooke [1997] 1 WLR
    700; [1996] 4 All ER 589; (1997) 29 HLR 249; (1997)
    96 LGR 379, QBD   5.94
R v Newham East JJ ex p Hunt; R v Oxted Justices ex p
    Franklin [1976] 1 WLR 420; [1976] 1 All ER 839;
    (1976) LGR 305, DC   5.49
R v Secretary of State for the Environment ex p Ward
    [1984] 1 WLR 834; [1984] 2 All ER 556; (1984) 48
    P&CR 212; (1983) 82 LGR 628   5.9
R v Smethwick JJ ex p Hands (1980) *Times* 4 December,
    DC   5.77
R v Southend Stipendiary Magistrate ex p Rochford
    District Council (1994) *Times* 10 May; [1994] Env LR
    D15, QBD   5.101
R v Southwark London Borough Council ex p Cordwell
    (1994) 27 HLR 594, CA   6.49
R v Wandsworth County Court ex p Munn (1994) 26
    HLR 697; [1994] COD 282, QBD   3.165, 3.170
R v Wheatley (1885) 16 QBD 34   5.26
R (on the application of Erskine) v Lambeth LBC [2003]
    EWHC 2479 (Admin); December 2003 *Legal Action* 9   6.77
R (on the application of Islington London Borough
    Council) v Inner London Crown Court [2003] EWHC
    2500 (Admin); [2003] All ER (D) 197 (Oct); [2004]
    HLR 31; December 2004 *Legal Action* 15; JPL B45, DC   5.92

R (on the application of Khatun) v Newham London
Borough Council [2004] EWCA Civ 55; [2005] QB 37;
[2004] HLR 29, CA   1.8

R (on the application of the Southwark Law Centre) v
Legal Services Commission; R (on the application of
Dennis) v Legal Services Commission [2007] EWHC
1715 (Admin); [2008] 1 WLR 1368; [2007] All ER (D)
325 (Jul)   4.28

R (on the application of Vella) v Lambeth London
Borough Council [2005] EWHC 2473 (Admin);
[2005] 47 EG 114 (CS); [2005] All ER (D) 171 (Nov),
DC   5.15

R (on the application of Weaver) v London and Quadrant
Housing Trust (Equality and Human Rights
Commission intervening) [2009] EWCA Civ 587;
[2009] 25 EG 137 (CS); [2009] All ER (D) 179 (Jun),
CA, *Affirming* [2008] EWHC 1377 (Admin); [2009] 1
All ER 17, DC   2.53

Rapid Results College v Angell [1986] 1 EGLR 53; (1986)
277 EG 856, CA   1.84

Ravenseft Properties Ltd v Davstone (Holdings) Ltd
[1980] QB 12; [1979] 2 WLR 897; [1979] 1 All ER 929;
(1978) 37 P&CR 502; (1979) 249 EG 51 QBD   1.23

Rayson v Sanctuary Housing association Ltd, March
1996 *Legal Action* 15, Ipswich County Court   8.66

Redland Bricks Ltd v Morris [1970] AC 652; [1969] 2
WLR 1437; [1969] 2 All ER 576, HL   3.99

Rimmer v Liverpool City Council [1985] QB 1; [1984] 2
WLR 426; [1984] 1 All ER 930; (1984) 12 HLR 23;
(1984) 47 P&CR 516; (1983) 269 EG 319; (1984) 82
LGR 424, CA   2.3, 2.5, 2.6

Robbins v Jones (1863) 15 CB (NS) 221   1.1, 1.37

Rookes v Barnard [1964] AC 1129, [1964] 1 All ER 367,
[1964] 2 WLR 269, HL, *Reversing in part* [1963] 1 QB
623, [1962] 2 All ER 579, CA, *Reversing* [1963] 1 QB
623, [1961] 2 All ER 825, [1961] 3 WLR 438, QBD   8.42

Rotherham Metropolitan Borough Council v Dodds
[1986] 2 All ER 867; [1986] 1 WLR 1367, CA   7.58

Rousou v Photi [1940] 2 KB 379; [1940] 2 All ER 528, CA,
Reversing [1939] 4 All ER 616, KBD   1.59

Rushton and Others v Southwark LBC, December 2006
Legal Action 24, Lambeth County Court   8.88

Ryan v Islington LBC [2009] EWCA Civ 578   8.8

Sachs v Brentfield Trust, December 2006 *Legal Action* 24   8.74

Salford County Council v McNally [1976] AC 379; [1975]
3 WLR 87; [1975] 2 All ER 860; (1975) 73 LGR 408,
HL   5.14, 5.85, 5.109

Salisbury Corp v Roles [1948] WN 412; (1948) 92 SJ 618,
   DC   5.108
Sampson v Hodson-Pressinger [1981] 3 All ER 710; 12
   HLR 40; 261 *Estates Gazette* 891, CA   2.14
Sampson v Wilson [1996] Ch 39; [1995] 3 WLR 455;
   (1995) 70 P&CR 359, CA, *Varying* (1994) 26 HLR
   486, Ch D   1.48, 8.61
Saner, J v Bilton (1878) 7 Ch D 815   1.112
Sarmad v Okello, November 2004 *Legal Action* 29   8.71, 8.94
Sarson v Roberts [1895] 2 QB 395   1.39
Sedleigh-Denfield v O'Callaghan, *sub nom* Sedleigh-
   Denfield v St Joseph's Society for Foreign Missions
   [1940] AC 880; [1940] 3 All ER 349; HL, *Reversing*
   [1939] 1 All ER 725, CA   2.16
Sharpe v Manchester Metropolitan District Council
   (1977) 5 HLR 71, CA   2.8, 2.14, 2.15
Sharratt v London Central Bus Co Ltd (The Accident
   Group Test Cases); Hollins v Russell [2003] 28 LS
   Gaz R 30; [2003] EWCA Civ 718, CA, *Affirming*
   [2003] 1 All ER 353; [2002] All ER (D) 468 (Nov), SC   4.98
Sheffield CC v Oliver Lands Tribunal LRX/146/2007,
   December 2008, *Legal Action* 31   1.83
Shefford v Nofax Enterprises (Acton) Ltd, December
   2006 *Legal Action* 24, Central London County Court   1.41, 8.73
Sheldon v West Bromwich Corp [1973] (1984) 13 HLR
   23; (1973) 25 P&CR 360, CA   1.89, 1.102, 1.105
Sheridan v Broadbridge, September 1995 *Legal Action* 16;
   Housing Law Casebook, para P14.5, Clerkenwell
   County Court   3.102
Sillitoe v Liverpool City Council (1988) 29 November,
   unreported, Liverpool County Court   7.91
Smith v Bradford Metropolitan Borough Council (1982) 4
   HLR 86; (1982) 44 P&CR 171; (1982) 80 LGR 713, CA   2.30, 2.31, 2.40
Smith v Littlewoods Organisation Ltd; Maloco v Same
   sub nom Smith v Littlewoods Organisation (Chief
   Constable, Fife Constabulary, third party) [1987] AC
   241; [1987] 2 WLR 480; [1987] 1 All ER 710, HL   7.98
Smith v Marrable (1843) 11 M & W 5   1.38, 1.40
Smyth v Farnworth, December 2009 *Legal Action* 23   8.89
Southwark London Borough Council v McIntosh [2002]
   08 EG 164; February 2002 *Legal Action* 22, Ch D   7.43
Southwark London Borough Council v Mills, Baxter v
   Camden London Borough Council (No 2) [2001] 1
   AC 1; [1999] 4 All ER 449; [1999] 3 WLR 939; [2000]
   LGR 138, HL, *Affirming* [2001] Ch 1; [1999] 1 WLR
   409; [1998] 3 EGLR 46, CA, *Reversing* [2001] Ch 1,
   [1998] 3 WLR 49, Ch   1.49, 2.14, 2.16,
                                        7.84

Southwark London Borough Council v Simpson (1998)
31 HLR 725; [1999] Env LR 553, DC   5.53

Springett v Harold [1954] 1 WLR 521; [1954] 1 All ER
568; (1954) 52 LGR 181, QBD   5.14

Stansbie v Troman [1948] 2 KB 48; [1948] 1 All ER 599,
CA   8.3

Stanton v Southwick [1920] 2 KB 642   1.65

Staves and Staves v Leeds County Council (1991) 23 HLR
107; [1992] 2 EGLR 37; [1992] 29 EG 119, CA   1.23, 1.80, 7.30

Stent v Monmouth District Council (1987) 19 HLR 269;
(1987) 54 P&CR 193; [1987] 1 EGLR 59; (1987) 282
EG 705, CA   1.21, 1.22, 1.24,
    1.33, 1.35

Stevens v Blaenau Gwent County Borough [2004] EWCA
Civ 715; [2004] HLR 1039; (2004) *Times* 29 June;
[2004] All ER (D) 116 (Jun), CA   2.10

Stockley v Knowsley Metropolitan Borough Council
[1986] 2 EGLR 141; 279 *Estates Gazette* 677, CA   2.10

Stone v Bolton *see* Bolton v Stone

Sone v Redair Mersey Agencies, May 1997 *Legal Action*
18; [1996] CLY 2244   8.84

Strandley Investments v Barpress Ltd [1987] 1 EGLR 69;
(1987) 282 EG 1124, CA   1.84

Street v Mountford [1985] AC 809; [1985] 2 WLR 877;
[1985] 2 All ER 289; (1985) 17 HLR 402; (1985) 50
P&CR 258; [1985] 1 EGLR 128; (1985) 274 EG 821,
HL   1.2

Sturolson & Co v Mauroux (1988) 20 HLR 332; [1988] 24
EG 102, CA   3.41, 8.23, 8.26,
    8.46, 8.76

Summers v Salford Corporation [1943] AC 283   1.64

Switzer v Law [1998] CLY, [1998] 7 CL 380   7.30

Sykes v Harry and Another [2001] EWCA Civ 167; [2001]
QB 1014; (2001) 33 HLR 80   2.40, 7.67, 8.30,
    8.47

Target v Torfaen BC (1991) 24 HLR 164, CA   2.5, 2.6

Taylor v Walsall and District Property and Investment
Co Ltd (1998) 30 HLR 1062, [1998] 06 LS Gaz R 24,
DC   5.101

Taylor v Webb [1937] 2 KB 283   1.83

Televantos v McCulloch (1991) 23 HLR 412; [1991] 1
EGLR 123; [1991] 19 EG 18, CA   3.13

Tennant Radiant Heat Ltd v Warrington Development
Corporation [1988] 1 EGLR 41; (1988) 11 EG 71, CA   2.14

Thornton & Jarrett v Birmingham County Council,
November 2004 *Legal Action* 27, Birmingham
County Court   1.50, 1.81, 2.54

Tower Hamlets London Borough Council v Greater
London Council (1983) 15 HLR 54, DC   5.81, 7.36

Vass v Pank, July 2001 *Legal Action* 25   8.31
Vergera v Lambeth LBC and Hyde Southbank Homes,
    August 2002 *Legal Action* 30, Lambeth County Court   8.68, 8.94
Victoria Square Property Co v LB Southwark [1978] 1
    WLR 463; [1978] 2 All ER 281; (1977) 34 P&CR 275;
    (1977) 247 EG 989; (1977) 76 LGR 349, CA   6.67
Vukelic v Hammersmith & Fulham LBC [2003] EWHC
    188 (TCC), November 2003 *Legal Action* 13   1.29
Vye v English Churches Housing Group, November 2003
    Legal Action 11, Lambeth County Court   8.4

Wadsworth v Nagle [2005] EWHC 26 (QB)   2.35
Wainwright v Leeds City Council (1984) 13 HLR 117;
    (1984) 270 EG 1289; (1984) 82 LGR 657, CA   1.97
Walker v Hobbs & Co (1889) 23 QBD 458   1.64
Walker v Lambeth LBC, September 1992 *Legal Action* 21,
    Lambeth County Court   8.63
Wallace v Manchester CC (1998) 30 HLR 1111, CA   8.16, 8.21, 8.24,
                                                        8.25, 8.32, 8.33,
                                                        8.50, 8.57, 8.69

Walton v Lewisham LBC, May 1997 *Legal Action* 20,
    Tunbridge Wells County Court   1.56
Warner v LB Lambeth (1984) 15 HLR 42, DC   5.81
Warren v Keen [1954] 1 QB 15   1.118
Warwick RDC v Miller-Mead *see* Miller-Mead v Minister
    of Housing and Local Government
Welsh v Greenwich LBC (2001) 33 HLR 40; (2000) 81 P
    & CR 144; [2000] All ER (D) 880, CA   1.15, 7.27
Wettern Electric Ltd v Welsh Development Agency [1983]
    1 QB 796; [1983] 2 WLR 897; [1983] 2 All ER 629;
    (1984) 47 P&CR 113   1.44
Whatling v Rees (1914) 84 LJKB 1122   5.26
Wheat v E Lacon Ltd [1966] AC 552; [1966] 2 WLR 581;
    [1966] 1 All ER 582, CA   2.21
Williams v Edwards [1997] CLY 561, Cardiff County Court   7.81
Willis and Willis v Fuller, May 1997 *Legal Action* 20,
    Hastings County Court   1.81
Wilson v Finch-Hatton (1877) 2 Ex D 336; 41 JP 583, 46
    LJQB 489, 25 WR 537, Ex D   1.38, 1.40
Woodar Investment Development Ltd v Wimpey
    Construction (UK) Ltd [1980] 1 All ER 571; [1980] 1
    WLR 277, HL   3.45
Wycombe Area Health Authority v Barnett (1982) 5 HLR
    84; (1982) 264 EG 619, CA   1.93

Yeomen's Row Management Ltd v Bodentien-Meyrick
    [2002] EWCA Civ 860, CA   1.111

Zenca and Others v Pouyiouros (1989) September *Legal
    Action* 24, QBD   7.63

Table of statutes

References in the right-hand column are to paragraph numbers.

Access to Justice Act 1999
    4.3–4.5, 4.13,
    4.25
  Pt 1   4.6
  s4(1)   4.3
  s5   4.6
  s8   4.5
  s19   4.6
  s27   4.73
  Sch 2   4.3
Access to Neighbouring Land Act
  1992   7.81
Agricultural Holdings Act 1948
  s14(3)   1.98
Building Act 1984   7.52
  ss21, 59   7.57
  s72   7.62
  s76   5.36
  ss77–83   7.47
  s79   7.50
Clean Neighbourhoods and
  Environment Act 2005
    5.1, 5.2
  s101   5.5
Contracts (Rights of Third Parties)
  Act 1999   3.44, 3.48
Control of Pollution Act 1974
    7.90
County Courts Act 1984
  s69   8.48
Courts and Legal Services Act 1990
    4.68
  s58   4.73, 4.74
  s58A(1)(a)   4.72, 5.104
Criminal Justice Act 1967
  s9   5.51, 5.74

Criminal Justice Act 2003
    5.72
Criminal Procedure and
  Investigations Act 1996
    5.72
  s1(2)   5.73
  s3   5.72
  s3(1)(b)   5.72
  s5(1)(a)   5.73
  s6   5.73
  s7   5.73
  s7A   5.72
  s8   5.73
  s13(1)(b)   5.72
Defective Premises Act 1972
    2.23, 2.30, 7.67
  s1   1.41, 2.7, 2.23,
    2.25, 2.27, 2.28,
    3.42, 3.90, 7.32,
    7.85
  s1(4)   1.105, 2.24
  s1(5)   2.27, 3.42
  s2   2.25
  s3   2.9, 2.28
  s4   2.29, 2.34, 2.35,
    2.41, 2.47, 3.42,
    3.46, 3.48, 3.90,
    3.161, 7.29, 7.31,
    7.67
  s4(1)–(3)   2.37, 2.42
  s4(2)   2.38
  s4(3)   2.30
  s4(4)   2.33, 2.42, 2.45,
    2.46
  s6(3)   2.36

Environment Act 1995
        5.1, 5.2
Environmental Protection Act 1990
        3.49, 4.16, 4.72,
  4.73, 5.2, 5.3, 5.5, 5.7, 5.9,
  5.14, 5.16, 5.24, 5.32, 5.35,
  5.37, 5.40, 5.44, 5.61, 5.66,
  5.98, 5.100, 5.104, 5.108,
  5.110, 5.112, 6.30, 7.4, 7.17,
  7.44, 7.73, 7.92, 7.102

Pt III	5.1, 7.83
s73	5.99
ss79–82	5.1
s79	5.8, 5.9, 5.19
s79(1)	5.44
s79(1)(a)	5.5–5.7, 5.11,
	5.16, 5.57
s79(1)(e)	5.5
s79(1)(g)	5.5
s79(1)(fa)	5.5
s79(1)(h)	5.5
s79(7)	5.7, 5.12, 5.27
s80(1)	5.25, 5.41, 5.44
s80(2)(a)	5.27
s80(2)(b)	5.28
s80(2)(c)	5.29
s80(3)	5.31
s80(4)	5.32
s80(5)	5.33
s81(1)	5.30
s81(3)	5.34
s81(4)	5.34, 5.35
s82	5.44–5.47, 5.49,
	5.51, 5.60, 5.88,
	5.94, 5.97,
	5.100, 5.109,
	5.111, 7.33, 7.35,
	7.102
s82(1)	5.62, 5.91
s82(2)	5.50, 5.67, 5.91
s82(2)(b)	5.67
s82(3)	5.87, 5.113
s82(4)	5.57
s82(4)(b)	5.82
s82(5)	5.57
s82(6)	5.56, 5.59, 5.94
s82(7)	5.56
s82(8)	5.50, 5.88, 5.89,
	5.91

Environmental Protection Act 1990
    continued

s82(12)	5.100
s160	5.56
s164(2)	5.1
Sch 3 para	
1(2)	5.31
Sch 3 para 2	5.23
Sch 15 para 4	5.5
Housing Act 1957	5.108, 6.49,
	6.77, 6.78, 7.44
Housing Act 1961	1.98, 5.108,
	6.49, 6.77, 6.78,
	7.44
s32	1.70
Housing Act 1969	5.108, 6.49,
	6.77, 6.78, 7.44
Housing Act 1985	5.108, 6.49,
	6.77, 6.78, 7.44,
	7.86, 7.87, 7.88
Pt 9	6.57
s96	3.10
ss97–98	7.71
s102	1.11
s102(1)	1.11
s265	6.57
s270	6.59
ss289–306	7.8
s289	6.60
s289(1)	7.8
s289(2ZA)	7.8
s289(2ZB)	7.8
s289(2ZC)	7.8
s289(2B)–(2F)	7.10
s289(4)	7.10
ss298–323	7.7
s300(1)	6.66
s302	1.68, 6.66
s604	1.41, 1.60
Housing Act 1988	1.71, 5.108,
	6.49, 6.56, 6.77,
	6.78, 7.44
s16	1.117
s21	6.12, 7.76
Sch 2,	
Ground 8	3.17, 4.37
Housing Act 1996	5.108, 6.49,
	6.77, 6.78
Pt VI	6.75

Housing Act 1996 *continued*	
Pt VII	3.34, 7.48
s135	3.10
s160(4)	6.75
s167(2)(c)	6.11
s175(3)	3.34, 6.11
s189	3.34
s193(2)	3.34
Housing Act 2004	4.16, 5.24, 5.44,
	5.108, 6.2, 6.3, 6.9, 6.12, 6.13,
	6.25, 6.28, 6.30, 6.31, 6.34,
	6.49, 6.57, 6.59, 6.65, 6.77–
	6.80, 7.4, 7.7, 7.17, 7.44, 7.61,
	7.68, 7.73, 7.76, 7.86, 7.92
Pt 1	6.15, 6.16, 6.77,
	7.38
s2(1)	6.31, 6.32
s2(4)	6.32
s2(5)	6.32
s3	6.16
s3(1)	6.13
s3(3)	6.13
s4	6.16, 6.21
s4(2)	6.15, 6.21
s4(3)	6.22
s4(6)	6.21, 6.25
s4(7)	6.25
s5(2)	6.43
s5(3)	6.45
s5(4)	6.45
s5(5)	6.45
s7	6.41
s8(2)–(4)	6.47
s9	6.16, 6.28
s11	6.53
s12	6.53
s13	6.53
s14	6.64
s20	6.55
s21	3.33, 6.55
s23	6.64
s28	6.51
s30	6.69
s32	6.69
s33	6.56
s40–42	6.62
s40(6)	6.28
s43	6.62
s46	6.57

Housing Act 2004 *continued*	
s47	6.60
ss73–74	7.76
s75	6.12, 7.76
s98	6.12
s213	3.33
s215	6.12
s216	7.87
s239(3)	6.28
s239(5)	6.28
s239(6)	6.28
Sch 3	6.71
Sch 16	1.41
Housing and Regeneration Act 2008	
	3.26
s193	3.26
s195	3.26
ss237–238	3.26
s239	3.26
Human Rights Act 1998	
	2.18, 2.52, 2.56,
	3.48, 7.55
s3(1)	2.48
s6	2.53
s6(1)	2.49
Sch 1, Art 8	2.48, 2.50, 2.52
Insolvency Act 1986	
s268(1)(a)	3.173
Justices of the Peace Act 1997	
s66	5.77
Land Compensation Act 1961	
	7.10
Land Compensation Act 1973	
	7.10
Pt III	6.76
s39	6.75
Landlord and Tenant Act 1985	
s1	3.36
s8	1.7, 1.58–1.60,
	1.64–1.68,
	1.100
s8(2)	1.62, 1.116
s8(5)	1.61
s8(6)	1.59
s810	1.63
ss11–17	1.70
s11	1.7, 1.54, 1.60,
	1.69,1.70, 1.72, 1.73, 1.75,
	1.80, 1.86, 1.95, 1.98, 1.99,

Landlord and Tenant Act 1985
s11 *continued*   1.100, 1.107,
      1.119, 2.33, 2.52, 3.48, 3.65,
      3.90, 5.86, 7.29, 7.30, 7.56,
      7.65, 7.67, 7.95
s11(1)   1.71
s11(1)(a)   1.71, 1.78, 1.86
s11(1)(b)–(c)   7.95
s11(1)(b)   1.71, 1.89, 1.92,
                  1.118
s11(1)(c)   1.71, 1.89, 1.92
s11(1A)   1.71, 1.72, 1.86,
                  1.94
s11(1A)(a)   1.78
s11(1A)(b)   1.91
s11(1B)   1.72
s11(3)   1.95
s11(3A)   1.94
s11(4)   1.73
s11(6)   1.73, 1.116
s12(1)(a)   1.73
s13(1)   1.98
s13(2)   1.98, 1.118
s14(4)   1.98
s16(b)   1.85
s17   3.163
s17(1)   3.162
s17(2)   3.163
s32(2)   1.98
Landlord and Tenant Act 1987
Pt II   3.20
s22   3.20
s24   3.20
s58   3.20
s60(1)   1.71
Law Reform (Contributory
      Negligence) Act 1945
                  8.47
Leasehold Reform, Housing and
      Urban Development Act 1993
s121   3.10
Limitation Act 1980 3.40
s2   2.27
s11   2.27, 3.43
s14A   2.27, 3.42
s33   3.43
Local Government and Housing Act
      1989   7.12
Pt VII   7.11

Local Government and Housing Act
      1989 *continued*
s89(1)   7.12
s89(3)   7.12
s93(3)   7.13
Local Government (Miscellaneous
      Provisions) Act 1976
s33   7.96
Occupiers' Liability Act 1957
                  2.19, 2.21, 2.22
s2   3.46
s2(1), (2)   2.19
s3(1)   2.20
Powers of Criminal Courts
      (Sentencing) Act 2000
s130   5.93
s130(3)   5.96
s131   5.93
s134(2)   5.97
Prevention of Damage by Pests Act
      1949   7.101
Prosecution of Offences Act 1985
s19A   5.107
Public Health Act 1936
                  5.1, 5.2, 5.5
Pt II   7.101
s45   7.93
s72   7.90
ss91–100   5.1
s99   5.45, 7.33
s141   5.5
s259   5.5
s268   5.5
Public Health Act 1961
s17   7.58
s22   7.58
Rent Act 1957   6.56, 6.59, 7.88
Rent Act 1965   6.56, 6.59, 7.88
Rent Act 1968   6.56, 6.59, 7.88
Rent Act 1977   1.26, 3.18, 6.56,
                  6.59, 7.88, 8.77
s67(3)(a)   3.18
s148   1.117
Supply of Goods and Services Act
      1982   1.56
Unfair Contract Terms Act 1977
                  1.8
Water Industry Act 1991
                  2.56

Table of statutory instruments

References in the right-hand column are to paragraph numbers.

Allocation of Housing (England) Regulations 2002
    SI No 3264
    reg 3(2)   6.75
Allocation of Housing (Wales) Regulations 2003 SI No
    239
    reg 3(a)   6.75
Cancellation of Contracts made in a Consumer's Home
    or Place of Work etc Regulations 2008 SI No 1816   4.74
    reg 7(1)   4.74
    reg 7(3)   4.74
Civil Procedure Rules 1998 SI No 3132   3.91
    r1.1(2)(c)   3.74
    r3.9   4.92
    r12.4(1)   3.135
    r12.4(2)   3.135
    r16.2–16.4   3.88
    r16.3   3.88
    PD 16   3.88
    PD 16, para 7.3   3.91
    PD 16, para 4.3   3.91
    r18   3.94
    r20.4(2)   3.117
    r21.5(3)   3.75
    Pt 23   3.135
    PD 23, para 12.4   3.104
    r24.2   3.136
    r25.1   3.168
    r25.1(1)(f)   3.172
    r25.6   3.134, 8.9
    r25.6.1(b)   4.35
    r25.7   3.134
    PD 25A, para 4.3   3.104
    r26.6–26.8   4.44
    r26.6   4.44
    r26.6(1)(b)   3.142

Civil Procedure Rules 1998 SI No 3132 *continued*

r26.6(5)	3.143
r31.6	3.149
r31.10(6)	3.150
r31.12	3.149
r31.16	3.75
PD 32, paras 17–20	3.151
r32.9	3.153
r32.14	3.152
PD 35, para 2.1	3.67
r35.3	3.64
PD 35, para 6A	3.147
Pt 36	3.125, 3.131, 3.132, 5.101
r36.2	3.125
r39.5	3.158
PD 39, para 3.1–3.10	3.158
PD 39, para 3.1	3.158
r40.13	3.124
r40.20	3.167
PD 43–48, para 6.6	3.141
PD 43–48, para 13.2	3.159
PD 43–48, para 19.2	4.91
PD 43–48, para 19.3	4.92
PD 43–48, para 19.4	4.92
PD 43–48, para 19.5	4.91
r43.2	4.91
r44.3	4.85, 4.91
r44.4	3.125
r44.15	4.91
PD 47, para 40.14	4.98
r48.1(2)	3.75
r48.1(3)	3.75
r56.2(1)	3.95
Pt 69	3.19, 3.173
Pt 72	3.173
Sch 1	3.171
Sch 2	3.165, 3.170, 3.173
Pre-action Protocol	3.49, 3.52–3.56, 3.60–3.63, 3.68, 3.75, 3.76, 3.82, 4.40, 6.26
para 1	3.76
para 3.1(b)	3.49–3.51
para 3.1(b)	3.49–3.51
para 3.2	3.56, 3.57
para 3.3	3.81
para 3.4	3.51
para 3.6	3.61

Civil Procedure Rules 1998 SI No 3132, Pre-action Protocol *continued*
    para 3.6(d)   3.61
    para 3.7   3.52
    para 3.148   3.77
    para 4.1(a)   3.77
    para 4.10   3.59
    Annex C   3.57
    Annex G   3.56
Collection and Disposal of Waste Regulations 1988
    SI No 819   7.90
Community Legal Service (Costs) Regulations 2000
    SI No 441   4.56
Community Legal Service (Financial) Regulations
    2000 SI No 516   4.56
Community Legal Service (Funding) (Amendment)
    Order 2008 SI No 1328   4.17
Community Legal Service (Funding) Order 2007
    SI No 2441
    Sch   4.17
County Court Rules 1981 SI No 1687
    Ord 26   3.173
    Ord 27   3.173
    Ord 29   3.170
    Ord 29 r1   3.165
Criminal Procedure Rules 2005   5.52
    r33   5.54
    r7.1(2)(a)   5.57
    r7.2.1   5.57
    r7.3(1)(a)(i), (ii), (b)   5.57
    r27   5.74
    r37   5.78
Gas Safety (Installation and Use) Regulations 1998
    SI No 2451   2.41, 7.69
    reg 36   7.66
Housing Health and Safety Rating System (England)
    Regulations 2005 SI 3208   6.9, 6.29, 6.41
    reg 2   6.36
    reg 3   6.36
    reg 5   6.29
    reg 6   6.36
    reg 7   6.36
    reg 8   6.36
    Sch 1   6.36, 6.37
    Sch 2   6.36
Insurance Companies (Legal Expenses Insurance)
    Regulations 1990 SI No 1159   4.66
Regulatory Reform (Fire Safety) Order 2005 SI No 1541   7.61
Regulatory Reform (Housing Assistance) (England and
    Wales) Order 2002 SI No 1860   7.11

Rules of the Supreme Court 1965 SI No 1776
   Ord 45 r8   3.171
Secure Tenants of Local Housing Authorities (Right to
   Repair) (Amendment) Regulations 1994 SI No
   844   3.10
Secure Tenants of Local Housing Authorities (Right to
   Repair) (Amendment) Regulations 1996 SI No
   73   3.10
Secure Tenants of Local Housing Authorities (Right to
   Repair) Regulations 1994 SI No 133   3.10
   Sch 1   1.106
Statutory Nuisance (Appeals) Regulations 1995 SI No
   2644   5.31
Unfair Terms in Consumer Contracts Regulations
   1999 SI No 2083   1.8, 1.42, 3.8
   reg 5   1.8

Table of European and international legislation

References in the right-hand column are to paragraph numbers.

European legislation

European Convention for the Protection of Human
     Rights and Fundamental Freedoms 1950   2.48, 2.53, 2.56
    Art 1, Protocol 1   2.56
    Art 8   2.50, 2.52, 2.53–
                              2.56, 3.48

International legislation

Civil Code of California
    s1942.5   6.12

Abbreviations

ADR	alternative dispute resolution
AJA	Administration of Justice Act 1999
AQ	allocation questionnaire
AST	assured shorthold tenancy
ATE	after-the-event
BTE	before-the-event
CCR	County Court Rules
CFA	conditional fee agreement
CLG	Communities and Local Government
CLS	Community Legal Service
CPIA	Criminal Procedure and Investigations Act 1996
CPR	Civil Procedure Rules
CrimPR	Criminal Procedure Rules
DMG	Decision Making Guidance
DPA	Defective Premises Act 1972
EHO	environmental health officer
ELR	Emergency Legal Representation
ENL	early notification letter
EPA	Environmental Protection Act
FC	Funding Code
FSA	Financial Standards/Services? Authority
HA	Housing Act
H&RA	Housing and Regeneration Act 2008
HHSRS Regs	Housing Health and Safety Rating System (England) Regulations 2005
HMO	house in multiple occupation
HRA	Human Rights Act 1998
HSE	Health and Safety Executive
IHO	Independent Housing Ombudsman
JP	Justice of the Peace
LA	Limitation Act 1980
LEI	legal expenses insurance
LGHA	Local Government and Housing Act
LOC	letter of claim
LSC	Legal Services Commission
LTA	Landlord and Tenant Act
OFT	Office of Fair Trading

OLA	Occupiers' Liability Act
PCCSA	Powers of the Criminal Courts (Sentencing) Act
PD	Practice Direction
PHA	Public Health Act 1936
PSOW	Public Service Ombudsman for Wales
RA	Rent Act
RSC	Rules of the Supreme Court
TSA	Tenant Services Authority
TSO	The Stationery Office
UTCC Regs	Unfair Terms in Consumer Contracts Regulations

Introduction

This introduction serves two functions. First, for those who are new to the book, it offers a brief word about the text and how to make best use of it. Second, for all readers, a short overview is offered of developments since 1999 (the date of the last edition), which may help put the content of the present edition in its proper context.

How to use this book

This book is about rented housing accommodation. It is concerned with disrepair and other adverse conditions affecting residents in such accommodation whether that accommodation is a house, maisonette, flat or simply a room.

Although the title would suggest it is exclusively about the rights of *tenants*, much of the text will help other occupiers of rented housing (the family members of tenants, their lodgers, subtenants, guests and visitors) and others who live near to poor rented housing and are affected by its condition.

Again, although the title suggests an exclusive focus on *repairs*, a good deal of the text addresses other adverse housing conditions including infestations, hazards, absence of amenities and so on. The structure is as follows.

Chapters 1 and 2 address the questions 'when must a landlord repair?', 'what must a landlord repair?' and 'how much work must a landlord do?' by reference to the rights of tenants given by the civil law of contract and tort. Where these rights come from legislation, the relevant extracts of the most important legislation are set out in appendix A.

Chapter 3 explains how remedies can be obtained to enforce those rights and deals primarily with taking action in the civil (county) courts. For some tenants, an important part of taking such action will be to secure compensation for the loss or hardship they have suffered and chapter 8 explains what damages are available from the civil courts and how they are calculated. Because taking action in the civil courts can be expensive, chapter 4 sets out what financial help is available to run such a case – with a particular focus on legal aid. The paperwork in pursuing a claim can be complex, so appendix D includes worked examples of the documentation used in all the main stages of enforcement of civil rights to repair using the courts system.

But the civil rights of tenants cannot and do not cover every conceivable problem with housing conditions and a civil court cannot always provide the (right) answer to a particular situation. Indeed, tenants in the private sector with limited security of tenure may find that their rights are rendered worthless by the fear of retaliatory eviction.[1] So, in chapters 5 and 6, readers will find descriptions of the powers available to local councils to address adverse housing conditions independently using environmental and housing legislation. Both chapters focus on what occupiers can do to propel councils into using their powers to achieve real improvements in living conditions. In some cases, securing the work necessary to achieve a safe and secure home will involve the council or the tenant prosecuting the landlord (which may even be the local council itself!). Chapter 5 explains how that can be done, with a step by step guide, and the appendices again contain both precedent documents and the core legislation.

From an occupier's viewpoint, what they will have is a 'problem' with their home that needs addressing – condensation, vermin, noise, vandalism or whatever. So in chapter 7 the text deals, in alphabetical order, with the main condition-related problems in rented housing, referring the reader back to other parts of the text or other sources in the hunt for legal and practical solutions.

Although it is written from a 'consumer' perspective, we hope that the text will help providers of accommodation to familiarise themselves with the law and practice relating to housing repair and housing conditions and that it will assist judicial and academic readers too. The book is light on legal theory and heavy on practicalities and deliberately so.

There is no expectation that the reader will digest the book from start to finish. It is intended to be practitioner-friendly and to be a resource to be dipped into, as and when necessary. The hope is that the detailed contents lists at the start of each chapter and the detailed index at the back will lead the reader to the most helpful point in the

---

1   Explained in chapter 6 at para 6.12.

text. The second part of this introduction may help put much of the work in context.

Sadly, as the text demonstrates, most of the relevant law is not simple. Housing disrepair has been the subject of numerous court decisions over many decades – as the footnotes and table of cases indicate. To keep matters as simple as possible we have only referred in the footnotes to a maximum of two reference points to each court case. Where there are further sources for that case they are given in the table of cases. Any reader who wishes to obtain the full text of any modern decision of the higher courts will find that available, free of charge, on the excellent website of the British and Irish Legal Information Institute.[2]

Although this is the fourth edition, it will not be the last. Feedback and comment from readers, particularly on suggestions for improvement or addition, would be warmly welcomed by the authors.

Housing disrepair: a decade of change?

When Stephen Knafler signed-off the third edition of this book in the early summer of 1999 the world of housing disrepair was a very different place from that addressed in this edition, over a decade later. The paragraphs that follow cannot, perhaps, do full justice to what has happened (or not happened!) but may provide the essential backdrop against which the current text can best be understood.

Simplification of the law

This has been a decade of missed opportunity. By 1999 there had been ample time for the Government to digest the comprehensive and compelling case for a simplification of the law on housing repair that the Law Commission had made in 1996. Its report in the Spring of that year had set out the problems that the state of the law was causing, the need for change, and had appended a draft *Landlord and Tenant Bill* suitable for swift introduction in, and passage through, Parliament.[3] Nothing happened.

A few months later, in July 1996, Lord Woolf, having been invited to review the way the courts handled civil housing cases reported that 'reform of the substantive law on housing could do more than anything to reduce delay'.[4]

2   www.bailii.org.
3   Law Com 238 *Landlord and tenant: Responsibility for State and Condition of Property,* 19 March 1996.
4   *Access to Justice: Final Report* July 1996 para 16.2.

In response, rather than start the process by bringing forward the Law Commission's proposed Landlord and Tenant Bill, the Government set the Law Commission the challenge of reviewing and codifying the whole law relating to rented accommodation.

That huge task was completed in the Spring of 2006. In its final report, *Renting Homes*,[5] the Law Commission not only called for implementation of the recommendations about repairs that it had made 10 years earlier[6] but also offered a new charter of clear rights and obligations relating to repair in rented housing[7] and, again, a draft Bill containing the necessary legislation. And again, nothing happened.

Any reform to the substantive law relating to the rights of tenants and obligations of landlords must now await the response to a further round of consultation on the report of the *Review of Private Rented Sector Housing*[8] that was itself published in October 2008. The consultation period on the Government's proposed response ended in August 2009. By the date this book went to print, once again, nothing further had happened. No legislation on housing was contained in the legislative programme for 2009/10 announced in the Queen's Speech delivered in November 2009.

The position on legislation and reform over the past decade has not been wholly bleak. In 2004 a Housing Act was passed to reform the law relating to housing conditions and to introduce mandatory licensing of houses in multiple occupation and some other rented housing. In 2006 it was brought into force giving councils new powers and duties to tackle adverse housing conditions through the broader medium of addressing housing hazards rather than fitness or repair and through licence conditions. But (as chapter 6 of this book describes) the assessment process is complex and enforcement is by no means straightforward. As the state of the private sector rented housing stock makes clear,[9] there is much that could and should be done. Too often the complexity of the new law, and the resources needed to enforce it, have together proved too daunting to busy local authorities with other priorities.

---

5   Law Com 297 *Renting Homes: The Final Report*, Cm 6781, 2006.
6   Law Com 297 *Renting Homes: The Final Report*, Cm 6781, 2006, Part 2 para 2.28.
7   Law Com 297 *Renting Homes: The Final Report*, Cm 6781, 2006, Part 8.
8   Available at www.york.ac.uk/inst/chp/Projects/PRSreview.htm.
9   See 'Unfinished business' below.

Transforming the state of social housing

A decade ago, this book would most often have been used by advisers helping tenants address problems with the housing let to them by *social* landlords: local housing authorities and (less commonly) housing associations. Some of the worst housing conditions were to be found on estates of social housing and in individual street properties neglected by cash-starved local authorities unable to invest in repair and improvement of them.

In the last 10 years, unprecedented investment has been made through both central government and private finance in improving the condition of social sector rented housing. Literally billions of pounds have been poured into the *Decent Homes* programme designed to ensure that every home let by a social landlord is a decent home in England by 2010. For Wales, the target date is 2012.[10]

No 'decent home' standard was ever enacted in legislation but from 2001 central government in England was determined to drive up the quality of the social housing stock by pumping-in or levering-in new investment. For local authorities it often came at a high price – disposal of the entire housing stock to a new breed of social landlord: the large scale voluntary transfer housing association. But for hundreds of thousands of tenants it has meant repaired or improved homes, albeit often at significantly higher rents.

Since its introduction in 2001, no tenant has been able to enforce the Decent Homes Standard beyond insisting on their other existing legal rights described in this book. But, as the programme of change reaches its conclusion, the Standard has at last been given some teeth in England. In his statutory directions to the Tenant Services Authority (TSA) in November 2009 the Secretary of State has required the TSA to include the Decent Homes Standard in the new national quality standards that all social housing providers must meet from April 2010.[11] The draft statutory national standards themselves are now out for consultation[12] and, once they are in force, tenants will be entitled to call on the TSA to enforce them using, if necessary, its powers to fine and award compensation.[13] That should

10 *The Welsh Housing Quality Standard*, Welsh Assembly Government, April 2002.
11 *Directions to the Tenant Services Authority: Summary of responses and Government response*, Communities and Local Government, November 2009.
12 *A new regulatory framework for social housing in England*, Tenant Services Authority, November 2009.
13 Briefly described in chapter 3 at para 3.26.

secure the final achievement of the decent homes targets. Debate has already begun on what will follow in 2010 and beyond.[14]

But the improvement in the condition of the stock has not been the only reason for a decline in the number of disrepair claims brought against social landlords. Many such landlords have done much to improve their responses to reports of repair and to react promptly and effectively to responsibly made claims. The process was spurred-on and assisted by helpful Good Practice Guidance issued by central government.[15]

The 'tolerated trespasser' issue

In the decade under review (1999–2009) many landlords found themselves equipped with a new defence to a disrepair claim. On receipt of such a claim, tenancy management records would be researched to see whether the history revealed an old possession order for the property – usually obtained years earlier for arrears of rent. That was because the wording of many such orders seemingly triggered loss of the tenancy either outright or on breach of the terms on which such an order had been suspended. After the tenancy was thus lost, the occupiers remained in possession as 'tolerated trespassers' with, it seemed, no rights to repair. Claims which pleaded that the occupier was a 'tenant' were routinely met, much to occupier's surprise, with defences asserting that they were not tenants at all, whatever the parties may have believed to be the case only a few days previously.

The trigger to address this absurd state of the law came in 2006 with a Court of Appeal decision that the standard form of suspended possession order being used daily by the civil courts was itself terminating all secure tenancies even if the terms *were complied with*.[16] Order was restored by two means. First, the House of Lords held that possession orders made against assured tenants (most private and many housing association tenants) did not end the tenancies until actual eviction.[17] Second, Parliament legislated that from May 2009 the same rule would apply for new possession orders made against secure tenants.[18]

---

14 See, for example, *Beyond Decent Homes: decent housing standards post-2010.* Chartered Institute of Housing, August 2009.

15 *Housing Disrepair: Legal Obligations, Good Practice Guidance,* Department for Transport Local Government and the Regions, January 2002.

16 *Harlow District Council v Hall* [2006] EWCA Civ 156; [2006] 1 WLR 2116, CA.

17 *Knowsley Housing Trust v White* [2008] UKHL 70; [2009] 1 AC 335.

18 Housing & Regeneration Act (H&RA) 2008 s299 and Sch 11.

But the problem has not entirely gone away. Where a secure tenancy was ended by a possession order prior to 20 May 2009 the former tenant will – from that date – be in occupation under a new replacement tenancy. There will, therefore, have been a gap from when the old tenancy was lost until 20 May 2009 when the new replacement tenancy started. In that gap, there will have been no tenancy and no repairing obligations. Parliament has given the judiciary the power to fill that gap in individual cases.[19] The first cases are now being heard in the county courts.[20]

The 'claims farmers' issue

After the third edition of this book was written in 1999, legal work on housing disrepair suffered much damage to its reputation by the arrival in the sector of 'claims farmers'. These were agents cold-calling at tenants' homes to drum up potential housing disrepair cases. Some social housing estates were subjected to a 'blitz' of such activity – to be followed some weeks or months later with a deluge of minor claims against local authority landlords, often financed under conditional fee agreements, and made by solicitors based at the other end of the country, whom the tenants had never met. It transpired that some agents were selling lists of prospective claimants to solicitors and insurers. Although some claims succeeded or were settled, many others led to protracted litigation. A whole 'costs war' developed between social landlords and those solicitors who were acting under multiple conditional fee agreements.[21] In some cases, tenants ended up in debt under credit agreements taken to meet legal costs insurance premiums.

To their credit, reasonable advisers stayed clear of these developments. The Housing Law Practitioners Association had long since revised its rules to keep out prospective members engaging in this work and the Law Society's Ethics Guidance steered responsible solicitors away from it. Those measures, coupled with later central government initiatives to regulate the claims management industry, have seen the virtual elimination of the phenomenon from the field of housing disrepair. However, it has left many social landlords with a lingering sense of injustice and a disposition to approach claims brought nowadays by responsible advisers with unnecessary caution.

19 H&RA 2008 Sch 11 Part II.
20 See, for example, *Lewisham LBC v Litchmore*, December 2009 *Legal Action* 31, Bromley County Court.
21 See chapter 4 for some of its aftermath.

A new dawn: the Disrepair Protocol

It was against the unhappy background just described, that representatives of landlords and tenants were brought together in the 1990s under the auspices of Lord Woolf's *Review of Civil Justice* to thrash out new arrangements for the sensible resolution of housing disrepair claims without the need for litigation. Negotiations were tortuous. Complete deadlock was reached on two topics. Lord Woolf had to address them, and resolve them, in his Final Report.[22]

Not least perhaps because the issues had been resolved contrary to the interests of landlords, negotiations (by then being brokered by the Law Society) dragged on for several more years. In his judicial capacity, Lord Woolf expressed dismay at the lack of progress in December 1999 and encouraged the parties to do better.[23]

With that prompt, negotiations resumed and eventually culminated in an agreed *Pre-Action Protocol for Housing Disrepair Cases,*[24] which was adopted by the Head of Civil Justice and became one of the protocols that stand with the Civil Procedure Rules.

It is intended to diminish use of the courts to resolve housing disrepair disputes. It is perhaps still too early to judge whether it has been entirely successful. But it is so essential now to the proper resolution of any such dispute that its requirements have been addressed in detail in chapter 3 of this edition.

Like almost every document drafted by a negotiating committee, formed of representatives of opposing parties, it is less than perfect and leaves many questions unanswered. But it has at least emerged with flying colours from its first scrutiny in the appellate courts.[25]

Tenants and their lawyers

When the last edition of this book was written, tenants of only modest means needing access to legal services could approach any solicitor offering legal aid services funded by the Legal Aid Board. That meant thousands of potentially available sources of help.

This Introduction is not the place to recount at any length the story of how the legal aid world has changed in the last decade. The number of available suppliers contracted with the Legal Services Commission to provide legal representation in housing cases has

---

22 *Access to Justice: Final Report* July 1996 paras 61–72.

23 *Field v Leeds City Council* [1999] EWCA Civ 3013; (2000) 32 HLR 618 at [23].

24 Available in amended form at www.justice.gov.uk/civil/procrules_fin/contents/protocols/prot_hou.htm.

25 *Birmingham City Council v Lee* [2008] EWCA Civ 891 [2009] HLR 15.

now diminished to a few hundred providers. Those suppliers work at sub-market rates of remuneration for advice-giving and are only adequately paid for the court cases in which they succeed. From October 2010 new and even more stringent contract requirements will apply and even more experienced housing litigators may leave the sector.

Two recent developments have had the potential to render housing disrepair work a virtual 'no-go' area for lawyers instructed by tenants.

The first was the possible raising of the 'small claims threshold' in the Civil Procedure Rules to catch yet more housing disrepair cases – with the result that the legal costs of successful claims would be irrecoverable by the winning tenant. Landlord representatives pressed hard for an increase.[26] Tenant's representatives lobbied strongly in the other direction. The Government eventually decided to maintain the status quo.[27]

The second is the possibility of the introduction of fixed legal costs for housing disrepair cases. The fixing of such legal costs is presently one option being considered by Lord Justice Jackson in his review of *Civil Litigation Costs*.[28] At the date of writing, the landlord lobby was again pressing hard for fixed costs or capped costs in housing disrepair cases to limit their potential liability for tenants' legal costs. A necessary consequence would be to render the work uneconomic for most tenant advisers. The review is due to report in the next few months.

Unfinished business

It had been hoped that, not least as a result of some of the developments described above (most particularly the Decent Homes initiative and the introduction of the Housing Act 2004), this edition might not have been necessary because the problem of extensive housing disrepair would have been eliminated or, at least, greatly diminished.

Improvements in some housing standards have certainly been achieved since 1999 and that progress has been well-charted.[29] But

26 See, for example, *Disrepair and the small claims threshold: Submissions to the DCA*, Social Housing Law Association, August 2006, asserting that 'nowadays there are few serious disrepair cases'.

27 For a good summary of when and why see: *The financial limit for small claims Standard Note:SN/HA/4141*, House of Commons Library, 30 October 2008.

28 See www.judiciary.gov.uk/about_judiciary/cost-review/.

29 *Fifteen years of the Survey of English Housing 1993/4 to 2007/8*, Communities and Local Government, September 2009.

housing disrepair remains unfinished business not only in the private rented sector but also in too many parts of the social housing sector. The latest available data shows that there are still over 1.2 million non-decent privately rented homes and over 1.1 million non-decent social rented homes.[30] The most common reason that homes in England fail the decent homes standard is that they contain Category 1 (the highest category) hazards.

It is the continuing needs of the more than two million households just mentioned that have prompted the writing of this fourth edition.

30 *English House Condition Survey 2007*, CLG, September 2009.

CHAPTER 1

Contractual rights

1.1	**Introduction**
1.2	**The contract of letting**
1.5	**Express terms**
1.18	**Meaning of 'repair' and 'disrepair'**
1.21	Inherent defects
1.24	Disproportionately extensive or costly work
1.27	Small defects
1.29	Repair and decoration
1.30	Prevention of future damage
1.31	Patch repairs or complete renewal
1.36	Blocked conduits
1.37	**Non-statutory implied terms for the benefit of tenants**
1.38	Lettings of furnished dwellings
1.44	Dwelling-houses held under a licence
1.45	Means of access and communal facilities
1.46	Ancillary property owned by the landlord
1.48	Quiet enjoyment/derogation from grant
1.52	Correlative obligations
1.56	Implied term on quality of repair work
1.57	**Statutory implied terms for the benefit of tenants**
1.58	Landlord and Tenant Act 1985 s8

continued

1.69   Landlord and Tenant Act 1985 s11
         Interpreting s11 • Standard for s11 repairs • Limitations of
         s11 • Important note for pre-1961 tenancies

1.100   Implied terms for the benefit of the landlord

1.100   The notice requirement

1.111   Access for the landlord
         Access at common law • Access by statute

1.118   Use in a tenant-like manner

Introduction

1.1   Fraud apart, there is no law against letting a tumble-down house, and the tenant's remedy is upon his contract, if any.[1]

Although this broad declaration must now be read subject to much statutory and judicial development, the terms of the tenancy remain the foundation of most tenants' rights in relation to repairs and of any subsequent legal claims.

The contract of letting

1.2   A tenant occupies premises under the terms of a contract of letting. This contract may be made orally or in writing or may even be inferred from the circumstances (for example, where a person occupies premises with exclusive possession and the landlord accepts money as rent).[2]

1.3   The terms of the contract or 'tenancy agreement' may be:

- expressly incorporated into the agreement either orally or in writing; or
- implied into the tenancy agreement either by statute or by the operation of common law.

1.4   Whether express or implied, these terms may impose an obligation on the landlord to carry out repairs, which the landlord is then contractually bound to perform.

Express terms

1.5   The common law (the judge-made law developed by the system of precedent) concerning rights to repair, which was formulated in the 18th and 19th centuries and which underpins present-day repairs law, rested on the fundamental principle of *caveat emptor*, ie let the buyer beware the bargain. In dealings with land and houses (as with other property) the onus was placed on the person intending to take the premises to have inspected them, assessed their quality, and then freely negotiated an appropriate contract accordingly.

---

1 *Robbins v Jones* (1863) 15 CB (NS) 221 at 240.
2 *Street v Mountford* [1985] AC 809, HL; *A-G Securities Ltd v Vaughan* [1990] 1 AC 417, HL.

1.6   It followed from the application of this principle that, once property had been accepted by the tenant, the landlord had almost complete immunity from repairing obligations other than those imposed by the contract (if any). Clearly, a strict application of the principle *caveat emptor* in today's society is wholly inappropriate and artificial, since the landlord and incoming tenant no longer (if they ever did in the past) bargain as equals over the letting of property. Intervention has come not from the common law but from statute.

1.7   Where repairing obligations are now imposed by law on landlords (eg, by the Landlord and Tenant Act (LTA) 1985 s11 or s8),[3] the statutes generally provide that these obligations cannot be transferred to tenants by way of express contractual terms and any attempt to do so is void.[4]

1.8   The Unfair Contract Terms Act 1977 does not apply to leases but the Unfair Terms in Consumer Contracts Regulations (UTCC Regs) 1999[5] do where the tenant takes as a consumer and the landlord lets as a business on standard terms.[6] These regulations can be used to render unenforceable written tenancy terms which are unfair,[7] where the tenancy was entered into after 30 June 1995 and the term was not individually negotiated. The regulations can therefore assist tenants by preventing landlords from relying on unfair contractual terms by which they might seek to qualify or undermine their own repairing obligations. In *Governors of the Peabody Trust v Reeve*[8] it was held that if a standard tenancy agreement allowed a landlord to vary the terms of a tenancy agreement unilaterally, such a term would be unfair.

1.9   For general guidance on the correct approach in determining whether terms on repair are fair, reference may usefully be made to the Office of Fair Trading (OFT)'s *Guidance on unfair terms in tenancy agreements*. This suggests, for example, that a term excluding a tenant's right to set off the cost of repairs against rent would be unfair.[9] This was indeed decided in *Cody v Philps*,[10] where the district

---

3 See paras 1.57–1.99.

4 *Islington LBC v Keane* December 2005 *Legal Action* 28; *Housing Law Casebook* para P5.27, Clerkenwell County Court.

5 1999 SI No 2083.

6 *R (Khatun) v Newham LBC* [2004] EWCA Civ 55; [2004] HLR 29.

7 See UTCC Regs 1999 reg 5; *Director General of Fair Trading v First National Bank plc* [2001] UKHL 52.

8 [2008] EWHC 1432 (Ch).

9 *Guidance on unfair terms in tenancy agreements* OFT356, OFT, September 2005, para 3.26.

10 December 2005 *Legal Action* 28; *Housing Law Casebook* para P12.11, West London County Court.

judge struck out a clause which prevented any set-off or deduction whatsoever against the rent, thereby enabling the tenant to defend a possession claim for rent arrears on the basis of a disrepair counter-claim. Advisers may also wish to refer to the OFT's investigations of tenancy terms in Newham and Wandsworth in 2005.[11]

1.10　　If the tenancy agreement contains an express term imposing a repairing obligation on the landlord, the adviser should consider whether the term covers the disrepair in question. This involves asking:

(a) what activity has the landlord contracted to perform? and
(b) on which parts of the dwelling has the landlord contracted to perform this activity?

1.11　The terms of a tenancy can be varied by agreement. Secure tenancy agreements can be varied unilaterally by the landlord under the Housing Act (HA) 1985 s102.[12] The adviser should therefore ascertain whether the original terms about repair have been varied.

1.12　　Various different formulations of wording, such as 'put in repair', 'keep in repair', 'good and substantial repair and condition' and many others, are used in express repairing obligations, and the meanings of the various permutations are examined in detail in the traditional legal textbooks.[13] Whatever the wording of an express term, a repairing covenant will never be construed to require the landlord to renew the whole property, ie, to turn an old and decaying house into a new and sound one.[14] Nor will it be construed to require the landlord to remove all potential hazards.[15] Accordingly, a repairing covenant is to be construed having regard to the condition of the property as it was at the date of letting.[16]

1.13　　In *Holding & Barnes plc v Hill House Hammond*,[17] the Court of Appeal reviewed the modern authorities on the proper approach to

---

11　See www.oft.gov.uk/advice_and_resources/resource_base/consumer-regulations/traders/1990/1/ and /www.oft.gov.uk/advice_and_resources/resource_base/consumer-regulations/traders/539/1/.

12　HA 1985 s102(1); *Palmer v Sandwell MBC* (1988) 20 HLR 74, CA; *R v Brent LBC ex p Blatt* (1992) 24 HLR 319, DC.

13　See Woodfall, *Landlord and Tenant,* Sweet & Maxwell, Volume 1-13.048; Hill and Redman, *Law of Landlord and Tenant,* Butterworth; Dowding and Reynolds, *Dilapidations the Modern Law and Practice,* 4th edn, Sweet & Maxwell, 2008.

14　*Lister v Lane* [1893] 2 QB 212, CA; *Pembery v Lamdin* [1940] 2 All ER 434, CA.

15　*Alker v Collingwood Housing Association* [2007] EWCA Civ 343; (2007) 29 HLR 430.

16　*Proudfoot v Hart* (1890) 25 QBD 42.

17　[2001] EWCA Civ 1334; [2002] L&TR 7.

the construction of contracts. It held that, in construing express repairing obligations, a common sense approach was required, having regard to the background factual matrix in which the contract was produced and disregarding the 'old intellectual baggage of "legal" interpretation'. This was applied in *Petersson v Pitt Place (Epsom) Ltd*,[18] where a judge's decision that both a landlord and tenant were obliged to repair a roof terrace was overturned. The Court of Appeal held that leases have to be construed so as to avoid overlapping repairing obligations.

1.14   It is common for landlords of residential property to (a) contract to carry out repairs (but not to carry out improvements, or to keep the premises in as good a state as when let, or to ensure that the dwelling remains suitable for human habitation); and (b) contract to repair only the structural or external parts of the dwelling (but not the internal, non-structural parts, eg, internal doors, kitchen fittings, decorations and so forth).

1.15   The adviser must check carefully whether the tenancy agreement contains repairing obligations which are more extensive. For example, in *Welsh v Greenwich LBC*,[19] the tenancy agreement provided that the landlord would 'maintain the dwelling in good condition and repair'. The landlord was held liable in civil proceedings for severe condensation and mould growth not involving structural or external disrepair. The Court of Appeal accepted that the phrase 'good condition' was intended to mark a separate concept and to make a significant addition to what was conveyed by the word 'repair'. Liability for condensation dampness was also established in *Johnson v Sheffield CC*,[20] where the tenancy agreement provided that the landlord would keep the dwelling 'fit to live in'.

1.16   Many tenancy agreements particularly those drafted by social landlords, contain express repairing obligations dealing with common parts. In *Long v Southwark LBC*,[21] the tenancy agreement provided that the landlord would 'take reasonable steps to keep the estate and common parts clean and tidy'. The landlord was held liable for rubbish left outside the rubbish chute, which, although in working order, was inadequate in size. It was not sufficient that the landlord had instructed contractors to clean because it did not have an adequate system for monitoring the contractors' performance.

18   [2001] EWCA Civ 86; [2002] HLR 52.
19   (2001) 33 HLR 40, CA.
20   August 1994 *Legal Action* 16, Sheffield County Court.
21   [2002] EWCA Civ 403; [2002] HLR 56.

1.17   Many social landlords also include lengthy definitions of exactly what is covered by their repairing obligations, which may be wider than the obligations implied by statute. For example, many social landlords agree that they are obliged to repair the plasterwork to demised premises. Other landlords may have contracted to keep parts of the interior in repair or to keep fittings in repair and working order. The message for all tenants and their advisers is: always check first exactly what the tenancy agreement says.

Meaning of 'repair' and 'disrepair'

1.18   What exactly does the word 'repair' cover and how is it to be applied? Ultimately, the question of whether a disputed item of required work is repair or renewal or maintenance or improvement will be one for the courts, based on the facts of the individual case, but some early decisions give a useful indication of the principles to be applied. For example, in *Lurcott v Wakeley*[22] it was said that repair means the restoration by renewal or replacement of subsidiary parts of the whole; whereas renewal, as distinguished from repair, means the reconstruction of the whole. In *Lurcott*, repair was held to cover the replacement of a deteriorated wall, since the wall was only a subsidiary part of the whole.

1.19   Denning LJ also gave guidance on the test to be applied:

> If the work which is done is the provision of something new for the benefit of the occupier, that is, properly speaking an improvement; but if it is only the replacement of something already there which has become dilapidated or worn out, then, albeit that it is a replacement by its modern equivalent, it comes within the category of repairs not improvements'.[23]

More recently, Sachs LJ said that the correct approach is to:

> ... look at the particular building, look at the state which it is in at the date of the lease, look at the precise terms of the lease, and then come to a conclusion whether, on a fair interpretation of those terms in relation to that state, the requisite work can fairly be called repair.[24]

1.20   It is clear that repair is the converse of disrepair. There must be disrepair before the landlord is liable to repair. Disrepair occurs when

22 [1911] 1 KB 905, CA.
23 *Morcom v Campbell-Johnson* [1956] 1 QB 106, CA.
24 *Brew Bros Ltd v Snax* [1970] 1 QB 612, CA.

there is deterioration, ie, when part of the building is in a worse condition than it was at some earlier time.[25]

Inherent defects

1.21   It follows that the landlord is not liable under a contractual repairing obligation simply because part of the dwelling was designed or constructed badly. If the dwelling has always had the defect in question, there has been no deterioration. In *Stent v Monmouth DC*[26] the front door did not have weatherboarding and permitted rain-water to penetrate into the dwelling but the landlord was not liable at that point because the door had always been defective in that respect. In *Post Office Properties Ltd v Aquarius Properties Ltd*[27] a defective kicker joint allowed ground water to penetrate laterally into a basement but the landlord was similarly not liable because the joint had always been defective.

1.22   It would, however, be going much too far to say that landlords are never liable to put right building defects which are 'inherent', ie, which have been present since construction. In *Stent v Monmouth DC*[28] the rain-water penetration eventually caused the door itself to rot, ie, deteriorate. Because the landlord was obliged under the terms of the tenancy agreement to keep the door in repair, it was required to repair the door. It was not relevant that the deterioration had been caused by an inherent defect. Furthermore, the court ordered the landlord to repair the door in such a way that future rain-water penetration and future disrepair to the door would not occur: by installing a proper, weather-proof door. In effect, the court ordered the landlord to rectify an inherent defect in order to remedy current disrepair and prevent future disrepair.

1.23   If the inherent defect causes disrepair to other parts of the building for which the landlord is responsible under the terms of the tenancy agreement, the court will usually require the landlord to remedy that damage.[29] If it would be practical and sensible to remedy the underlying defect to prevent it from causing the same disrepair over and over again, then the courts will order the landlord to remedy the

25   *Post Office v Aquarius Properties* [1987] 1 All ER 1055, CA; *Quick v Taff-Ely BC* [1986] 1 QB 809, CA.

26   (1987) 19 HLR 269, CA.

27   [1987] 1 All ER 1055, CA.

28   (1987) 19 HLR 269, CA.

29   *Staves and Staves v Leeds CC* (1991) 23 HLR 107, CA.

inherent defect.[30] The only exception occurs when the work involved is disproportionately extensive and/or costly.

Disproportionately extensive or costly work

1.24 It is always a question of degree whether that which the landlord is being asked to do can properly be described as a repair, or whether on the contrary it would involve producing a wholly different thing from that which was demised: *Stent v Monmouth DC*.[31] Examples of work which has been held to be too extensive or costly to be a 'repair' are: complete replacement of foundations;[32] complete replacement of cladding to a high-rise building;[33] the replacement of the whole of a steel frame;[34] and the installation of a damp-proof course.[35] Whether or not the work required is too extensive or costly in any given case will depend on exactly what work is required, what it is likely to cost, how long it will prolong the life of the dwelling and what the terms of the tenancy agreement are.[36]

1.25 The most recent guidance is given in *McDougall v Easington DC*,[37] where Mustill LJ said:

> It is my opinion that three different tests may be discerned, which may be applied separately or concurrently as the circumstances of the individual case may demand, but all to be approached in the light of the nature and age of the premises, their condition when the tenant went into occupation, and the other express terms of the tenancy:
> (i) whether the alterations went to the whole or substantially the whole of the structure or only to a subsidiary part;
> (ii) whether the effect of the alterations was to produce a building of a wholly different character than that which had been let;
> (iii) what was the cost of the works in relation to the previous value of the building and what was their effect on the value and lifespan of the building?

---

30 *Ravenseft Properties v Davstone (Holdings) Ltd* [1980] QB 12, QBD; *Elmcroft Developments Ltd v Tankersley-Sawyer* (1984) 15 HLR 63, CA; cf *Quick v Taff-Ely BC* [1986] QB 809, CA.
31 (1987) 19 HLR 269, CA.
32 *Lister v Lane* [1983] 2 QB 212.
33 *Holding & Management Ltd v Property Holding & Investment Trust Ltd* (1989) 21 HLR 596, CA.
34 *Plough Investments Ltd v Manchester CC* [1989] 1 EGLR 244.
35 *Eyre v McCracken* (2001) 33 HLR 169, CA.
36 *Holding & Management Ltd v Property Holding & Investment Trust Ltd* (1989) 21 HLR 596, CA.
37 (1989) 21 HLR 310, CA.

1.26   In *McDougall v Easington DC*,[38] considerable work had been undertaken to a council house of system-built, concrete panel construction,
namely the removal of the whole of the front and rear elevations, the
replacement of the roof structure, and rain-water system, replacement of windows and doors, and stripping out of the interior fittings.
These works were held to constitute an improvement rather than a
repair, as the house 'not only looked different but was different ... The
outcome was a house with a substantially longer life and worth nearly
twice as much as before.' The works had given the house 'a new life
in a different form'.[39] A similar view was taken in *Eyre v McCracken*,[40]
where the Court of Appeal reviewed the authorities on the installation
of damp-proof courses and found that to require a Rent Act protected
tenant to insert a damp-proof course into a property in 2001 would
be to require him to give back to the landlord a different thing from
that demised to him in 1976 and would therefore be an improvement
rather than a repair. This case is not, however, authority for the proposition that a landlord will not be obliged to insert a damp-proof course
under the landlord's repairing obligations because the court held that
'the circumstances are very different from those involved in the consideration of the landlord's covenant in *Elmcroft Developments*'[41] (see
paragraph 1.32), where such works were held to be a repair.

Small defects

1.27   Conversely, small defects such as nail holes and minor cracking (to
plaster or rendering) are in many cases not considered to be sufficiently serious to amount to disrepair.

1.28   The reason is that the courts have qualified the meaning of disrepair. It does not mean any degree of deterioration, but deterioration
which as a matter of fact and degree is unacceptable after taking into
account and making allowances for the age of the premises, their
character, the local area and the type of tenants likely to want to rent
them.[42]

---

38   (1989) 21 HLR 310, CA.
39   *McDougall v Easington DC* (1989) 21 HLR 310, CA, per Mustill LJ at 316.
40   (2001) 33 HLR 169, CA.
41   *Eyre v McCracken* (2001) 33 HLR 169, CA, per Pill LJ at para 46.
42   *Anstruther-Gough-Calthorpe v McOscar* [1924] 1 KB 716, CA.

Repair and decoration

1.29 An obligation to repair includes, if necessary, an obligation to carry out decoration required to preserve whatever is to be repaired.[43] It should also be noted that the requirement to 'repair' carries with it an obligation on the landlord to make good or redecorate on completion of repair works.[44] On the extent of a landlord's obligation to redecorate, see *Vukelic v Hammersmith and Fulham LBC*.[45] There is no liability to redecorate after improvement works (which are not considered to be works of repair) save where such redecoration is negotiated as a condition for granting a landlord permission to do improvement works.[46]

Prevention of future damage

1.30 An obligation to repair can include an obligation to prevent future damage.[47]

Patch repairs or complete renewal

1.31 The obligation to repair can sometimes require the landlord completely to renew or to replace part of a dwelling instead of carrying out a temporary or patch repair.

1.32 In *Elmcroft Developments Ltd v Tankersley-Sawyer*,[48] for example, the landlords conceded that their obligation to repair the structure required them to hack off and replace wall plaster each time it became damp but denied that it required them to tackle the source of the dampness (rising damp) by installing a damp-proof course. Ackner LJ said:

> The patching work would have to go on and on, because as the plaster absorbed (as it would) the rising damp, it would have to be renewed and the cost to the [landlords] in constantly being involved in this sort of work, one would have thought, would have outweighed easily the cost in doing the job properly. I have no hesitation in rejecting the

---

43 *Irvine v Moran* (1991) 24 HLR 1, QBD.

44 *McGreal v Wake* (1984) 13 HLR 107, CA; *Bradley v Chorley BC* (1985) 17 HLR 305, CA.

45 [2003] EWHC 188 (TCC); November 2003 *Legal Action* 13.

46 *McDougall v Easington DC* (1989) 21 HLR 310, CA.

47 *Holding & Management Ltd v Property Holding & Investment Trust Ltd* (1989) 21 HLR 596, CA; *McDougall v Easington DC* [1989] 21 HLR 310, CA.

48 (1984) 15 HLR 63, CA.

submission that the appellant's obligation was repetitively to carry out futile work instead of doing the job properly once and for all.

1.33 The notion that patch repairing was sufficient to discharge the duty was similarly rejected in *Stent v Monmouth DC*.[49] In that case there had been a problem for over 30 years of rot to a wooden front door and frame. The landlords had repeatedly cut out and repaired parts of the door and frame and from time to time replaced the rotten wooden door with another wooden door which then rotted. The Court of Appeal had no hesitation in holding that, on the facts, the obligation to 'repair' was not discharged by these patch repairs. The council 'had the obligation to make good the design defect which caused the collection of water which occasioned the rotting'.[50] This was achieved by installing a self-sealing aluminium door.

1.34 *Quick v Taff Ely BC*[51] does not fit happily with this line of authority. In that case a window sill and wall plaster required replacement because of acute condensation dampness. That in turn could be cured by double glazing, insulation etc. However, insufficient findings of fact had been made in the county court to show that the only 'proper' way of tackling the limited disrepair which had been proved was the major work urged by the tenant.

1.35 In summary, the test of whether patch repairs will suffice is whether tackling the root cause would be a 'mode of repair which a sensible person would have adopted; and the same reasoning applies if for the word "sensible" there is substituted some such word as "practicable" or "necessary"'.[52] The burden is on the tenant to lead the evidence which shows that further patch repairs will not suffice and that a more radical repair or replacement is necessary.[53] The tenant was unable to discharge this burden in *Dame Margaret Hungerford Charity Trustees v Beazeley*[54] where it was held that, since the property was to be completed reconstructed in the near future, further patch repairs were sufficient, even though ordinarily the replacement of the roof would have been required.

49 (1987) 19 HLR 269, CA.
50 *Stent v Monmouth DC* (1987) 19 HLR 269, CA, per Sir John Arnold at 286.
51 [1986] 1 QB 809.
52 *Stent v Monmouth DC* (1987) 19 HLR 269, CA, per Stocker LJ at 284–5; see also *Carmel Southend Ltd v Strachen and Henshaw* [2007] EWHC 1289 (TCC).
53 *Murray v Birmingham CC* (1988) 20 HLR 39, CA.
54 (1994) 26 HLR 269, CA.

Blocked conduits

1.36   Gutters and flues which are blocked are in disrepair.[55]

Non-statutory implied terms for the benefit of tenants

1.37   At common law, the landlord has no duty to repair or to ensure that the dwelling is habitable.[56] Neither is the landlord under a common law duty of care to take reasonable steps to ensure that any occupier of the rented premises does not suffer personal injury or damage to his or her property as the result of defects to the premises.[57] This is historically why the terms of the contract are of such importance to a tenant with repairing problems. There are, however, a number of exceptions to the common law immunity of the landlord achieved by implying terms which impose obligations on landlords.

Lettings of furnished dwellings

1.38   Where the landlord lets a furnished dwelling for immediate occupation it will be an implied term of the contract of letting that the premises are fit for human habitation at the start of the tenancy.[58]

1.39   The term does not apply to lettings of unfurnished dwellings.[59] Furthermore, the obligation is strictly an initial one, ie, that the premises were fit when they were let.[60] However, the term will be broken if the dwelling is initially unfit but the lack of fitness becomes obvious only at a later stage of the tenancy.[61]

1.40   The courts have held that dwelling-houses are unfit for human habitation at common law if they are infested by bugs,[62] have a

---

55 *Melles & Co v Holme* [1918] KB 100, KBD; *Bishop v Consolidated London Properties Ltd* (1933) 102 LJKB 257; *Greg v Planque* [1936] 1 KB 669, CA; *Passley v Wandsworth LBC* (1998) 30 HLR 165, CA.

56 *Cavalier v Pope* [1906] AC 428, HL; *Robbins v Jones* (1863) 15 CB(NS) 221.

57 *McNerny v Lambeth LBC* (1989) 21 HLR 188, CA.

58 *Smith v Marrable* (1843) 11 M&W 5; *Hart v Windsor* (1844) 12 M&W 68; *Wilson v Finch-Hatton* (1877) 2 Ex D 336.

59 *McNerny v Lambeth LBC* (1989) 21 HLR 188, CA.

60 *Sarson v Roberts* [1895] 2 QB 395.

61 *Harrison v Malet* (1886) 3 TLR 58.

62 *Smith v Marrable* (1843) 11 M&W 5.

defective drainage[63] or sewerage system,[64] or carry an infection,[65] or if there is a lack of safety,[66] or an insufficiency of water supply.[67] Note, however, that the obligation is confined to fitness for habitation and that the implied term does not require the landlord to ensure that the premises are in structural repair when let, eg, cracked ceiling plaster will not be covered.

1.41   Guidance on whether premises are unfit at common law may be obtained from the case-law on statutory provisions referring to that term in a housing context.[68] In its modern application, the implied term will still be of use to tenants of furnished dwellings whose homes were in very poor condition when let.[69] Examples would include premises which were affected by penetrating dampness, infested with cockroaches or fitted with dangerous electrical wiring.

1.42   Generally, implied terms can be excluded from any letting by an express term to the contrary. However, the OFT Guidance suggests that it would be unfair for a landlord to use an express term to avoid this implied term in lettings to which the UTCC Regs 1999 apply.[70]

1.43   As long ago as 1996 the Law Commission proposed a general implied term about fitness.[71] But to date its recommendations have not been implemented. In *Lee v Leeds CC*,[72] the Court of Appeal held that there was no basis for implying into tenancies of social housing let by public authorities an obligation to keep a dwelling in good condition or to remedy defects which make it unfit for human habitation. Any such extension to the law will have to come from Parliament, which seems unlikely at the present time.

---

63 *Wilson v Finch-Hatton* (1887) 2 Ex D 336.

64 *Harrison v Malet* (1886) 3 TLR 58.

65 *Bird v Greville* (1884) C & E 317; *Collins v Hopkins* [1923] 2 KB 617.

66 *Edwards v Etherington* (1825) Ry & M 268.

67 *Chester v Powell* (1885) 52 LT 722.

68 See case-law on HA 1985 s604 (repealed in England by HA 2004 Sch 16, with effect from 6 April 2006) and Defective Premises Act 1972 s1, eg *McMinn v Bole & Van den Haak v Huntsbuild Ltd & Money* [2009] EWHC 483 (TCC).

69 See, eg, *Shefford v Nofax Enterprises (Acton) Ltd* December 2006 *Legal Action* 24; *Housing Law Casebook* para P11.53, Central London County Court.

70 *Guidance on unfair terms in tenancy agreements* OFT356, para 3.14.

71 Law Commission, *Landlord and Tenant: Responsibility for State and Condition of Property* LC238, HMSO, 1996.

72 [2002] EWCA Civ 6; [2002] 1 WLR 1488.

Dwelling-houses held under a licence

1.44   Where there is a licence and not a tenancy, a term may be implied in the licence requiring the licensor to take reasonable care to ensure that the condition of the dwelling does not cause personal injury to any of the occupiers or damage their property.[73]

Means of access and communal facilities

1.45   It is an implied term for most tenancies of residential accommodation that the landlord is obliged to take reasonable care to keep means of access and communal facilities (eg, shared rubbish chutes or lifts) in repair and proper working order, if that is not already required by an express term.[74]

Ancillary property owned by the landlord

1.46   The courts will generally imply a term imposing a duty on the landlord to take reasonable care to ensure that the condition of ancillary property retained in his or her ownership (eg, the roof of a block of flats, common hall, water tanks, heating plant or drains) does not deteriorate so as to cause personal injury to the tenant or damage to his or her property.[75]

1.47   There will, however, be no grounds for implying a term about repair of the common parts where provision is comprehensively made for such repairs in a written tenancy agreement.[76]

Quiet enjoyment/derogation from grant

1.48   A landlord either expressly or by necessary implication contracts to give the tenant 'quiet enjoyment' of the rented premises for the duration of the letting. This may be breached in circumstances of disrepair, for example by a landlord failing to keep watertight the building containing the tenant's flat, thereby allowing the flat to be penetrated

---

73   *Greene v Chelsea BC* [1954] 2 QB 127, CA. See also *Wettern Electric Ltd v Welsh Development Agency* [1983] 1 QB 796, QBD; *Morris-Thomas v Petticoat Lane Rentals* (1987) 53 P&CR 238.

74   *Miller v Emcer Products* [1956] Ch 304, CA; *Liverpool CC v Irwin* [1977] AC 239, HL; *King v South Northamptonshire DC* (1992) 24 HLR 284, CA; cf *Duke of Westminster v Guild* [1985] QB 688, CA.

75   *Dunster v Hollis* [1918] 2 KB 795; *Cockburn v Smith* [1924] 2 KB 119; *Duke of Westminster v Guild* [1985] QB 688, CA.

76   *Gordon v Selico Ltd* (1986) 18 HLR 219, CA.

by rain-water or dampness,[77] or by carrying out work on other parts of the building, causing noise and nuisance to the tenants.[78]

1.49   The covenant of quiet enjoyment is prospective in nature and does not apply to things done before the grant of the tenancy even though they may have continuing consequences.[79] Accordingly, in *Southwark LBC v Mills*,[80] the landlord did not breach the covenant by failing to install effective soundproofing. The doctrine of *caveat lessee* applied: the tenant took the premises in the state in which they were let and could not complain about any pre-existing defect.

1.50   The covenant does not create new repairing obligations. But if the landlord fails to perform his or her obligations or carries out those obligations so as to interfere unreasonably with the tenant's occupation there will be a breach of the covenant of quiet enjoyment in addition to other causes of action.[81] In *Goldmile Properties v Lechouritis*,[82] the Court of Appeal held that a lease containing a landlord's repairing obligation and a covenant for quiet enjoyment had to be construed to give effect to both provisions. Accordingly, a landlord had to take all reasonable precautions to prevent disturbance being caused by repairs but could not be required to take every possible precaution. In *Thornton and Jarrett v Birmingham CC*,[83] HHJ McKenna found that the council had breached the covenant of quiet enjoyment when it had failed to rehouse the tenant while repair works were carried out, even though she had not asked to be rehoused; not all reasonable steps to minimise the risks had been taken having regard to the tenant's children, aged 8 and 10.

1.51   A landlord shall not 'derogate from his grant' of a tenancy to the tenant. This implied term may be breached in relation to disrepair if a landlord allows premises retained in his or her ownership or occupation to be in such a state as to interfere with the tenant's tenancy. The principle of non-derogation from grant cannot be used to create new repairing obligations.[84]

77   *Booth v Thomas* [1926] Ch 397, CA; *Gordon v Selico Ltd* (1986) 18 HLR 219, CA.
78   *Mira v Aylmer Square Investments* (1990) 22 HLR 182, CA; *Sampson v Wilson* [1996] Ch 39.
79   *Southwark LBC v Mills* [2001] 1 AC 1, HL.
80   [2001] 1 AC 1, HL.
81   *Duke of Westminster v Guild* [1985] 1 QB 688, CA.
82   [2003] EWCA Civ 49, CA.
83   November 2004 *Legal Action* 27; *Housing Law Casebook* para P11.58, Birmingham County Court.
84   *Duke of Westminster v Guild* [1985] 1 QB 688, CA.

Correlative obligations

1.52   If the tenancy agreement requires the tenant to pay for certain works or services, it will usually be implied that the landlord will actually perform those works or services.[85] In *Edmonton Corporation v Knowles*,[86] the tenant was obliged to pay to the landlord the cost of redecorating the exterior in every third year of the term. It was held that there was a correlative obligation on the landlord to carry out the redecoration. Similarly in *Collins v Northern Ireland Housing Executive*,[87] tenants were obliged to pay standing charges and amounts for consumption of heating and hot water provided through a central system. It was held that it was an implied term of a collateral contract, which existed between the parties, that the landlord authority would provide and maintain the heating system.

1.53   Other tenant's obligations can also result in terms being implied which are binding on the landlord. In general, a term will be implied into a contract where the implication of the term is necessary to give business efficacy to a transaction and where both parties would have agreed to its insertion had its absence been pointed out to them when they concluded the contract.[88]

1.54   In *Barrett v Lounova (1982) Ltd*,[89] the tenant was contractually bound to carry out all inside repairs and leave the inside of the premises in good repair and condition. There were no express repairing obligations binding on the landlord and LTA 1985 s11 (see paragraphs 1.69–1.99) did not apply because the tenancy began before 24 October 1961. The dwelling was in a poor state of repair, suffering from severe rain-water penetration as the result of roof defects. The Court of Appeal held that it was an implied term of the agreement that the landlord would keep the structure and exterior of the dwelling in repair:

> It is obvious, as shown by this case itself, that sooner or later the covenant imposed on the tenant in respect of the inside can no longer be complied with unless the outside has been kept in repair ... In my view, it is therefore necessary, as a matter of business efficacy, to make this agreement workable, that an obligation to keep the outside in repair must be imposed on someone.[90]

85   *Edmonton Corporation v Knowles* (1962) 60 LGR 124.
86   (1962) 60 LGR 124.
87   [1987] 2 NIJB 27 CA(NI); *Housing Law Casebook* para P4.14.
88   *Liverpool CC v Irwin* [1977] AC 239, HL.
89   [1990] 1 QB 348, CA.
90   *Barrett v Lounova* (1982) Ltd [1990] 1 QB 348, CA, per Kerr LJ at 358C.

1.55   The extent to which correlative obligations such as this may be imposed remains unclear,[91] but the modern trend is against the implication of new implied terms, see, eg, *Adami v Lincoln Grange Management Ltd*[92] (a long leaseholder case), where it was held that the decision in *Barrett v Lounova*[93] should be confined to its own facts. More recently in *Lee v Leeds CC*,[94] the Court of Appeal declined to imply a term that the landlord remedy design defects or keep the dwelling in a condition which enabled the tenant to perform her obligations under the tenancy, namely to keep the inside of her home clean and in a reasonable state of decoration. The court relied on the fact that the landlord was already liable to repair the exterior, whereas in *Barrett v Lounova*[95] there was no exterior repairing covenant.

Implied term on quality of repair work

1.56   It has been held at county court level that there is an implied term to do repairs with reasonable care and skill and proper materials.[96] The Supply of Goods and Services Act 1982 also creates a duty on those providing goods to ensure that they are of satisfactory quality and on those providing services to do so with reasonable care and skill.

Statutory implied terms for the benefit of tenants

1.57   As we have seen, the basic rule at common law is that the landlord is not liable for housing defects except in so far as expressly provided in the tenancy agreement. The common law exceptions to this rule, described above, are piecemeal and limited in scope. As a result, Parliament has legislated to imply limited and basic repairing obligations into certain types of tenancy.

Landlord and Tenant Act 1985 s8

1.58   Section 8 of the LTA 1985 implies into lettings at a low rent (for example, certain periodic tenancies) two separate contractual terms which are absolute and non-excludable:

91   *Demetriou v Poolaction Ltd* (1991) 25 EG 113, CA.
92   (1997) 30 HLR 982, CA.
93   [1990] 1 QB 348, CA.
94   [2002] EWCA Civ 6; [2002] 1 WLR 1488, CA.
95   [1990] 1 QB 348, CA.
96   *Walton v Lewisham LBC* May 1997 *Legal Action* 20; *Housing Law Casebook* para P4.13, Tunbridge Wells County Court.

- that the premises are fit for human habitation on the date of letting; and
- that the premises will be kept fit for habitation, by the landlord, throughout the duration of the tenancy.

See appendix A for the full text of s8.

1.59 Both terms apply to lettings of whole houses or parts of houses.[97] The apparently wide scope of s8 is, however, limited by the narrow range of lettings to which it applies. In order to have the benefit of these implied terms the annual rent (irrespective of who pays the rates[98]) must be less than the maximum amounts shown below:

Date of letting	Maximum annual rent
Before 31 July 1923	£40.00 in London £26.00 in boroughs or districts with over 5,000 people £16.00 elsewhere
On or after 31 July 1923 and before 6 July 1957	£40.00 in London £26.00 elsewhere
On or after 6 July 1957 and before 1 April 1965	£80.00 in London £52.00 elsewhere
On or after 1 April 1965	£80.00 in inner London £52.00 in outer London and elsewhere

1.60 If the letting was originally at a rent not greater than the maximum figure shown above, the tenant has the benefit of the implied terms. The current rent is irrelevant. As will be apparent, very few periodic tenancies remain which can benefit from s8. The failure to uprate the rent levels to give protection to more recent tenants has attracted judicial comment in the Court of Appeal.[99] The Government has declined to increase the rent levels, because in its view the s8 provisions are 'effectively out of date', having been overtaken by the more modern provisions of s11.[100] The Law Commission has recommended[101] that, subject to certain exceptions, legislation should impose a term on leases of dwellings for less than seven years that the landlord will

---

97 LTA 1985 s8(6).
98 *Rousou v Photi* [1940] 2 KB 379, CA.
99 *Quick v Taff Ely BC* [1986] 1 QB 809, CA.
100 Lord Skelmersdale, HL Debs col 370, 22 October 1986.
101 Law Commission, *Landlord and Tenant: Responsibility for State and Condition of Property* LC238, HMSO, 1996, at para 7.7.

keep the dwelling fit for human habitation, applying the statutory definition of unfitness which used to be contained in HA 1985 s604. The Law Commission's proposals have yet to be acted on.

1.61   Section 8 is not applicable to a letting for a fixed term of three years or more where it is expressly agreed that the tenant will put the premises into a condition reasonably fit for habitation (s8(5)). If the letting contains no such term, the benefit of s8 extends to any long lease which fulfils the low rent condition.

1.62   The section gives the landlord an express power to enter and inspect premises after giving the tenant or occupier 24 hours' notice in writing of his or her intention to do so (s8(2)).

1.63   In determining whether a house is fit for human habitation, regard is to be had to its condition in respect of: repair, stability, freedom from damp, internal arrangement, natural lighting, ventilation, water supply, drainage/sanitary conveniences, facilities for the preparation and cooking of food, and facilities for the disposal of waste water. The house is deemed to be unfit for human habitation if, and only if, it is so far defective in one or more of these respects that it is not reasonably suitable for occupation in that condition: LTA 1985 s10.

1.64   Breaches of the terms implied by s8 have been successfully established in a wide range of cases, for example: a small house in which the sole window in a main room could not be safely opened;[102] premises where plaster had fallen from the ceiling;[103] the complete collapse of a ceiling;[104] and accommodation in which a sanitary convenience was defective and serious dampness had accrued from defective guttering.[105]

1.65   It should be noted that liability arises only in relation to the defects within the premises let to the tenant, so that, for example, defective common staircases[106] and occasional incursions of vermin from elsewhere[107] will be outside the scope of the terms implied by s8.

1.66   A 'rule of thumb' guide to the standards required by s8 was set out by Atkin LJ in 1926:

> If the state of repair of a house is such that by ordinary use damage may naturally be caused to the occupier, either in respect of personal

---

102 *Summers v Salford Corporation* [1943] AC 283, HL.

103 *Walker v Hobbs & Co* (1889) 23 QBD 458.

104 *Fisher v Walters* [1926] 2 KB 315, KBD.

105 *Horrex v Pidwell* [1958] CLY 1461.

106 *Dunster v Hollis* [1918] 2 KB 795, KBD.

107 *Stanton v Southwick* [1920] 2 KB 642, KBD.

injury to life or limb or injury to health, then the house is not in all respects reasonably fit for human habitation.[108]

1.67 The courts have, however, developed a serious limitation to the usefulness of s8 by confining its application to premises which can be made fit by the landlord at reasonable expense.[109] This controversial decision rests on a concession made in argument and has no foundation within s8 itself. It has stood unchallenged for over three decades and is ripe for review.

1.68 Advisers should note that s8 is not applicable to tenants of temporary accommodation owned by local authorities in clearance areas or subject to prohibition orders.[110]

Landlord and Tenant Act 1985 s11

1.69 This is the main statutory repairing obligation which is implied into all tenancies of less than seven years beginning on or after 24 October 1961. Nowadays, most tenants can rely on this repairing obligation, even if their tenancy agreement contains no express repairing obligations.

1.70 LTA 1985 s11 implies into tenancy agreements an obligation on landlords to effect certain repairs which is both absolute and non-excludable. Section 11 replaced HA 1961 s32. For the full text of LTA ss11–17 see appendix A.

1.71 The obligation is as follows (as amended by the HA 1988 in respect of tenancies entered into on or after 15 January 1989):

11(1) In a lease to which this section applies ... there is implied a covenant by the lessor –
(a) to keep in repair the structure and exterior of the dwelling-house (including drains, gutters and external pipes),
(b) to keep in repair and proper working order the installations in the dwelling-house for the supply of water, gas and electricity and for sanitation (including basins, sinks, baths and sanitary conveniences but not other fixtures, fittings and appliances for making use of the supply of water, gas or electricity), and
(c) to keep in repair and proper working order the installations in the dwelling-house for space heating and heating water.

(1A) If a lease to which this section applies is a lease of a dwelling-house which forms part only of a building, then subject to

108 *Morgan v Liverpool Corporation* [1927] 2 KB 131, CA.
109 *Buswell v Goodwin* [1971] 1 WLR 92, CA.
110 HA 1985 s302.

subsection (1B), the covenant implied by sub-section (1) shall have effect as if –

(a) the reference in paragraph (a) of that subsection to the dwelling-house included a reference to any part of the building in which the lessor has an estate or interest; and

(b) any references in paragraphs (b) and (c) of that subsection to an installation in the dwelling-house included a reference to an installation which, directly or indirectly, serves the dwelling-house and which either –

　(i) forms part of any part of a building in which the lessor has an estate or interest; or

　(ii) is owned by the lessor or under his control.

(1B)　Nothing in subsection (1A) shall be construed as requiring the lessor to carry out any works or repairs unless the disrepair (or failure to maintain in working order) is such as to affect the lessee's enjoyment of the dwelling-house or of any common parts, as defined in section 60(1) of the Landlord and Tenant Act 1987, which the lessee, as such, is entitled to use.

1.72　Tenancies which pre-date 15 January 1989 do not have the benefit of s11(1A) and s11(1B), so the obligation to repair is limited to the structure and exterior of the dwelling and the installations therein. However pre-1989 tenants not covered by the amendments to s11, may be able to rely on the common law implied terms described in paragraphs 1.37–1.56.

1.73　The landlord cannot exclude the obligation imposed by s11 by the use of express contractual terms. Any term purporting to exclude liability (s12(1)(a)) or transfer it to the tenant (s11(4)) is void.[111]

1.74　The landlord or the landlord's agent is given a statutory right to enter premises for the purpose of viewing the condition and state of repair on giving the tenant 24 hours' notice in writing: s11(6).

Interpreting s11

1.75　Owing to the breadth of the implied terms contained in s11, the component parts have been subject to close scrutiny.

1.76　**'keep in repair'** The covenant to keep in repair is a continuing obligation to keep up the standard of repair in the dwelling throughout the duration of the tenancy. Moreover, it also requires the landlord to put the premises into repair if they were not in good repair at the outset of the tenancy.[112]

111　*Irvine v Moran* (1991) 24 HLR 1, QBD; *Islington LBC v Keane* December 2005 *Legal Action* 28; *Housing Law Casebook* para P5.27, Clerkenwell County Court.

112　*Proudfoot v Hart* (1890) 25 QBD 42.

1.77   For the scope of works covered by the term 'repair' see paragraphs 1.18–1.36.[113]

1.78   **'the structure and exterior'** For s11(1)(a) or s11(1A)(a) to apply it must be shown that there is actually some part of the structure or exterior which is in a state of disrepair and therefore requires 'repair', ie, 'the covenant will only come into operation where there has been damage to the structure and exterior which requires to be made good'.[114] Evidence of damage to decoration, clothing, bedding, curtains, etc is all to no avail unless some part of the structure or exterior can be shown to require repair.

1.79   The **structure** is less than the whole dwelling but more than just the load-bearing elements. It is usually taken to refer to:

> those elements of the overall dwelling-house which give it its essential appearance, stability and shape. The expression does not extend to the many and various ways in which the dwelling-house will be fitted out, equipped, decorated and generally made to be habitable ... in order to be part of the structure of the dwelling-house a particular element must be a material or significant element in the overall construction.[115]

1.80   It is the opinion of the Law Commission that internal plaster should be treated as part of the structure for the purposes of LTA 1985 s11[116] and there are a number of cases in which concessions have been made to that effect or the court has assumed that plaster was part of the structure.[117] In *Hussein v Mehlman*[118] it was held that the contention that bedroom ceiling plaster was not part of the structure was untenable. However, the only binding authority directly on the point held that plaster is not part of the structure for the purposes of LTA 1985 s11, but more in the nature of a decorative finish.[119] But even in that case, it was held that 'to some extent, in every case there will be a degree of fact to be gone into to decide whether or not something is or is not part of the structure of the dwelling-house'.[120]

---

113 See too *Brunskill v Mulcahy* [2009] EWCA Civ 686.

114 *Quick v Taff Ely BC* [1986] QB 809, CA, at 818E.

115 *Irvine v Moran* (1991) 24 HLR 1, QBD, at 5. See also *Pearlman v Governors of Harrow School* [1979] QB 56, CA.

116 Law Commission, *Landlord and Tenant: Responsibility for State and Condition of Property* LC238, HMSO, 1996, at p69.

117 *Staves v Leeds CC* (1991) 23 HLR 107, CA; *Quick v Taff-Ely BC* [1986] QB 809, CA; *Palmer v Sandwell MBC* (1988) 20 HLR 74, CA.

118 [1992] 2 EGLR 87; [1992] 32 EG 59, Wood Green Trial Centre.

119 *Irvine v Moran* (1991) 24 HLR 1, QBD.

120 *Irvine v Moran* (1991) 24 HLR 1, QBD, at 5.

1.81   It was hoped that this issue might be resolved in *Niazi Services v Van der Loo*[121] but in the end the Court of Appeal declined to say anything about the cracks in the plaster in that case while acknowledging that the issue whether plasterwork was part of the structure was 'not free from difficulties of its own'.[122] In practice, the issue appears to depend on the extent and degree of the damage to any plasterwork with major problems being held to be structural.[123]

1.82   The **exterior** is the outside or external part of the dwelling-house. The liability under the covenant extends to all outside parts of the demised dwelling.

1.83   The interpretation of the words 'structure' and 'exterior' may be illustrated as follows:

- A partition wall between the dwelling and another house or flat is part of the structure or exterior.[124]
- Floor joists in a dwelling are part of the structure; the structure is not limited to items in the ownership of the landlord.[125]
- In relation to a house, the path and steps which are the immediate and ordinary means of access are within the 'exterior'[126] but the paving of the backyard is not.[127]
- The roof (if any) is part of the structure of a house as is any skylight it contains (see paragraph 1.84 for roofs of flats).[128]
- The walls are part of the structure, together with any cement rendering.[129] But a plasterboard false wall which had been nailed to the wall surface was not: it was affixed to the structural wall; it had not become part of it.[130]

---

121 [2004] EWCA Civ 53; [2004] 1 WLR 1254, CA.

122 *Niazi Services v Van der Loo* [2004] EWCA Civ 53; [2004] 1 WLR 1254 at para 7.

123 See, eg, *Willis and Willis v Fuller* May 1997 *Legal Action* 20; *Housing Law Casebook* para P5.30, Hastings County Court; *Thornton v Birmingham CC* November 2004 *Legal Action* 27; *Housing Law Casebook* para P11.58, Birmingham County Court; *Hyde Southbank Homes v Oronkaye and Obadiara* December 2005 *Legal Action* 28; *Housing Law Casebook* para P11.36, Bow County Court; cf *Morgan and Daniels v Birmingham CC* December 2007 *Legal Action* 29, Birmingham County Court.

124 *Green v Eales* [1841] 2 QB 225.

125 *Marlborough Park Services Ltd v Rowe and Another* [2006] EWCA Civ 436; [2006] HLR 30, CA.

126 *Brown v Liverpool Corporation* [1969] 3 All ER 1345, CA.

127 *Hopwood v Cannock Chase DC* [1975] 1 WLR 373, CA.

128 *Taylor v Webb* [1937] 2 KB 283.

129 *Granada Theatres Ltd v Freehold Investment (Leytonstone) Ltd* [1959] Ch 592, CA.

130 *Fincar SRL v 109/113 Mount Street Management Co Ltd* [1999] L&TR 161; [1998] EGCS 173, CA.

- External joinery will usually be part of the structure, and failure to paint it so as to protect it from rot will be a failure to repair.[131]
- Windows will be part of the structure if they are a substantial and integral part of the wall.[132] On the other hand, the ordinary windows in a house or flat are part of the exterior of the dwelling.[133] But external windows will usually be both part of the structure and exterior.[134]

1.84 Where the dwelling-house is a flat, 'structure and exterior' has been held to extend to: the outside wall(s) of the flat, the outside of the inner party wall of the flat, the outer sides of the horizontal divisions between the flat and the flats above and below, and ceilings and walls of the flat,[135] and the whole of the roof terraces of flats except for their tiled surface areas.[136] Where the ceiling and roof of a top-floor flat form an inseparable structural unit, the roof will be within the structure or exterior of the flat. In the case of other flats, whether a common roof is within the covenant will be a question of fact according to the particular circumstances.[137]

1.85 **'the dwelling-house'** This means the building or part of a building which is let to the tenant wholly or mainly as a private residence: LTA 1985 s16(b).

1.86 The 'structure and exterior' with which s11(1)(a) is concerned, then, is the 'structure and exterior of the dwelling-house' let to the tenant, ie, the tenant's own house or flat. Usually, therefore, the provision could not be used by the tenant of the lower of two flats to get the roof over the upper flat repaired, even if the disrepair was causing damage to the lower flat, since on any view the roof would not be part of the structure or exterior of the lower flat. The position is different for tenancies commencing on or after 15 January 1989. In these tenancies, the term implied by s11 is extended to include not only the structure and exterior of the demised premises but also

---

131 *Irvine v Moran* (1991) 24 HLR 1, QBD.

132 *Boswell v Crucible Steel Co of America* [1925] 1 KB 119, CA; *Holiday Fellowship v Hereford* [1959] 1 WLR 211, CA.

133 *Ball v Plummer* (1879) 23 SJ 656.

134 *Sheffield CC v Oliver* Lands Tribunal LRX/146/2007, December 2008 *Legal Action* 31.

135 *Campden Hill Towers v Gardner* [1977] QB 823, CA.

136 *Ibrahim v Dovecorn Reversions Ltd* (2001) 82 P&CR 362, ChD.

137 *Douglas-Scott v Scorgie* [1984] 1 WLR 716, CA; *Rapid Results College v Angell* [1986] 1 EGLR 53, CA; *Straudley Investments v Barpress Ltd* [1987] 1 EGLR 69, CA; *Hatfield v Moss* [1988] 2 EGLR 58, CA.

the remaining parts of the building in which the landlord retains an estate or interest (s11(1A)), providing the disrepair is in fact affecting the lessee's enjoyment of his or her own dwelling-house or the common parts. So in the example above, if water was penetrating into the lower flat owing to defects in the roof above the upper flat, the tenant of the lower flat could use s11(1A) to get the roof over the upper flat repaired, (even though it was not part of the structure or exterior of the lower flat), provided that the landlord of the lower flat owned or had some other interest in the roof above the upper flat as well.

1.87   **'keep in … proper working order'** These words necessarily presuppose that at the start of the tenancy the relevant installations were in proper working order, so that, if by reason of disrepair or design fault an installation has never been in proper working order, a landlord with knowledge of the defect will be in continuing breach of the implied term.[138]

1.88   But what if an installation for the supply of water, gas or electricity has been in proper working order but ceases to work properly owing to changes in supply? In *O'Connor v Old Etonians Housing Association Ltd*,[139] the Court of Appeal held that an installation would be in proper working order if it was able to function under those conditions of supply that it was reasonable to anticipate would prevail. If a variation to the supply occurred which could not have been reasonably anticipated, the landlord's duty to keep an installation in proper working order might require him or her to make modifications to the installation depending on the circumstances of the case, including the duration of the variation and the cost of modification.

1.89   **'the installations in the dwelling-house'** The landlord is obliged to keep in repair and in working order the installations specifically mentioned in s11(1)(b) and (c). The provision also extends to other installations for the supply of water, gas, electricity, sanitation, heating and hot water. Thus, water or gas pipes, electrical wiring, water tanks,[140] boilers, radiators and other space heating installations, such as vents for underfloor heating, will be within the repairing obligation.

1.90   The installations must usually be *in* the tenant's dwelling. However, some tenants (and particularly those in high-rise flats) experience major problems as a result of the failure of installations serving blocks or estates but sited outside their homes, for example, central

---

138 *Liverpool CC v Irwin* [1977] AC 239, HL.
139 [2002] EWCA Civ 150; [2002] Ch 295.
140 *Sheldon v West Bromwich Corporation* (1984) 13 HLR 23, CA.

heating boilers. The courts have declined to extend the benefit of the repairing covenant to such tenants. In the *Campden Hill Towers* case,[141] Megaw LJ said:

> .... the installations in the physical confines of the flat must be kept in repair and capable, so far as their own structural and mechanical condition is concerned, of working properly. But no more than that.

1.91   The requirement that the defective installations must be in the dwelling has been lifted for more recent tenants. If the tenancy was granted on or after 15 January 1989, the obligation to repair and keep in proper working order is extended to any installation which (a) either directly or indirectly serves the dwelling and (b) is either owned by or under the control of the landlord or forms part of any part of a building in which the landlord has an estate of interest, providing that the defect is in fact 'such as to affect the lessee's enjoyment of the dwelling-house or of any common parts' (s11(1A)(b)). This provision effectively overcomes the restrictions of the *Campden Hill Towers* decision. It gives these more recent tenants rights to require repairs to, for example, the communal heating boiler, the pump in the district heating system and the water tank on the roof of the tower block. However, it does not assist tenants where the defect to an installation is in a part of a building in which the landlord has no estate or interest. In *Niazi Services Ltd v Van der Loo,*[142] the landlord of a flat above a restaurant was held not liable for poor water pressure where this was because of works in the restaurant below, in which the landlord had no interest.

1.92   Apart from the installations specifically mentioned in the section, the repairing obligation does not extend to fixtures, fittings, and appliances for making use of water, gas, electricity and sanitation (s11(1)(b)).

1.93   In *Wycombe Area Health Authority v Barnett,*[143] the Court of Appeal held that the obligation in s11(1)(b) and (c) to keep the installations in the premises in proper working order did not impose a duty on the landlord to lag water tanks and pipes so as to avoid damage in exceptionally severe cold weather. The court did indicate, however, that a landlord would be liable if the pipes were prone to burst within the normal temperature range, and that since there was in any event no liability on the part of the tenant to do so, any prudent landlord would insulate the pipes to avoid damage being caused to his or her reversion.

---

141 *Campden Hill Towers v Gardner* [1977] QB 823, CA at 835H.
142 [2004] EWCA Civ 53; [2004] 1 WLR 1254.
143 (1982) 5 HLR 84, CA.

1.94   Even though the landlord will be presumed to know of the disrepair in the parts of the property he or she retains (so that there is no need for actual notice of such disrepair to be given), it is not certain that the courts will presume that the landlord knows of the effect on the individual tenants. It may, therefore, be advisable to ensure that the landlord has actual knowledge (preferably by notice) of both the defect and effect before proceeding for breach of s11(1A). It is a defence for the landlord to show in such proceedings that, despite using reasonable endeavours, he or she was unable to obtain the right to carry out the works to the particular part of the building concerned (eg, where the disrepair emanates from a flat of which the landlord is the freeholder but where the leaseholder is exercising a right to refuse access): s11(3A).

Standard for s11 repairs

1.95   The repairing obligations implied into tenancy agreements by s11 are subject to the important qualification that, in determining the standard of repair to be required, regard is to be had to the age, character, and prospective life of the dwelling-house and the locality in which it is situated: s11(3). Reference to age, character and locality does no more than re-state the position which applies in any event at common law: see paragraph 1.28. This is an area in which expert evidence may be required. In *Montoya v Hackney LBC*,[144] a finding that twisting of the doors and windows amounted to disrepair was overturned in the light of evidence from the single joint expert that the defects were commensurate with the age and type of property and so they did not amount to disrepair; the judge should not have departed from the only expert evidence in the case.

1.96   At least where disrepair is materially affecting the tenant's comfortable enjoyment of the dwelling-house, its 'prospective life' is only relevant if demolition is imminent.[145] On the other hand, the fact that complete reconstruction is envisaged is a good reason for patch repairing the roof in the meantime, even though ordinarily replacement would have been required.[146]

1.97   The standard of repair is no higher for a social landlord than it is in the private rented sector.[147]

---

144 December 2005 *Legal Action* 28, QBD.
145 *Newham LBC v Patel* (1978) 13 HLR 77, CA; cf *McClean v Liverpool CC* (1988) 20 HLR 25, CA.
146 *Dame Margaret Hungerford Charity Trustees v Beazeley* (1994) 26 HLR 269, CA.
147 *Wainwright v Leeds CC* (1984) 13 HLR 117, CA.

Limitations of s11

1.98   The operation of s11 is circumscribed in a number of ways:

- No liability can be imposed on the landlord for breach of s11 until the landlord has knowledge of the defects complained of and fails to effect repairs within a reasonable period of time thereafter (but see paragraphs 1.100–1.110).
- The provision applies only to tenancies commencing on or after the passage of the HA 1961, ie, 24 October 1961 (s13(1)).
- It applies only to periodic tenancies and fixed-term leases of less than seven years. Lettings for longer periods are also covered where the landlord has an option to end the letting within seven years of commencement. But, by s13(2), lettings for less than seven years may fall outside s11 if the tenant can renew for a further term, making more than seven years in total. These provisions, together with those relating to renewed lettings, are somewhat complex and an adviser should pay close attention to the terms of ss12–15 before giving a conclusive opinion.
- Section 11 does not apply to certain agricultural tenancies within the Agricultural Holdings Act 1948 (s14(3)).
- Except in the case of post-15 January 1989 tenancies, it does not extend to common parts of the building containing the accommodation let to the tenant, nor to parts of the premises retained by the landlord but which the tenant is permitted to use.
- Section 11 does not extend to any item which the tenant is entitled to remove from the premises, for example, a tenant's own electric fire (although the position would be different if the fire was provided by the landlord). Nor does it relieve the tenant of the obligation to use the premises in a tenant-like manner (see paragraphs 1.118–1.119). Nor does it require the landlord to reinstate premises destroyed by act of God or inevitable accident etc (s11(2)).
- Section 11 does not assist most business tenants (s32(2)).
- Section 11 does not apply to certain properties let *to* local authorities and other public bodies (s14(4)).
- Section 11 does not bind the Crown. It cannot therefore be relied on by the tenants of most government departments and agencies.[148]

But this may be discriminatory in breach of article 14 of the European Convention on Human Rights.[149]

---

148 *Department of Transport v Egoroff* (1986) 18 HLR 326, CA.
149 *Larkos v Cyprus* (1999) 7 BHRC 244; [1998] EHRLR 653.

Important note for pre-1961 tenancies

1.99   Tenancies which would otherwise be outside s11 because they started before 24 October 1961 may nevertheless gain the benefit of the provision. For example, where a fair rent has been registered on the basis that the tenancy is subject to s11 and the landlord has accepted rent following that registration, the landlord will be bound by the repairing obligation.[150] Alternatively, a pre-1961 tenant may be able to show that he or she is covered by s11 because the earlier tenancy has been determined and replaced by one commencing after 1961. This will be the case for all local authority tenants because in the 1960s and 1970s council rent increases were achieved by a process of notice to quit and re-grant. Pre-1961 tenants not covered by s11 may be able to rely on one of the common law implied terms described above.

Implied terms for the benefit of the landlord

The notice requirement

1.100   It is an implied term of all tenancy agreements which impose an obligation on the landlord to repair property rented out to a tenant that the landlord is not liable to carry out any repair unless and until he or she (1) has been put on notice or in any other way has knowledge of the need for repair and (2) has failed to carry out the repair within a reasonable period of time thereafter.[151] Although a common law rule, it has been consistently held to apply also where the repairing obligations are imposed by statute, eg, by LTA 1985 ss8 and 11. The burden of proving both these matters is on the tenant.[152]

1.101   The landlord's knowledge of the defect must be proved even if the disrepair is latent. Thus, a tenant injured by the collapse of a ceiling which no one could have expected to be liable to fall cannot recover damages from his or her landlord for breach of repairing obligations.[153]

1.102   It should be noted that it is the 'knowledge' of the landlord which is important. Usually this knowledge will arise from notice of disrepair given by the tenant. However, a landlord may be imputed with

---

150   *Brikom Investments v Seaford* [1981] 1 WLR 863, CA; *Johnstone v Charlton and Taylor* May 1998 *Legal Action* 21, Sunderland County Court.

151   *Makin v Watkinson* (1870) LR 6 Ex 25; *O'Brien v Robinson* [1973] AC 912, HL; *Morris v Liverpool CC* (1988) 20 HLR 498, CA.

152   *Morris v Liverpool CC* (1988) 20 HLR 498, CA.

153   *O'Brien v Robinson* [1973] AC 912, HL.

knowledge if the disrepair is brought to the attention of his or her workmen,[154] rent-collector or any other person (eg, a resident care-taker) employed by the landlord and having express or implied authority to receive complaints of disrepair on behalf of the landlord.

1.103   The route by which the landlord receives knowledge of the disrepair is not significant, except that it has been suggested that the informant must be a 'responsible source'.[155] In *Dinefwr BC v Jones*,[156] the council was held to have actual notice of the disrepair seen at the property by the council's environmental health officer (EHO) even though the EHO was not from the housing department and was inspecting the property after complaints relating to cleanliness rather than disrepair. The EHO, however, was not treated as having implied knowledge on behalf of the council about defects other than those obviously visible (ie not those which would have been discovered only on a thorough inspection). A tenant cannot necessarily rely on the proposition that, because the premises were inspected by the landlord or landlord's unqualified agent, it follows that the landlord knew of the defects in the premises. It is for the tenant to show that the landlord or unqualified agent saw the defect.

1.104   The *Jones*[157] case also indicates that knowledge will be established where the landlord receives information about the defects in a property from an independent valuer (in that case from the valuation officer following a right-to-buy application). This was confirmed in *Hall v Howard*,[158] where the landlord received an offer to purchase from a private tenant, accompanied by a surveyor's valuation report listing (and costing) repairs needed. Receipt of the report was sufficient to fix the landlord with knowledge of the defects. Similarly, service by a local authority of some form of statutory repair notice is sufficient to establish knowledge on the part of the landlord and thus, liability.[159]

1.105   The information received by the landlord must be sufficient to put a reasonable person on enquiry about whether works of repair are needed.[160] It will therefore be useful or usual for the tenant to make the

---

154 *Sheldon v West Bromwich Corporation* (1973) 13 HLR 23, CA.
155 *Dinefwr BC v Jones* (1987) 19 HLR 445, CA.
156 (1987) 19 HLR 445, CA.
157 *Dinefwr BC v Jones* (1987) 19 HLR 445, CA.
158 (1988) 20 HLR 566, CA.
159 *McGreal v Wake* (1984) 13 HLR 107, CA.
160 *O'Brien v Robinson* [1973] AC 912, HL; *Sheldon v West Bromwich Corporation* (1973) 13 HLR 23, CA; *British Telecommunications plc v Sun Life Assurance Society plc* [1996] Ch 69, CA.

landlord aware of the disrepair needing to be tackled, but the notice given need not particularise the degree or extent of the disrepair nor the remedial works required.[161] Where the tenant informs the landlord that he or she will be preparing a detailed list of items of disrepair and estimates for the works required, the landlord is not treated as having knowledge of the defects until the list and estimates are served.[162] Where no notice or knowledge can be established, the Defective Premises Act 1972 s4 may be helpful (see paragraphs 2.37–2.41).

1.106   Even after a landlord has knowledge of disrepair, there is no breach of the repairing obligation until 'a reasonable time has elapsed in which the repair could have been carried out'.[163] There is no prescribed 'reasonable time', so the length of the period for completion of repairs will vary according to the circumstances in each case. A useful guide to what the Government considers a reasonable period for ordinary minor repairs is given in Schedule 1 to the Secure Tenants of Local Housing Authorities (Right to Repair) Regulations 1994.[164]

1.107   If the landlord has given some advance indication to the tenant of the times within which particular repairs will usually be completed (perhaps by showing 'target periods' in a tenants' handbook) these will be strongly indicative of what a 'reasonable time' would be for repairs falling within those categories. Some landlords may even have placed such time limits within the tenancy agreement (in which case they can be directly enforced). In other cases, the courts (and initially those advising tenants) will determine the reasonable period, taking into account a variety of factors. Obviously the scale and severity of the disrepair will be critical factors but also relevant will be: whether the tenant is actually living in the property: the availability of replacement parts; and (in the case of social landlords) the overall workload.[165] The burden of proving that a reasonable time has been exceeded lies on the tenant. This will require firm evidence rather than inference. For example, even where the repair required is the replacement of a missing or damaged front door and door frame, it does not necessarily follow that a landlord allowing a week to pass before effecting final repairs is in breach of s11, where a temporary repair has been made.[166]

161 *Griffen v Pillet* [1926] 1 KB 17, KBD.
162 *Al Hassani v Merrigan* (1988) 20 HLR 238, CA.
163 *Calabar Properties v Stitcher* [1984] 1 WLR 287, CA at 298.
164 1994 SI No 133.
165 *Morris v Liverpool CC* (1988) 20 HLR 498, CA.
166 *Morris v Liverpool CC* (1988) 20 HLR 498, CA.

1.108   It is important to recognise that the implied term about knowledge applies only to parts of a building which have been rented to the tenant. It does not apply to parts which have been retained in the control of the landlord. When there is disrepair to part of a building which (a) the landlord is contractually obliged to repair, and (b) the landlord continues to control, then the landlord is liable immediately disrepair occurs whether or not he or she knows or could have known of the need for repairs.[167]

1.109   This will be particularly important where a tenant is unable to prove knowledge, but failure by the tenant to draw the defect to the landlord's attention in this type of case can in some circumstances be taken into account as a failure to mitigate.[168] It is also important in those disrepair cases where the majority of the damage occurs immediately a defect arises and before any reasonable time to carry out a repair has elapsed, eg, in flooding cases.[169] In any event, reliance on the fact that there is no need for notice will increase the period of breach, because time will start to run immediately a defect occurs rather than after a reasonable time has elapsed, and may thereby increase any damages which may be recovered.[170]

1.110   It has recently been suggested in *Charalambous v Earle (Addendum to judgment)*[171] that this rule may need modification to take account of the practicalities of the modern relationship of residential landlords and tenants but this was said in the context of a long lease where there is a reciprocal obligation on lessees to contribute to the costs of the remedial works.

Access for the landlord

1.111   For the purposes of carrying out repairs or inspecting for repairs, landlords may have rights of access at either common law or under statute. In the absence of an express term, or some relevant statutory

---

167 *Melles & Co v Holme* [1918] 2 KB 100, KBD; *Bishop v Consolidated London Properties Ltd* (1933) 102 LJKB 257; *Loria v Hammer* [1989] 2 EGLR 249, ChD; *British Telecommunications plc v Sun Life Assurance Society plc* [1996] Ch 69, CA; *Passley v Wandsworth LBC* (1998) 30 HLR 165, CA; *Charalambous v Earle (Addendum to judgment)* [2006] EWCA Civ 1338; [2007] HLR 8, CA.

168 *Minchburn v Peck* (1988) 20 HLR 392, CA.

169 See, eg, *Passley v Wandsworth LBC* (1998) 30 HLR 165, CA.

170 *Charalambous v Earle (Addendum to judgment)* [2006] EWCA Civ 1338; [2007] HLR 8.

171 [2006] EWCA Civ 1338; [2007] HLR 8, CA.

provision, a landlord has no power to enter tenanted property in order to carry out improvements.[172]

Access at common law

1.112   The landlord who is subject to an express or implied duty to keep premises 'in repair' will have the right at common law to enter to carry out those works (but no others):

> I have construed that covenant to mean that he shall put them into good condition if necessary and it is my judgment that the covenant carries with it an implied licence to the lessor to enter upon premises of the lessee and to occupy them for a reasonable time to do what he has covenanted to do.[173]

1.113   The right to enter to do repairs is subject to an obligation to give the tenant reasonable notice and must be exercised reasonably, although the tenant is not usually entitled to a copy of the specification of works.[174]

1.114   The landlord has the right to temporary vacant possession in order to carry out repairs only when vacant possession is essential.[175]

1.115   In the case of periodic tenancies of dwelling-houses, the landlord has an implied right to enter to repair defects which might cause personal injury.[176]

Access by statute

1.116   Most statutory repairing obligations carry within them express rights of entry for the landlord (see particularly the discussions of LTA 1985 ss8(2) and 11(6) at paragraphs 1.62 and 1.74).

1.117   In addition, s148 of the Rent Act 1977 s148 gives landlords an express right to enter for the purpose of carrying out repairs in the case of protected or statutory tenancies. HA 1988 s16 gives the same right of access to the landlord of an assured tenant.

Use in a tenant-like manner

1.118   Under LTA 1985 s11(2), a landlord is not obliged to do repairs which the tenant is liable to do by virtue of his or her duty to use the premises

172 *McDougall v Easington DC* (1989) 21 HLR 310, CA; *Yeoman's Row Management Ltd v Bodentien-Meyrick* [2002] EWCA Civ 860.

173 *Saner v Bilton* (1878) 7 ChD 815 at 824.

174 *Granada Theatres v Freehold Investments (Leytonstone) Ltd* [1959] Ch 592, CA.

175 *McGreal v Wake* (1984) 13 HLR 107, CA.

176 *McAuley v Bristol CC* [1992] QB 134, CA.

in a tenant-like manner. In *Warren v Keen*,[177] Denning LJ described this duty as an obligation 'to do the little jobs around the place which a reasonable tenant would do' and included in his definition turning the water off when the tenant went away, cleaning chimneys and windows, mending fuses and unblocking the sink. A local authority's view that changing a tap washer might be added to that list was rejected in *Islington LBC v Keane*,[178] where it was held that changing a tap washer was part of repairing a tap and its component parts and something most people would call a plumber to do; it therefore fell within s11(1)(b); the express term suggesting that the tenant was liable for this defect was accordingly void.

1.119   Earlier, in *Churchill v Nottingham CC*,[179] it was held that, while cleaning a chimney might still be part of a tenant's duty to act in a tenant-like manner in respect of a small cottage on the moors where wood or coal was still burned and the chimney used in the old fashioned way, in modern housing a tenant was not obliged to disconnect a fixed gas fire, remove the back plate and clean the flue behind it; this obligation fell on the landlord under s11.

---

177 [1954] 1 QB 15, CA.

178 December 2005 *Legal Action* 28; *Housing Law Casebook* para P5.27, Clerkenwell County Court.

179 January 2001 *Legal Action* 25; *Housing Law Casebook* para P5.25, Nottingham County Court.

CHAPTER 2

Rights beyond the contract

2.1	**Introduction**	
2.2	**Common law rights**	
2.2	Negligence	
	The landlord builder • *Works after letting* • *Works before letting* • *Common parts* • *Limits on actions in negligence*	
2.13	Nuisance	
2.19	**Statutory rights**	
2.19	Occupiers Liability Act 1957	
2.23	Defective Premises Act 1972	
	Defective Premises Act 1972 s1 • *Defective Premises Act 1972 s4*	
2.48	Human Rights Act 1998	

Introduction

2.1   Beyond the contractual rights conferred expressly or impliedly by the terms of a tenancy agreement, English law has been extremely slow to impose any further obligations on landlords, or even to give tenants remedies for injury sustained as a result of disrepair. Indeed, landlords letting premises were initially given a very broad exemption from any liability to repair or prevent injury to occupiers. However, in recent years substantial progress has been made, through both the common law and statute, in piercing the landlord's 'cloak of immunity from responsibility' in respect of shoddy housing.

Common law rights

Negligence

2.2   The developments made at common law have taken place in the field of negligence. The English common law of tort provides that a person injured physically or materially by the negligence of another can recover recompense from that other if a duty of care is owed, the damage was foreseeable and the wrongdoer failed to take reasonable care. Throughout its development, the common law avoided including tenants and their families among the class of persons to whom a landlord owed a duty of care. It is only relatively recently that case-law has made significant changes to this approach.

2.3   A landlord who lets a defective, dangerous or unsafe property on which he or she has done no work is immune from any action in negligence.[1] In *Rimmer v Liverpool CC*,[2] the Court of Appeal expressed the view that the immunity of the landlord, although questionable, is still 'too deeply entrenched in our law for any court below the highest to disturb or destroy it' and that to do so would possibly be 'so great a change in the law as to require legislation'. More recently in *McNerney v Lambeth LBC*,[3] an attempt to show that the immunity of the landlord had been overtaken by developments in case-law failed. In that case, the landlord had not negligently constructed the building but it was unable to cope with modern usage and was prone to chronic condensation dampness. The Court of Appeal held that the

1   *Cavalier v Pope* [1906] AC 428, HL.
2   [1985] QB 1, CA.
3   (1989) 21 HLR 188, CA.

fundamental immunity of the landlord in the law of negligence had survived into the modern age and could be removed only by a change in law made by statute.

2.4   Although the general immunity of a bare landlord in negligence still survives today, there are now a number of ways in which a landlord can be held liable in negligence in special circumstances.

The landlord builder

2.5   If the landlord designed or built the dwelling he or she owes subsequent occupiers the same duty of care as is owed by builders who do not subsequently become the landlord of the dwelling, that is, a duty to take reasonable care to ensure that the dwelling does not contain any latent defects which cause personal injury or property damage.[4]

2.6   A tenant's knowledge of, or the opportunity for inspection of, a defect may negative the duty of care or break the chain of causation but only where it is reasonable to expect a tenant to remove or avoid the danger and unreasonable for the tenant to run the risk of being injured by the danger. This will not usually be the case.[5]

2.7   The duty of care will not be breached where works were carried out according to the standards of reasonably skilled workmen at the time the works were done.[6] This common law duty of care has largely been overtaken by the statutory duty imposed by the Defective Premises Act 1972 s1 (see paragraphs 2.23–2.28).

Works after letting

2.8   The landlord who carries out work after the tenancy begins will also probably be held to owe to his or her tenant the same duty of care that any contractor would owe to the occupier, that is, a duty to take reasonable care to ensure that defective workmanship or materials do not cause personal injury or property damage.[7] The duty extends to using reasonable material to ensure that the work is effective. So, for example, where a landlord tries to treat an infestation of bugs with inadequate materials, the landlord will be liable to the tenant for subsequent damage caused.[8]

---

4 *Rimmer v Liverpool CC* [1985] QB 1, CA; *Murphy v Brentwood DC* [1991] 1 AC 398, HL; *Targett v Torfaen BC* (1991) 24 HLR 164, CA.

5 *Rimmer v Liverpool CC* [1985] QB 1, CA; *Targett v Torfaen BC* (1991) 24 HLR 164, CA.

6 *Adams v Rhymer Valley DC* (2001) 33 HLR 446, CA.

7 *Billings (AC) & Sons v Riden* [1958] AC 240, HL.

8 *Sharpe v Manchester MDC* (1977) 5 HLR 71, CA.

Works before letting

2.9   The common law has not yet expressly imposed on landlords who did not construct or design the premises any liability in tort to tenants or others for defective work carried out before the letting, but any such remaining immunity has been removed by statute (Defective Premises Act (DPA) 1972 s3, see paragraph 2.28).

Common parts

2.10   The general immunity of landlords in negligence does not extend to protect a landlord who negligently fails to repair or maintain the common parts of a property with the result that a tenant or others using the common parts are injured or their property is damaged.[9] There is a general duty on landlords in relation to hazards occurring on their land to do whatever is reasonable in the circumstances having regard to their capacity to act and their ability to abate or deal with the hazard. In *Stockley v Knowsley MBC*,[10] a landlord was held liable in negligence for failing to prevent frozen water pipes in the roof from bursting and flooding a tenant's flat. The council owed the tenant a duty of care to prevent flooding because in the circumstances it had been reasonable for them to abate or deal with the potential hazard. Simply telling a tenant to turn off the stopcock without advising her where it was or how to do so was insufficient to discharge the duty. But in *Stevens v Blaneau Gwent CBC*[11] there was held to be no duty to install safety locks to windows as there was no emergency or external threat which imposed a duty on the council to act. Given that the windows were part of the premises let, it would not appear that the council would have owed a duty of care, even if this had been the case, although this was not the reason given by the Court of Appeal for rejecting liability.

Limits on actions in negligence

2.11   There is no liability in negligence at common law unless and until harm is caused to the person or property of a victim. Being a duty owed in tort, the duty will extend only to personal injury or property

---

9   *Cockburn v Smith* [1924] 2 KB 119, CA; *Duke of Westminster v Guild* [1985] QB 688, CA; *Lips v Older* [2004] EWHC 1686 (QB).
10   [1986] 2 EGLR 141, CA.
11   [2004] EWCA Civ 715; (2004) HLR 1039.

damage, not to pure economic loss or defects to the dwelling itself which might make occupation uncomfortable or distressing.[12]

2.12 A landlord will not be liable in negligence for the acts of an independent subcontractor.[13]

Nuisance

2.13 At common law, a private nuisance is an activity or state of affairs existing on land or premises which unduly interferes with the use or enjoyment of neighbouring land or premises.

2.14 A landlord will be liable for any common law nuisance arising on ancillary property owned by him or her and impinging on the tenant's dwelling-house.[14]

2.15 Tenants most commonly bring claims in nuisance against their landlords in respect of pest infestations. In *Sharpe v Manchester MDC*,[15] the landlord was held liable in nuisance for a cockroach infestation which probably entered a tenant's flat through the service ducts in the common parts of the block of flats. However, there was no such liability in *Habinteg Housing Association v James*,[16] where there were no common parts retained by the landlord and the reserved rights of entry over the other tenanted flats did not given the landlord sufficient control over them for it to be liable for failure to treat any infestation emanating from them.

2.16 A landlord may be liable if he or she causes a nuisance by creating it or continues a nuisance by failing to take steps to abate the nuisance when he or she is aware or ought to be aware of its existence.[17] A landlord will not be liable where the defect causing the nuisance predates the grant of the tenancy because the principle of *caveat lessee*[18] will be held to apply, ie, that the lessee takes subject to any defects

---

12 *Murphy v Brentwood DC* [1991] 1 AC 398, HL; *D&F Estates v Church Commissioners* [1989] AC 177, HL; *Department of the Environment v Thomas Bates & Son* [1991] 1 AC 499, HL.

13 *D&F Estates v Church Commissioners* [1989] AC 177, HL.

14 *Sharpe v Manchester MDC* (1977) 5 HLR 71, CA (cockroach infestation); *Sampson v Hodson-Pressinger* [1981] 3 All ER 710, CA; cf *Southwark LBC v Mills* [2001] 1 AC 1, HL (noise); *Guppy's Bridport Ltd v Brookling* (1984) 14 HLR 1, CA (major building works); *Gordon v Selico Co Ltd* (1986) 18 HLR 219, CA (water penetration); *Tennant Radiant Heat Ltd v Warrington Development Corporation* (1988) 11 EG 71, CA (water penetration).

15 (1977) 5 HLR 71, CA.

16 (1995) 27 HLR 299, CA.

17 *Sedleigh-Denfield v O'Callaghan* [1940] AC 880, HL at 897.

18 See paras 1.5–1.6.

existing at the date of the lease.[19] In *Jackson v JH Watson Property Investment Ltd*,[20] the landlord was not liable in nuisance for water penetration caused by faulty construction work to common parts by his predecessor in title because it predated the grant of the lease.

2.17   A landlord may also be liable for a nuisance caused by disrepair within demised premises which arises after the grant of a lease and affects another tenant's property, but only where the landlord has an obligation to repair or has reserved the right to enter and repair, either expressly or by implication.[21] Accordingly, a landlord will be liable in nuisance for water penetration to a tenant's flat caused by plumbing leaks in the flat above which he or she has failed to remedy, where the landlord has an obligation or right to repair the plumbing leaks in the flat above.

2.18   Only persons with exclusive possession of land can bring an action in private nuisance.[22] Accordingly, no claim in nuisance can be brought by the children of a tenant,[23] but they may be able to bring a claim arising under the Human Rights Act 1998.[24]

Statutory rights

Occupiers Liability Act 1957

2.19   Under the Occupiers Liability Act (OLA) 1957 the 'occupier' of land or premises owes a 'common duty of care' to all visitors except to the extent that he or she lawfully restricts liability: OLA 1957 s2(1). The 'common duty of care' is a duty to take such care as is reasonable in all the circumstances to ensure that the visitor will be reasonably safe when on the premises for the purpose for which he or she was invited: OLA 1957 s 2(2).

2.20   The statute prohibits any attempt by a landlord to exclude or reduce his or her obligations to people not party to the contract who are visitors under the terms of the tenancy agreement: OLA 1957 s3(1).

---

19   See *Southwark LBC v Mills* [2001] 1 AC 1, HL.

20   [2008] EWHC 14 (Ch); December 2008 *Legal Action* 31.

21   *Nelson v Liverpool Brewery Co* (1877) 2 CPD 311; *Mint v Good* [1951] 1 KB 517, CA.

22   *Hunter v Canary Wharf* [1997] AC 655.

23   *Murphy and Peers v Stockport* August 2002 *Legal Action* 27, Stockport County Court.

24   See *Dobson and others v Thames Water Utilities Ltd and another* [2009] EWCA Civ 28.

2.21   For the purposes of the OLA 1957, the landlord remains the occupier of the common parts of any building which he or she owns.[25]

2.22   Although the 1957 Act imposes a liability on the landlord for injury caused by defects in the part of a building 'occupied' by the landlord, it does not provide a mechanism by which the landlord may be
forced to repair such defects in the common parts in advance of the
accident.

Defective Premises Act 1972

Defective Premises Act 1972 s1

2.23   Section 1 of the DPA 1972 imposes a duty on all those, including
landlords, who undertake work for or in connection with the provision of a dwelling to:

(a) do the work in a professional or workmanlike manner;
(b) use proper materials; and
(c) ensure that the dwelling is fit for human habitation when
completed.[26]

See appendix A for the full text of DPA 1972 s1. The origins of the
statute lie in a Law Commission report: *Civil Liabilities of Vendors and
Lessors of Defective Premises*[27] that may usefully be referred to when
interpreting or construing the Act.[28]

2.24   The duty is owed by builders as well as architects, surveyors,
specialist sub-contractors and any others taking on work in connection with the provision of a dwelling. It is also owed by the employer,
eg, the local authority or property development company which en-
gages the builder to do the work: DPA 1972 s1(4). The duty is owed
to the person for whom the dwelling is initially provided and to all
persons subsequently acquiring a legal or equitable interest in it. The
duty is owed in respect of work which commenced after 1 January
1974 and can apply to a failure to undertake necessary works.[29]

2.25   The scope of DPA 1972 s1 is restricted by DPA 1972 s2, which excludes all dwellings covered by the National House Builders scheme

---

25   *Wheat v E Lacon Ltd* [1966] AC 552; *Dear v Newham LBC* (1987) 19 HLR 391,
QBD; *Jordan v Achara* (1988) 20 HLR 607, CA.

26   See, eg, *McMinn Bole & Van den Haak v Huntsbuild Ltd & Money* [2009] EWCA
Civ 1149.

27   Law Com No 40.

28   *Alker v Collingwood Housing Association* [2007] EWCA Civ 343; (2007) 39 HLR
29, CA per Carnwath LJ at para 20.

29   *Andrews v Schooling* [1991] 1 WLR 783, CA.

(which covers nearly all new private sector development). DPA 1972 s1 is, accordingly, only likely to apply to newly built public sector buildings and both public and private sector conversions/alterations.

2.26   Damages recoverable for breach of section 1 may include damages for economic loss and damages for the loss of enjoyment of the premises.[30]

2.27   The cause of action is treated as accruing when the work (or any post-completion remedial work) is completed: DPA s1(5).[31] The limitation period will be six years under Limitation Act 1980 s2, since liability is strict. As a claim under the DPA 1972 s1 is a claim for breach of statutory duty rather than a claim in common law negligence, no advantage can be taken of any possible extension of time under Limitation Act 1980 s14A to extend the limitation period to three years from the date of knowledge. If the action includes a claim for personal injuries, Limitation Act 1980 s11 should apply.

2.28   The duty under DPA 1972 s1 is not extinguished by any disposal of the reversion: DPA 1972 s3. DPA 1972 s3 therefore abolishes the immunity of landlords in respect of work carried out before the letting and provides that, in respect of such work, the landlord is liable to any person who might be reasonably expected to be affected by negligent work, eg, the tenant's family and visitors as well as the tenant him or herself. The full text of section 3 is in appendix A.

Defective Premises Act 1972 s4

2.29   Section 4 of the DPA 1972 serves two distinct purposes, which can be broadly summarised as follows: (1) in some circumstances it makes landlords liable for personal injury or property damage caused by disrepair even though the landlord did not have knowledge of the need for repair; and (2) in some circumstances it creates new obligations to prevent the condition of the dwelling causing personal injury or property damage. The full text of DPA 1972 s4 is in appendix A.

The basic duty

2.30   The DPA 1972 applies from 1 January 1974, whether or not the tenancy began before that date: DPA 1972 s4(3). It applies to all of the land let, not just the dwelling-house. For example, it applied to the

---

30 *Murphy v Brentwood DC* [1991] 1 AC 398, HL per Lord Bridge at 480H-B; *Bayoumi v Protim Services Ltd* (1996) 30 HLR 785, CA.

31 *Alexander v Mercouris* [1979] 1 WLR 1270, CA; *Alderson v Beetham Organisation* [2003] EWCA Civ 408, CA.

patio at the rear of the dwelling-house in *Smith v Bradford MBC*.[32] It does not apply to land which is not let, eg, the common parts.

2.31   The duty is owed to 'all persons who might reasonably be expected to be affected by defects in the state of the premises': that includes the tenant as well as the tenant's family members and visitors.[33]

2.32   The duty is a duty to 'take such care as is reasonable in all the circumstances' to see that the persons owed the duty are reasonably safe from personal injury or property damage caused by a 'relevant defect' of which the landlord knew or 'ought ... to have known'.

2.33   A 'relevant defect' is a defect which the landlord is either (1) bound to repair or maintain under the express or implied terms of the contract including Landlord and Tenant Act (LTA) 1985 s11 or (2) bound to repair or maintain under DPA 1972 s4(4) (see paragraph 2.42).

2.34   A landlord's obligation under a tenancy agreement to repair and maintain the property or to keep it in good condition does not impose an obligation to put it in a safe condition and a defect is not a relevant defect simply because it is hazardous.[34] DPA 1972 s4 does not impose a statutory warranty that premises are reasonably safe.

2.35   A tenant of one property can rely on section 4 in relation to relevant defects in other properties owned by the same landlord where the landlord has repairing obligations in relation to the defect in the other property or has reserved a right to enter and repair in default. In *Wadsworth v Nagle*,[35] the tenant of a lower flat affected by water penetration from the flat above claimed damages from the landlord who was also the landlord of the flat above. The claim failed because the upper flat was let on a long lease with the repairing obligation for internal repair falling on the tenant and the landlord had no express or implied right to enter the upper flat to repair the defective bath sealant which caused the water penetration.

2.36   The landlord cannot exclude or modify the duty: DPA 1972 s6(3).

The duty where the landlord ought to have known of the defect

2.37   Subsections 4(1), (2) and (3) of the DPA 1972 create no new repairing or maintaining obligations[36] but they do superimpose a duty to take care on top of existing repairing obligations in such a way that the

---

32 (1982) 4 HLR 86, CA.

33 *Smith v Bradford MBC* (1982) 4 HLR 86, CA.

34 *Alker v Collingwood Housing Association* [2007] EWCA Civ 343; (2007) 29 HLR 29, CA.

35 [2005] EWHC 26 (QB).

36 *McNerny v Lambeth LBC* (1989) 21 HLR 188, CA; *Boldack v East Lindsey DC* (1999) 31 HLR 41, CA.

landlord can be liable for personal injury or damage to property when he or she 'ought ... to have known' of the likelihood of such injury or damage. This goes beyond the usual requirement that the landlord has actual knowledge of the defect (see paragraph 1.100).

2.38   DPA 1972 s4(2) provides that: 'The said duty is owed if the landlord knows (whether as a result of being notified by the tenant or otherwise) or if he ought in all the circumstances to have known of the relevant defect'.

2.39   The courts expect landlords to take positive steps to inspect for latent defects when the landlord is aware that a problem might exist, but not to inspect for unforeseeable dangers.[37]

2.40   Cases in which, on special facts, the landlord ought to have known of the risk of personal injury are *Clarke v Taff Ely BC*[38] (failure to undertake simple routine inspection of the floor in an older house prone to floorboard rot); *Smith v Bradford MC*[39] (failure to undertake proper pre-letting inspection of void premises in which a former tenant had built a defective patio) and *Sykes v Harry*[40] (failure to service a gas heater).

2.41   In the case of gas installations, the Gas Safety (Installation and Use) Regulations 1998[41] require landlords to inspect gas appliances annually. Failure to inspect is likely to result in the court holding that a landlord 'ought to have known' of any defect causing personal injury or property damage for the purposes of DPA 1972 s4.

Additional obligations

2.42   DPA 1972 s4(4) provides:

> Where premises are let under a tenancy which expressly or impliedly gives the landlord the right to enter the premises to carry out any description of maintenance or repairs of the premises, then, as from the time when he first is, or by notice, or otherwise can put himself, in a position to exercise the right and for so long as he is or can put himself in that position, he shall be treated for the purposes of subsections (1) to (3) above (but for not other purposes) as if he were under an obligation to the tenant for that description of maintenance or repair of the premises; but the landlord shall not owe the tenant any duty by virtue of this subsection in respect of any defect in the state of the premises

37 *Morley v Knowsley BC* May 1988 *Legal Action* 22; *Housing Law Casebook* para P10.6, CA.
38 (1980) 10 HLR 44, QBD.
39 (1982) 4 HLR 86, CA.
40 [2001] EWCA Civ 167; [2001] QB 1014.
41 1998 SI No 2451.

arising from, or continuing because of, a failure to carry out an obligation expressly imposed on the tenant by the tenancy.

2.43 This section has the result that, where a landlord is expressly or impliedly permitted to enter the premises let, to carry out work of repair or maintenance, the landlord comes under a positive duty to ensure that his or her failure to carry out that type of repair or maintenance does not cause personal injury or property damage. This section has no application to parts which are not let, for example, exterior paths.[42]

2.44 Advisers should therefore consider carefully what rights to enter the premises have been granted to the landlord by the tenancy agreement. Usually, express rights of entry are limited to inspection and carrying out repairs. This was the case in *Boldack v East Lindsey DC*,[43] where another right of entry granted by the tenancy agreement was the right to remove any articles left on the premises at the end of the tenancy, but this did not provide a relevant right of entry because it only arose at the end of the tenancy when the council were entitled to possession of the premises. Accordingly, there was no duty to remove the paving slab which had caused injury to the tenant's sons, because it was neither work of repair nor work of maintenance.

2.45 However, in *Dunn v Bradford MDC*,[44] there was an express term that tenants would permit their landlord to enter the premises for the purpose of executing 'repairs or improvements'. It was claimed that this gave the landlord the right to carry out improvements and that the landlord therefore had a duty to carry out such improvements as were necessary to eradicate condensation dampness. The court held that s4(4) could not be used to compel a landlord to remedy design defects or to impose a duty on a landlord to carry out works of improvement going beyond such repair and maintenance as was necessary to maintain the house in the condition in which it was first let.

2.46 The scope of DPA 1972 s4(4) is potentially quite wide because the Court of Appeal held in *McAuley v Bristol CC*[45] that the landlord of a council house let on a periodic tenancy had an implied right to enter the house to carry out any works of repair which were necessary to remove a 'significant risk' of personal injury to the tenant, his or her family or visitors. By virtue of DPA 1972 s4(4) that right was converted into a duty, breach of which resulted in the landlord being

---

42 *King v South Northamptonshire DC* (1992) 24 HLR 284, CA.
43 *Boldack v East Lindsey DC* (1999) 31 HLR 41, CA.
44 [2002] EWCA Civ 1137; [2003] HLR 154, CA.
45 (1991) 23 HLR 586, CA.

held liable for personal injury to one of the tenants. This does not, however, impose any obligation on a landlord to remedy a design defect which poses a danger to health unless the works necessary to remedy that defect are works of maintenance or repair. The fact that a landlord may be entitled to enter to abate a statutory nuisance[46] does not give rise to a deemed obligation to the tenant to remedy the statutory nuisance unless the works necessary to do so are works of maintenance or repair as the duty under DPA 1972 s 4(4) is limited to works of maintenance or repair.[47]

2.47   The duty under DPA 1972 s4 can be enforced proactively by an application for an injunction to cure the defect, before it causes harm.[48]

Human Rights Act 1998

2.48   Section 3(1) of the Human Rights Act (HRA) 1998 provides that all legislation must, so far as possible, be read and given effect in a way which is compatible with certain rights set out in Schedule 1 of the Act (largely taken from the European Convention on Human Rights ('the Convention')).

2.49   HRA 1998 s6(1) provides that it is unlawful for a public authority to act in a way which is incompatible with a Convention right.

2.50   Article 8 of HRA 1998 Sch 1 provides that:

1   Everyone has the right to respect for his private and family life, his home and correspondence.
2   There shall be no interference by a public authority with the exercise of this right except such as is in accordance with the law and is necessary in a democratic society in the interests of national security, public safety or the economic well-being of the country, for the prevention of disorder or crime or for the protection of the rights and freedoms of others.

2.51   In a number of cases, the European Court of Human Rights has held that severe environmental pollution may prevent individuals from enjoying their homes to such a degree as to affect their private and family life adversely and that there may be positive obligations, inherent in effective respect for private and family life, to take action to stop such harm.[49]

46   *Lee v Leeds CC* [2002] EWCA Civ 6; [2002] 1 WLR 1488, CA.
47   *Alker v Collingwood Housing Association* [2007] EWCA Civ 343; (2007) 39 HLR 29, CA.
48   *Barrett v Lounova (1982) Ltd* [1990] 1 QB 348, CA.
49   *Lopez Ostra v Spain* (1994) 20 EHRR 277; *Guerra v Italy* (1998) 26 EHRR 357.

2.52   Attempts, so far, to extend a landlord's liability for defects by virtue of the HRA 1998 have been unsuccessful. In *Lee v Leeds CC*,[50] It was held that LTA 1985 s11, as construed in *Quick v Taff Ely BC*[51] (namely that the obligation to keep in repair the structure did not extend to the rectification of design faults), was not incompatible with Article 8 and that the HRA 1998 did not require that LTA 1985 s11 be reinterpreted.

2.53   It was accepted that HRA 1998 s6 imposed on a public authority (which may now include registered social landlords as well as local authorities[52]) an obligation to take steps to ensure that the condition of a dwelling-house which is let for social housing is such that the tenant's Convention rights under Article 8 are not infringed, but such an obligation is not unqualified; the steps which a public authority must take to ensure compliance with Article 8 must be determined in each case, by having due regard to the needs and resources of the community and of individuals.[53]

2.54   Therefore, it is possible that, in exceptional circumstances, a landlord which is a public authority could be in breach of an occupier's right to respect for his or her home under Article 8 where it allowed a property to deteriorate into very poor condition. Conditions were not considered to be sufficiently bad for there to be a breach of Article 8 in either *Lee v Leeds CC*[54] (where the premises had been found to be prejudicial to health by reason of condensation dampness) or *Thornton and Jarrett v Birmingham CC*[55] (where there was major dampness but the premises were no longer prejudicial to health at the relevant time).

2.55   More recently, in *Fadeyeva v Russia*[56] the European Court of Human Rights has held that that, although an applicant had no medical evidence directly linking her ill health to toxins produced by the steel plant near her home, the applicant's prolonged exposure to the toxins 'inevitably made her more vulnerable to various diseases' and 'adversely affected the quality of her life at home'. On that basis, the actual detriment to the applicant's health and well-being reached a level sufficient to bring it within the scope of Article 8. This would

50   [2002] EWCA Civ 6; [2002] 1 WLR 1488, CA.
51   [1986] 1 QB 809.
52   *R (Weaver) v London & Quadrant Housing Trust* [2009] EWCA Civ 587, CA.
53   *Lee v Leeds CC* [2002] EWCA Civ 6; [2002] 1 WLR 1488, CA at paras 48–49.
54   [2002] EWCA Civ 6; [2002] 1 WLR 1488, CA.
55   November 2004 *Legal Action* 27; *Housing Law Casebook* para P11.58, Birmingham County Court.
56   October 2005 *Legal Action* 18, ECHR; *Housing Law Casebook* para A3.5.

suggest that the threshold for a claim under Article 8 may not be as high as previously thought and could well be attained by a tenant adversely affected by condensation dampness.

2.56   Although there has yet to be a successful claim brought for housing defects under the HRA 1998, a successful result was achieved in the field of nuisance in *Marcic*, where the Court of Appeal found Thames Water liable to an owner-occupier, for the recurrent flooding of his property by overflowing sewage, in common law nuisance and on the basis that the water authority's failure to act was a breach of the owner's Convention rights under Article 8 and Protocol 1 Article 1.[57] However, the House of Lords subsequently rejected all the claims in that case on the basis that liability in nuisance would be inconsistent with the statutory scheme for regulation of water and sewage undertakers which also provided a fair balancing mechanism for the assessment of priority and enforcement, so there was no breach of the Convention.[58] More recently, in *Dobson and Others v Thames Water Utilities Ltd and Another*,[59] it was held as a preliminary issue that the principle in *Marcic* did not preclude claims in nuisance involving allegations of negligence or claims under the HRA 1998 where the exercise of adjudicating on those causes of actions was not inconsistent with and did not involve conflicts with the statutory process under the Water Industry Act 1991. The Court of Appeal considered the principles for the award of damages in nuisance claims and under the HRA 1998 and held that it was unlikely that any further award for damages under the HRA 1998 would be made where there had already been an award of damages for nuisance.

---

57 *Marcic v Thames Water Utilities Ltd* [2002] QB 929, CA.
58 *Marcic v Thames Water Utilities Ltd* [2003] UKHL 66, HL.
59 [2009] EWCA Civ 28, CA.

CHAPTER 3

Civil remedies for disrepair

3.1   Introduction

3.3   Direct action

3.4   Using rent to pay for repairs

3.11   Withholding rent

3.13   Set-off against rent

3.18   Reduction in rent

3.19   Appointing a receiver or manager

3.21   Using the ombudsmen and/or the Tenant Services Authority
         Using the ombudsmen • Using the Tenant Services Authority

3.27   Court proceedings

3.30   Taking initial instructions

3.40   Matters to consider after the first interview
         Limitation periods • Who will be the claimant?

3.49   Pre-action Protocol for housing disrepair cases

3.55   First contact with the landlord

3.58   Legal aid

3.59   Landlord's response

3.60   Instruction of expert(s)

3.64   Choice of an expert

3.68   Chronology and witness statement

3.75   Obtaining evidence

3.76   Negotiations

continued

3.78   Use of counsel

3.80   Contact with the client

3.81   Letter of claim

3.84   Response to letter of claim

3.85   Issuing proceedings
          Final preparations • The claim form • Particulars of claim • Which court?

3.96   Interim injunctions
          Injunction procedure

3.116   Counterclaims

3.125   Settlements

3.134   Interim applications

3.138   Allocation and ADR

3.149   Disclosure

3.151   Witness statements

3.154   Preparations for trial

3.156   Continuing negotiations

3.157   Trial

3.161   Final orders
          Mandatory orders for works • Declarations • Damages and costs • Remedies for breach of orders

Introduction

3.1 This chapter assumes:

- that the landlord is legally liable to undertake the particular repair needed;
- that, where notice is necessary, the tenant has given notice of the disrepair and the need for remedial works; and
- that the landlord has failed to carry out the necessary repairs within a reasonable period (where such a period is applicable).[1]

3.2 In these circumstances, the landlord is in breach of a legal obligation to repair and the tenant has a right to both financial compensation (damages) and an order requiring the landlord to carry out the necessary repairs (where any remain outstanding).

Direct action

3.3 The tenant's adviser should first consider the possibility of using remedies other than issuing court proceedings. These include:

- using rent to pay for repairs;
- withholding rent;
- set-off against rent;
- reduction in rent;
- appointing a receiver or manager;
- using the ombudsmen and/or the Tenant Services Authority.

Using rent to pay for repairs

3.4 Where it is clear that the landlord is in breach of contractual repairing obligations, the tenant has a right at common law to carry out the necessary repairs (either personally or by engaging a contractor) and to recover the costs and expenses incurred by deducting them from future rent. The availability of this right to tenants was reaffirmed in the case of *Lee-Parker v Izzet*.[2]

3.5 In order to rely on this right, tenants need show that they have behaved reasonably. Therefore, certain preliminary steps should be followed in order to exercise it:

- Inform the landlord of the intention to take this form of action if repairs are not carried out.

1 See paragraphs 1.100 and 1.106.
2 [1971] 1 WLR 1688; [1971] 3 All ER 1099, Ch.

- Allow a further reasonable period for the landlord to comply with the repairing obligations.
- Obtain three estimates from properly qualified contractors for the cost of carrying out the remedial works and send copies of these to the landlord with a 'final warning'.
- Engage the contractor at the lowest reasonable tender to have the work carried out.
- Submit a copy of the contractor's invoice to the landlord and request reimbursement.
- If no money is forthcoming, settle the invoice and recoup the cost by deducting it from future rent.

3.6   This right, which is wholly separate from the right to 'set off against rent' (see paragraphs 3.13–3.17) will provide a tenant who is sued for unpaid rent with a complete defence to the landlord's action.

3.7   This remedy can be invaluable where a relatively low-cost repair is needed (eg, replacing a part to a central heating boiler or mending a leaking toilet). However, it has the disadvantage that the tenant is then responsible for any shortcomings in the standard of repair and only a court would be able to decide at what point a landlord would resume responsibility for further repair to the item that has been repaired. It will be rare for a tenant to be able to afford to carry out a more expensive repair without first saving up rent with a view to eventually paying a contractor, as was the case in *Asco Developments & Newman v Lowes, Lewis and Gordon.*[3]

3.8   Some tenancy agreements attempt to exclude the right to withhold rent in this way. However, such a term is likely to offend the Unfair Terms in Consumer Contracts Regulations 1999.[4] Indeed, a similar term prohibiting 'set-off' (see paragraphs 3.13–3.17) was held to be unenforceable in the county court case of *Cody v Philps.*[5]

3.9   This procedure is not available to council tenants in receipt of housing benefit because their rent is paid by way of a rent rebate, in effect by a credit to the rent account.

3.10   Since 1 January 1986 secure tenants, and from 12 February 1997 introductory tenants, of local authorities have been able to use a statutory scheme allowing them to arrange minor repairs and recover the cost. The scheme is explained in the government booklet *A Better*

---

3   (1978) 248 EG 683 Ch.
4   1999 SI No 2083 and see para 1.9.
5   December 2005 *Legal Action* 28, West London County Court.

Deal for Tenants: Your Right to Repair.[6] In most respects it is more limited than the common law right. It is found in the Housing Act (HA) 1985 s96[7] and HA 1996 s135, but it is hardly ever used in practice. Its scope is limited to repair work costing less than £250 and it requires the service of notices and counter-notices[8]. In most respects it gives fewer rights than those already existing in common law.

Withholding rent

3.11   A tenant has no right in law simply to withhold rent in protest at a landlord's failure to carry out repairs. In addition to inviting possession proceedings, tenants encouraging others to withold rent could be taken to court for unlawful interference with the contracts (ie, the tenancy agreements) of other tenants.[9]

3.12   An adviser should not encourage a tenant to withhold rent: to do so invites possession proceedings, in which the tenant will be a defendant and therefore at a disadvantage. All too often a tenant withholding rent is unable to resist spending any money set aside on other outgoings and, if the damages awarded do not exceed the amount withheld, there is a real risk of a possession order. The dangers are well illustrated by the case of *Al Hassani v Merrigan*,[10] where the counterclaim for damages was dismissed, the money set aside could not meet the arrears, and the judge found it reasonable in the circumstances to grant a possession order for arrears of rent.

Set-off against rent

3.13   In many cases, the tenant seeks advice only when possession proceedings have been started as a result of rent arrears. If there is disrepair, it will be possible to reduce or even extinguish the arrears by counterclaiming a sum equal to the damages to which the tenant is entitled as a result of the landlord's default. This is the case even though the damages are unliquidated, in that they have not yet been valued by

---

6 Communities and Local Government, August 2002, available only online at www.communities.gov.uk/publications/housing/betterdeal2.

7 As amended by Leasehold Reform, Housing and Urban Development Act 1993 s121.

8 Further details can be found in the Secure Tenants of Local Housing Authorities (Right to Repair) Regulations 1994 SI No 133 as amended by 1994 SI No 844 and 1997 SI No 73.

9 See *Camden Nominees v Forcey* [1940] Ch 352.

10 (1988) 20 HLR 238, CA.

the court.[11] Where the amount of damages matches or exceeds the rent arrears, the tenant is entitled to an equitable set-off amounting to a complete defence to the landlord's possession action.[12]

3.14   Equitable set-off has the advantage over the common law right to recoup from rent discussed above, in that it goes beyond costs of remedial works and can include ordinary (general) damages for inconvenience and distress to which the tenant is entitled as a result of the landlord's default. The set-off should be raised formally in the defence to the landlord's claim and will usually be accompanied by a counterclaim setting out the breach complained of and the damage suffered.[13]

3.15   It must be shown that the right to set-off emerges from a landlord's breach of the tenancy and that it would be unfair (inequitable) to allow the landlord to recover the amount claimed in the face of the landlord's breach of obligation and the tenant's counterclaim. Such conditions will usually be automatically satisfied in the case of damages resulting from the landlord's breach of a contractual repairing obligation.

3.16   Note that, where the tenancy has been assigned to a new landlord, the tenant is not entitled to set off damages arising before the assignment in a claim for rent arrears which have arisen after the assignment.[14] However, if rent arrears are assigned to the new landlord, then the tenant can set off damages for disrepair that arose when those arrears accrued.[15]

3.17   This remedy is invaluable where the landlord is relying on the 'potentially draconian'[16] power in HA 1988 Sch 2 Ground 8 to seek possession against an assured tenant (where the judge usually has no choice but to grant a possession order if two or more months' arrears are outstanding) and where the set-off could extinguish the arrears or reduce them to less than two months' rent.

Reduction in rent

3.18   A tenant protected by the Rent Act 1977 can apply to the rent officer for a reduction in the registered rent if there has been a 'change in

11   *British Anzani v International Marine* [1979] 2 All ER 1063, QBD.
12   *Televantos v McCulloch* (1991) 23 HLR 412; [1991] 1 EGLR 123, CA.
13   See the defence and counterclaim in appendix D.
14   *Edlington Properties Ltd v Fenner & Co Ltd* [2006] EWCA Civ 403.
15   See *Muscat v Smith* [2003] EWCA Civ 962.
16   *North British Housing Association v Matthews* [2004] EWCA Civ 1736; [2005] HLR 17, per Dyson LJ at para 33.

the condition of the dwelling' since the last assessment.[17] However, this rarely arises nowadays, given the dwindling numbers of Rent Act tenants.

Appointing a receiver or manager

3.19   In the private sector, situations can arise where the identity of the landlord is not known, or the landlord cannot be traced and urgent repairs require attention. In such cases, the remedy is to apply for the appointment of a receiver. The court has power to do this in any case where it appears just and convenient: see Part 69 of the Civil Procedure Rules (CPR). This remedy is not available to tenants of local authorities.[18] On the remuneration of the receiver, see *Evans v Clayhope Properties*.[19]

3.20   For situations where there are two or more flats in a single block owned by a non-resident landlord, the procedure for appointment of a manager is now codified in the Landlord and Tenant Act (LTA) 1987 Part II. This requires, in the usual case, that a preliminary 'warning notice' be served on the landlord or agent (s22). If this does not produce the required effect, a leasehold valuation tribunal may, on application, appoint a manager to take over and run the block for the purpose of making good the disrepair (s24). The appointment can be registered against the title of the property as a notice at the Land Registry to prevent the landlord avoiding the consequences of the order by selling on. Unfortunately, local authority and registered social landlords are exempt from this provision (s58).

Using the ombudsmen and/or the Tenant Services Authority

Using the ombudsmen

3.21   Council tenants aggrieved by their landlords' failure to carry out repairs, and private tenants concerned at the failure of local authorities to intervene to improve their housing conditions, may seek redress against the council concerned from the Local Government Ombudsmen (formerly Commissioners for Local Administration).[20] Tenants of registered social landlords (principally housing associations) have

---

17 Rent Act 1977 s67(3)(a).
18 *Parker v Camden* LBC [1985] 2 All ER 141, CA.
19 (1988) 20 HLR 176, CA.
20 See www.lgo.org.uk.

access to the Housing Ombudsman Service.[21] This service operates in broadly similar fashion to the Local Government Ombudsmen. In Wales, both local authorities and registered social landlords are subject to complaints to the Public Services Ombudsman for Wales.[22]

3.22   Ombudsmen have the power to investigate complaints of maladministration, delay or injustice made against local authorities and registered social landlords by tenants. In both cases, the tenant must first complete the landlord's internal complaints procedure before the ombudsman can intervene. This is a daunting process but, in relatively minor cases, it may be a more proportionate remedy than court proceedings. The tenant or adviser must be familiar with the internal complaints process of the landlord, which can usually be found on its website.

3.23   If there is a genuine dispute over the cause of disrepair or the appropriate remedy, the ombudsman may appoint an independent surveyor to help in the investigation of a complaint. The Local Government Ombudsmen have published good practice guides on repairs and remedies, which include sections on repairs (Part II) and environmental health (Part VIII).[23]

3.24   Even though the full investigation of a complaint can take over a year, the formal process of instituting a complaint is often sufficient to propel a recalcitrant landlord or local authority into action. The local government ombudsmen have made it clear that they do not expect tenants to take court action in order to get repairs done. Accordingly, they are prepared to investigate complaints even in cases where the tenant could clearly bring legal proceedings. Perhaps most usefully, they will investigate complaints of maladministration where there is no redress by way of civil action, eg, complaints of condensation dampness[24] or in relation to improvement works.

3.25   Advisers should be cautious about assisting tenants to make complaints to the ombudsmen using public funding because the ombudsmen will not usually award costs and therefore the statutory charge (explained at paragraph 4.56) may apply.[25]

---

21 See www.housing-ombudsman.org.uk.

22 www.ombudsman-wales.org.uk.

23 Commission for Local Administration in England *Council Housing Repairs: Guidance on Good Practice 3* (1993); *Remedies: Guidance on Good Practice 6* (2005).

24 *Local Government Ombudsman Investigation report, Bristol City Council* 06B05370, December 2007.

25 See *Local Government Ombudsman Investigation report, Stonebridge Housing Action Trust* 05A7668, September 2006, December 2006 *Legal Action* 25.

Using the Tenant Services Authority

3.26   The Housing and Regeneration Act (H&RA) 2008, which does not come into force fully until April 2010, creates a new regulator, the Tenant Services Authority (TSA), which will regulate social housing provided by registered providers in England. The TSA will be responsible, among other things, for setting standards for the provision of social housing and for monitoring compliance with them. These standards may require registered providers to comply with specified rules, including rules about the terms of tenancies, maintenance and estate management.[26] The TSA may issue codes of practice in relation to standards[27] and may require landlords to pay compensation where they have failed to meet the standards set.[28] However, the TSA cannot award compensation where the ombudsman has awarded compensation, except if such compensation has not been paid as recommended.[29] There is nothing in the H&RA 2008 which requires that tenants and their advisers must complain to their landlord before making complaints directly to the TSA, as is the position with the complaints to the ombudsmen. In November 2009 the Secretary of State directed the TSA that its National Standards must address the quality of accommodation provided by registered providers and later that month the TSA began a consultation exercise on the precise terms of the standards which will apply from April 2010.

Court proceedings

3.27   Most disrepair claims will start as civil actions in the local county court although many will be brought as counterclaims to possession proceedings for rent arrears. Although court proceedings take longer than some of the other remedies mentioned above, they can be a powerful way of securing a remedy for a tenant who has suffered at the hands of a recalcitrant landlord. The court can order a landlord to repair a property, can award damages and can make declarations. All of these remedies will be considered below.

3.28   Given the complexity of the court process, particularly where an order for repairs is being sought, a tenant would be well advised to seek legal representation. The remainder of this chapter assumes

26 H&RA 2008 s193.
27 H&RA 2008 s195.
28 H&RA 2008 ss237–8.
29 H&RA 2008 s239.

that a tenant has consulted an adviser who is able to represent him or her in court proceedings. It will also be assumed that the tenant will be funding the case with legal aid.

3.29   Advisers have differing approaches to managing disrepair cases. The tactics set out in this chapter have worked well in practice but are by no means the only way of conducting a successful claim. They may need to be adapted to suit different advisers or indeed the approaches of different county courts. Of course, the procedural rules cannot be approached with the same flexibility.

Taking initial instructions

3.30   At an early stage the adviser will have to check whether the tenant is financially eligible for legal aid and, if so, the adviser will need to complete a Controlled Work 1 form (CW1) available to all legal aid providers from the Legal Services Commission (LSC). Proof of the tenant's income and savings will need to be attached to the form. If the tenant is financially eligible this will entitle the adviser to obtain initial instructions and to apply for further funding by obtaining a legal representation certificate. If the tenant is not eligible for legal aid the adviser will have to consider whether there is any other way of funding the case, for example, with a conditional fee agreement or through legal expenses insurance, see paragraphs 4.68 onwards.

3.31   Some advisers send the tenant a questionnaire to complete and bring to the first meeting. This works well with some tenants but could be off-putting for a tenant disadvantaged by language or literacy difficulties. A sample questionnaire is contained in appendix D.

3.32   It is important that the adviser establishes the tenant's requirements at the first interview. Sometimes the tenant does not want repairs carried out, but would prefer a transfer to other accommodation. Unfortunately, there is no private law remedy to obtain such a result and the possibility of a judicial review of a refusal to grant a transfer only arises in the most extreme circumstances. Judicial review proceedings are outside the ambit of this book.

3.33   It is sadly the case that the remedies in this book will rarely be of use to tenants of private landlords. Such tenants are likely to have assured shorthold tenancies (ASTs) with limited security. Tenants with ASTs will therefore need to be warned that any action to secure repairs may well lead to the termination of their tenancy. ASTs are likely to be of relatively short duration. It is therefore rare for the value of any damages claim to be enough to justify the expense of court proceedings. However, the adviser should bear in mind that, if the tenancy began or was renewed after 6 April 2007 and the landlord has not protected any deposit paid, as required by HA 2004 s213, then the landlord will be unable to rely on a notice served under HA 1988 s21. Until the landlord protects the deposit, the tenant's position will be more secure.

3.34   In cases of significant loss or extreme disrepair, the tenant may be willing to risk losing the tenancy rather than endure the conditions and an interim injunction should be considered, see below. Where a tenant is in priority need as defined by HA 1996 Part 7 s189, if the property is in very poor condition, the local authority may have a duty to secure that suitable accommodation is made available.[30]

3.35   For the remainder of this chapter it will be assumed that the tenant wants either to take county court action or to defend and counterclaim in proceedings brought by a landlord.

3.36   It is important to establish the landlord's identity as early as possible and the tenant should be asked to bring the original tenancy agreement, together with any other tenancy documents, to the first interview with the adviser. If there is any uncertainty about the identity of the landlord, the adviser can use LTA 1985 s1 to force the person receiving the rent to supply the tenant with the landlord's name and address. Official copies of the register of title (also known as Office Copy Entries) can be obtained online from the Land Registry to establish the ownership of the property but the adviser should remember that the landlord may him or herself be the tenant of the person named on the title register.

3.37   The tenant should be advised to keep a diary of all future contact with the landlord, of the continuing effects of the disrepair and of any unnecessary inconvenience and distress caused by work of repair when it is eventually carried out.

3.38   The adviser may want to give the tenant a list to complete of any expenses and losses arising from the disrepair, see appendix D. The tenant should be warned against the temptation of exaggerating such losses. In practice, the general damages, that is, the amount the court awards for inconvenience and distress, are often much larger than the financial losses, and any dishonesty at this stage will affect the credibility of the whole case. Often the tenant will not have retained receipts and will have thrown goods away before giving the landlord the opportunity to inspect them. This can cause difficulties. For example, in *Heffernan v LB Hackney*,[31] a claimant was refused his claim

---

30 See HA 1996 ss175(3) and 193(2).
31 [2009] EWCA Civ 665.

for losses because of a lack of evidence. Sedley LJ said it was:

> not permissible to come to court with bald assertions of the kind with which the Judge ... was presented, unsupported by a single document showing payment or loss, and to leave him, as Bowen LJ once put it, like a blind man searching for a black hat in a dark room ...

3.39   Even so, non-inflated claims for goods destroyed can be successfully made without receipts because most judges accept the reality that tenants rarely keep them. When completing the list, the tenant might want to use a catalogue or the internet to obtain estimates for the replacement value of goods rather than spending hours going round the various shops where the goods were originally bought.

Matters to consider after the first interview

Limitation periods

3.40   The adviser needs to bear in mind that the landlord will have a potential defence to any claim for disrepair that the tenant suffered before the limitation date. The basic limitation periods are three years in personal injury claims and six years in other cases, running from when the cause of action accrues and ending with the date on which the claim is issued (Limitation Act (LA) 1980). The key date, therefore, is that on which the cause of action accrues, and this may vary.

3.41   The cause of action under a tenancy agreement accrues at the date of breach of the obligation to repair. Where premises are in disrepair, breach usually occurs when the landlord has knowledge of the disrepair and failed to remedy it within a reasonable period.[32] If repairs are not carried out, the cause of action is a continuing one but proceedings should be started within six years of the initial breach in order to ensure that the tenant is compensated for the whole period. If there has been a continuing breach of obligation for more than six years, the damages will be limited to the circumstances over the six years preceding the launch of proceedings if the landlord relies on a limitation defence.[33]

3.42   Where the claim is founded in tort, the same principles apply whether the duty of care which has been breached arises in common law or by statute. Actions based on a breach of the duty imposed by Defective Premises Act (DPA) 1972 s1 are subject to the usual rules

32 See paragraph 1.106.
33 As in *Sturolson & Co v Mauroux* (1988) 20 HLR 332, CA, at 334.

on limitation, so the cause of action in most cases arises at the date of completion of the works (s1(5)). Where the claim is for damage to property, eg, under DPA 1972 s4, the initial six-year limitation period runs from the date of damage.[34] If the damage was not discoverable at that date, this rule has been modified by LA 1980 s14A to give the claimant three years from the date that he or she first had the knowledge needed to bring the action. However, there is a longstop of 15 years from the date of the tortious act, after which the claim cannot be statute-barred.

3.43   Where a claim arises from a personal injury, the three-year limitation period runs from the date of injury, even though the landlord's tortious act may have occurred many years earlier.[35] Disrepair claims often involve both personal injury and other heads of damages. If all of these claims are brought in one action, LA 1980 s11 will apply a three-year limitation period to all causes of action, including a claim for inconvenience and distress. The solution is to ask the opponent to agree not to raise the limitation point. Alternatively, the claimant can make an application under LA 1980 s33 to extend the three-year limitation period.[36] Some advisers start two separate legal actions, one for personal injury and the second for any other claims and then ask the court to consolidate the two actions and hear them together.

Who will be the claimant?

3.44   A remedy in contract is usually only available to the parties to the contract. It follows that a tenant can be the claimant or, in the case of a joint tenancy, all or any of the tenants can be claimants. Third parties such as children or lodgers may enforce contractual provisions only if they can bring themselves within the terms of the Contracts (Rights of Third Parties) Act (C(RTP)A) 1999. They can sometimes do this if they are named as authorised occupiers in the tenancy agreement.

3.45   The cases of *Jarvis v Swan Tours Ltd* and *Jackson v Horizon Holidays*[37] have been applied to housing disrepair cases to allow tenants

34 *Pirelli General Cable Works v Faber (Oscar) & Partners* [1983] 1 All ER 65, HL; *Ketteman v Hansel Properties* [1984] 1 WLR 1274, HL.

35 *Rimmer v Liverpool CC* [1984] 1 All ER 930, CA.

36 See, eg, *Millington v Islington LBC* August 1999 *Legal Action* 25; *Housing Law Casebook* para P1.6, Clerkenwell County Court.

37 *Jarvis v Swan Tours Ltd* [1973] 1 All ER 71; *Jackson v Horizon Holidays* [1975] 1 WLR 1468, CA, as explained in *Woodar Investments v Wimpey* [1980] 1 WLR 277, HL.

to claim damages for inconvenience and distress not only for themselves, but also for their families.

3.46   In cases where a non-tenant has suffered injury or damage to
property (as opposed to inconvenience and distress or economic
loss), that person may have a right to bring a claim in his or her own
name using the DPA 1972 s4 or the Occupiers Liability Act 1957 s2.

3.47   In *Chin v Hackney LBC*,[38] a tenant brought an action for damages
for disrepair and the claim was settled on terms that the landlord
would carry out agreed works and pay damages. The tenant's disabled daughter then issued new proceedings for damages for personal injury caused to her by the housing conditions. The Court of
Appeal allowed the daughter to bring her claim, stating that the new
case was not 'res judicata' (ie, already decided) because it was not between the same parties as the earlier case. However, the court made it
clear that, where more than one member of a household has a claim
arising from the same facts, these should all be brought in a single
action and a wasted costs order should be considered where separate
actions are issued. Even so, where separate actions are brought to
preserve the six-year limitation period for the disrepair claim, it is
unlikely that a court would consider such a sanction.

3.48   *Murphy and Peers v Stockport MBC*[39] contains a useful analysis
of the obstacles facing non-tenants who wish to be parties in housing disrepair actions. Mrs Murphy was the tenant and brought an
action for damages for disrepair against her council landlord. Her
children, who endured the disrepair along with their mother, were
named as the second and third claimants. It was held that, in the
absence of any claim for personal injury or damage to their personal
property, the children could not rely on the duty of care in DPA 1972
s4. They could not sue in nuisance because they had no proprietary
interest in their home. They could not rely on any express term as
they were not parties to the tenancy agreement with the council and
the C(RTP)A 1999 did not apply because the children were not identified by name, class or description in the agreement. They could not
rely on the implied term in LTA 1985 s11 and, applying *Lee v Leeds
CC*,[40] that statute was not to be read as in any way extended by the
Human Rights Act 1998 and Article 8 of the European Convention
on Human Rights. The best that the children could expect would be

38 [1996] All ER 973, CA.
39 August 2002 *Legal Action* 27, Stockport County Court.
40 [2002] EWCA Civ 6.

to have 'some element of a remedy on the coat-tails' of Mrs Murphy, by application of the rule in *Jackson* (see paragraph 3.45).

Pre-action Protocol for housing disrepair cases

3.49 Except in real emergencies,[41] the judge at court will expect the tenant to have followed a procedure known as the Pre-action Protocol for Housing Dispreair Cases before starting court proceedings. The Protocol can be found on the Ministry of Justice website.[42] It applies to all civil disrepair claims, but not to counterclaims nor to proceedings in the magistrates' court brought under the Environmental Protection Act 1990.[43] It aims to encourage the early exchange of information in the hope that the parties can achieve a settlement without the need for court action.

3.50 The Protocol requires a letter to be sent to the landlord at the earliest opportunity, warning of the possible claim. If the tenant has all the information needed to start proceedings this can be a letter of claim (LOC) but more usually the letter is a preliminary early notification letter (ENL) setting out as much information as is available at an initial stage. The Protocol provides for an expert to be jointly selected by the parties and instructed to prepare a report where necessary. It builds at least one and in some cases two delays of 20 working days into the procedure to give the parties the opportunity to settle the issues between them. The adviser can usually follow the disrepair Protocol after obtaining a legal representation certificate because the general rule that pre-action protocols must be followed under Legal Help[44] does not apply to housing cases.[45]

3.51 The Protocol does not extend the statutory limitation period, so, if that is about to expire, the tenant should issue proceedings immediately rather than following the Protocol, unless the landlord quickly confirms that he or she will not rely on limitation as a defence (see paragraph 3.4 of the Protocol). For guidance on limitation periods see paragraph 3.40–3.43.

3.52 Paragraph 3.7 of the Protocol makes it clear that if, as a result of following the Protocol, the tenant's claim settles without litigation on

41 In which case see interim injunctions at paragraph 3.96.
42 www.justice.gov.uk/civil/procrules_fin/contents/protocols/prot_hou.htm, although it is often quicker to type 'disrepair protocol' into an internet search engine.
43 Protocol para 3.1(b).
44 See chapter 4, paragraph 4.13 onwards.
45 See CLS Funding Code para 15.2.

terms that would have justified bringing it, the landlord will pay the tenant's reasonable costs and expenses. In *Birmingham CC v Lee,*[46] the landlord carried out repairs during the Protocol period and then declined to pay the tenant's legal costs, given that the value of her claim was less than £5,000 and the claim therefore would be decided on the small claims track where costs would not usually be payable (see paragraph 3.142). The Court of Appeal held that costs were properly payable up until the point that the repairs were carried out, even though the damages part of the claim was technically a small claims track claim.

3.53　　Advisers should be careful not to allow the Protocol to delay the issue of proceedings unreasonably. It is important that the tenant sees that progress is being made because, if the momentum is lost through ineffective exchanges of correspondence, the tenant may lose confidence in the adviser and even give up a legitimate claim altogether.

3.54　　For the remainder of this chapter the Protocol will be dealt with alongside other matters that the adviser will have to consider as the case progresses. It will also be assumed that the adviser is not in a position to send a LOC at an early stage and therefore sends a ENL.

First contact with the landlord

3.55　　The tenant will not usually be granted a legal representation certificate until a letter complaining about the disrepair has been sent to the landlord.[47] Given that the Protocol requires the tenant to give the landlord 20 working days to respond to the ENL, it makes sense to send this letter while the tenant is still funded by Legal Help and then allow the 20-working-day period to run while the LSC considers the legal representation application. The ENL can be attached to the application form, thus avoiding the duplication of a detailed statement in support of the application.

3.56　　A specimen ENL is set out in the Protocol and is reproduced in a slightly adapted form in appendix D; it should contain the following information[48]:

- Tenant's name, address of property, tenant's address if different, tenant's telephone number and when access is available.

46　[2008] EWCA Civ 891.
47　See paragraph 4.40.
48　Protocol para 3.2.

- Details of the defects, including any defects outstanding. The Protocol has a schedule that can be used for this purpose (known as Annex G).
- Details of any notification previously given to the landlord;
- The name of a proposed expert (see paragraph 3.61).
- Proposed letter of instruction to expert (the standard letter in Annex C of the Protocol can be used for this purpose).
- Tenant's disclosure of any relevant documents that are readily available.

3.57   The ENL should also request disclosure from the landlord of all relevant records or documents; paragraph 3.2(b) of the Protocol sets out a list. The ENL should also include the tenant's authorisation for release of the information.

Legal aid

3.58   As soon as the adviser has enough information to apply for a representation certificate, the legal aid application should be sent off. See chapter 4 for more detail. Once legal aid is granted, the adviser should continue negotiations with the landlord while at the same time preparing to start proceedings should that prove necessary.

Landlord's response

3.59   The landlord should usually reply to the ENL within 20 working days[49] of receiving it, disclosing all relevant records or documents and responding to the tenant's proposal for instructing an expert. If there is no response, then the adviser can continue to gather evidence and then send a LOC as soon as there is enough information to do so.

Instruction of expert(s)

3.60   Once the 20-working-day period allowed in the ENL has passed, the next step will usually be to instruct an expert. The Protocol suggests that this will not always be necessary and photographs or video footage of any defects may be enough. However, most tenants do not have the technical knowledge needed to prove that the poor housing conditions in photographs are caused by actionable disrepair. Evidence from an expert carries weight and it is not usually possible for the adviser to be certain of the merit of the case without it. Only

49 See Protocol para 4.10 for a definition of 'working days'.

in the simplest of matters should the adviser dispense with the need to instruct an expert.

3.61   Paragraph 3.6 of the Protocol sets out detailed steps to take if the parties are communicating with each other. They are supposed to try to agree a single expert who will be jointly instructed by both of them, with each party bearing half of the cost. If this is not possible, each party should instruct their own expert, but a joint inspection should be agreed. The Protocol states that the inspection should take place within 20 working days of the landlord's response to the ENL.[50]

3.62   There are advantages and disadvantages to agreeing the identity of the expert with the opponent. The advantage is that it minimises costs, because the expert's fee is shared equally between the parties. The disadvantage is that the adviser cannot discuss the case with the expert, for example, by telephoning to obtain a 'feel' of just how serious the disrepair is. Any discussions with a joint expert should be recorded in writing and sent to the opposing party. Advisers should, therefore, follow the Protocol but not allow the opponent to veto the adviser's choice of expert.

3.63   The specimen letters in the Protocol require a landlord to give reasons if he or she objects to the expert proposed by the tenant. Tenants' advisers should not allow the landlord to reject an expert without giving an explanation because it is an advantage to the tenant for the adviser to choose an expert known to be unbiased and reliable.

Choice of an expert

3.64   There is no advantage to a tenant in instructing a 'tame' expert who is tenant- biased. This is only likely to lead to an unsuccessful outcome at trial. CPR 35.3 states:

> It is the duty of an expert to help the court on the matters within his expertise.
> This duty overrides any obligation to the person from whom he has received instructions or by whom he is paid.

The adviser should instruct an expert who is aware of these duties and who will present the facts impartially. The expert must identify the causes of the disrepair and it can be fatal to the case if he or she does not appreciate this.

3.65   For example, in *Ball and Another v Plymouth CC*,[51] Mr and Mrs Ball complained of cold and damp. Their surveyor's report stated

---

50 See Protocol para 3.6(d).
51 [2004] EWHC 134 (QB).

'sweepingly' that the flat was suffering from condensation caused by damp penetration through external walls which in his professional opinion was section 11 disrepair. No further details of the damp penetration were given. The landlord's expert reported that he could find no evidence of disrepair. It was a fast track trial, so neither surveyor gave evidence at court. The judge held that the burden of proof had not been satisfied and the tenants' claim failed.

3.66   If the adviser has not used an expert before it is wise to seek recommendations from other practitioners specialising in housing disrepair. Usually the appropriate expert in a housing disrepair case will be a qualified chartered surveyor with experience of (or training in) how to give evidence in court. However, some environmental health officers (EHOs) also have the necessary experience and knowledge to perform this function,[52] although there is always a danger that if the landlord instructs a chartered surveyor, the judge might consider the landlord's expert to be more qualified. In cases involving an element of condensation dampness or infestations the advantage of obtaining an EHO's report outweighs the risk because EHOs are trained in public health matters and the report can be used in a magistrates' court prosecution if it turns out that there is no civil remedy.

Example

The tenant complains of water dripping from the ceiling in wet weather and of damp and mould throughout the property. The adviser suspects penetrating damp but cannot rule out the possibility that the property is suffering from condensation due to bad design. It could be that the drips are in fact water condensing on the cold ceiling as a result of the increased humidity in cold and wet conditions. The adviser instructs an EHO with experience of giving evidence in the county court. If the report shows that the dampness is caused by a combination of disrepair and condensation then the adviser can use the report in the county court. If the report discloses only condensation damp not attributable to disrepair then, as long as the EHO states that the property is prejudicial to health, the adviser can use the report to bring a prosecution in the magistrates' court (see chapter 5). Alternatively, the adviser can send a copy of the report to the local housing authority and ask that action be taken under the Housing Acts (see chapter 6).

---

52 The Health and Housing Group have a list of such EHOs. Contact: 37 Star Street, Ware, Hertfordshire SG12 7AA, tel: 01920 465384.

3.67   CPR Practice Direction (PD) 35.2.1 sets out the form and content of an expert's report which must contain a statement of truth and details of the expert's qualifications.

Chronology and witness statement

3.68   If the landlord complies with pre-action disclosure as set out in the Protocol, then a large amount of documentary information, sometimes going back many years, will be sent to the adviser. An increasing number of tenants now correspond by email and this can add to the weight of paper evidence. All of these documents have to be collated and considered because they may help or weaken the tenant's case. The best way to deal with such documentation is to prepare a chronology setting out the dates and most important events, cross-referencing them to the documents. A sample chronology is set out in appendix D.

3.69   Whether or not a chronology is used, a proof of evidence (sometimes referred to as a file statement) will need to be prepared. This should set out the full history of the disrepair, and the inconvenience and distress suffered by the tenant. The dates and some of the facts can be based on the tenant's questionnaire and the chronology, but an interview will usually be necessary to bring out the ways in which the disrepair has affected this particular tenant.

3.70   The adviser should consider whether a home visit can be justified to assist with the preparation of the proof of evidence. A much clearer statement will be prepared and the inconvenience and distress will be much better articulated if the adviser has seen the disrepair and the layout of the premises. Landlords' representatives invariably object to the cost of such a home visit when the costs are assessed, but costs officers are usually prepared to allow the cost of one home visit by the adviser.

3.71   The proof of evidence will eventually form the basis of a witness statement to be shown to the opponent, and it should therefore be in the tenant's own words as far as possible. If the tenant is unable to recall exact dates, then this should be made clear in the proof of evidence. At this stage the proof should disclose the weaknesses as well as the strengths of the case although, when it is turned into a witness statement, unhelpful information will be privileged and should be omitted. Advisers might want to put in italics items that they know should eventually be excluded from the witness statement.

3.72   The proof of evidence should refer to any items that have been damaged by the disrepair, such as electrical devices destroyed by water or clothing destroyed by damp.

3.73   Both the chronology and the proof of evidence will need to be updated when the expert's report is available so that the tenant can comment on it and confirm its accuracy.

3.74   The adviser should also consider obtaining proofs of evidence from other members of the tenant's family, friends and possibly even health visitors and social workers about the effect of the disrepair on the tenant. The cost of this exercise has to be balanced against the value of the claim because the courts expect the costs to be broadly proportionate to the amount of money involved and the complexity of the issues.[53]

Obtaining evidence

3.75   If the landlord does not respond or refuses to provide disclosure under the Protocol, the adviser may feel that there is not enough evidence to issue proceedings. If so, an application for pre-action disclosure under CPR 31.16 should be considered. This will not be necessary if the expert's evidence clearly indicates disrepair and if the tenant is likely to make a convincing witness. The adviser should note that CPR 48.1(2) states that the general rule is that the applicant for disclosure will pay the costs of the person against whom the order is sought, although it is possible to persuade the court to make a different order.[54] Failure to comply with a Protocol is a relevant factor that should overturn this presumption.

Negotiations

3.76   Where the landlord is co-operating with the Protocol, the adviser will likely to be well aware of the need to keep negotiating while at the same time preparing the case for the prompt issue of proceedings. However, negotiations may not be enough to satisfy the court that the Protocol has been followed. Paragraph 1 of the Protocol makes it clear that litigation should be a last resort, and the parties should consider whether some form of alternative dispute resolution procedure (ADR) would be more suitable than litigation. ADR is defined as mediation, or another dispute resolution method, which seeks to settle disputes without the need for court proceedings.

53 CPR 1.1(2)(c).
54 CPR 48.1(3).

3.77   ADR has not featured much in disrepair litigation to date but the pressure is increasing to use it. This will be discussed in more detail in paragraph 3.139. There can be costs sanctions for failing to consider ADR at the pre-action stage[55] so it might be wise for the adviser to propose it or to make a note on file if it seems inappropriate in a particular case.

Use of counsel

3.78   An inexperienced adviser should consult a barrister specialising in housing disrepair well before proceedings are issued. The barrister should be instructed to advise in writing on merits and value (which is still archaically referred to as 'quantum' by most lawyers). If there is no approved list of housing counsel within the adviser's organisation, or the adviser cannot obtain a personal recommendation, then the annual 'Repairs round-up' published in *Legal Action* in December each year has a list in its footnotes of barristers who have been active in recent cases and this is a good place to start.

3.79   Even an experienced housing adviser will often instruct counsel before issuing proceedings, either because of a restriction on the legal aid certificate or because legal expenses insurers require a barrister's advice on the merits before insuring a case.

Contact with the client

3.80   While the adviser is gathering the information necessary to issue proceedings, it is important to keep in contact with the tenant. Often the landlord will be carrying out repairs, sometimes to a poor standard, and the adviser will have to take details, since these may increase the claim further. The adviser may have to deal with allegations that the tenant has refused admission to workmen and to persuade the tenant to continue to give access.

Letter of claim

3.81   Once the adviser has investigated the case, paragraph 3.3 of the Protocol requires that a LOC should be sent. This letter should give any details that were omitted from the ENL, full details of the disrepair, a full history of notice given and a summary of the inconvenience, distress and financial losses suffered by the tenant as a result of the

---

55   See Protocol para 4.1(a).

disrepair. If any personal injury has been suffered this should be set out. The letter should ask for proposals for compensation and should ask for a full schedule of works, together with the anticipated date for completion of the works proposed.

3.82   Although not required by the Protocol, the letter should make it clear that if satisfactory proposals are not received from the landlord within 20 working days, court proceedings will be started without further notice.

3.83   If the adviser is using counsel, this is the point at which instructions to draft court papers should be sent off, so that the adviser is ready to start proceedings as soon as the 20 working days expire. Similarly, if there is a limitation on the legal aid funding certificate, this is the point at which the adviser should apply for the restriction to be lifted, unless the adviser's organisation has devolved powers to do this itself.

Response to letter of claim

3.84   The landlord is supposed to reply to the LOC within 20 working days, stating whether liability is admitted and, if not, the reasons why it is denied. The landord should make any allegation about lack of knowledge of the repair or difficulties in gaining access. A full schedule of intended works including anticipated start and completion dates and a timetable for the works should be included, as should any offer of compensation and costs. If such a letter is not received, the tenant's adviser should issue proceedings as soon as possible.

Issuing proceedings

Final preparations

3.85   The adviser should check the scope and costs limitation on any legal representation certificate or any restriction on any legal expenses insurance certificate before issuing the claim. The adviser should also ensure that a notice of funding has been served, and if not, one should be prepared and served with the court papers.

3.86   Once the court timetable starts running the adviser will have to meet tight deadlines. It is therefore wise to ensure that the tenant and any witnesses have confirmed the accuracy of, and signed, their proofs of evidence, see paragraph 3.71.

3.87   The adviser should remember that any proceedings brought on behalf of a child need to be brought by a person acting as the child's litigation friend and a Certificate of Suitability[56] needs to be filed.[57]

The claim form

3.88   The claim form is in form N1 and can be found on the Courts Service website.[58] It can be completed online and then printed. It must:

- Contain a concise statement of the nature of the claim.
- Specify the remedy which the claimant seeks.
- Where the claimant is making a claim for money, contain a statement of value in accordance with CPR 16.3.
- Include an address at which the claimant resides.
- Where the landlord is an individual, include an address (with postcode) at which the landlord resides or carries on business (if this is known). This applies even if the landlord's solicitors agree to accept service on the landlord's behalf.
- Where the landlord is an individual, include the landlord's date of birth, if known.[59]

A court fee will be payable to 'HM Courts Service'.[60]

Particulars of claim

3.89   In disrepair cases it is not practical to include full particulars of the claim in the claim form and a separate document setting out the particulars of claim should be prepared. There is no reason why this should not be served at the same time as the claim form.

3.90   The particulars of claim should include:

- all causes of action which are relevant, including express obligations, LTA 1985 s11, DPA 1972 s4, breach of covenants for quiet enjoyment, nuisance and where applicable, DPA 1972 s1;
- a description of the property, the occupiers and the current rent level; and
- details of disrepair, notice and damage.

---

56 County court form N235.
57 CPR 21.5 (3).
58 The easiest way to locate this form is to type 'Form N1' into an internet search engine.
59 CPR 16.2–16.4 and the Practice Direction (PD) to Part 16.
60 For the amount of the fee, see leaflet EX50 on the Courts Service website. The easiest way to check the fee is to type 'court form EX50' into an internet search engine.

3.91   The following documents should be annexed to and served with the particulars of claim:

- the repairing clause and other relevant clauses of any written tenancy agreement;[61]
- if a personal injury claim is included, a CPR compliant medical report;[62] and
- a detailed statement of any losses and expenses.[63]

It is also good practice to file the expert's report as an annex to the particulars of claim.

3.92   If exemplary or aggravated damages are to be claimed (see paragraph 8.42) then these must be specifically pleaded. A statement of value is required on the claim form only, but is usually also included in the particulars of claim. Interest must be specifically claimed, or the tenant might lose the right to it.

3.93   A specimen particulars of claim is set out in appendix D.

3.94   If at all possible, advisers should avoid the need to amend the particulars subsequently, because this can have adverse costs consequences. Also, if enough detail is given at this stage, it reduces the chance of the case being delayed by requests for further information under CPR 18.

Which court?

3.95   The county court has jurisdiction to hear claims of any value and it is the obvious forum for disrepair claims. The claim must be started in the county court for the district in which the property in disrepair is situated.[64]

Interim injunctions

3.96   In cases of severe disrepair causing serious and continuing interference with the tenant's enjoyment of the property, the court can make an order forcing the landlord to carry out repairs before the full merits of the case have been tested at trial. This emergency remedy is known as an interim or interlocutory injunction. An application for such an injunction will ensure that the matter is brought before a judge in a matter of days rather than months.

61 CPR PD 16 para 7.3.
62 CPR PD 16 para 4.3.
63 CPR PD 16 para 4.3.
64 CPR 56.2(1).

3.97   Despite the attractions of this method for securing immediate remedial works, the tenant needs to be aware that the injunction is granted purely to avoid the risk of further danger or damage and that, for these purposes, the landlord may successfully convince the court that basic 'patch' repairs will be enough.

3.98   The case of *American Cyanamid Co v Ethicon Ltd*,[65] sets out the matters that the tenant will be required to satisfy in order to obtain a mandatory interim injunction, namely that:

- There is a serious question to be tried (ie, a more than frivolous assertion that the landlord is in breach of a repairing obligation).
- Damages alone would not be adequate compensation (eg, because of a serious risk to health) or that the landlord would not be in a financial position to meet the damages to which the tenant would be entitled.
- The tenant will be in a position to meet the costs incurred by the landlord in performing works required by the injunction, if it is later found that the order should not have been made.
- If there is doubt about these last two factors, the balance of convenience (ie, comparative hardship) favours the tenant.

3.99   The leading authority on injunctions in disrepair cases is *Parker v Camden LBC*[66] and this, together with *Redland Bricks Ltd v Morris*,[67] requires that:

- The repair work required must be agreed by the parties or it must be clear what needs to be done (so there must be no substantial dispute between experts).
- The court will not order substantial works, eg, the replacement of an entire heating system.
- The circumstances must be exceptional, eg, an immediate risk to health and safety.
- The terms of order sought must be sufficiently clear for the landlord to know exactly what remedial work has to be done and by what date.
- The cost of carrying out works has to be taken into account.

3.100   In practice, the courts have not followed such a strict approach and, for example in London, interim injunctions are routinely made by some courts against social landlords. Furthermore, where it is not possible to specify exactly what repair work is needed, the tenant

---

65 [1975] AC 396, HL.
66 [1986] 1 Ch 162, CA.
67 [1970] AC 652.

can apply for an injunction requiring the landlord to investigate the cause of disrepair and then by a specified date provide the court with a report setting out the work needed to remedy it with proposals for doing so.[68] This often proves just as effective as making an application for specified work to be ordered.

3.101   In *Parker*, the court stated that an injunction may be granted where there is:

> an undoubted breach of covenant giving rise to actual and immediate major discomfort and inconvenience and to a real risk of damage to health flowing from the admitted breach ...

3.102   An example of the procedure being usefully employed can be found in the county court case of *Sheridan v Broadbridge*.[69] There the landlord accepted that a range of remedial work was needed but did not accept that the works should be subject to an injunction. The judge was satisfied that at least one item (a rear staircase in danger of collapse) was sufficiently serious to pass the *Parker* test and made a mandatory order in respect of that and all the other outstanding works. He expressly held that, provided at least one item justified the making of the order, the injunction should cover all the work agreed to be required.

3.103   If the application fails, the evidence put before the court suggesting risk to health or safety should at least justify a direction for an early trial. Any costs awarded against the tenant may be set off against a final award of costs or damages and in a legal aid case will not be assessed until the end of the case. The adviser should not hesitate to make an application for an injunction where there is a real risk to health or safety.

Injunction procedure

3.104   In an extremely urgent case, it is possible to go before the court without any paperwork, although the judge is likely to make the adviser undertake to file papers on the same or the next working day.[70]

3.105   In slightly less urgent cases, the adviser will need to complete a form N16A, a specimen of which appears in appendix D. The court will also expect to see a draft order and a witness statement from the tenant, explaining the reason for the urgency, confirming the injury

---

68 See appendix D for an example of an injunction.
69 September 1995 *Legal Action* 16; *Housing Law Casebook* para P14.5, Clerkenwell County Court.
70 CPR PD 25A para 4.3.

or damage that will result if the work is not ordered and explaining why the tenant cannot carry out the work and then bring a damages claim. The expert's report should be exhibited to the tenant's witness statement or a separate witness statement should be prepared and signed by the expert. Once again, the statement should make it clear why there is immediate danger to the tenant.

3.106   In legal aid cases the adviser must ensure that the scope of the legal aid as set out on the representation certificate includes applying for an injunction. If it does not, an application for an amendment must be granted by the LSC before the injunction application is made, otherwise the adviser will not be paid.

3.107   As a result of *American Cyanamid Co v Ethicon Ltd*,[71] it has become the practice for an injunction order to include an undertaking by the applicant to reimburse the respondent for any expense incurred as a result of obeying the injunction, should it later be decided that the order should not have been made. This is not an appropriate undertaking for a tenant of limited means to make and, if this is pointed out, most judges accept that it should not be required. However, a legally aided tenant should be warned that, as already mentioned, if the application is unsuccessful or the judge makes no order on costs, then the costs of the injunction application could come out of any damages that the tenant later recovers.

3.108   If the injunction application is successful, then the adviser must ensure that the order includes an order for costs. If the injunction order is silent on the question of costs, then no costs will be payable, even if the tenant goes on to win the final claim. Judges often make an order for 'costs reserved', which means that, at the end of the case, the settlement order or the final court order will need to provide that those costs are payable by the defendant. A note should be made on the file so that these costs are not forgotten.

3.109   If the court proceedings are already under way when the injunction application is made, a court fee will be payable. If the application is made at the same time as the claim is lodged, then a fee additional to the usual one will be payable. Leaflet EX50, which can be viewed on the Court Service website,[72] sets out the level of fees, but it is surprisingly unclear about the fee for an injunction. Most courts expect the tenant to pay the fee for a money claim, ie, for the damages part of their case and an additional fee based on the amount set out for

---

71 [1975] AC 396, HL.
72 The easiest way to locate this is to type 'court form EX50' into an internet search engine.

a county court non-money claim for the injunction application. It might be wise for the adviser to check on the telephone with their local county court because interpretations do appear to differ in different parts of the country.

3.110 The adviser will have to decide whether to make the application for an injunction 'on notice', in which case the court is likely to set a date some weeks ahead or 'without notice' (also known as *ex parte*), in which case the court will fix the first available date to put the case before the judge. Often the only way of securing a realistically early hearing date is to apply without notice, even though the adviser should still notify the landlord both of the intention to seek the injunction and of the hearing.

3.111 The adviser must ensure that the landlord is served with a copy of the notice of application for the injunction including notice of the hearing date and with all the supporting papers. A certificate of service[73] should be filed at court before the hearing.

3.112 Although it is not usual for oral evidence to be given at an interim injunction hearing, the adviser should arrange for both the tenant and the expert to be at court. The tenant needs to be there to give instructions to the adviser and so that the judge can see that the case matters to the tenant. The expert needs to be there because it is usual for the landlord to come to court and try to negotiate some form of order or undertaking and the expert's assistance will be needed when wording an injunction/undertaking which identifies particular work.

3.113 The adviser should be wary of accepting an undertaking from a corporate body unless someone with executive responsibility, such as a director of a company or the head of housing of a local authority, is present at court to give the undertaking. Otherwise, it may well not be enforceable at a later date.

3.114 If the landlord will not submit to an injunction, and if an undertaking is not acceptable to the tenant, then it is unlikely that an order will be made at the first hearing and the application will probably be adjourned to a later date with more time available. Usually, by the time the matter is scheduled to return to court the works will have been done, because landlords take injunction applications extremely seriously.

3.115 If an injunction order is obtained, the adviser will want the court to endorse it with a penal notice and the order must be served personally on the landlord, if an individual, or on an officer with executive

73 See form N215.

powers to carry out the order, if the landlord is a corporate body. For more details on enforcing an injunction, see paragraph 3.165.

Counterclaims

3.116   Many disrepair claims are counterclaims brought in defence of possession proceedings based on rent arrears. The defence should include a paragraph asking the court to set off the tenant's right to damages for the counterclaim against any rent arrears. A specimen defence and counterclaim is set out in appendix D.

3.117   A court fee based on the value of the counterclaim is payable and CPR 20.4(2) states that the defendant will need permission to make a counterclaim unless it is filed with the defence.

3.118   A term in the tenancy agreement prohibiting set-off may be unfair, see *Cody v Philps*.[74] As mentioned at paragraph 3.16, a tenant is not entitled to set off damages for disrepair incurred when the property was owned by a previous landlord in a claim brought by a new landlord, unless the new landlord has been assigned, and is suing for the old arrears. [75]

3.119   The defence and counterclaim may well have to be drafted without the benefit of an expert's report, because even if a court has given 28 days for the defence and counterclaim to be filed, it is unlikely that the adviser will be able to obtain and consider a report within that period.

3.120   The value of the counterclaim is not considered by the court when ascertaining 'value' for the purposes of allocating the case to a procedural track.

3.121   The adviser should check the wording of any legal aid certificate carefully to see whether it authorises the making of a counterclaim. It is not sufficient for it to state that the funding is to defend a possession claim.[76] If necessary the adviser should apply for an amendment of the scope of the certificate before starting work.

3.122   Filing a counterclaim will buy the tenant precious time in a rent arrears possession claim, because any decision about possession will usually be delayed until after the trial of the counterclaim. *Al Hassani v Merrigan*,[77] mentioned in paragraph 3.12, illustrates how important

74   December 2005 *Legal Action* 28; *Housing Law Casebook* para P12.11, West London County Court.

75   *Edlington Properties Ltd v Fenner and Co Ltd* [2006] EWCA Civ 403.

76   *LSC Manual* vol 3f–001.

77   (1988) 20 HLR 238, CA.

it is that such time is used wisely by the tenant. In particular, the adviser should ensure that the tenant now pays the rent as and when it falls due and that any problems with budgeting or housing benefit are addressed. Even if the adviser believes that the counterclaim is likely to exceed the amount of the rent arrears, the tenant should be advised to reduce the arrears by making regular payments. Judges can be inconsistent in the amount of damages awarded and if the adviser's prediction about damages proves to be over-optimistic, the tenant may end up relying on reasonableness as a defence to the possession claim, rather than on the counterclaim. In such circumstances, unless the tenant can demonstrate that his or her finances are now under control and that paying both rent and arrears has been established as a regular habit, the tenant's tenancy will be in jeopardy.

3.123   For similar reasons, the adviser should not be tempted to treat a counterclaim as a reason for allowing the trial to be delayed any longer than is absolutely necessary. If a case drifts, the danger is that the tenant will fall behind with the rent again and may even be in the appalling position of owing more rent by the time the case comes to trial than was owed when the possession proceedings were started.

3.124   If, when the case comes to trial, the damages awarded under the counterclaim exceed the arrears, any possession claim based on arrears of rent should be dismissed. If the court gives judgment for specified amounts on both the claim and the counterclaim, then the judge can make a separate order on costs against each party, see CPR 40.13. This could mean that the tenant's costs are reduced or even extinguished by the costs awarded to the landlord. Separate orders should therefore be avoided.

Settlements

3.125   Part 36 of the CPR encourages early settlements of litigation by placing costs and interest penalties on a party who refuses to accept a reasonable offer. There are good reasons for a tenant to take advantage of this provision: the interest penalty can benefit the tenant by increasing the damages, and the costs penalty can mean that costs which might otherwise be borne by the tenant are paid by the landlord on the 'indemnity basis'.[78] An offer under Part 36 can be made before the proceedings are issued but, in any event, serious consideration should be given to making such an offer when the particulars of

---

78 For an explanation of the difference between 'standard' and 'indemnity' costs see CPR 44.4.

claim are served. There are formalities that should be observed when wording a Part 36 offer, see CPR 36.2.

3.126   Usually the tenant will have been advised that there is a bracket within which the damages are likely to fall. One strategy is to pitch the financial part of the offer at the low end of this bracket, to increase the chances of beating it in court if the matter proceeds to trial and to tempt the landlord into a settlement. On the other hand, it may be better to pitch the settlement offer at the very top of the bracket because, if the adviser makes an offer at the low end of the scale and it is not accepted, this is likely to lower the landlord's expectations of what might be awarded and consequently lower the likely eventual settlement.

3.127   The correct approach in any particular case will depend on the tenant's temperament and attitude to the court case. Many tenants would rather have less money at an earlier stage than endure the anxiety and uncertainty of litigation, especially once the repairs have been carried out. The adviser must take instructions, explain the pros and cons of both strategies and then let the tenant decide.

3.128   Any offer in respect of damages should be put on the understanding that, if the repairs have not been carried out by the required date, further damages will be claimable.

3.129   The offer may invite the landlord to submit to a court order requiring outstanding repair work to be completed within a specified time period. The landlord is likely to want such terms to be included in a Tomlin order[79] as opposed to an order for specific performance, which is effectively a mandatory injunction.

3.130   A Tomlin order recites that a settlement has been achieved, but all the details of the settlement are included in a schedule to the order, which is not a public document. It can include provisions that go beyond the power of the court; for example, it can provide that the work has to be done to the satisfaction of the tenant's expert or that the landlord has to re-house the tenant. It can therefore be a useful form of settlement. However, if it includes repair works, which the landlord then fails to carry out, the tenant will have to apply for a further order to turn the Tomlin order into an injunction. While it will be almost impossible for the landlord to resist such an application, this will cause delay in the proceedings, and so Tomlin orders should be resisted in cases of serious disrepair. If a Tomlin order is used, the adviser must ensure that it gives permission to restore the case

---

79   Named after Mr Justice Tomlin, from his judgment in *Dashwood v Dashwood* [1927] WN 276.

for enforcement purposes. Permission may be required to restore in other circumstances. See appendix D for a precedent

3.131 A well advised landlord will take the initiative by making a Part 36 offer. A tenant who fails to accept a reasonable offer which is not then bettered at trial will be ordered to pay the landlord's costs incurred from 21 days after the date of the offer. Even a legally aided tenant will have to pay such costs out of any damages awarded. This could significantly reduce or even extinguish the amount recovered. Where the case is funded by legal aid, the tenant may well be compelled by the LSC to accept an offer at the lower end of the damages bracket. All of this must be fully explained to the tenant.

3.132 It is possible for the landlord to make an offer under Part 36 to settle the financial part of the claim while still defending the claim for specific performance. The fact that works are still outstanding and the case must continue to trial should not be an excuse for failing to accept a reasonable Part 36 offer for damages.

3.133 If the adviser recommends a settlement to the tenant in a legally aided case, he or she should be sure to warn that it will be some months before the tenant receives the money and that the statutory charge, which entitles the LSC to take its costs out of any damages, will apply until such time as the costs have been paid by the landlord. The adviser should tell the tenant that any shortfall between the costs obtained from the landlord and the true costs of the case will have to come out of the damages. Similar warnings should be given in conditional fee cases. If the tenant is not advised of these matters before agreeing to the settlement, the tenant is likely to feel ambushed and this will cause unnecessary and unfortunate friction between the tenant and the adviser.

Interim applications

3.134 If a defence is filed, the adviser should consider making an application for an interim payment under CPR 25.6 and 25.7. The court can award an interim payment only if the defendant has admitted liability, judgment has been obtained or the court is satisfied that, if the matter went to trial, the tenant would be likely to obtain judgment for a substantial amount. This is often the case in disrepair claims and the psychological advantage of obtaining an interim payment at this stage is tremendous. In legally aided cases, permission will be needed from the LSC to release any interim payment to the tenant, but this is often forthcoming, for example, where the tenant needs the money to replace destroyed carpets or essential furniture.

3.135   If the tenant's claim is purely for money and the landlord fails to file a defence, the tenant's adviser should enter judgment in default; see CPR 12.4(1). If there is outstanding disrepair and a claim for specific performance is therefore being made, the adviser will have to apply on notice for the defendant to be debarred from defending, see CPR 12.4(2) and CPR 23. In either case, the court will still have to consider the claim at a disposal hearing[80] and may direct that certain steps be taken to enable it to do this, such as that a witness statement is filed.

3.136   If a defence is filed but the adviser thinks that it is very weak, an application for judgment can be made at this stage. CPR 24.2 allows a court to give summary judgment if it considers that the defendant has no real prospect of successfully defending the claim and there is no other compelling reason why there should be a trial. There is, therefore, a high burden on the tenant but an application can be a useful tactic where the adviser knows from experience that the landlord is simply buying time and ultimately will not fight a trial.

3.137   The adviser should ensure that the tenant is aware that costs could be awarded in favour of the landlord if the application for an interim remedy is unsuccessful and this will reduce any damages eventually obtained.

Allocation and ADR

3.138   Once the court has seen the landlord's defence, an allocation questionnaire (AQ) will be sent to each party. The purpose is for the court to obtain enough information to manage the case actively from this point. It is very important that the completed form is returned to court within the time specified because the court can strike out the tenant's claim if the adviser fails to do this.

3.139   The AQ asks the parties whether they want a one-month stay to attempt to settle the case and whether the court should arrange a mediation appointment. ADR is regarded with some suspicion by tenants' advisers, who see requests for stays as delaying tactics on the part of landlords. Where repairs are still outstanding by this stage, many months after the adviser's first contact with the landlord, nothing short of a mandatory order is likely to resolve the matter. It is doubtful that a landlord will agree through mediation to an order that could ultimately result in imprisonment for default. The tenant's adviser will therefore want to press on towards trial without risking further delay through mediation.

80 CPR PD 23 para 12.4.

3.140 Where the repair work has been done and the claim is purely financial, mediation can bring a settlement about in much less time and at much less cost than through litigation and is to be encouraged. The legal aid certificate can be amended to cover the cost of mediation. The procedure at a mediation is non-adversarial and the adviser's role will be very different from the role of representing the tenant at a trial. Even so, the adviser will need to prepare the case for the mediation, warning the tenant of both the strengths and weaknesses and helping the tenant to decide how far to compromise in order to reach a settlement. Further information about mediation can be obtained from the National Mediation Helpline.[81]

3.141 The AQ asks for an estimate of the likely trial costs. The adviser will have to offer an explanation on assessment if the actual costs exceed the estimate by more than 20 per cent,[82] so care must be taken not to underestimate such costs. An allocation fee is payable by the claimant at this stage. The adviser should attach suggested directions to the completed AQ.

3.142 A district judge will consider the AQ to decide which of the court's three procedural tracks is the most appropriate for the case. If there are repairs outstanding, then as long as the cost of the repairs exceeds £1,000, the claim will be allocated to the fast track or to the multi-track. If the cost of repairs is likely to be less than £1,000, then the case will be allocated to the court's small claims track, unless the value of the damages claim exceeds £1,000. If there are no repairs outstanding, then the case will be allocated to the small claims track *unless* the value of the claim exceeds £5,000.[83] Costs are not payable on the small claims track and the LSC will not usually fund a case that is allocated to it.

3.143 CPR 26.6(5) states that the fast track is the normal track for cases with a value of less than £25,000 if they can be tried in less than a day and there is no need for oral evidence from an expert. Judges seem to allocate disrepair cases to the fast track as a matter of course, even though most of them have a complex history and are unlikely to be disposed of in one day. Advisers should argue in the AQ that any case including a claim for specific performance is too complex to be allocated to the fast track. Even claims purely for damages for historic disrepair may not be suitable for the fast track, unless a joint expert

81 Telephone: 0845 60 30 809.
82 CPR PD 43–48 para 6.6
83 CPR 26.6(1)(b).

has been appointed, in which case it should just about be possible to complete the trial within a day.

3.144   It is good practice for the adviser to serve a copy of the proposed AQ on the landlord's representative as soon as possible and in any event a few days before it is due to be filed at court. Both parties should try, if possible, to agree the timetable for carrying out the steps necessary to prepare the case for trial (these steps are known as 'directions').

3.145   If the parties have not selected a joint expert, the directions should provide either that one is now appointed or that the parties have permission to rely on their own expert evidence.

3.146   Once the AQ and fee have been filed at court, there is likely to be a delay of a few weeks while the papers are put before the district judge and a directions order is made. Of course, the adviser can start carrying out the proposed directions while waiting for the sealed order, but if the landlord delays there is no sanction.

3.147   CPR PD 35.6A requires that the directions order is served on the expert. In an exceptional case, where an expert fails to comply with court directions, a costs order can be made against him or her.[84]

3.148   Once the sealed directions order is received, the adviser should diarise the directions and ensure compliance with them. The adviser should not hesitate to apply to the court if the landlord fails to comply with the time limits. Maintaining the pressure on the opponent is likely to bring the landlord to the negotiating table and, if repairs are outstanding, the sooner that a mandatory order is obtained, the better for the tenant's welfare.

Disclosure

3.149   The directions will provide for each party to disclose any documents that have not already been revealed in the Protocol process, see CPR 31.6. Corporate landlords often fail to divulge all relevant documents that they have in their possession. For example, the tenant may have made a formal complaint, in which case the landlord's complaints department will have a file relating to the disrepair. Similarly, any expert employed by a corporate landlord is likely to have a separate file and unless the papers were prepared in contemplation of court proceedings, the documents will be disclosable. The adviser has to consider carefully at this stage whether the cost of forcing the landlord to produce such documents is justified by the improvement in

84   *Phillips v Symes* [2004] EWHC 2330 (Ch).

the tenant's prospects of success. In disrepair cases, there may be enough evidence almost to guarantee a successful outcome without the need for specific disclosure. In heavily contested cases, however, this possibility should not be overlooked. See CPR 31.12.

3.150 Advisers should remember that tenants are obliged to disclose all relevant documents that either help or hinder their case, unless the documents are privileged.[85] The tenant must sign the disclosure form personally[86] and must resist any temptation to omit unhelpful documents from the list. The duty of disclosure is ongoing and any documents that come into existence after the list has been served must be disclosed unless they are privileged.

Witness statements

3.151 The proofs of evidence that have already been prepared now need to be put in a form that is suitable for witness statements.[87] The tenant's proof of evidence will need to be updated so that the tenant comments on any allegations made in the defence and on any documents disclosed by the landlord. The tenant will also need to update the position of the works of repair and mention any distress caused by repair works that have been carried out in an inconsiderate manner.

3.152 Any witness statement needs to be signed by the witness and to contain a statement of truth declaring that the witness believes the statement to be true. It is a contempt of court punishable by imprisonment for a witness deliberately to make false statements in a witness statement.[88]

3.153 It is hoped that the adviser will not be in a position where a witness is no longer co-operating. However, CPR 32.9 provides for service of a witness summary setting out what the adviser expects the witness to say if a signed witness statement cannot be obtained.

Preparations for trial

3.154 Once witness evidence has been exchanged, the adviser should consider instructing a barrister to advise on the strength of the case in the light of all the papers. This is sometimes called a 'case to counsel

---

85 Legal privilege includes communications between the tenant and adviser and papers prepared in contemplation of litigation. Further detail is beyond the scope of this book.

86 CPR 31.10(6).

87 CPR PD 32 paras 17–20.

88 CPR 32.14.

to advise'. If the tenant is legally aided, the certificate is likely to be limited to this point and an application to extend the certificate to cover all steps up to and including trial will have to be supported by positive advice from counsel. It is quite possible for the adviser to be in a position where the trial date is approaching and the LSC is still imposing this limitation, so delay should be avoided. The adviser might want to arrange a site visit by the barrister. Some barristers are reluctant to spend the time in doing this, but others say that it is invaluable.

3.155   The court will send out a Listing Questionnaire, also known as the pre-trial checklist [89] which must be completed and returned within a tight time-scale. It serves as a checklist to ensure that the case is ready to be tried. Advisers must be in no doubt that the court will regard postponement of a trial as a last resort. The adviser should consider whether any further directions are required, for example, that the tenant should have permission to call oral evidence from the expert. A detailed cost estimate must be filed with the checklist and in multi-track cases a trial timetable must be filed. The trial advocate is the most appropriate person to draft this timetable. A pre-trial checklist fee *and* a hearing fee are payable when the checklist is filed.

Continuing negotiations

3.156   The adviser should never be tempted to delay progress at this stage while negotiating with the landlord or landlord's representatives. The best settlements are achieved while the landlord is under the pressure of an approaching trial.

Trial

3.157   As soon as the hearing date is notified by the court, the adviser must inform the tenant, all witnesses, the expert and counsel. The adviser should discuss with the barrister the latest date by which the barrister will want to receive the brief for trial.

3.158   If the tenant is the claimant, the adviser must prepare four identical bundles of all documents that either party might want to refer to a trial; these are known as trial bundles. CPR 39.5 and PD to rule 39 paragraphs 3.1–3.10 set out the contents of the bundles. The adviser should supply counsel with the draft index to the bundle for com-

89 Form N170.

ment. Note that these must be filed at court not more than seven and not less than three working days before trial[90] and that the copy that is provided to the landlord's representative must be identical to the two that will go to the court for the use of the judge and the witnesses.

3.159 If the tenant is not funded with legal aid, the court rules require that 24 hours before a fast track trial a schedule of costs in form N260 must be served on the opponent.[91]

3.160 The trial takes place before a district or circuit judge, who considers the evidence, both in the form of written statements and under cross-examination, listens to the arguments on both sides and then delivers judgment.

Final orders

Mandatory orders for works

3.161 If any repair work remains outstanding, the tenant's representative will seek an order at trial that the landlord comply with the contractual repairing obligation. The order will be for specific performance of the express or implied terms of the tenancy agreement. For non-contractual repairing obligations, the equivalent remedy is a mandatory injunction. The duty imposed by the DPA 1972 s4 (see chapter 2) can also be enforced by injunction.[92] Specific performance is a remedy available at common law[93] and by statute.

3.162 Section 17(1) of the LTA 1985 provides:

> In proceedings in which a tenant of a dwelling alleges a breach on the part of his landlord of a repairing covenant relating to any part of the premises in which the dwelling is comprised, the court may order specific performance of the covenant, whether or not the breach relates to a part of the premises let to the tenant and notwithstanding any equitable rule restricting the scope of the remedy, whether on the basis of a lack of mutuality or otherwise.'

3.163 Several points arise:

- For the purposes of s17, 'tenant' includes subtenants and statutory tenants (s17(2)).
- Specific performance of obligations to maintain common parts can be ordered on the application of a single tenant.

90 CPR PD 39 para 3.1.
91 CPR PD 43–48 para 13.2.
92 *Barrett v Lounova (1982) Ltd* [1990] 1 QB 348; [1989] 1 All ER 351, CA.
93 *Jeune v Queens Cross Properties* [1974] Ch 97; [1973] 3 All ER 97, CA.

- The old equitable rules that 'the applicant must have clean hands' (ie, must not also be in breach of obligations, eg, for payment of rent) and that 'an order must be capable of supervision by the court' may be abrogated by the proviso to s17, but the grant of specific performance remains entirely at the discretion of the court.

3.164   It will not be a defence for the landlord to raise the prospect of severe financial hardship as a result of the terms of the order. Indeed, in *Francis v Cowliffe Ltd*,[94] an order for the provision and maintenance of lifts was made notwithstanding the very real prospect of bankruptcy of the landlord as a result of compliance.

3.165   Any mandatory order must be served personally on the landlord and, in cases of corporate landlords, on a person with executive power to ensure that the work is done. It has been usual practice for a penal notice stating the consequences of disobeying an injunction to be added to any injunction order. CCR Order 29 rule 1(3) (which has been retained in CPR schedule 2) states that such a penal notice *shall be* endorsed on any mandatory order at the request of the person in whose favour it has been made; this has been confirmed to be an executive act which should be carried out by a court official on request.[95] However, a penal notice is not a pre-requisite to committal proceedings and in *MSA v Croydon LBC*[96] Collins J said:

> I do not think that a penal notice is necessary in orders made against a public body. A failure to comply with an order can be dealt with by an application to the court for a finding of contempt and, if necessary, a further mandatory order which may contain an indication of what might happen should there be any further failure to comply. Adverse findings coupled with what would probably be an order to pay indemnity costs should suffice since it is to be expected that a public body would not deliberately flout an order of the court. Were that to happen, the contemnor could be brought before the court and, were he to threaten to persist in his refusal, an order could be made which made it clear that if he did he would be liable to imprisonment or a fine.

The judgment related to judicial review proceedings but the wording of the county court rule is the same as the rule for those proceedings so it will inevitably be argued that it applies in disrepair cases. This does not prevent an adviser from serving the mandatory order without a penal notice and enforcing it if necessary.

94 (1976) 239 EG 977, DC.
95 See *R v Wandsworth County Court ex p Munn* (1994) 26 HLR 697; [1994] COD 282, QBD.
96 [2009] EWHC 2474 (Admin).

3.166   The adviser should also ensure that any time limits set out in an injunction should run from the date that the order is served rather than from the date it is made.

Example

On 2 April the tenant obtains an order compelling the landlord to overhaul a roof by 26 April. The sealed order with penal notice is not received by the adviser until 15 April and the landlord then proves elusive and the adviser is unable to effect service until 27 April. By that time the order has expired and if the landlord does not comply with it, it will be unenforceable unless the adviser applies to court for new time limits. This can be avoided if the order said that the roof had to be overhauled within 28 days of service of the order upon the landlord.

Declarations

3.167   The county court has power to make a binding declaration, even if it is the only relief sought.[97] Where a mandatory order is unlikely to be effective (because it either cannot be served or will not be complied with) and the tenant would prefer to carry out the works and recoup the costs from future rent, or simply where an injunction is refused, the grant of a declaration may be a useful alternative remedy. In a disrepair case the court should be invited to make a declaration providing that:

(1) the landlord is in breach of a specified repairing obligation;
(2) the tenant is entitled to do the necessary works of repair in default;
(3) the works may be financed by deduction from future rent; and
(4) the tenant's compliance with stages (2) and (3) will not constitute breach by the tenant of any express terms of the tenancy agreement which prima facie prohibit such action.

3.168   The court has power to make an interim declaration.[98]

Damages and costs

3.169   The court can, of course, award damages and costs. Damages are discussed in chapter 8. The adviser should ensure that any settlement or judgment order provides for the landlord to pay costs as agreed or

---

97 CPR 40.20.
98 CPR 25.1.

assessed by the court. The costs will include the costs of implementing a court order, which may involve liaising with the tenant while work is being carried out.

Remedies for breach of orders

3.170   Failure to perform works directed in an order of specific performance or by injunction is punishable by committal for contempt. It is unlikely that a landlord will be put in prison on a first non-compliance and a court may impose a fine as an alternative. Even so, proceedings to commit the landlord for contempt of court are a very effective way to ensure that the repair work is done. To deal with circumstances in which the landlord is a local authority or company, the initial injunction should be served on an officer with executive power, who can be committed for breach.[99] The procedure is set out in CCR Order 29, which is retained in CPR Schedule 2. All requirements should be carefully followed, because technical defences by a landlord are likely to succeed.

3.171   As an alternative to the use of committal, Rules of the Supreme Court Order 45 r8[100] allows a court faced with a breach of a mandatory order to direct that the necessary action be taken by or on behalf of the tenant at the expense of the landlord defendant. The court may select and direct the individual or company which is to carry out the action required. The availability of this remedy for repairs cases was confirmed in *Parker v Camden LBC*.[101] The court may enforce the financial element of the Order 45 r8 procedure, either by directing a payment into court (as in *Barrett v Lounova (1982) Ltd*[102]) or by an order of sequestration on the landlord's assets.

3.172   If there is a real risk that the landlord will sell a property to avoid the effect of judgment, or will dispose of assets to avoid an award of damages, the tenant can apply in the High Court for a freezing injunction.[103]

3.173   If damages or costs are not paid by the landlord, the adviser can use a variety of remedies to secure payment:

---

99   *R v Wandsworth County Court ex p Munn* (1994) 26 HLR 697, QBD, but also see *MSA v Croydon LBC* [2009] EWHC 2474 (Admin).

100   Which has been preserved in CPR Schedule 1.

101   [1986] Ch 162; [1985] 2 All ER 141, CA.

102   [1990] 1 QB 348, CA.

103   CPR 25.1(1)(f).

- a warrant of execution to seize goods held by the landlord;[104]
- a third party debt order, which is often very effective against local authorities;[105]
- a charging order, which can be very effective against private landlords who own the premises;[106]
- an attachment of earnings order;[107]
- the appointment of a receiver;[108]
- a statutory demand[109] threatening to petition for bankruptcy, but only if the intention is to follow it through with such an application.

3.174   The costs of *enforcing*, as opposed to *implementing*, the final order will not be included and must be separately applied for. Similarly, the legal representation certificate will need to be amended before any enforcement action is taken.

---

104 CCR Order 26, retained in CPR Schedule 2.
105 CPR 72.
106 CPR 73.
107 CCR 27, retained in CPR Schedule 2.
108 CPR 69.
109 Insolvency Act 1986 s268(1)(a).

CHAPTER 4

Funding

4.1	**Legal aid**
4.6	Funding Code
4.13	Legal Help
4.18	Help at Court
4,21	The boundary between Legal Help and Legal Representation
4.25	Legal Representation
4.43	Small claims
4.46	Emergency Legal Representation
4.51	Amending certificates
4.53	Notice of issue of certificate
4.54	Responsibilities of the assisted person
4.56	The statutory charge
4.63	**Before-the-event insurance**
4.68	**Conditional fee agreements**
4.73	Requirements of a CFA
4.77	Model CFA
4.80	Assessing the risk
4.84	Setting the success fee
4.87	Insurance
4.91	Notice of funding
4.93	Paying for disbursements and counsel
4.97	Challenges to CFAs

Legal aid

4.1   Since 1 July 2007 most housing advice and representation work has been carried out by organisations that have signed a contract with the government's Legal Services Commission (LSC) to provide publicly funded legal services, now once again known as legal aid. The contract between the LSC and each organisation is known as the Unified Contract.[1]

4.2   For the purposes of housing disrepair, legal aid comes in two main types: Legal Help, also known as controlled work, which enables the adviser to provide a limited amount of legal advice and assistance to a tenant but not to take steps in court proceedings, and Legal Representation, also known as licensed or certificated work, which enables the adviser to take a case to court.

4.3   The LSC was created by the Access to Justice Act (AJA) 1999 to 'establish, maintain and develop a service known as the Community Legal Service (CLS)',[2] which is the vehicle for funding and providing legal advice and representation in civil matters. The LSC replaced the Legal Aid Board. The AJA 1999 allows the LSC to fund services relating to disputes about legal rights and duties. It also contains a list of services which may not be funded as part of the CLS.[3]

4.4   A number of regulations and orders have been made under the AJA 1999. In addition, the Lord Chancellor has issued a number of requirements under the Act about how the LSC should distribute legal aid and advice. The Act, regulations, orders and requirements can be accessed online on the LSC website.[4]

4.5   The AJA 1999 provides that the LSC should prepare a code about the provision of funded services.[5] The resulting Funding Code (FC) is the set of rules the LSC uses to decide which individual cases it will fund through civil legal aid.

Funding Code

4.6   The Funding Code (FC) comes in three parts, all of which are accessible online via the LSC website (see paragraph 4.9):

• **Part 1: FC Criteria**, which define what services the LSC will fund, ranging from basic legal advice to representation in court

---

1   www.legalservices.gov.uk/civil/unified_contract_civil.asp.
2   AJA 1999 s4(1).
3   AJA 1999 Sch 2.
4   www.legalservices.gov.uk/civil/legislation.asp.
5   Section 8.

proceedings. Section 5 of Part 1 is the 'General Funding Code' which sets out the fundamental criteria applicable to any application for public funding. Section 10 of Part 1 deals with housing cases;

- **Part 2: FC Procedures**, which set out how the LSC makes decisions about funding civil legal aid; and
- **Part 3: FC Decision Making Guidance**, which helps inform practitioners working under the FC about the general approach they should follow in funded cases and what approach to take on specific topics.

The Decision Making Guidance (DMG) has been divided into several parts, of which the most relevant for housing disrepair is section 19.8.

4.7   The FC is reproduced in volume 3 of the *LSC Manual*, which is a required reference tool for publicly funded advisers in England and Wales. The *Manual* is published in four volumes by TSO (The Stationery Office) and is available by annual subscription in loose-leaf volumes, on CD or online. Volume 1 of the *Manual* contains the legislative framework of the legal aid scheme; volume 2 contains the contractual documents relevant to legal aid providers; volume 4 relates to criminal legal aid. The *Manual* is amended from time to time. However, many of its key components – in particular the Funding Code – can be accessed without charge via the LSC website.

4.8   The references to the *LSC Manual* set out below are correct at the time of going to print but may well be altered by the LSC at a later date.

4.9   To access these documents online, advisers can visit the LSC home page at www.legalservices.gov.uk. From here advisers should select the link to the CLS page and, when this appears, select the link called 'What cases do we fund?' on the left-hand side of the screen. The chapters of the *Manual* containing the FC Criteria and the FC Procedures appear in portable document format (pdf) files on the right of the screen. When opened, each can be searched by section, paragraph number or key word.

4.10   By further selecting the links on the left-hand side of the screen for 'General funding principles,' 'Standard funding criteria' and 'Non family guidance' advisers can access various pdf files of the chapters of the *Manual* containing the DMG, which again appear on the right.

4.11   The FC is divided into parts and sections: FC Part 2 (Procedures) is sub-divided into further parts (A, B, C, etc). The *Manual* repeats these, but confusingly adds its own numbering system. So, for example, FC Part 1 (Criteria), section 5.2.1 appears at paragraph 3A-025 of the *Manual* (ie, *Manual* vol 3, part A, para 25). Footnotes in this chapter give both references.

4.12   Housing cases are given special attention in FC Part 1 (Criteria)[6] and in FC Part 3 (DMG).[7]

Legal Help

4.13   Legal Help (also known as controlled work) is a level of service under the AJA 1999 and the FC which allows advice and assistance to be given to tenants who are financially eligible. It excludes the provision of general information about the law and the legal system, the issuing or conducting of court proceedings, advocacy or instructing an advocate in proceedings.[8]

4.14   In order to receive Legal Help, the tenant must be financially eligible and will need to produce proof of income and savings so that the adviser can confirm this. Advisers can make use of an online legal aid eligibility calculator on the LSC website, to help work out eligibility for those levels of help where the provider is responsible for means assessment.[9] The calculator can provide an indication of eligibility but it is not a replacement for the detailed financial eligibility guidance in volume 2, part F of the *Manual* (a link to which will be found on the eligibility calculator webpage).

4.15   The adviser will also have to show that the case satisfies the 'sufficient benefit test':

> Help may only be provided where there is sufficient benefit to the client, having regard to the circumstances of the matter, including the personal circumstances of the client, to justify work or further work being carried out.[10]

4.16   It follows that the adviser will not be paid for assisting with trivial legal problems. However, Legal Help will cover most aspects of a tenant's disrepair problems, for example, the preliminary investigation of a claim for damages or an order for specific performance, initial

---

6 FC Part 1 (Criteria), section 10 (*Manual* para 3A-051).

7 FC Part 3 (DMG), section 19 (*Manual* para 3C-156).

8 FC Part 1 (Criteria), section 2.1 (*Manual* para 3A-004).

9 The LSC eligibility calculator is available at: www.legalservices.gov.uk/civil/guidance/eligibility_calculator.asp.

10 FC Part 1 (Criteria), section 5.2.1 (*Manual* para 3A-025).

correspondence with the landlord (see paragraph 3.55), the completion of legal aid application forms, advice on bringing claims under the Environmental Protection Act (EPA) 1990 (see chapter 5), advice to resolve the existence of hazards under the housing, health and safety rating system (under the Housing Act (HA) 2004) (see chapter 6) or help with a complaint about housing conditions to an ombudsman.

4.17   Payment to advisers is set at standard fixed fees per case, which are based on past national averages for housing work.[11] Extra payment is not usually made for exceptional cases, unless the costs on hourly rates are three times the standard fixed fee,[12] in which case providers can apply to be paid separately at hourly rates.

Help at Court

4.18   Help at Court is a level of service the grant of which authorises help and advocacy for a client in relation to a particular hearing, without the adviser formally acting as legal representative in the proceedings.[13]

4.19   The criteria for Legal Help (financial eligibility and sufficent benefit – paragraphs 4.14 and 4.15 above) apply, with the addition of the following two criteria:[14]

- Help at Court may only be provided if the nature of the proceedings and the circumstances of the hearing and the client are such that advocacy is appropriate and will be of real benefit to the client.
- Help at Court may not be provided if the contested nature of the proceedings or the nature of the hearing is such that, if any help is to be provided, it is more appropriate that it should be given through Legal Representation.

4.20   The use of Help at Court is likely to be limited in housing disrepair claims, but see paragraph 4.43.

---

11 Currently £174 per case from 1 July 2008. See the Schedule to the Community Legal Service (Funding) Order 2007 SI No 2441, as substituted by the Schedule to the Community Legal Service (Funding) (Amendment) Order 2008 SI No 1328.
12 Currently £522 from 1 July 2008.
13 FC Part 1 (Criteria), section 2.1 (*Manual* para 3A-004).
14 FC Part 3 (DMG), section 5.3 (*Manual* para 3A-026).

The boundary between Legal Help and Legal Representation

4.21   Legal Help will allow initial investigative work to be carried out to the point where sufficient information is available to allow the adviser to assess whether the criteria in the FC are satisfied for full Legal Representation or Investigative Help (see paragraph 4.25 onwards) including certifying the prospects of success.

4.22   As long as the case seems strong on merit, advisers are not expected to follow the disrepair protocol under Legal Help.[15] This is contrary to the position with most Legal Help work so LSC officers may need to be reminded of this from time to time.

4.23   Nor is the adviser expected to carry out extensive investigations under Legal Help.[16] In particular, there is no general requirement that experts' reports have to be obtained before an application is made for Legal Representation.[17] In cases where investigations are needed before the adviser can assess the merit of the case, Investigative Help which is another form of legal aid, should be used (see paragraph 4.26), notwithstanding the guidance that few housing cases will satisfy the criteria for Investigative Help and most cases requiring a certificate will proceed straight from Legal Help to Legal Representation.[18]

4.24   Work under Legal Help should include establishing the strength of the tenant's case and reasonable endeavours to determine the identity of the landlord, the ownership of the property in question, whether the landlord is likely to be able to meet any money judgment or is insured (if these can be ascertained), whether liability is likely to be contested and, if so, on what basis and with what merit. This does not mean engaging in extensive correspondence or waiting indefinitely for a response from the other party.

Legal Representation

4.25   Legal Representation (also known as licensed work or certificated work) is a level of service under the AJA 1999 and the FC, the grant of which authorises legal representation for a party to proceedings or for a person who is contemplating taking proceedings.

15 FC Part 3 (DMG), section 19.8.3 (*Manual* para 3C-163).
16 FC Part 3 (DMG), section 19.3.5 (*Manual* para 3C-158).
17 FC Part 3 (DMG), section 19.8.7 (*Manual* para 3C-163).
18 FC Part 3 (DMG), section 19.3.5 (*Manual* para 3C-158).

4.26   Legal Representation takes two forms: Full Representation and Investigative Help. Investigative Help is limited to investigation of the strength of a proposed claim. It includes the issue and the conduct of proceedings only so far as necessary to obtain disclosure of relevant information or to protect the client's position in relation to any urgent hearing or time limit for the issue of proceedings[19].

4.27   Applications for Legal Representation and Investigative Help are both made on form CLSAPP1 which can be obtained from the LSC website.[20] As with Legal Help, eligibility for this form of legal aid depends on the tenant's finances, which in straightforward cases the adviser can assess using the LSC online eligibility calculator (see paragraph 4.14).[21]

4.28   Advisers should remember that a tenant's outgoings include the net rent payable (after receipt of housing benefit), whether or not actual payments have been made to the landlord, plus any instalments currently being paid towards arrears.[22]

4.29   The usual criteria in the General Funding Code for the grant of Investigative Help and Legal Representation in FC Part 1 are in section 5 and they are supplemented by housing-specific criteria in FC Part 1 section 10.[23]

4.30   Guidance on Legal Representation in housing disrepair cases is contained in section 19.8 of the FC Part 3 (DMG) (*Manual* para 3C-163). The following sections in FC Part 3 (DMG) are also relevant:

Section	Subject	*Manual* reference
4	Merits, Costs and Damages	3C-028 to 3C-037.1
5	Public Interest	3C-038 to 3C-044
6	The Human Rights Convention	3C-045 to 3C-048
10	Investigative Help	3C-077 to 3C-082
12	Emergency Representation	3C-088 to 3C-103

4.31   FC Part 3 (DMG) section 19.5 states that unless the case is urgent the client should consider alternative methods of dispute resolution,

19 FC Part 1 (Criteria), section 2.1 (*Manual* para 3A-004).
20 www.legalservices.gov.uk/civil/forms.asp.
21 The LSC eligibility calculator is available at: www.legalservices.gov.uk/civil/ guidance/eligibility_calculator.asp.
22 *Southwark Law Centre, R (on the application of) v Legal Services Commission* [2007] EWHC 1715 (Admin).
23 FC Part 1 (Criteria), section 10 (*Manual* paras 3A-051 to 3A-054).

such as mediation or the ombudsmen. An application for Full Representation may not be appropriate if pursuing alternative options would be 'a sensible step which a reasonable private client would take'.[24] However, even where ombudsman or mediation schemes exist, Full Representation will not automatically be refused if it can be demonstrated that the courts might be best able to deliver what the client needs.

4.32   The merits test for all housing cases is simply that the likely benefits of the proceedings must justify likely costs.[25]

4.33   As mentioned above (paragraph 4.23) if the costs of investigation of the merits are likely to be substantial then an application for Investigative Help should be considered. The usual merits test does not apply for this form of Legal Representation. It is especially useful where the remedy is uncertain.[26]

Example

A tenant is complaining of 'damp' in the bathroom and, despite careful questioning by the adviser, the cause is not clear. The adviser knows that it could be due to disrepair such as rising dampness but it could be condensation due to bad design, where no civil remedy will be available. See chapter 7.

4.34   In such cases Investigative Help can pay the cost of an expert's report to establish whether there is a civil remedy. However, the FC DMG makes it clear that not all cases need to go through the stage of Investigative Help and that it is less important for housing claims.[27] It may be more appropriate to apply for full Legal Representation and pursue the Disrepair Pre-action Protocol (see paragraphs 3.49–3.54), provided that:

- there is clear evidence of prior notice having been given to the landlord of the relevant defects by or on behalf of the tenant;
- the prospects of success are clear; and
- the value of damages can be estimated.[28]

4.35   Where there is disrepair that has not been remedied then, subject to the client's financial eligibility and merits, a full Legal Representation certificate will be granted so long as the case is likely to proceed on the

---

24 FC Part 3 (DMG) section 19.5 (*Manual* para 3C-160).
25 FC Part 3 (DMG) section 19.4.1(b) (*Manual* para 3C-159).
26 FC Part 3 (DMG) section 4.4 (*Manual* para 3C-031).
27 FC Part 3 (DMG) section 10.1 (*Manual* para 3C-077).
28 FC Part 3 (DMG) section 19.8.3 (*Manual* para 3C-163).

fast track or multi-track[29] (ie, where an order for works is sought and the cost of repairs or damages are likely to exceed £1,000[30]).

4.36 Once the disrepair has been remedied, a certificate will not be granted (or be allowed to continue) unless:[31]

- the damages are likely to exceed £5,000; or
- the case has already been allocated to the fast track or multi-track.

4.37 In possession cases, where the adviser wants to counterclaim for disrepair, there is no strict requirement that the client must have at least a 50 per cent prospect of success in defending the case. Funding will be refused only if the client has no substantive legal defence to the possession claim.[32] Even where the repairs have already been carried out, the tenant is likely to be allowed to pursue a small disrepair counterclaim if it will 'significantly reduce' the outstanding rent arrears by way of set-off.[33] This will be the case especially where it is the only way of defeating a possession claim founded on Ground 8 of HA 1988 Sch 2, the mandatory ground for possession based on two months' rent arrears.

Example

A tenant is faced with possession proceedings. The landlord is a housing association relying on Ground 8 on the basis that £1,500 of rent arrears exist. This is more than two months' rent. The tenant does not have the means to reduce the arrears to less than the two months' rent threshold. The adviser asks whether there have been any disrepair problems and the tenant confirms that, despite complaints, a year ago there was no hot water and heating at the property for three months, but the problem has now been fixed. This would not justify a free-standing application for legal aid to bring a claim, because the damages are likely to be well below £5,000. It *will* justify applying for legal aid to *defend* and counterclaim in the proceedings because the damages awarded on the counterclaim will reduce the arrears to below two months' rent and will therefore make it much more likely that a court will refuse an order for possession.

---

29 FC Part 3 (DMG) section 19.8.6 (*Manual* para 3C-163).
30 CPR 26.6.1(b).
31 FC Part 3 (DMG) section 19.8.6 & 19.8.8 (*Manual* para 3C-163).
32 FC Part 3 (DMG) section 19.4.1(a) (*Manual* para 3C-159).
33 FC Part 3 (DMG) section 19.7.8 (*Manual* para 3C-162).

4.38   At present, funding will not be refused in any housing case on the grounds that it could be funded by way of a conditional fee agreement (CFA).[34] CFAs are explained in paragraphs 4.68–4.99.

4.39   The main rules relating to funding housing disrepair litigation are set out in FC Part 3 (DMG) section 19.8 (*Manual* para 3C-163). Legal Representation is still available for a claim for personal injury made within disrepair proceedings, even if a separate application for representation needs to be made, for example, by children of the tenant.[35]

4.40   Section 19.8.7 of the FC Part 3 (DMG) sets out a checklist of the information which the adviser is expected to provide in an application for Legal Representation:[36]

- an adequate statement of case setting out the allegations of disrepair in detail;
- the date(s) when the landlord was put on notice and the method by which this was done;
- an indication of whether there have been any previous proceedings, eg, in the magistrates' court and, if so, details of the outcome and copies of any expert(s) report(s) already obtained in connection with the issues of disrepair;
- details of the availability of local arbitration or mediation arrangements or ombudsman scheme or why it is inappropriate to pursue these;
- where there have been previous proceedings, an explanation of why further action is justified;
- an estimate of the value of the claim, with reference to the severity of the disrepair, the small claims limit and relevant case-law;
- copies of any relevant correspondence with the landlord or agents;
- details of the opponent's financial circumstances and ability to pay, in all cases where compensation or costs will be claimed (this is particularly important where the opponent is a private landlord); and
- confirmation of whether the Disrepair Pre-actionProtocol applies or the justification for departing from the protocol in the particular case.

---

34 FC Part 3 (DMG) section 19.4.1(d) (*Manual* para 3C-159).
35 FC Part 3 (DMG) section 19.8 4(*Manual* para 3C-163).
36 LSC forms can be accessed at: www.legalservices.gov.uk/civil/forms.asp.

4.41 The adviser will be expected to give the LSC the standard wording of the scope of the certificate, for example, 'to be represented in an action for housing disrepair against the opponent' and to suggest the appropriate limit on the steps that can be taken before the LSC reviews the certificate. In a case where there is some doubt about the merits or prospects of the case, the scope is likely to be limited to obtaining further evidence and thereafter counsel's opinion. No adviser, however experienced, is likely to be given a free rein and at the very least the certificate will be limited to all steps up to but not including trial.

4.42 Where all the disrepair has been remedied, the value of a damages claim will be considered closely. While the cost benefit ratios in the General Funding Code do not apply directly to cases concerning disrepair to the client's own home, they may still be taken into account as guidelines as to whether a case is cost effective.[37] Those cost benefit ratios are the ratios between the likely costs and the prospects of success, as follows.[38]

Prospects of success	Minimum damages to costs ratio
Very good – 80% or more	1:1
Good – 60% to 80%	2:1
Moderate – 50% to 60%	4:1

Example

A tenant complains of past disrepair which has since been remedied. The adviser values damages at £6,000 and predicts the prospects of success at more than 80 per cent. If the adviser then estimates that the likely costs at legal aid rates will be £12,500, legal aid will be refused, despite the strong merit, because the cost of the case exceeds the likely damages. If there is any disrepair still to be remedied then, as long as the cost of carrying out the repair is more than £1,000, legal aid is likely to be granted in this situation.[39]

---

37 FC Part 3 (DMG) section 19.8.8 (*Manual* para 3C-163).
38 FC Part 3 (DMG) section 4.5.5 (*Manual* para 3C-032).
39 FC Part 3 (DMG) section 19.8.6 (*Manual* para 3C-163) and CPR 26.6.1(b).

Small claims

4.43   Legal Representation will be refused if the case has been or is likely to be allocated to the small claims track.[40] Indeed, the LSC has no power to issue a certificate for a case proceeding in the small claims track, though clients can sometimes receive Help at Court for a case in that track.[41]

4.44   In deciding whether a case is likely to be allocated to the small claims track, the approach should be as set out in rules 26.6 to 26.8 of the Civil Procedure Rules (CPR). These provide that the small claims track is the normal track for any claim which has a value of not more than £5,000. However, several matters have to be taken into account by the court when deciding the track for a claim. In particular, if an order for repairs is being sought the threshold will be £1,000. Other matters include the likely complexity of the facts, law or evidence, the amount of oral evidence which may be required and the circumstances of the parties.[42]

4.45   In exceptional circumstances, for example, to enable a tenant with language difficulties to have proceedings issued and be represented when arguing the issue of allocation to track, an application might still be made for Legal Representation. The adviser will need to argue persuasively that the case is likely to be allocated to the fast track. More likely, and certainly in other cases, the adviser is expected to assist the tenant to act in person under the Legal Help scheme or represent the tenant under Help at Court, and then apply for Legal Representation if the case is allocated to the fast track.

Emergency Legal Representation

4.46   Emergency Legal Representation (ELR) is dealt with at section 5.5 of the General Funding Code and at section 12 of the FC Part 3 (DMG).[43] It may be justified if representation is needed in injunction or other emergency proceedings, in relation to an imminent hearing in existing proceedings or because the limitation period is about to expire.[44]

4.47   Where a legal aid provider has devolved powers to grant ELR in an appropriate case, it must do so.[45] Otherwise, an emergency

40 FC Part 1 (Criteria), section 5.4.6 (*Manual* para 3A-027).
41 FC Part 3 (DMG) section 9.16 (*Manual* para 3C-076).
42 See CPR 26.8.
43 *Manual* paras 3C-088 onwards.
44 FC Part 3 (DMG) section 12.2.1 (*Manual* para 3C-089).
45 FC Part 3 (DMG) section 12.1.6 (*Manual* para 3C-088).

application must be submitted to the local LSC Office, though in real emergencies, ELR can be granted by fax or over the telephone.[46] In such a case, the adviser must first ensure that the client has signed the usual legal aid application forms and means assessment forms and has provided all of the information that the adviser will require to complete and submit such forms after the grant of ELR. Otherwise, there is a risk that if the client fails to co-operate after the event, forms cannot be submitted to the LSC and the adviser will not be paid for an emergency action undertaken.

4.48   In order to justify the grant of ELR, it must be necessary to do the work before a substantive application for legal representation could be made and determined. LSC Offices vary in how long this takes but almost all applications are decided within 30 working days. An emergency certificate will be issued only if the likely delay (as a result of any failure to grant ELR) would mean:

- a risk to the physical safety of the tenant, his or her family or the roof over their heads; or
- a significant risk of miscarriage of justice, unreasonable hardship or irretrievable problems in handling the case; and
- there are no other appropriate options available to deal with the risk.[47]

4.49   Delay by the tenant in dealing with the proceedings could be a ground for refusing an emergency certificate, but only if the further delay necessary to process a full application would not cause the sort of risks referred to above.[48]

4.50   The scope of an emergency certificate, setting out the steps that can be taken, can be amended by an organisation that has been given devolved powers (together with a consequent amendment to the costs limit) but the duration of the certificate (four weeks) cannot be extended except by the LSC Office. [49] The adviser must take care to diarise the date that the certificate will expire and, if a full certificate has not been received to replace it, ensure that an application for an extension is lodged well before that date (this can also be done by telephone). If the emergency certificate expires without the date being extended, it ceases to be in force and no further work may be carried out under it.[50] This is a trap of which the adviser needs to be aware.

46 FC Part 2 (Procedures) Parts C11-13 (*Manual* paras 3B-041 onwards).
47 FC Part 3 (DMG) section 12.2.6 (*Manual* para 3C-089).
48 FC Part 3 (DMG) section 12.2.9 (*Manual* para 3C-089).
49 FC Part 2 (Procedures) Part C13.1 (*Manual* para 3B-043).
50 FC Part 2 (Procedures) Part C13.2 (*Manual* para 3B-043).

Amending certificates

4.51   An authorised solicitor with devolved powers can amend the scope limitation[51] (and a consequential amendment to the costs limit up to £10,000) of a non-emergency certificate under the devolved powers, but only if the certificate has certain scope wordings, usually limited to obtaining counsel's opinion.

4.52   In all other cases, only the LSC Office can amend the certificate and to obtain an amendment the adviser must complete a lengthy CLSAPP8 form.[52] Much of the information sought on the form has to be repeated on each application so it is worth subscribing to a computerised forms service, so that the form can be saved and later amended. Advisers should take care to apply for amendments many weeks before they are needed. If the adviser carries out work beyond the current scope of the certificate he or she will not be entitled to recover the cost of that work either from the LSC or from the opponent.

Notice of issue of certificate

4.53   The FC Part 2 (Procedures) requires a legally aided party to give notice to the opponent of the fact that the case is being funded by the LSC when first notifying the opponent of the proposed claim.[53] The notice must tell the opponent that only the client's solicitor or the LSC can give a valid receipt for any damages or costs paid. Failure to serve such a form before the issue of proceedings can affect the tenant's right to recover the legal costs from the landlord. All amendments to the scope of a certificate must be similarly notified to the opponent, but the adviser should not reveal the limitations because these are privileged and would give the opponent a tactical advantage.

Responsibilities of the assisted person

4.54   Some certificates require clients to make monthly financial contributions towards the cost of legal representation. It is important to stress to clients the need to keep up regular payments. If they do not do so, the certificate is likely to be suspended, so that no further work may be done by the adviser, and ultimately discharged.

---

51 FC Part 2 (Procedures) Part C37 (*Manual* para 3B-067).
52 www.legalservices.gov.uk/civil/forms.asp.
53 FC Part 2 (Procedures) Part C16 'Notice of issue of certificates' (*Manual* para 3B-046).

4.55   Clients must also be reminded that they have an ongoing duty to notify any changes in circumstances to the LSC for the duration of their case. Some changes may result in a review of the client's financial eligibility, for example, if the client starts to live with another adult, so that their joint incomes should be aggregated for the purpose of assessing eligibility, or if the client takes a new job at a different rate of pay.

The statutory charge

4.56   Where the client is funded by the LSC it has first call on any property recovered or preserved for the client (usually damages in housing disrepair cases) as a result of work carried out by the adviser. This is known as the 'statutory charge'.[54]

4.57   The statutory charge does not apply to any property recovered or preserved under Legal Help alone, ie, where no other level of service is granted before that recovery or preservation.[55]

4.58   However, any property recovered or preserved on behalf of the client as a result of work carried out under a Legal Representation certificate will be subject to the statutory charge. The charge will also cover work done under Legal Help, if the work was in connection with the same dispute or proceedings for which the Legal Representation certificate was subsequently issued.[56]

4.59   Damages recovered should be paid to the LSC, where they will be utilised to pay any costs and disbursements which the LSC is liable to pay to the adviser and any counsel. In practice, where costs are recovered from an opponent, solicitors retain the client's damages on client account and give an undertaking to the LSC on form CLSADMIN3 (Application to suspend contributions/ undertaking as to costs)[57] that the claim for legal aid costs will not exceed a certain amount (usually the legal aid only costs which are not recoverable from the opponent and the Legal Help costs).

4.60   Once such an undertaking has been given to the LSC, the balance of any damages may be released to the client. However, advisers should be wary of releasing damages in this way before costs are actually recovered from an opponent. If, for any reason, the opponent

---

54 See the Community Legal Service (Financial) Regulations 2000 and the Community Legal Service (Costs) Regulations 2000 (in both cases as amended and replaced from time to time).

55 Unified Contract – Civil Specification, para 9.1.

56 Unified Contract – Civil Specification, para 9.5.

57 www.legalservices.gov.uk/civil/forms.asp.

does not pay (eg, because of insolvency), the adviser will be held to the undertaking to the LSC, which will act as a limit on the costs payable by the LSC to the adviser.

4.61   It is usual for winning tenants to recover costs from their landlord. However, these 'party' costs will exclude costs relating purely to funding issues and, for example, costs of hearings where no orders for costs against the opponent were made, or disbursements for reports that were unhelpful and could not be used in the litigation.

4.62   It is, therefore, important to advise clients in writing at the outset of their case and at regular intervals throughout it that the statutory charge will bite on their damages. Any costs not recovered from the opponent will reduce the client's compensation. It follows that it is vital for the adviser to seek appropriate costs orders against opponents, whether at interim hearings, at trial or as part of any settlement.

Before-the-event insurance

4.63   Some tenants who seek advice will already have 'before-the-event' (BTE) legal expenses insurance (LEI). In an appropriate case, a claim might be made on this insurance in the hope that the insurer will be prepared to meet the tenant's own legal costs of bringing a disrepair claim. This possibility should be explored in every case.

4.64   BTE insurance might take the form a stand-alone LEI policy, or it may be an addition to some other insurance, for example, home contents insurance. Occasionally, LEI is provided as an incidental benefit of having a credit card or bank account, but cover is usually limited to telephone legal advice from a solicitor on the insurance company's panel.

4.65   Some BTE policies exclude landlord and tenant disputes, in which case the policyholder cannot use the LEI to fund a disrepair dispute. Most policies require notification of a possible claim within 90 days of the date that the policyholder first becomes aware of it. Since tenants usually endure disrepair for many months before consulting an adviser, most tenants find that the insurer declines cover on the basis that it has suffered prejudice as a result of delay.

4.66   The Insurance Companies (Legal Expenses Insurance) Regulations 1990[58] require an insurer to give a policyholder freedom of choice of a solicitor, but most insurance companies insist that the policyholder consults a solicitor on an approved panel, and they will only allow

---

58   1990 SI No 1159.

freedom of choice at the point where litigation is about to commence. The Financial Services Authority (FSA) takes the view that the operation of pre-action protocols does not form part of litigation and that insurance companies are within their rights to place this restriction on their policyholders. The FSA accepts that there are cases where freedom of choice is essential from the outset, for example, where a policyholder is disabled and needs to consult a local solicitor.

4.67 Once BTE LEI funding is in place, there will be no need for the adviser and client to apply for legal aid or sign a CFA (see paragraphs 4.68–4.99). However, if a disrepair claim is pursued with the benefit of BTE LEI, the adviser must become acquainted with the sometimes onerous reporting conditions that may apply to such insurance, and keep to those conditions. It is important that both client and adviser are clear about any restrictions that the policy may place on their freedom to conduct the litigation, especially where opponents' offers to settle are concerned. Policies sometimes give insurers the right to withdraw insurance cover unless an offer is accepted, even if the adviser considers it too low.

Conditional fee agreements

4.68 These agreements, known as CFAs (and more popularly as 'no win, no fee' agreements) were introduced by the Courts and Legal Services Act 1990. They allow a solicitor to agree not to charge unless the client wins the case. To that extent, the Act modifies the indemnity principle under which a solicitor cannot submit a bill to an opponent for more than the client would be liable to pay.

4.69 Few tenants are able to afford to pay a solicitor privately so, where a tenant is ineligible for legal aid and has no BTE legal expenses insurance, a CFA may be the only way of funding a disrepair case. However, before signing a CFA solicitors are under a professional duty to discuss with the client how the client will pay the solicitor's fees, in particular whether the client may be eligible and should apply for public funding (and whether the client's own costs are covered by insurance or may be paid by someone else, such as an employer or trade union).[59]

4.70 It should be noted that counterclaims are rarely suitable for CFAs, unless the counterclaim for damages far exceeds the rent arrears on

---

59 Solicitors' Code of Conduct 2007 2.03(1)(d), see: www.sra.org.uk/code-of-conduct.

which a possession claim is based and the tenant is unlikely to allow the arrears to increase.

4.71 Under a CFA the solicitor is entitled to charge a 'success fee' (also known as an 'additional liability') if the case is won in civil proceedings. This is to compensate for the risk of not being paid at all if the case had been lost. The success fee is a percentage of the profit costs, namely, the costs that the solicitor is charging, excluding expenses such as court fees and VAT.

4.72 Prosecutions under the EPA 1990 are specifically permitted to be funded under a CFA, although no success fee can be charged.[60]

Requirements of a CFA

4.73 Section 58 of the Courts and Legal Services Act 1990 (as amended by AJA 1999 s27) requires that CFA agreements:

- are in writing;
- do not relate to criminal or family proceedings (except for prosecutions under the EPA 1990); and
- specify the success fee, which must not exceed that specified by the Lord Chancellor (currently 100 per cent).

4.74 If the section 58 requirements are not met then the agreement is unenforceable and, by virtue of the indemnity principle, the losing party is not liable for the winning party's costs. In *Forde v Birmingham City Council*[61] a housing case, it was held that it is possible to rectify a defect in a CFA by asking a client to sign a replacement agreement (though at the time of writing that decision is under appeal). If a CFA is signed during or following a home visit, it is possible that consumer regulations could render the CFA unenforceable, unless additional requirements are met.[62] Where the regulations apply, the client must be given a written notice of the right to cancel the contract within seven days of it being made. The notice must be in a particular form and contain specified information.[63] Any adviser making a home visit should consider the regulations carefully.

4.75 CFAs signed before 1 November 2005 had further requirements which, if not satisfied, meant that the agreement was unenforceable. As a result, it was extremely easy for a small technical breach to prevent

---

60 Courts and Legal Services Act 1990 s58A(1)(a).

61 [2009] EWHC 12 (QB).

62 Cancellation of Contracts made in a Consumer's Home or Place of Work etc Regulations (CCCHPW Regs) 2008 SI No 1816 reg 7(1).

63 CCCHPW Regs 2008 reg 7(3).

solicitors from being paid for their work. This led to a 'costs war' which to an extent is still continuing. For examples of this costs war in disrepair cases see *Bowen v Bridgend CBC*[64] and *Crook v Birmingham CC*.[65]

4.76 There are further professional requirements relating to CFAs which apply to all solicitors. These are set out in rule 2.03(2) of the Solicitors' Code of Conduct 2007[66] and they require that the adviser explains the following to the client, both at the outset and, when appropriate, as the matter progresses:

- the circumstances in which the client may be liable for the costs and whether the solicitor will seek payment of these from the client, if entitled to do so;
- if the solicitor intends to seek payment of any or all of the costs from the client, the client's right to an assessment of those costs; and
- where applicable, the fact that the solicitor is obliged under a fee sharing agreement to pay to a charity any fees which are received by way of costs from the client's opponent or other third party.

Model CFA

4.77 The Law Society has produced a 'model' CFA for use in personal injury cases and an explanatory leaflet to be given to clients called 'What you need to know about a CFA',[67] both of which will need to be adapted by advisers to make them suitable for housing disrepair claims.

4.78 The model CFA is a one page agreement containing the statutory and basic requirements. Advisers will also need to draft a 'client care letter' to provide the further information that is required by the Solicitors' Code of Conduct. Some solicitors prefer to incorporate all the necessary information into one letter, which becomes the CFA. The Law Society has issued a Practice Note to guide practitioners about the use of client care letters.[68]

4.79 The adapted CFA should contain a term stating that the client will give access for works to be carried out and will ensure that no rent arrears accrue or, if there are modest arrears, that these are cleared by

64 [2004] EWHC 9010 (Costs) (25 March 2004).
65 [2007] EWHC 1415 (QB).
66 See: www.sra.org.uk/code-of-conduct.
67 To access these documents make an internet search for 'payment by results Law Society'.
68 To access this, go to the Law Society's home page (www.lawsociety.org.uk), click on *practice notes* and then *client care letters*.

the client, if necessary by regular instalments. The solicitor would be well advised to withdraw from the arrangement if the client breaches these terms, because the likelihood is that the claim will fail and neither damages nor costs will be recovered.

Assessing the risk

4.80   Before the adviser enters into a CFA with a client, it is essential that a thorough risk assessment is carried out. The risk assessment should be a pro forma document, kept on the file, assessing the all facets of the case on which the adviser is about to embark.

4.81   In particular, the adviser must address at the outset:

- any issues of limitation;
- the identity and solvency of the proposed defendant;
- how the facts can be proved, whether the client will make a good witness and whether expert evidence will be necessary;
- how liability will be proved;
- any issues of causation;
- the likely value of the claim and the likely track to which proceedings will be allocated;
- the likelihood of the case settling or going to trial;
- general litigation risk; and
- any other special factor that might affect the prospects of success.

4.82   This risk assessment will inform the adviser about the advisability of undertaking the case on the speculative basis which a CFA represents. A copy should be discussed with and approved by a senior colleague before a CFA is offered to the client; and a copy should be given to the client before he or she signs the CFA.

4.83   Not only will the risk assessment help the adviser to avoid taking on a weak or, worse, a hopeless case, it will also prove invaluable in the task of setting the appropriate success fee for the CFA and justifying that success fee if the costs are challenged by the opponent at the end of the case.

Setting the success fee

4.84   The level of the success fee in the CFA should reflect the risk of pursuing the case. The Practice Direction to CPR Part 44 sets out the principles that the adviser should consider when setting the success fee.[69] Staged success fees are now common. In *Forde v Birmingham*

---

69   This is found in the PD for CPR Parts 43–48, para 11.

CC,[70] the CFA under consideration in a disrepair claim provided for a success fee of 100 per cent of basic charges if the claim concluded at trial, or 75 per cent if the claim concluded before a trial had commenced but after proceedings had been issued, or 50 per cent if the claim concluded before proceedings were issued.

4.85   In *Designer Guild Ltd v Russell Williams (Textiles) Ltd (trading as Washington DC) (No 2)*,[71] an Appellate Committee of the House of Lords went so far as to say:

> there is an argument for saying that in any case which reached trial a success fee of 100 per cent is easily justified because both sides presumably believe that they have an arguable and winnable case.

It is therefore generally accepted that any case that goes to trial justifies a 100 per cent success fee. Whatever level is chosen, the adviser will need to show his or her reasons.[72]

4.86   Some parts of the success fee are not recoverable from the opponent, for example, any amount charged to the client for postponing payment of fees until the end of the case, or for paying disbursements in advance on the client's behalf.

Insurance

4.87   When acting for a client under a CFA, it is advisable to have legal expenses insurance (LEI) in place to protect the client against the risk of having to pay the opponent's costs if the case is unsuccessful.

4.88   A list of after-the-event (ATE) insurance providers is printed from time to time in the Law Society's publication *Litigation Funding* but, rather than approach insurers directly, the usual course is to submit an application to a specialist broker, such as 'The Judge'. Their website[73] contains a downloadable proposal form, which must be signed by both solicitor and client. A case summary and counsel's advice on merits are often needed to support an application, and a fee is payable to the brokers for their services.

4.89   ATE insurance is expensive. Premiums are often one-third of the estimated likely costs of the opponent, or more. However, most ATE policies now offer deferred premiums, which do not have to be paid until the end of the case, and which are self-insured, so that they are not payable if the client loses. Having said this, if the client wins

---

70 [2009] EWHC 12 (QB).

71 [2003] EWHC 9024 (Costs), 20 February 2003, SCCO.

72 CPR 44.3B(1)d.

73 www.thejudge.co.uk/

the case, the premium becomes payable immediately by the client, regardless of how long it takes to recover it from the opponent, or whether it is recovered at all. As with all insurance products, the adviser and client should pay very close attention to the often detailed small print of each policy in order to understand the terms and conditions on which insurance is offered.

4.90   There is no guarantee that any insurer will offer to insure a disrepair claim. The reality is that ATE LEI is hard to find for most cases of modest value and the risk of having to pay the opponent's costs, if unsuccessful, should be fully explained to the client. So long as the client is willing to take the risk, the adviser may consider that the disrepair claim is sufficiently strong to proceed under a CFA, without insurance.

Notice of funding

4.91   The CPR Practice Direction relating to Pre-Action Conduct provides that a party should inform their opponent 'as soon as possible' about any funding arrangement entered into. This should be, either within 7 days of entering the funding arrangement concerned or, where a claimant enters into a funding arrangement before sending a letter before claim, in the letter before claim.[74] In the housing context the 'letter before claim' will be the early notification letter, see paragraph 3.50. A 'funding arrangement' for this purpose is defined in CPR 43.2(1)(k) and includes entering into a CFA or taking out an insurance policy. Former provisions which allowed a party to wait until the issue of proceedings before notifying their opponent no longer apply. The sanction for failing to advise an opponent of a funding arrangement is contained in CPR 44.3B namely that, unless the court otherwise allows, any additional liability (such as the success fee or insurance premium) will not be recoverable 'for any period during which that party failed to provide information about a funding arrangement'. CPR 44.15 and para 19.4 of the Costs Practice Direction to Parts 43–48 set out the information that has to be disclosed, namely:

- the date of the CFA and the claim or claims to which it relates (including Part 20 claims if any);
- the name and address of any legal expenses insurer, the policy number and the date of the policy and the claim or claims to which it relates (including Part 20 claims if any);

74 Practice Direction: Pre-Action Conduct, para 9.3.

- the level of cover provided by any such insurance; and
- whether the insurance premiums are staged and, if so, the points at which increased premiums are payable.

4.92 The Costs Practice Direction to CPR Parts 43–48 at para 19.2 provides that the information may be given by using Form N251 (notice of funding), a copy of which must (in addition) be filed with the court when the claim form is issued, and served on the opponent when the claim form is served. The adviser does not need to disclose the percentage success fee in the CFA or how it is calculated, at this stage, nor give the amount of the insurance premium. This is because until the case is finished the opponent is not entitled to know the adviser's view of the strength of the case. Where a party has entered into more than one funding arrangement in respect of a claim, for example a CFA and an insurance policy, a single notice containing the information set out in Form N251 may contain the required information about both or all of them.[75] Para 19.3 provides that if there is any change in the funding arrangement (for example, if a second CFA were signed which supersedes the first CFA, or a different insurance policy were taken out), then notice of change in Form N251 must be given to the opponent. Advisers must be aware that at the conclusion of the case, when serving a notice of commencement of assessment of a bill of costs, Costs Practice Direction para 32.5 requires that the opponent is also served with relevant details of the additional liabilities at that stage (i.e. with the notice of commencement), including:

- a statement of the reasons for the percentage increase in the CFA (ie, the success fee); and
- a copy of the insurance certificate showing whether the policy covers the receiving party's own costs; his opponents costs; or his own costs and his opponent's costs; and the maximum extent of that cover, and the amount of the premium paid or payable.

A failure to do so will prevent recovery of the additional liability, unless a separate application is made to a costs judge for relief from sanctions under CPR 3.9.

Paying for disbursements and counsel

4.93 Where the client has adequate savings, the adviser may ask him or her to meet disbursements as they occur, but this arrangement needs to be agreed in advance. If the client cannot afford to pay for

75 See Costs PD for CPR Parts 43-48, para 19.4(5).

disbursements, the adviser will have to do so on the client's behalf. The client might be asked to make small monthly instalment payments towards the disbursements by standing order. The adviser will either have to bear the disbursements or apply for specialist 'disbursement funding' which is offered by several banks and brokers.

4.94   As mentioned above, an element of the success fee can reflect the fact that the adviser is carrying the cost of disbursements until the end of the case (when it is hoped that they will be recovered from the opponent); payment of this is likely to come out of the client's damages.

4.95   Many barristers are willing to undertake work under a CFA. Barristers will want to consider the papers and carry out their own risk assessment before agreeing to take the case on. They will assess their own success fee (usually staged) and will enter into a CFA with the solicitor, rather than with the client.

4.96   If the client wins the case, the solicitor will be liable to pay the barrister under the CFA, regardless of whether the barrister's fees and success fee are recovered from the opponent. The solicitor may wish to retain sufficient damages from the client, until those costs are recovered. Paying parties are as likely to challenge the level of the barrister's success fee as they are to challenge the level of the solicitor's success fee.

Challenges to CFAs

4.97   As mentioned above, a vigorous 'costs war' has developed in recent years, where paying parties seek to challenge the validity of CFAs on technical grounds. If a CFA is declared to be unenforceable by the court, then the solicitor will not be entitled to payment of his or her costs (at all), though disbursements incurred on behalf of clients are still usually recoverable.

4.98   In *Hollins v Russell*,[76] it was recommended that a copy of the agreement should be produced to the paying party as part of the costs assessment procedure at the end of the case. As a result of technical challenges, many solicitors refuse to produce the agreement to the opponent on the ground of privilege. However, if they do this the court may put the solicitor to an election at the costs assessment hearing either to disclose the CFA, or to prove its contents and therefore the validity of the retainer by some other means, for example, by the oral evidence of the solicitor who conducted the case. This is

76 [2003] EWCA Civ 718.

known as the Pamplin procedure after the judgment in *Pamplin v Express Newspapers*,[77] but the procedure is now embodied in the Practice Direction to CPR Part 47, para 40.14.

4.99   If faced with a serious challenge to the validity of the CFA, the adviser may wish to consult specialist costs counsel.

77 [1985] 1 WLR 689.

CHAPTER 5

Proceedings under the Environmental Protection Act 1990

5.1	**Introduction**
5.5	**Statutory nuisance**
5.7	Elements of s79(1)(a)
	'Any premises' • *'in such a state'* • *'prejudicial to health'* • *'or a nuisance'*
5.23	**Action by local authorities**
5.23	Abatement notices
5.35	High Court actions
5.36	Emergency procedure
5.40	Recurring nuisances
5.42	**Action by tenants and other occupiers**
5.42	Private sector tenants and occupiers
5.45	Public sector tenants and occupiers
5.46	Section 82 proceedings
5.50	**Overview of procedure**
5.51	**Preparatory work**
5.52	**Procedure**
5.53	The expert
5.56	Notice of the intended proceedings

continued

5.57   The information
5.63   The first hearing
5.71   Preparing for the trial
5.78   Trial

5.83   Nuisance orders
5.88   Enforcement

5.91   Penalties

5.93   Compensation

5.99   Appeals

5.100   Costs

5.108   Environmental Protection Act 1990 and the Housing Acts

5.110   Note of warning

Introduction

5.1   Since the mid-19th century, Parliament has sought to protect the general public from the worst effects of slum housing (ie, disease, overcrowding and dangerous buildings) through public health legislation. These laws, which were largely consolidated into the Public Health Act (PHA) 1936, have been amended subsequently and are now recast in the Environmental Protection Act (EPA) 1990 Part III.[1] See appendix A for the text of EPA 1990 ss79–82. These provisions replace those found in PHA 1936 ss91–100 and came into force on 1 January 1991.[2]

5.2   Much of this legislation can be used by tenants, occupiers and their neighbours to force landlords of bad housing to carry out necessary repairs, and to improve the condition of property which they own. The Act is concerned with attacking the effects of bad housing, that is, the poor conditions which occupiers and others face as a result of deterioration in the structure of dwellings and other housing defects.

5.3   The EPA 1990 can be a useful weapon in those circumstances where premises are unhealthy but there is no civil remedy because there is no actionable disrepair. In particular, the EPA 1990 has proved invaluable in assisting tenants living in damp housing where the cause was condensation due to bad design. The black mould produced by such conditions has been shown to cause ill health such as asthma (see chapter 7). Fortunately, condensation-ridden housing has declined over the last 15 years. This, coupled with the limits that recently decided cases[3] have placed on using the Act, means that EPA 1990 prosecutions have become less common.

5.4   The key to the use of this public health legislation, by tenants against landlords responsible for bad housing, is the concept of the 'statutory nuisance'.

Statutory nuisance

5.5   Statutory nuisances are defined as arising in the specific circumstances set out in the EPA 1990 and related legislation. The following,

---

1   As amended by the Environment Act 1995 and the Clean Neighbourhoods and Environment Act 2005.

2   EPA 1990 s164(2).

3   Eg *Birmingham CC v Oakley* [2000] UKHL 59, see paragraph 5.11.

contained in the EPA 1990 and PHA 1936, are the most immediately relevant to housing conditions (statutory references are to the EPA 1990 unless otherwise stated):

- 'any premises in such a state as to be prejudicial to health or a nuisance' (s79(1)(a));
- 'any accumulation or deposit which is prejudicial to health or a nuisance' (s79(1)(e));
- 'any insects emanating from relevant industrial, trade or business premises and being prejudicial to health or a nuisance' (s79(1)(fa));[4]
- 'any other matter declared by any enactment to be a statutory nuisance' s79(1)(h);
- 'any tent, van, shed or similar structure used for human habitation which is in such a state or so overcrowded as to be prejudicial to health; or the use of which, by reason of the absence of proper sanitary accommodation or otherwise, gives rise, whether on the site or on other land, to a nuisance or to conditions prejudicial to health' (PHA 1936 s268, as amended by EPA 1990 Sch 15 para 4);
- 'any well, tank, cistern or water-butt used for the supply of water for domestic purposes which is so placed, constructed or kept as to render the water therein liable to contamination prejudicial to health' (PHA 1936 s141, as amended by EPA 1990 Sch 15 para 4);
- 'any pond, pool, ditch, gutter or watercourse which is so foul or in such a state as to be prejudicial to health or a nuisance' (PHA 1936 s259, as amended by EPA 1990 Sch 15 para 4);
- 'noise emitted from premises so as to be prejudicial to health or a nuisance' (s79(1)(g).

Most 'species' of statutory nuisance contain two distinct limbs, which are to be read as alternatives and treated quite separately, ie, 'prejudicial to health' or a 'nuisance'.

5.6   Several of the listed statutory nuisances deal with matters likely to be common in dwellings out of repair (blocked gutters, polluted water tanks, defective cisterns etc) but the one of most relevance to unhealthy housing is contained in s79(1)(a). Each element of s79(1)(a) requires close attention, especially as some of its elements are replicated in the other forms of statutory nuisance.

4 Added by Clean Neighbourhoods and Environment Act 2005 s101.

Elements of s79(1)(a)

'Any premises'

5.7 Premises are defined by the EPA 1990 to include all land and vessels.[5] Thus both private and public sector housing are covered. The courts have held that the Act directs attention to the condition of the premises, rather than to the way in which they are used.[6] Indeed, the premises need not even be occupied.[7]

5.8 In the case of a block of flats, the 'premises' for the purposes of s79 may be an individual flat or flats. It is possible to allege a statutory nuisance in relation to an entire block only if either the tenants are complaining of the condition of the common parts or if there is a problem 'not confined to any one constituent unit in the block and which can only be related to the entire block'.[8]

5.9 An open site without any permanent buildings (eg, a travellers' site) may also be 'premises' for the purpose of s79. Thus the EPA 1990 powers may be used to eliminate statutory nuisances on caravan sites and other areas of land used for residential purposes.[9]

'in such a state'

5.10 A statutory nuisance arises if the state of the premises as a whole is such as to be prejudicial to health or a nuisance. This may arise either from a single major item of disrepair (eg, a collapsing ceiling) or from the accumulation of a number of minor items. It should be noted that it is the effect of the defects which gives rise to the nuisance rather than the simple fact of disrepair.

5.11 In *Birmingham CC v Oakley*,[10] it was stated that the object of s79(1)(a) is to provide a means for the summary removal of noxious matters and the Act must be restricted to public health matters. So, a poor arrangement of rooms, where a toilet without a washhand basin was situated next to a kitchen could not render premises in a 'state' so as to be prejudicial to health. Similarly, in *R v Bristol CC ex p Everett*,[11] a steep staircase, where there was a likelihood of accident, could

---

5   EPA 1990 s79(7).
6   *Birmingham CC v Oakley* [2000] UKHL 59; [2001] 1 AC 617.
7   *Coventry CC v Doyle* [1981] 1 WLR 1325, DC.
8   *Birmingham DC v McMahon and Others* (1987) 19 HLR 452, QBD at 457.
9   *R v Secretary of State for the Environment ex p Ward* [1984] 2 All ER 556, QBD at 560.
10 [2000] UKHL 59; [2001] 1 AC 617.
11 [1999] 1 WLR 92; [1999] 2 All ER 193, CA.

not be considered a statutory nuisance. Where the landlord is not the local housing authority, the circumstances in both these cases can be addressed using the provisions discussed in chapter 6 of this book.

'prejudicial to health'

5.12   A statutory nuisance will arise where premises are in such a state, through disrepair or otherwise, as to be 'prejudicial to health' which is defined by the EPA 1990 s79(7) to mean 'injurious or likely to cause injury, to health'. Thus, both actual and potential ill health are covered.

5.13   The courts have held that the requirement of being 'prejudicial to health' will be satisfied simply where it can be shown that the state of the premises is such as would cause a well person to become ill or the health of a sick person to deteriorate further.[12] Accordingly, a statutory nuisance exists where *any* premises are so defective as to cause potential or actual detriment to the health of the tenant or other occupiers. The test is, however, objective in the sense that no account is taken of any occupier's particular vulnerability.[13]

5.14   'Health', although not defined by the EPA 1990, should be interpreted broadly to include physical and mental health, particularly to incorporate the medically recognized stress associated with living in bad housing. Mere interference with comfort will not bring a case within the 'health' limb[14] nor will defects which are merely decorative (such as stained wallpaper[15]) or which simply constitute an 'eyesore'.[16]

5.15   Examples of premises which are 'prejudicial to health' include those suffering from dampness, condensation or mould growth and infestations[17] but not those which lack sound insulation.[18]

---

12 *Malton Urban Sanitary Authority v Malton Farmers Manure Co* (1879) 4 Ex D 302.

13 *Cunningham v Birmingham CC* (1988) 30 HLR 158, DC.

14 *Salford CC v McNally* [1975] 3 WLR 87, HL, per Wilberforce LJ.

15 *Springett v Harold* [1954] 1 All ER 568, QBD.

16 *Coventry CC v Cartwright* [1975] 2 All ER 99, DC.

17 See, eg, *Dent v Haringey LBC* December 1999 *Legal Action* 18; *Housing Law Casebook* para P16.38, Wood Green Crown Court; *Ogunlowo v Southwark LBC* December 2005 *Legal Action* 29 ; *Housing Law Casebook* para P16.44, Camberwell Magistrates' Court.

18 *R (Vella) v Lambeth LBC and London and Quadrant Housing Trust* [2005] EWHC 2473 (Admin), which overruled *Southwark LBC v Ince* (1989) 21 HLR 504.

'or a nuisance'

5.16   The EPA 1990 does not define 'nuisance'. In *National Coal Board v Neath BC*,[19] the Divisional Court held that to fall within s79(1)(a), the 'nuisance' must be either:

- a public nuisance at common law; or
- a private nuisance at common law.

5.17   At common law a public nuisance arises where an act or omission affects adversely the comfort or quality of life of the public generally, or a class of citizens.

5.18   At common law a private nuisance is a substantial interference by the owner or occupier of property with the use and enjoyment of neighbouring property.

5.19   Given this restrictive interpretation of 'nuisance' in s79, it follows that a statutory nuisance based on this limb 'cannot arise if what has taken place affects only the person or persons occupying the premises.'[20] Thus, if the conditions in the premises are a nuisance only to the tenant or other occupier, a 'statutory nuisance' will not arise unless the prejudice to health 'limb' of s79 can be satisfied as an alternative.

5.20   Moreover, only certain types of nuisance may be within the section. The courts have required that the nuisance be of such a nature as to relate to matters of public health.[21] Conditions short of prejudice to health such as offensive smells, noise and dirt may be within the definition. Traffic noise is not actionable.[22]

5.21   Even within the narrow definition of a 'nuisance', action can be taken against 'statutory nuisance' arising from disrepair in immediately adjacent property (including common parts retained by the landlord). Examples include: leaking lavatory overflows, unhygienic rubbish chutes, back-surges of sewage, blocked pipes and gutters, and noisy central heating boilers.

5.22   Where premises are in such a state as to cause potential or actual injury to health, or constitute a nuisance, the consequent statutory nuisance may be tackled, either by action by the local authority, or through direct action by the occupier.

---

19 [1976] 2 All ER 478, DC.

20 *National Coal Board v Thorne* [1976] 1 WLR 543, DC, per Watkins J at 546.

21 *Great Western Railway v Bishop* (1872) LR 7 QB 550; *Bishop Auckland Local Board v British Auckland Iron and Steel Co Ltd* (1883) 10 QBD 138, considered in *Coventry CC v Cartwright* [1975] 2 All ER 99, DC.

22 *Haringey LBC v Jowett* (2000) 32 HLR 308, DC.

Action by local authorities

Abatement notices

5.23   The existence of statutory nuisances may be brought to the attention of local authorities either by their own systematic inspections of their districts (for example, in renewal areas) or, more commonly, by complaints from tenants and others. The investigation of statutory nuisances and enforcement of environmental protection legislation are usually delegated to individual environmental health officers (EHOs). For these purposes, EHOs have a right to enter and inspect premises which may be in such a state as to be a statutory nuisance.[23]

5.24   Once satisfied of the existence of a statutory nuisance (or the likelihood of a statutory nuisance arising or recurring), a local authority is legally bound to take action,[24] using the powers available to it under the EPA 1990 or the Housing Act (HA) 2004 (see chapter 6). Although obliged to follow the statutory procedures to tackle statutory nuisances, some authorities will first give the landlord an 'informal notice' that EPA 1990 sanctions are being considered.

5.25   The first formal step is service by the local authority of an abatement notice under EPA 1990 s80(1) on the person responsible for the nuisance. The notice requires the person served (in practice, usually the landlord) to abate the nuisance (or prevent it arising or recurring) and to execute 'such works, and the taking of such other steps as may be necessary' for that purpose. The notice also gives a time limit for completion of remedial works.

5.26   The abatement notice must be sufficiently clear in all the circumstances of the case to enable the recipient to understand what is required, bearing in mind the risk of exposure to penal sanctions for non-compliance. In straightforward cases the notice need not spell out precisely what works are required, but can simply require a certain result to be achieved.[25] In more complex cases, however, the abatement notice must specify the works required and these works must be capable of remedying the nuisance.[26]

5.27   The local authority is required to serve the abatement notice on 'the person responsible for the nuisance': s80(2)(a). He or she is

---

23   EPA 1990 Sch 3 para 2.
24   *Cocker v Cardwell* (1869) LR 5 QB 15.
25   *Budd v Colchester BC* [1999] LGR 601; (1999) *Times* 14 April, CA.
26   *Network Housing Association v Westminster CC* (1994) 27 HLR 189, DC. See also *Millard v Wastall* [1898] 1 QB 342; *Whatling v Rees* (1914) 84 LJKB 1122; *R v Wheatley* (1885) 16 QBD 34.

defined by EPA 1990 s79(7) as being 'the person to whose act, default or sufferance the nuisance is attributable'.

5.28   In cases of structural defects (eg, statutory nuisances arising from disrepair), the abatement notice must be served on the 'owner',[27] ie, the person who does (or would) receive the rent.[28]

5.29   If the person causing the nuisance cannot be found (as is frequently the case with property in gross disrepair) the authority can serve notice on the owner *or* occupier.[29]

5.30   Where more than one person is responsible for a statutory nuisance, notice may be served on each person whether or not his or her conduct or default alone would amount to a nuisance.[30]

5.31   The person served with an abatement notice has a right of appeal to a magistrates' court (to be exercised within 21 days of the date notice is served[31]) by way of complaint.[32] The grounds of appeal are set out in the Statutory Nuisance (Appeals) Regulations 1995.[33] The grounds include defect or error in the abatement notice and that the notice might lawfully have been served on a third party as well as the appellant. The magistrates have power to quash or vary the abatement notice or dismiss the appeal.

5.32   If the abatement notice is neither appealed nor complied with, the person served is guilty of an offence if the failure to comply is without reasonable excuse.[34] The EPA 1990 imposes no statutory duty to prosecute for non-compliance with abatement notices and is silent about whether private prosecutions may be brought by occupiers directly in place of local authorities unwilling to take action.

5.33   If the offence of failure to comply is proven, the landlord or other person served is liable to a fine up to level 5 on the standard scale and a further fine of one-tenth the level 5 scale for each further day of non-compliance following conviction.[35] The original abatement notice continues to bind the person served and the incentive for compliance with it is the prospect of incurring daily fines. There is, accordingly, no need for a nuisance order.

---

27 EPA 1990 s80(2)(b).
28 *Camden LBC v Gunby* [1999] 4 All ER 602, QBD.
29 EPA 1990 s80(2)(c).
30 EPA 1990 s81(1).
31 EPA 1990 s80(3).
32 EPA 1990 Sch 3 para 1(2).
33 1995 SI No 2644.
34 EPA 1990 s80(4).
35 EPA 1990 s80(5).

5.34   Whether or not it prosecutes for non-compliance, the authority can itself abate the nuisance 'and do whatever may be necessary' for execution of the original abatement notice.[36] It can then recover its costs from the person served or from the present owner of the property.[37]

High Court actions

5.35   If the local authority is satisfied that it would be inappropriate to deal with a statutory nuisance by using the magistrates' court procedure outlined above, it may take any necessary legal proceedings against the owner in the High Court.[38] Such proceedings have the advantage of giving access to broader equitable remedies, eg, injunctions, and wide-ranging means of enforcement. They are useful where the owner persistently defaults or repeatedly delays the summary process before the magistrates' court. For the procedure in a High Court action under the EPA 1990, see *Warwick RDC v Miller-Mead*.[39]

Emergency procedure

5.36   Frequently, the delays inherent in the enforcement procedures described above render them inappropriate for tackling situations of 'prejudice to health'. A streamlined procedure for these urgent cases is to be found in s76 of the Building Act 1984, set out in appendix A.

5.37   Thus, where an authority is satisfied (usually as a result of an urgent tenant complaint) that a statutory nuisance exists and that unreasonable delay would be caused by following the EPA 1990 procedure, it may serve the landlord with a notice stating its intention to do the remedial works and specifying the defects it intends to remedy.

5.38   *Nine days* after service, the local authority may carry out all the necessary work identified in the notice and may recover its costs and expenses from the person on whom the notice is served. Landlords can prevent this procedure taking effect only if, within seven days of service of the notice, they serve a counter-notice on the authority indicating that they intend to remedy the defects. The authority cannot act thereafter unless:

• the landlord fails to start remedial works within a reasonable time, or

36 EPA 1990 s81(3).
37 EPA 1990 s81(4).
38 EPA 1990 s81(4).
39 [1962] 2 WLR 284, CA.

- having been started, remedial works proceed unreasonably slowly or make no progress at all.

In either of these circumstances, the local authority can proceed directly and carry out the works, and recover the full cost from the landlord.

5.39   Advisers assisting tenants in situations where disrepair is sufficiently gross to constitute a statutory nuisance by reason of prejudice to health, should always consider pressing the environmental health department to use this 'nine-day notice' procedure.

Recurring nuisances

5.40   Under the EPA 1990 a local authority can serve an abatement notice requiring works, not only when it is satisfied that a nuisance exists, but also where it is satisfied that:

- a nuisance is likely to occur; or
- a nuisance is likely to recur.

5.41   The notice can either prohibit or restrict the nuisance arising or recurring and require the necessary works for those purposes.[40]

Action by tenants and other occupiers

Private sector tenants and occupiers

5.42   Private sector or housing association tenants will usually look to the EHOs employed by local authorities to take the necessary administrative and legal proceedings to eradicate statutory nuisances arising at their homes, using the powers described above.

5.43   Accordingly, advisers consulted by private tenants suffering prejudice to health or nuisance should consider involving the local authority's EHO by requesting a visit and inspection of the tenant's property. The tenant must be warned that taking such action could lead to the ending of the tenancy, for example if the tenant has limited security or if the premises are in such poor condition as to lead to an order that they should no longer be occupied. If a referral is made, the adviser should liaise closely with the EHO and ensure that the abatement procedures are fully used, including the nine-day notice procedure for urgent cases. In any subsequent prosecution of the landlord, the tenant may well be a witness for the local authority.

40   EPA 1990 s80(1).

5.44   There are five situations, however, which may give rise to difficulty:

- *The EHO fails to carry out an inspection, or there is an unreasonable delay before a visit is made* A local authority is required to investigate individual complaints (s79(1)). In the event of a clear default, a complaint may be made to the Secretary of State,[41] who may direct the authority to inspect. Alternatively a complaint may be made to the Local Government Obudsman.[42] In the interim, consideration can be given to bringing a private prosecution (see paragraph 5.46 onwards).

- *The EHO carries out an inspection but does not agree that a statutory nuisance has arisen* In such circumstances, advisers should ask for the matter to be reconsidered, ensuring that the EHO is supplied with all the available medical information about the prejudice to the health of the tenant, or complaints from other tenants about the nuisance. An EHO may be persuaded to revisit and reconsider if presented with a convincing report from an independent expert engaged by the tenant.

- *The EHO is not prepared to find that premises constitute a statutory nuisance, even after reconsideration* In this eventuality, the EHO should be asked whether there are any Category 1 or Category 2 hazards for the purposes of HA 2004 and, if so, what action will be taken: see chapter 6. Alternatively, the tenant will need to establish the existence of the nuisance by instructing an independent EHO and, if satisfied that a statutory nuisance can be proved, take proceedings directly against the landlord using the s82 procedure (see paragraphs 5.46 onwards).

- *The EHO agrees that there is a statutory nuisance, but fails to take remedial action within a reasonable time using the EPA 1990 procedures* The duty of the local authority to serve an abatement notice is a mandatory statutory duty.[43] The tenant can challenge the failure to take action, if aggrieved by the breach of statutory duty, and apply in judicial review proceedings in the High Court for an order directing the local authority to use the powers avail-

---

41 Currently the Secretary of State for the Department of Environment Food and Rural Affairs or, in Wales, the Welsh Minister for Environment, Sustainability and Housing.

42 Or, in Wales, the Public Services Ombudsman for Wales.

43 *Cocker v Cardwell* (1869) LR 5 QB 15; *McPhail v Islington LBC* [1970] 2 WLR 583, CA, at 586.

able to it.[44] Alternatively, complaint may be made to the Local Government Ombudsman.[45] However, this may be secondary to the urgent need to remedy the statutory nuisance, in which case the tenant should initiate summary proceedings directly against the landlord in the magistrates' court, using the s82 procedure, and secure the attendance of the EHO as a witness (see paragraph 5.46 onwards).

- *The EHO behaves improperly or unprofessionally* If the difficulty for the tenant arises from the improper or unprofessional behaviour of the EHO (eg, where the tenant is subject to racist remarks or has some evidence of corruption), complaint should be made to the chief EHO of the authority concerned. If this produces no satisfaction, the matter should be raised with the professional association of EHOs, the Chartered Institution of Environmental Health.

Public sector tenants and occupiers

5.45 Council tenants are largely outside the protection of the public health legislation simply because EHOs, as local government officers, cannot serve statutory notices on their own local authorities.[46] The council tenant must therefore use the enforcement procedure contained in EPA 1990 s82 (formerly PHA 1936 s99): see paragraph 5.46 onwards.

Section 82 proceedings

5.46 The procedure for direct action by tenants against their local authority or private landlord is contained in EPA 1990 s82 which is set out in appendix A.

5.47 Under this section, action may be taken against a local authority by a council tenant for the abatement of a statutory nuisance, even though the authority is providing the accommodation in exercise of its powers as a housing authority.[47] Similarly, s82 can be used by a private sector or housing association tenant where the local authority is not itself taking proceedings to compel the landlord to deal with a statutory nuisance at the property.

---

44 EPA 1990 s80(1).
45 Or, in Wales, the Public Services Ombudsman for Wales.
46 See *Cardiff CC v Cross* (1982) 6 HLR 1, CA.
47 *R v Epping (Waltham Abbey) JJ ex p Burlinson* [1947] 2 All ER 537, KBD.

5.48   Proceedings may be initiated by any person aggrieved by the statutory nuisance. Although this will usually be the tenant or licensee, the provision extends to all other occupiers of the premises, such as the tenant's family or lodgers.

5.49   Under s82, proceedings brought by individual tenants are criminal proceedings from the outset[48] even though the Act itself refers to an action started by way of complaint.[49] The document starting a magistrates' court prosecution is usually described as an '*information*' but since both the terms 'complaint' and 'information' are referred to in the legislation and case-law, they will also be used interchangeably in this chapter.

Overview of procedure

5.50   •   Thetenant sends a letter to the landlord giving notice that a statutory nuisance exists and giving the landlord 21 days to abate it.
   •   The tenant asks the magistrates' court to issue a summons by serving an information and supporting documents on the court officer.
   •   The court allocates a date for both the parties to attend.
   •   At the first hearing if the defendant pleads guilty, a nuisance order is made. If there is a dispute over compensation or costs, that part of the case is adjourned to a later date.
   •   If the defendant pleads not guilty, the court adjourns the case to a date when there is sufficient time for the case to be tried.
   •   If successful, the proceedings produce a nuisance order under s82(2), breach of which constitutes a further criminal offence: s82(8).

Preparatory work

5.51   The form of legal aid known as Legal Representation[50] is *not available* for the private prosecution of criminal cases, or for the enforcement of orders made under s82. Preparatory work can be undertaken using the other form of legal aid, known as Legal Help. Preparation will usually include:

48 *Botross v Hammersmith and Fulham LBC* (1994) 27 HLR 179, DC.
49 *R v Newham East JJ ex p Hunt* [1976] 1 All ER 839, DC and Magistrates' Courts Act 1980 s50.
50 See chapter 4.

- The engagement of an independent EHO to inspect the premises, take photographs and samples, and prepare a report.[51]
- Preparation of statements of the tenant and other members of the household relating to conditions at the premises, including statements which may be submitted under the Criminal Justice Act (CJA) 1967 s9.
- Preparation of a schedule of items destroyed or damaged by disrepair, including other financial loss, to be submitted for consideration of a compensation order.
- Assisting the tenant to disclose information to which the defendant is entitled.

Procedure

5.52   See appendix D for precedents. The procedure in the magistrates' court is regulated by the Criminal Procedure Rules 2005 (CrimPR) which can be found on the Ministry of Justice website.[52]

The expert

5.53   The proceedings before the magistrates will turn mainly on factual and expert information about 'prejudice to health' or 'nuisance' and the tenant's adviser will want to obtain and rely on a written expert's report on the condition of the premises. It was held in *O'Toole v Knowsley MBC*[53] that an EHO is qualified to assess whether premises are prejudicial to health and no additional medical evidence, for example from a GP (general practitioner), is necessary. In *Southwark LBC v Simpson*,[54] it was stated that a chartered surveyor without expertise in public health matters will not have the knowledge required to give admissible opinion in an EPA 1990 case.

5.54   The tenant's adviser must serve the expert's report on the court and on the landlord[55] and must then inform the EHO that the report has been so served.[56] The EHO's duties to the court are set out in CrimPR 33 and are much the same as in civil proceedings.

51 Advisers may find such EHOs via the Health and Housing Group, Star Street, Ware, Hertfordshire, SG12 7AA, tel: 01920 465384.
52 Current website address: www.justice.gov.uk/criminal/procrules_fin.
53 (2000) 32 HLR 420, QBD.
54 (1999) 31 HLR 725, DC.
55 CrimPR 33.4.
56 CrimPR 33.4.

5.55   Magistrates are not entitled to reject the evidence of an EHO called on behalf of the tenant unless that evidence is challenged or contradicted by an EHO for the respondent:

> when it comes to deciding whether the condition of premises is or is not liable or likely to be injurious to health one is moving outside the field where a tribunal is entitled to draw on its own experience. That is a matter upon which the tribunal needs informed expert evidence.[57]

Notice of the intended proceedings

5.56   Before the person aggrieved starts court proceedings the landlord must be given at least 21 days' notice specifying the matter complained of: EPA 1990 s82(6) and (7). The notice must provide reasonable details of the alleged statutory nuisance but need not be comprehensive or set out what remedial works are required.[58] The notice must be served on the person responsible for the nuisance. EPA 1990 s160 provides that where the defendant is the local authority, the notice must be served on a clerk to that authority. Since most town clerks have been replaced by chief executives, this can pose a problem. There are two conflicting cases on this point.[59] Advisers should take the precaution of sending one copy of the notice to the chief executive's office but addressed to 'the clerk' and a second copy to the council's solicitor.

The information

5.57   The person aggrieved by the existence of a statutory nuisance serves an information in writing at the magistrates' court.[60] This is a straightforward process involving completion of a prescribed information form which is served on the court officer at the tenant's local magistrates' court.[61] The information must contain a statement of the offence, setting out:

- An indication of the capacity in which the defendant is to be served (ie, as the person responsible for the nuisance or the 'owner' if

---

57 *Patel v Mehtab* (1982) 5 HLR 78, QBD, per Donaldson LJ at 82.
58 *East Staffordshire v Fairless* [1998] EWHC 954 (Admin).
59 *R v Birmingham CC ex p Ireland* [1999] 2 All ER 609, QBD; *Leeds v Islington LBC* (1999) 31 HLR 545, DC.
60 CrimPR 7.2(1).
61 CrimPR 7.2(1).

either the nuisance arises from a structural defect, or the person responsible for the nuisance cannot be found).[62]

- The nature of the alleged nuisance in ordinary language[63] and enough detail for the defendant to understand what is being complained of,[64] but note that the information does not need to specify the work needed to abate the nuisance.[65] The EHO report, if attached to the information, will usually be more than adequate.

- That the statutory nuisance arises under s79(1)(a) (prejudice to health or a nuisance) rather than one of the other subsections (smoke, effluvia, noise etc), if that is the case.[66]

5.58   It would be usual for the tenant to be in occupation of the premises at the date the summons is requested, but the absence of the tenant (perhaps driven to live elsewhere temporarily by the poor conditions) is not fatal to an application.[67]

5.59   It is permissible to send an information immediately after expiry of the notice period under s82(6).[68]

5.60   Although many metropolitan magistrates' courts are familiar with applications made under EPA 1990 s82, advisers should be careful not to take the issue of a summons for granted in other areas. It is good practice to ensure that the information is accompanied by a statement from the tenant, the expert's report, a copy of EPA 1990 s82 and a request for an early hearing date.

5.61   On receipt of the information, the court should issue a summons to require the parties to attend a hearing on a specified date.[69] The function of magistrates, or the justices' clerk, when issuing a summons is judicial, ie, there is a discretion to issue, or to refuse to issue the summons, which must be exercised judicially. It would, however, be wrong to refuse to issue a summons merely because the landlord also faced civil proceedings, at least when the scope of the civil proceedings is not co-extensive with the scope of the EPA 1990 proceedings.[70]

---

62 EPA 1990 s82(4) and (5).

63 CrimPR 7.3(1)(a)(i).

64 CrimPR 7.3(1)(a)(ii).

65 *East Staffordshire BC v Fairless* [1998] EWHC 954 (Admin).

66 CrimPR 7.3(1)(a)(ii).

67 *Jones v Public Trustee* September 1988 *Legal Action* 21, Hastings Magistrates' Court.

68 *R v Dudley Magistrates' Court ex p Hollis* [1998] 1 All ER 759, DC.

69 CrimPR 7.1(2)(a).

70 *R v Highbury Corner Magistrates Court ex p Edwards* (1994) 26 HLR 682, DC.

5.62   In order to have jurisdiction the court must be satisfied that at the date of the information there is a statutory nuisance (rather than the prospect of a nuisance arising or recurring)[71] and that the tenant was 'aggrieved' by the statutory nuisance *at that date*.[72] Thus, if any work is carried out by the landlord after the date of the EHO's inspection report, it may be necessary to arrange a re-inspection by the EHO before the information is put before the court.

The first hearing

5.63   The court will usually inform the tenant directly of the hearing date, so the adviser should ensure that the tenant realises that he or she must pass this date on to the adviser as soon as possible.

5.64   Even if the remedial works are started after the laying of the information, the tenant and adviser should attend on the hearing date to secure an order for costs (see below). Note that the case could proceed to hearing even if the tenants have been re-housed, since removing the tenant does not remedy the statutory nuisance.[73]

5.65   Advisers may well find that, at the first hearing date, the case appears in a list of many others, on the basis that it will be effective only if there is a guilty plea and agreement on matters such as the works to be covered by an order.

5.66   The tenant may feel able to present the case at an uncontested hearing. If not, both solicitors and barristers have the right to address the court. Some barristers are willing to act in EPA 1990 prosecutions under a conditional fee agreement (CFA).[74] If a barrister is instructed without a CFA, the adviser will be liable for his or her fee.

5.67   The adviser should try to find out from those representing the landlord if the intention is to plead guilty. If so, it may be possible to agree a works schedule and at the hearing the magistrates can be invited to make an order requiring the defendant to abate the nuisance within a specified time and to carry out the works necessary for that purpose.[75] If by the hearing date the nuisance has abated (whether naturally or as a result of remedial measures) but the court is satisfied that recurrence is likely, it can make an order prohibiting

---

71   EPA 1990 s82(1).

72   *Hilton v Hopwood* (1899) 44 SJ 96.

73   *Lambeth LBC v Stubbs* (1980) 255 EG 789; (1980) 78 LGR 650, DC, followed and applied in *Coventry CC v Doyle* [1981] 2 All ER 184, DC.

74   See chapter 4 on funding.

75   EPA 1990 s82(2).

recurrence and requiring works to prevent recurrence.[76] It will be apparent that the court's powers at this stage mirror those of the authority itself to serve an abatement notice as described at paragraph 5.24 (save that the magistrates have no jurisdiction to prevent first occurrence of a nuisance). In order to secure the most appropriate orders, tenants and their advisers should have drafts available for the court to consider.

5.68   If the defendant landlord does *not* plead guilty at the first hearing, he or she may well request an adjournment. Magistrates are not entitled to adjourn simply to allow for works to be done before trial and thus deprive the tenant of the right to a compensation order.[77] Even so, if the tenant opposes an adjournment then the defendant can be sure of obtaining one from the court by pleading not guilty, in which case the court is likely to fix a one-day or two-day trial well into in the future. The tenant should be reminded not to lose sight of the primary object of the proceedings, namely to force the landlord to do work. One approach is to agree to one short adjournment of perhaps 14 or 21 days and, if the defendant is not prepared to plead guilty by the second hearing, to insist (at that second hearing) on an effective trial date being fixed. Only as an adviser becomes familiar with a regular opponent will the best tactics become apparent.

5.69   The tenant must have a list of dates when the EHO will be unable to attend court so that the trial date can be fixed for a date when the EHO is available.

5.70   A misguided tenant might at this stage try to prevent the landlord from carrying out work before trial in order to secure a conviction. Such a strategy will backfire because it will be held that the landlord is not liable for the continuance of the nuisance and the summons will be dismissed.[78]

Preparing for the trial

5.71   Unless the tenant is going to present the case, an advocate should be booked as soon as the trial date is known. The adviser should also ensure that the EHO is informed of the trial date and asked to attend.

5.72   The Criminal Procedure and Investigations Act (CPIA) 1996 requires the prosecuting tenant 'as soon as is reasonably practicable

---

76   EPA 1990 s82(2)(b).

77   *R v Dudley Magistrates' Court ex p Hollis* [1998] 1 All ER 759, DC.

78   *Quigley v Liverpool Housing Trust* [1999] EWHC 593 (Admin); *Jones v Walsall MBC* [2002] EWHC 1232 (Admin).

after ... the accused pleads not guilty'[79] to disclose to the defendant any information or documents that may undermine the tenant's case.[80] This duty of disclosure continues until the end of the case.[81] If there is no such material the tenant must confirm this to the landlord in a written statement.[82]

Examples

(1) An adviser learns from a witness that the tenant's flat became affected by damp only when the tenant overcrowded the flat by sub-letting rooms. The subtenants have now left and the landlord is unaware of the subletting. This evidence cannot be ignored; the adviser must tell the tenant to either abandon the prosecution or provide the landlord with details of the witness and the substance of the evidence.

(2) An adviser obtains a report from an EHO stating that the tenant's home is *not* prejudicial to health. The tenant offers to pay for a second report in the hope that the second EHO will have a more helpful opinion. The adviser must tell the tenant that even if a second report is obtained, the first one will have to be shown to the defendant landlord.

5.73　Because this is a summary prosecution, the defendant landlord is not obliged to give the tenant notice of what issues he or she is going to raise in the defence.[83] This means that the tenant has to prepare to prove every element of the offence, as set out in paragraph 5.79. However, if the landlord wants further information from the tenant then the voluntary disclosure procedure set out in CPIA 1996 s6A can be used. The landlord will serve a statement setting out the general nature of the defence; a copy must be sent to the court. On receipt of the defence statement, the tenant prosecutor must either:

- disclose any material which in the light of the defence statement might be reasonably expected to assist the defence; or
- confirm in writing that there is no such material.

CPIA 1996 s8 has a procedure that the landlord can use to force the tenant to produce documents or information if the landlord believes

---

79　CPIA 1996 s13(1)(a).
80　CPIA 1996 s3 as amended by CJA 2003.
81　CPIA 1996 s7A.
82　CPIA 1996 3(1)(b).
83　CPIA 1996 ss1(2) and 5(1)(a).

that the tenant is withholding something that would assist his or her case.

5.74 Section 9 of the CJA 1967 allows written statements to be tendered in evidence at a magistrates' court trial. The adviser may want to make use of this provision to rely on evidence from a witness who would prefer not to attend trial. The statement must be in a prescribed form and must be sent to the court as soon as possible. The court officer will then serve it on the defendant, who has seven days in which to object to the statement being tendered in evidence.[84] If an objection is made, the evidence will not be admissible unless the witness attends court.

5.75 About two weeks before the date set for the trial, the adviser should try to find out from the landlord's representative whether the intention is still to fight the case. If in fact the landlord is now going to plead guilty, then, as long as the landlord's representative confirms this in writing, the court can be informed and some of the time set aside can be allocated to another matter.

5.76 If the intention is still to plead not guilty, the advocate will want to see a full proof of evidence from the tenant and any other witnesses. Although a trial bundle[85] is not strictly required for a magistrates' court trial, many advocates expect to be given one to assist with the preparation of the case.

5.77 In a contested case it is worth checking that none of the sitting justices are in any obvious way associated with the interests of the defendant.[86] In particular, where the case is being brought against a local authority none of those sitting should be members of that authority.[87]

Trial

5.78 The procedure for a magistrates' court trial is set out in CrimPR 37 and the adviser should read it carefully.

5.79 At the close of the evidence, the justices are required to make certain findings, including:

- The actual condition of the premises: (i) at the date of the serving of the tenant's information and (ii) at the date of hearing.

---

84 CrimPR 27.
85 See paragraph 3.158.
86 *R v Smethwick JJ ex p Hands* (1980) *Times* 4 December, DC.
87 Justices of the Peace Act 1997 s66.

- Whether the condition at the date of the serving of the information constituted a statutory nuisance, and whether the statutory nuisance still exists.
- Identifying the person responsible for the statutory nuisance, or the owner.

5.80   The existence of a statutory nuisance and the cause of that nuisance have to be proved to the criminal standard of proof, ie, beyond reasonable doubt.

5.81   The landlord will not be the 'person responsible' if the court decides that the real cause of the nuisance is the tenant's failure to use the heating system supplied or otherwise to behave reasonably.[88]

5.82   The fact that the matter complained of does not arise from any breach of the landlord's obligation to repair may be persuasive in showing that it was not caused by any act or default of the landlord, but is not conclusive.[89] However, where the nuisance arises from any defect of a structural nature (eg, dampness resulting from a hole in the roof), the landlord is liable in the capacity of 'owner', irrespective of repairing obligations, once a statutory nuisance is proved.[90] It is necessary to have evidence at the trial to prove ownership.

Nuisance orders

5.83   If the matters listed at paragraph 5.79 are found in favour of the tenant, the court must make an order against the defendant requiring:

- such work as the court considers necessary to abate the nuisance, within a stipulated time limit, or
- sufficient works to prevent a recurrence of the nuisance.

5.84   The work required must be specified by the court in the nuisance order,[91] and so advisers should ensure that the court is supplied with a full and detailed draft order. Where there has been agreement on the facts, advisers should arrange that the fullest possible order is agreed in advance with the landlord and put before the justices. Much may be achieved through hard bargaining on the terms of orders 'at

---

88 *Dover DC v Farrar* (1982) 2 HLR 32, DC; *GLC v Tower Hamlets LBC* (1983) 15 HLR 54, DC; *Warner v Lambeth LBC* (1984) 15 HLR 42, DC; *Carr v Hackney LBC* (1996) 28 HLR 747, DC

89 *Birmingham DC v Kelly and Others* (1985) 17 HLR 572, QBD, at 579.

90 *Coventry CC v Doyle* [1981] 2 All ER 184, DC and EPA 1990 s82(4)(b).

91 *Network Housing Association v Westminster CC* (1995) 27 HLR 189, DC.

the door of the court' and the tenant's expert can assist with negotiations on the wording of the order. Whether or not the order is agreed, evidence in support of it must be given, since the decision about the extent of the works necessary to abate the nuisance should be made by the court itself.[92] The order may properly require works to be done which go beyond the terms of any contractual repairing obligation on the landlord. The order can for instance, require improvement work or the installation of fixtures, fittings and facilities not present at the commencement of the tenancy.[93]

5.85   The court has a wide discretion about the form and content of the order and, in considering the remedial works to be specified, can properly have regard to the future life of the property. The justices must 'look at the whole circumstances of the case and try and make an order which is in its terms sensible and just, having regard to the entire prevailing situation'.[94] If the order is being made against a local authority, the court is also entitled to have regard to the general obligations that the council owes to its tenants and to the extent of its resources.[95]

5.86   Although, in many cases, the landlord will attempt to convince the court that simple 'patch' repairs will cure the statutory nuisance, advisers should be bold in pressing for substantial orders for work sufficient to prevent recurrence of the nuisance. With the assistance of expert witnesses, tenants in past cases have been able to persuade courts to make formidable orders for remedial works, including improvements which, because of the restrictions of the Landlord and Tenant Act 1985 s11, would not have been achieved in the county court. For example, in *Birmingham DC v Kelly and Others*,[96] the magistrates ordered installation of gas-fired central heating, secondary double glazing, roof insulation, filling of cavity walls and electrical re-wiring.

5.87   Where the only effective way to abate the statutory nuisance is to have the whole property demolished, a nuisance order requiring demolition may be made.[97] Where the property is unfit, the court can

---

92 *Birmingham DC v Kelly and Others* (1985) 17 HLR 572, QBD.
93 *Birmingham DC v Kelly and Others* (1985) 17 HLR 572, QBD.
94 *Nottingham Corporation v Newton* [1974] 2 All ER 760, QBD, per Widgery LCJ at 766.
95 *Salford CC v McNally* [1975] 3 WLR 87, HL; *Birmingham DC v Kelly and Others* (1985) 17 HLR 572, QBD.
96 (1985) 17 HLR 572, QBD.
97 *Brown v Biggleswade Union* (1879) 43 JP 554.

prohibit occupation.[98] It is therefore wise, when a property is in very poor condition, to ensure that the tenant realises that re-location may be the consequence of bringing proceedings.

Enforcement

5.88   It is hoped that the landlord will comply with the terms of the nuisance order before expiry of the time stated in the order. If he or she fails without reasonable excuse to comply with 'any requirement' of an order made in s82 proceedings, the landlord commits a further criminal offence: EPA 1990 s82(8). The tenant may then bring a prosecution for that non-compliance in the same magistrates' court where the order was made. Indeed, if the order in the earlier part of s82 proceedings was made against a private or housing association landlord, the local authority could bring the further prosecution even though it was the tenant who first obtained the order in default of the authority acting. The prosecution is launched by serving a further information. If the magistrate is satisfied that an offence has occurred, the magistrates' court (or its clerk) will issue a summons requiring the attendance of the landlord for trial. Tenants should press for early hearing dates as the daily fine,[99] which is the real pressure on the landlord to comply with the order, bites only from the date of conviction, not from when the order is breached or the information laid.

5.89   Tenants should try to establish in advance whether the landlord will be pleading guilty or not guilty to the offence of non-compliance. In particular tenants should be alert to the prospect of the defendant relying on s82(8), the 'reasonable excuse' defence. This is undefined and potentially very wide ranging.

5.90   If the magistrates are satisfied about non-compliance or there is a guilty plea, a further conviction will be entered.

Penalties

5.91   Where the initial prosecution under s82(1) results in a nuisance order, the court enters a conviction and may impose a fine of up to level 5[100] on the standard scale: s82(2). The penalty for failure to comply with a nuisance order made by the court is a fine of up to level 5

---

98 EPA 1990 s82(3).

99 EPA 1990 s82(8).

100 Currently (November 2009) £5,000.

on the standard scale plus one tenth of that scale for each subsequent day on which compliance remains outstanding (s82(8)). The magistrates have discretion whether to impose the daily fine[101] and will be assisted by any information about the landlord's earlier convictions relating to other properties owned.

5.92 The level of fine is for the magistrates to decide, but some guidance was provided in *R (Islington LBC) v Inner London Crown Court*.[102] In that case, the premises had been fitted with new windows that provided inadequate ventilation and, as a result, the tenant's flat was suffering from condensation and mould growth, conditions that Lord Justice Brooke described as 'deplorable'. He stated that a fine in the region of £500 would be 'clearly too low', but he quashed a fine of £4,000 as being too high, given that the premises were fit for human habitation, the council had pleaded guilty and at the time of sentencing had nearly completed the schedule of works. The case was remitted for sentencing to the Crown Court, where the fine was reduced to £1,500.

Compensation

5.93 In addition to any penalty, a compensation order[103] may be made in favour of the tenant for damage suffered to person and property. In a 'prejudice to health' case, actual ill health will usually have been proved and recompense should follow. A compensation order provides a 'speedy, summary and cheap' method of obtaining financial compensation without the need to bring separate civil proceedings.[104] Full details of any personal injury should be provided,[105] although in the absence of such evidence an award for anxiety and distress can be made.[106] Up to £5,000 may be awarded by magistrates[107] (there is no limit in the Crown Court). It is not necessary to show that the landlord would have been liable in civil proceedings to pay compensation,[108]

---

101 *Canterbury CC v Ferris* [1977] JPL B45, DC.

102 [2003] EWHC 2500 (Admin); [2004] HLR 31; December 2004 *Legal Action* 15, DC.

103 Powers of Criminal Courts (Sentencing) Act (PCCSA) 2000 s130; *Herbert v Lambeth LBC* (1991) 24 HLR 299, DC; *Botross v Hammersmith and Fulham LBC* (1994) 27 HLR 179, DC.

104 *R v Dorton* [1988] Crim LR 254, CA.

105 *R v Cooper* [1982] Crim LR 308, CA.

106 *Bond v Chief Constable of Kent* [1983] 1 All ER 456, DC.

107 PCCSA 2000 s131.

108 *R v Chappell* [1984] Crim LR 574, CA.

but some evidence of the actual loss suffered must be available: mere representations are insufficient.[109]

5.94   The decision in *R v Liverpool Crown Court ex p Cooke*[110] has greatly limited the value of compensation awards and effectively means that the longest period of inconvenience and distress that can be claimed is six months and often will be much shorter. In *Cooke*, the Divisional Court held that, when assessing compensation, magistrates were not entitled to take into account the whole period for which the nuisance existed. Since there is no 'offence' under s82 unless a nuisance is proved to exist on the date of hearing, it follows that the earliest date that compensation can be awarded from will be the date that the 21-day statutory notice expires, see paragraph 5.56. If the statutory notice has expired more than six months before the information was laid, then compensation will run from six months before the date that the information was laid. The Divisional Court reiterated earlier warnings from appeal courts that the power to make compensation orders should be exercised only in simple and clear cases. The Divisional Court indicated in *Cooke* that in the context of the relatively short period of liability 'many, if not most' claims ought to be simple and straightforward.

5.95   Even so, the Divisional Court in *Davenport v Walsall MBC*[111] dismissed an appeal from magistrates who refused to make a compensation order on the ground that the case was too complicated, even though it was a relevant factor that there was likely to be no civil remedy. It was a feature of the case that the defendant had pleaded guilty and so the magistrates did not have a substantial pool of information about the case. The Divisional Court indicated that it did not wish to encourage magistrates to be 'over-eager to resort to assertions of complexity' but that it would only interfere if the 'decision falls outside the scope of their legitimate discretion'.

5.96   Magistrates are required to give reasons if refusing to award compensation, whether or not an application has been made.[112]

5.97   Care should be taken in identifying the actual loss in respect of which compensation is sought because, in any subsequent civil action for damages, credit will have to be given for the amount of the compensation order where the award is for the same 'injury, loss or damage'.[113] If a civil claim is going to be brought, the magistrates

109 *R v Horsham Justices ex p Richards* [1985] 2 All ER 1114, DC; *R v Amey* [1983] 1 All ER 865, CA.

110 [1996] 4 All ER 589, QBD.

111 (1995) 28 HLR 754, DC.

112 PCCSA 2000 s130(3).

113 PCCSA 2000 s134(2).

should always be asked to award compensation for those items which will not attract civil damages. The adviser should take care not to compromise the civil damages claim when coming to a settlement of the s82 prosecution. However, there is county court authority for the assertion that the clearest evidence would be needed to show that an agreement reached in the magistrates' court would extend to producing a compromise in a prospective civil claim.[114]

5.98   In *Issa v Hackney LBC*,[115] the tenant's home was prejudicial to health owing to bad design, even though there was no breach of the tenancy agreement. The council landlord was fined and ordered to carry out remedial works. The tenant's children had suffered asthma and they brought a county court claim against the council for damages. They relied as their cause of action on the council's failure to comply with the EPA 1990 and the conviction that their parent had obtained. The Court of Appeal held that the EPA 1990 does not give rise to a private law right of action. There is no civil liability on landlords unless there is actionable disrepair.

Appeals

5.99   An appeal against conviction may be made to the Crown Court.[116] Indeed, any 'person aggrieved' by the outcome of the proceedings before the magistrates may appeal and so a tenant who is unsuccessful with a prosecution may appeal to the Crown Court.[117] The appeal takes the form of a rehearing but the court concerns itself only with the matters as they stood at the date of the hearing before the justices.[118] Appeal also lies to the Divisional Court of the Queen's Bench Division by way of case stated. Alternatively, the procedure for judicial review by the High Court is available. Judicial review may be necessary, for example, to compel the magistrates in EPA 1990 proceedings to award costs.[119] Any order made by the magistrates' court to take effect before an appeal can be heard must be complied with.[120]

---

114 *Middlemast v Hammersmith and Fulham LBC Housing Law Casebook* para P16.48, West London County Court.

115 [1997] 1 All ER 999, CA.

116 EPA 1990 s73.

117 *Cook v Southend BC* (1989) 11 CL 323, CA.

118 *Northern Ireland Trailers v Preston County Borough* [1972] 1 All ER 260.

119 See *R v Dudley Magistrates' Court ex p Hollis* [1998] 1 All ER 759, DC.

120 *Hammersmith LBC v Magnum Automated Forecourts* [1977] 1 All ER 401, CA.

Costs

5.100   The EPA 1990 makes specific provision for costs awards in s82 proceedings. Where the court is satisfied that the statutory nuisance existed at the date that the information was laid then, irrespective of whether the nuisance still exists or is likely to recur, the court must order the defendant to pay the costs. The sum ordered to be paid is 'such amount as the court considers reasonably sufficient to compensate the tenant for any expenses properly incurred by him in the proceedings'.[121]

5.101   These should be sufficient to cover experts' fees, legal costs, tenant's loss of earnings etc. Several thousand pounds of costs were awarded in *Ogunlowo v Southwark LBC*.[122] There is no formal procedure to assess the costs and the magistrates have a wide jurisdiction. Decisions on costs can be reached without the need for pleadings or formal bills[123] but in *Taylor v Walsall and District Property and Investment Co*[124] it was made clear that the informant is expected as 'a matter of routine' to give advance notice to the defendant of any claim for costs and the defendant should indicate in advance whether that claim is accepted or challenged. The same case encouraged the use of the equivalent of Part 36 offers. Perhaps the best way for the adviser to approach costs is to produce a schedule similar in form to that used for summary assessment of costs in the county court.[125]

5.102   Although legal aid for representation is not available to tenants in the magistrates' court, it is available to the tenant to resist any appeal to the Crown Court[126] or to the Divisional Court or to participate in any challenge brought by judicial review.

5.103   Costs remain 'properly incurred' when the tenant pursues an application for a compensation order at an adjourned hearing, even though the magistrates decide not to make a compensation order, providing the application was proper, ie, was not 'doomed from the outset'.[127]

5.104   Costs will only be 'properly incurred' if the complainant has signed a valid conditional fee agreement[128] or is liable under a private

---

121   EPA 1990 s82(12).
122   December 2005 *Legal Action* 29; *Housing Law Casebook* para P16.44, Camberwell Magistrates' Court.
123   *R v Southend Stipendiary Magistrate ex p Rochford DC* [1994] Env LR D15, QBD.
124   (1998) 30 HLR 1062, DC.
125   See County Court form N260.
126   *R v Inner London Crown Court ex p Bentham* (1988) 21 HLR 171, QBD.
127   *Davenport v Walsall MBC* (1995) 28 HLR 754, DC.
128   Courts and Legal Services Act 1990 s58A(1)(a).

retainer to pay those costs to the solicitor. A success fee cannot be charged for an EPA 1990 prosecution.[129] Costs are not properly incurred if there is an unlawful contingency fee arrangement. In *Hughes v Kingston upon Hull Council*,[130] a magistrate made a finding that Mr Hughes, a pensioner on income support, was not aware of any liability for costs to his solicitor. The Court of Appeal held that Mr Hughes was unable to seek an order for costs against the council because the agreement with his solicitors was a contingency fee and therefore contrary to public policy.

5.105   The adviser can reserve the right to waive payment of fees, but there must be a letter of retainer setting out the client's liability to pay costs, win or lose, together with applicable rates. In *Carr v Leeds CC; Wells and Coles v Barnsley MBC*,[131] the court decided that a retainer was not a sham where the tenants did not have the means to pay their solicitors but clearly believed themselves to have a liability for costs.

5.106   Where the court has made an order for costs or compensation to be paid, the defendant must send any payments to the magistrates' court office. A court official will then send costs or compensation direct to the client, rather than to the adviser. This can leave the adviser out of pocket because the tenant may well think that the whole sum is compensation and spend it. Some courts will agree to send the costs to the adviser if the tenant signs a letter of authority to that effect. Even with such a letter some magistrates' courts will keep to their usual procedure. Where the case is compromised, the adviser can make it a condition of the settlement that the defendant pays the costs to the adviser rather than the client. In these circumstances, the tenant's representative should tell the magistrates that there is no need for a costs order because they have been agreed privately between the parties. If the costs were not paid by the defendant the tenant could instruct the adviser to bring a civil claim to sue on the compromise.

5.107   The magistrates have no general discretion to award costs against an unsuccessful tenant. However, there is power to do so if, in the magistrates' opinion, the landlord's costs were incurred as a result of an unnecessary or improper act or omission on the part of the tenant.[132] If the magistrates believe that the fault lies on the part of the

---

129 Conditional Fee Agreements Order 2000 SI No 823.
130 [1999] 2 All ER 49, CA.
131 (2000) 32 HLR 753, DC.
132 *R v Enfield Justices ex p Whittle* June 1993 *Legal Action* 15; *Housing Law Casebook* para P16.30, DC.

tenant's legal adviser or representative then they can make a 'wasted costs order' against that person.[133] Such orders are rare.

Environmental Protection Act 1990 and the Housing Acts

5.108   As has been seen, local authorities have a statutory duty to take action where premises are in such a state as to be a statutory nuisance under the EPA. However, if any premises are in such poor condition as to amount to a Category 1 hazard, the local authority has a statutory duty to take action under the HA 2004.[134] The courts have made it clear that local authorities should not use the statutory nuisance procedure to force full-scale repairs on landlords of unfit housing[135] but must instead use the Housing Act procedure.[136]

5.109   On the other hand, the fact that *council* property is unfit or hazardous (even to the extent of simply awaiting demolition) is no bar to the tenant taking proceedings under s82, although in such cases justices are invited to take into account, in drawing up orders, the prospective life of the property.[137]

Note of warning

5.110   EPA 1990 procedures provide a swift and straightforward remedy for bad housing and impose salutary penalties on landlords, including local authorities, but several problems are relevant to tenants considering such action.

5.111   EPA 1990 s82 proceedings are *criminal* proceedings and carry a higher burden of proof. Advisers should be certain of their evidence before starting prosecutions. If the case is contested, the trial could take several days and the tenant's expert could be required at court for the whole period. At trial, if any element of the offence is not proven by the tenant, for example that the landlord is the owner of the property, then the magistrates will dismiss the case. If the proceedings result in an acquittal, the tenant's adviser will have incurred

---

133 Prosecution of Offences Act 1985 s19A.
134 See chapter 6.
135 *Salisbury Corporation v Roles* [1948] WN 412; (1948) 92 SJ 618, DC.
136 *R v Kerrier DC ex p Guppys (Bridport)* (1976) 32 P&CR 411, CA.
137 *Salford CC v McNally* [1975] 3 WLR 87, HL.

heavy costs and expenses, which the tenant will not have to pay if the adviser is acting under a CFA, and which the tenant will be unlikely to be able to afford if the adviser was acting under a private retainer.

5.112   Most advisers use the EPA 1990 when it is the only available remedy, for example because the statutory nuisance is caused by a design fault rather than by disrepair.

5.113   In cases of very poor standard housing, the prosecution may result in a finding of unfitness and an order from the court prohibiting occupation of the property: s82(3). This would prevent the tenant returning to the property until it was made fit.

CHAPTER 6

Bad housing and the Housing Act 2004

6.1   Introduction

6.8   Getting prepared to take action

6.13   Mobilising the local housing authority

6.30   Assessment of the premises

6.40   Selecting the appropriate action

6.51   Forms of action and their enforcement

6.51   Hazard awareness notice

6.53   Improvement notice

6.55   Prohibition order

6.57   Demolition order

6.60   Declaring a clearance area

6.62   Emergency action

6.64   Suspending action

6.66   Purchase of the property

6.68   Enforcement

6.72   Rehousing and compensation for displaced tenants

6.77   Council tenants

6.80   Conclusion

Introduction

6.1   Poor standards in rented housing are not only of concern to the tenants who occupy that housing. The wider community rightly takes an interest in the quality and safety of housing being made available to rent. In our modern society, we are collectively interested to ensure that:

- the third of all households who are living in rented housing enjoy basic minimum standards;
- those who visit them at their homes are safe to do so;
- children growing up in rented housing develop and thrive in safe conditions;
- the elderly living in rented housing can continue to do so free from unnecessary risks; and
- rented housing does not become an eyesore or otherwise adversely impact on the local environment.

6.2   To ensure that these objectives are attained, there have been on the statute book for over a century numerous Housing Acts and other measures designed to achieve basic minimum conditions in, and standards of safety for, rented housing. The standards prescribed and the methods of achieving them have changed over time and it is not necessary to trace the history. The modern approach is largely contained in the Housing Act (HA) 2004 which has been brought into force in stages over the past few years.

6.3   In this chapter, those aspects of this housing legislation of most assistance to the individual tenant or other occupier will be considered. The text seeks to show how the provisions can be used to help tenants who want to enjoy improved standards of safety, comfort and security in their homes where action is not forthcoming from landlords. A particular advantage and attraction of use of the HA 2004 provisions is that they:

- are not limited to disrepair;
- carry no obligation of prior notification;
- cover latent or inherent defects;
- operate irrespective of the tenure of the occupiers;
- deal with problems of design, layout and facilities; and
- apply at no financial cost or financial risk to the tenant.

6.4   Before turning to the detail, however, it is essential to emphasise that very little of the housing legislation imposes obligations on landlords which are directly enforceable by tenants. Rather, the legislation works by casting powers and duties on local housing authorities (primarily district and borough councils). These powers and duties range from initial inspection of residential premises to applying the ultimate sanctions of emptying or demolishing housing stock which does not meet minimum standards.

6.5 It is therefore essential that tenants and their advisers understand how to trigger action by the relevant local housing authority. It is much more important to understand how to get the local housing authority to take up issues and pursue them than to examine the minutiae of the technical assessments that local housing authority housing inspectors undertake. It is results that count, more than the method by which they are achieved.

6.6 For that reason, this chapter first outlines how to prepare to take action and how the powers of local housing authorities can best be invoked, before turning to describe the applicable duties and the available powers.

6.7 There is no lack of enthusiasm on the part of the courts for upholding or enforcing the legislation relating to housing conditions. Indeed, the judiciary has sanctioned policies of bold use of the Housing Act legislation in attempts to eradicate bad housing. Lord Denning MR said over 30 years ago:

> It seems to me that the policy of Parliament was to make the owners of houses keep them in proper repair. Not only so as to keep up the stock of houses, but also to see that protected tenants should be able to have their houses properly kept up. It would be deplorable if there were no means of compelling owners of old houses to keep them in proper repair; or if the owners could let them fall into disrepair as a means of evicting tenants. Of course, if the state of the house is so bad that it should be condemned whoever was occupying it then let it be demolished or closed or purchased. But if it is worth repairing, then it should be repaired, no matter whether it is occupied by a protected tenant or an unprotected tenant.[1]

Getting prepared to take action

6.8 Before taking even the first steps to invoke the exercise of local housing authority powers, tenants and their advisers need to understand what might be achievable and what consequences might follow from involving the authorities.

---

1 *Hillbank Properties v Hackney LBC* [1978] QB 998 at 1009; (1982) 3 HLR 73 at 82, CA.

6.9   In terms of marshalling the necessary information, tenants and their advisers will find that a broad outline of local housing authority powers and duties under the HA 2004 is given in the remainder of this chapter. But that is no substitute for the need to have access to the primary materials. In discussion and correspondence with local housing authorities, advisers will certainly need to make reference to extracts from the HA 2004, to the regulations[2] and the orders made under it, and to the statutory guidance issued on its implementation. Although much of the primary material is available on the internet, those seeking a detailed treatment will need access to a good textbook or handbook such as *Using the Housing Act 2004.*[3]

6.10   Each adviser will also, before invoking action by a local housing authority, need some appreciation of how the local housing authority is structured to utilise its Housing Act powers and enforce statutory requirements. Most local housing authorities have delegated their Housing Act responsibilities to their local environmental health officers (EHOs). Advisers will need to know where the EHOs are based, how they are deployed (whether by geographical patch or by regulatory subject area), when and how they may best be contacted, and what local procedures have been adopted for the exercise of enforcement powers.

6.11   But, perhaps most crucially, the focus must be on what the tenant wishes to achieve and whether involving the local housing authority will help or hinder that objective. If the tenant actually wants to secure rehousing (often from the private rented sector into social rented housing), invoking the Housing Act powers of the local housing authority may prove counter-productive. If the measures taken do actually improve the condition of the tenant's home, that may result in a lowering of priority on any waiting list if priority has been given on account of unsatisfactory housing conditions.[4] Likewise, if it might be possible to have the tenant accepted as homeless because conditions are so poor that it is not reasonable to remain in occupation,[5] the prospects of success with that approach will reduce if conditions are improved. On the other hand, some enforcement activity may result in permanent displacement of the tenant, triggering an obligation on the local housing authority to secure re-housing and possibly pay compensation (see paragraph 6.72 below).

---

2   Particularly the Housing Heath and Safety Rating System (England) Regulations 2005 SI No 3208 (HHSRS Regs 2005).

3   Carr, Cottle and Ormandy, *Using the Housing Act 2004*, Jordans, 2008.

4   HA 1996 s167(2)(c).

5   HA 1996 s175(3).

6.12   Even more important, if the tenant is a private sector tenant with only the limited security of an assured shorthold tenancy (or even an unprotected tenancy) there may be the need to consider the real risk that, if the local housing authority is called in to take action, however minimal, the landlord may retaliate by seeking recovery of possession[6] (or perhaps by seeking an increased rent at the next opportunity). In some cases, this possibility of repossession can be precisely what the tenant in fact wants. If the tenant is in a priority need category for the purposes of homelessness legislation, she or he may be pleased to have the prospect of an unanswerable possession claim generated as the landlord's response to the local housing authority's enforcement of Housing Act powers. If the landlord does 'retaliate' by serving a notice seeking possession under HA 1988 s21 and the tenant does not want to leave, an adviser should check whether (1) the premises are in an unlicensed building which should be licensed under HA 2004 (see paragraph 7.74) or (2) the landlord has failed to register any deposit paid with an approved deposit holder. In either of those two circumstances the landlord will be unable to rely on the HA 1988 s21 notice.[7]

Mobilising the local housing authority

6.13   All local housing authorities are under a statutory duty to keep housing conditions in their area under review, with a view to identifying any action that may be needed under the HA 2004 and related legislation.[8] Sadly, very few local housing authorities interpret this as requiring a systematic inspection of all housing in their districts, whether by a rolling programme of inspections or otherwise. It is often said that they lack the resources to undertake such exercises or deal with the consequences they may throw up. Accordingly, the Secretary of State and the Welsh Assembly Government have reserved powers to give directions to local housing authorities about undertaking their review duties.[9]

6.14   More commonly, individual properties are brought to the attention of local housing authorities by complaints from tenants and their advisers or by others (such as fire authorities and other regulators).

---

6 This concept of 'retaliatory eviction' is described in D Crewe 'The tenant's dilemma Warning: your home is at risk if you dare complain', *Citizens Advice*, June 2007. In some countries it provides a defence to possession proceedings: see, eg, Civil Code of California, section 1942.5.

7 HA 2004 ss75, 98 and s215.

8 HA 2004 s3(1).

9 HA 2004 s3(3).

6.15   If a local housing authority considers, whether by reason of a complaint or as part of its own review of its district, that it would be appropriate for any residential premises to be inspected under the HA 2004 Part 1 (Housing Conditions), the local housing authority must arrange for an inspection to be carried out.[10]

6.16   The statutory Enforcement Guidance[11] rather curiously describes the duty to inspect in these terms:

> While there is not an express duty on local authorities to inspect properties where they think there might be hazards, sections 3 and 4 of the Act, when taken together, imply that an authority should have good reason not to investigate further.[12]

The better view is that where the information that it has received causes the local housing authority to consider that an inspection would be appropriate, then it is under a mandatory statutory duty to inspect.

6.17   The Enforcement Guidance recognizes that requests for inspections may be received at a rate too great for a local housing authority to carry out an immediate inspection on receipt of each request. It suggests that:

> Authorities will need to prioritise inspections and in doing so may have regard to their wider housing strategies and the individual circumstances of the case before them. Local authorities may feel that priority should be given to complaints or referrals from sources such as social services child protection teams, the police, the fire and rescue authority and Warm Front managers, and also from other occupiers, directly or indirectly through local councillors.[13]

6.18   Research has suggested that tenants will benefit from the request for inspection (and any pressure for subsequent action) being channelled through and pursued by an adviser. One report found that:

> a majority of the authorities investigated maintained that it was the presence of a local voluntary housing advice centre or law centre which encouraged strictest compliance with statutory powers.[14]

6.19   Although authorities have substantial powers to tackle unsatisfactory rented housing, a frequent difficulty for advisers is in mobilising an

---

10   HA 2004 s4(2)
11   Communities and Local Government (CLG), *Housing Health and Safety Rating System Enforcement Guidance, Housing Act 2004 Part 1: Housing Conditions* (Enforcement Guidance), February 2006, issued under HA 2004 s9.
12   Enforcement Guidance para [2.6].
13   Enforcement Guidance para [2.8].
14   Hawke and Taylor, 'Compulsory repair of individual physically substandard housing' [1984] *Journal of Social Welfare Law* 129 at 132.

authority into taking any action, even an initial inspection. Accordingly, advisers must be prepared to press the local housing authority forcefully on the need for action. Initially, this may take the form of letters and telephone calls to the local housing authority's EHOs. If the officers fail to act, approaches to local councillors may be necessary.

6.20   If such pressure produces no response within a reasonable period, advisers should consider obtaining and presenting an 'official complaint'. This is *not* a complaint under the local housing authority's ordinary complaints procedure.

6.21   Under HA 2004 s4, a Justice of the Peace (JP) for an area may make an 'official complaint' to the local housing authority that an HA 2004 Category 1 or Category 2 hazard (see paragraph 6.33) is present on the premises. On receipt of such an official complaint, the authority is bound to:

* inspect the premises[15]; and
* consider a report from the inspecting officers if the officers are of the opinion that such a hazard does exist at the premises.[16]

6.22   A similar official complaint may be made by a parish or community council, with like effect.[17] See appendix D for a draft request for an official complaint and the text of a sample complaint.

6.23   It is not procedurally difficult to arrange for such an official complaint to be made. Advisers can draft all necessary documents themselves and need only satisfy a JP, parish council or community council that particular premises have a Category 1 or Category 2 hazard. That can be done by inviting a visit to the premises or by providing a short report (perhaps with photographs).

6.24   As far as official complaints made by JPs are concerned, practice varies considerably in arrangements made at magistrates' courts for dealing with these cases. Most justices' clerks will simply make an *ad hoc* arrangement for a magistrate to be available to consider a paper or personal request. However, the speediest method is to set up an official complaint on an informal basis with a JP known personally to the adviser or tenant or to arrange for a local parish or community councillor to raise the matter at a parish council or community council meeting.

6.25   Unfortunately, the HA 2004 contains no statutory timetable or deadline within which local housing authorities must respond to

---

15   HA 2004 s4(2).
16   HA 2004 s4(6).
17   HA 2004 s4(3).

invitations to inspect or to official complaints. All the Act provides is that where, following an official complaint, the inspecting EHO concludes that there are hazards on the premises he or she must report to the authority without delay and the authority must consider this report as soon as possible.[18]

6.26   If a local housing authority is dilatory in arranging an inspection on request, or in responding to an official complaint (see paragraph 6.22), or even in taking action following an inspection, the tenant will need to bring a claim for judicial review in the Administrative Court (after giving notice by way of a pre-action protocol letter[19]) seeking a mandatory order requiring the local housing authority to act. Experience would suggest that receipt by a local housing authority's legal department of notice of intention to take such proceedings is usually sufficient to galvanize the local housing authority into action.

6.27   In certain cases, particularly those exemplifying systemic delay or inaction, complaint through the local housing authority's own complaints procedure and ultimately to the Local Government Ombudsmen (or, in Wales, the Public Services Ombudsman for Wales) may be worthwhile. Failure by a local housing authority to act when it is known that a property may require statutory action is maladministration, notwithstanding the resource implications for local housing authorities of enforcing the legislation.

6.28   Two common explanations tendered by local housing authority staff for failure to take prompt and effective action are (1) problems securing access to premises and (2) the need to follow elaborate procedures set out in the local enforcement protocol. Advisers should be ready to meet both these points:

1) **Access** Obviously the local housing authority should be furnished with all necessary contact details so that the tenant can give access to the tenanted areas. Beyond that, and for access in relation to common parts and other parts retained by the landlord or let to others, HA 2004 s239(3) gives local housing authority officials powers of entry to premises at any reasonable time. Although 24 hours' notice should usually be given,[20] immediate access may be obtained without notice when it is necessary to ascertain whether certain offences are being committed[21] or where emergency

---

18 HA 2004 ss4(6) and 4(7).
19 Civil Procedure Rules, Pre-action Protocol for Judicial Review.
20 HA 2004 s239(5).
21 HA 2004 s239(6).

remedial action is required.[22] Further detail about procedure for undertaking the inspection, once access is secured, is given in the statutory Operating Guidance.[23]

2) **Procedural delay** Each local housing authority will have adopted its own local policy and procedure code regulating its enforcement activities (including HA 2004 enforcement). Advisers should secure a copy. Appropriate compliance with the published procedures should produce speedy rather than delayed action. Advisers will need to ensure that any time-scales published in the local code are complied with.

6.29   Obviously, at the end of an inspection the tenant and adviser will want to know what has been noted and what action will be taken. Although it is good practice rather than a legislative requirement that copies of inspection records be provided, the Housing Health and Safety Rating System Regulations (HHSRS Regs) 2005 require that inspection records are prepared and retained[24] and the Operating Guidance advises that:

> any inspection should ensure that sufficient clear information is recorded to substantiate the findings and provide the evidence to support the judgments and decisions. That information should be recorded in a form which is logical and readily understandable, in particular by occupiers and owners.[25]

Assessment of the premises

6.30   Under the legislation which the HA 2004 replaced, local housing authority inspectors were looking to see whether premises were 'unfit for human habitation' or 'in substantial disrepair'. As described in chapter 5, such local housing authority inspectors are still using the Environmental Protection Act 1990 to identify whether the premises are a 'statutory nuisance'. However, an inspection and assessment under HA 2004 Part 1 seeks to identify and address what it terms as 'hazards'.

6.31   For the purposes of the HA 2004 a 'hazard' means any risk of *harm* to the *health* or safety of an actual or potential occupier of a

---

22 HA 2004 s40(6).

23 CLG, *HHSRS Operating Guidance – Housing Act 2004: Guidance about inspections and assessment of hazards given under Section 9* (Operating Guidance), February 2006, chapter 4 and annex B.

24 HHSRS Regs 2005 reg 5.

25 Operating Guidance, annex B, para [B2].

dwelling which arises from a *deficiency* in the dwelling or in any *building* or land in the vicinity.[26]

6.32   The Act provides supplementary interpretations on each of the words italicized. Harm includes temporary harm.[27] Health includes mental health.[28] Building includes parts of a building.[29] Deficiency may arise as a result of construction, absence of maintenance, want of repair or otherwise.[30]

6.33   The task of the local housing authority is to identify whether any hazards are present and then to classify them. The most serious hazards are Category 1 hazards. The next most serious hazards are classified as Category 2. In short, if a Category 1 hazard is identified, the local housing authority will be under a duty to act. If a Category 2 hazard is found the local housing authority is under no obligation to act but has the statutory power to do so. In most circumstances, therefore, the tenant will want the assessment to produce a finding that there is a Category 1 hazard.

6.34   The process of assessment is highly technical (arguably, unnecessarily so). It is carried out by local housing authority officials in accordance with detailed provisions in the Act, the regulations made under it, the Operating Guidance, and the Enforcement Guidance, together running over many hundreds of pages.

6.35   In short summary, the process is as follows:

1) An assessment is made of the likelihood of a person suffering any harm as a result of the hazard.
2) An assessment is then made of the range of probable harmful consequences of that hazard.
3) The results of the two strands of assessment are combined to produce a numerical score (using a prescribed methodology).
4) The numerical score is considered against a range of scores grouped into prescribed bands.
5) If the banding is A, B or C, the hazard is a Category 1 hazard.
6) Any lower banding is a Category 2 hazard.

6.36   For the purposes of illustration only, take a property affected by dampness and mould growth. 'Damp and mould growth' is a hazard of a prescribed description if there is a risk of harm from exposure

26 HA 2004 s2(1).
27 HA 2004 s2(4).
28 HA 2004 s2(5).
29 HA 2004 s2(4).
30 HA 2004 s2(1).

to house dust mites, damp, mould or fungal spores.[31] The classes of potentially relevant harmful consequences are listed in the regulations and range from 'death' and 'regular severe pneumonia' in Class 1 to regular serious coughs and colds in Class 4.[32] The task of assessment involves calculation of the degree of risk of harm from the dampness or mould growth and the likely severity of the harm it may cause. That assessment is then reduced to numbers and percentages.[33] The numbers then fall into numerical score ranges identifying the appropriate band for those numbers.[34] If the dampness is assessed as falling in bands A, B or C it will be a Category 1 hazard.[35] If in any other band, it will be a Category 2 hazard.

6.37   Other prescribed descriptions of hazards include virtually all common defects in dwellings including deficient lighting, excess cold, electrical hazards, risks of falling, hygiene problems and many more.[36]

6.38   This short description of the assessment process should suffice to demonstrate that assessment is something of an 'art' as well as a science. It is not a field into which the non-specialist should trespass unguided. Those seeking to delve a little further will greatly benefit from both the House of Commons Library Briefing Note *Housing Health and Safety Rating System (HHSRS) Standard Note: SN/SP/1917*[37] and the *Housing Health and Safety Rating System – Guidance for Landlords and Property Related Professionals.*[38]

6.39   If the tenant or adviser is dissatisfied with an assessment, the best course is to ask for a re-assessment by a second officer of the local housing authority or, failing that, to commission an inspection and report from an independent environmental health expert such as those participating in the Health and Housing Group.[39] Advisers personally taking on the daunting task of seeking to influence the making of, or a revision of, an assessment will need to become

31 HHSRS Regs 2005 reg 3 and Sch 1.
32 HHSRS Regs 2005 reg 2 and Sch 2.
33 HHSRS Regs 2005 reg 6.
34 HHSRS Regs 2005 reg 7.
35 HHSRS Regs 2005 reg 8.
36 HHSRS Regs 2005 Sch 1.
37 Available at: www.parliament.uk/commons/lib/research/briefings/snsp-01917. pdf.
38 CLG, 2006, available at: www.communities.gov.uk/publications/housing/ housinghealth.
39 Health and Housing Group, 37 Star Street, Ware, Hertfordshire SG12 7AA, tel: 01920 465384, fax: 01920 462730.

very familiar with the extensive statutory guidance contained in the Operating Guidance[40] which is the primary negotiating tool on the subject.

Selecting the appropriate action

6.40   Once a local housing authority has made its assessment of the hazard, the results will dictate the necessity for action. If a Category 1 hazard has been identified, the local housing authority must act by taking what it considers to be the most appropriate enforcement action from the available statutory menu of options (considered below). If the assessment has identified a Category 2 hazard, the local housing authority has a power (but is not under a duty) to take enforcement action.

6.41   The tenant or adviser faced with an assessment of only a Category 2 hazard should not assume that no action will be taken. The Enforcement Guidance expressly states that:

> Authorities have a general power under section 7 to take enforcement action in relation to Category 2 hazards. But aside from hazards which are at the upper range, in band D for example, residential property may contain a number of more modestly rated hazards which appear to create a more serious situation when looked at together. There may for example be a minor hazard to health from damp in the bathroom ceiling, plus a moderate fall hazard from a loose but not actually broken handrail on the stairs, plus a food hygiene hazard from old-fashioned preparation facilities in the kitchen. In this example, the hazards do not combine in any measurable way. However the situation in the property may be considered unsatisfactory because the occupants encounter one hazard after another as they move around. Such a property may be perceived as less safe than one with a single high-scoring hazard.
>
> There may be pressure on authorities, particularly from tenants, to act against a number of moderate hazards on the grounds that they present a picture of a run-down property, even though no single hazard is evidence of a serious risk to health and safety. HHSRS is designed to deal with all hazards, no matter how serious, which arise from deficiencies in and around the home. Therefore, *even minor Category 2 hazards need not go un-addressed* if the local authority considers that it is appropriate in all the circumstances to take action in relation to those hazards. Authorities can use their powers to deal with single or multiple Category 2 hazards. More generally, authorities may also

40 See note 23.

decide that they will *always* act on certain bands of Category 2 hazards.[41] [Emphasis added]

6.42   If reference to that Guidance does not produce the desired result from the tenant's or the adviser's perspective where an initial Category 2 assessment has been made, the local housing authority can be asked in any event to exercise its discretion and take action given particular factual circumstances. A local housing authority that responded that it *never* took action in respect of Category 2 hazards notwithstanding the Enforcement Guidance – perhaps on the basis of a lack of resources – would be unlawfully fettering its discretion and should be made subject to judicial review proceedings. If a reasoned explanation is proffered for why no action is going to be taken on the Category 2 hazard in the particular case, the preferred course may be to invite a further inspection (perhaps following a tenant's representations) or to commission an independent inspection and report – with a view to reconsideration and the assessment moving into Category 1.

6.43   The range of enforcement actions available to the local housing authority includes:[42]

- service of a hazard awareness notice;
- issuing an improvement notice;
- making a prohibition order;
- making a demolition order;
- declaring a clearance area;

and (where a Category 1 hazard is present and posing an immediate risk):

- emergency remedial action; or
- making an emergency prohibition order.

6.44   The different alternatives are described more fully below. Advisers seeking to contend for one course of action to be pursued in preference to others should become familiar with the extensive statutory guidance contained in the Enforcement Guidance[43] which is the primary negotiating tool on the subject.

6.45   If only one option is possible, the local housing authority must take that action.[44] In all other circumstances, the local housing authority has a choice to make as to which is the most appropriate course

---

41 Enforcement Guidance paras 4.16–4.17.
42 HA 2004 s5(2).
43 See note 11.
44 HA 2004 s5(3).

of action and it must take the form of action it selects.[45] Although no two options can be pursued at the same time in respect of the same hazard, the choice is not once-and-for-all. If the preferred measure does not secure the desired result, the local housing authority may then try again with the same action or select a different one.[46] In determining which route to pursue, the local housing authority is required to have regard to guidance issued by the Secretary of State or the Welsh Assembly Government. The current guidance is given in the Enforcement Guidance.

6.46   The process of option selection is intended to be both participatory and transparent. On participation, the Enforcement Guidance says:

> Enforcement policies should take account of the circumstances and views of *tenants*, landlords and owners. Policies should also provide for consultation [with] social services, tenancy support, housing needs and housing management officers, *where there are vulnerable occupants*, for the purposes of *agreeing* a suitable approach to hazards.[47] [Emphasis added]

6.47   In respect of transparency, the local housing authority must draw up a statement explaining why a particular option was selected rather than the others.[48] That statement then accompanies any notice served in pursuit of the preferred option.[49]

6.48   Obviously, either tenant or landlord may be disappointed by the selection made by the local housing authority. If the selection results in service of an improvement notice, a prohibition order, an emergency prohibition order or the taking of emergency remedial action 'the person served' (which may include the tenant) has, in each case, a right of appeal to the Residential Property Tribunal. That tribunal can confirm, vary or quash the notice. But the tenant is unlikely to wish to appeal against a notice that has actually been served. More likely, the tenant will wish to have achieved a more compelling form of action than that adopted or a more immediate one.

6.49   The tenant would certainly have sufficient interest in a decision about which course of action to adopt to seek to challenge it by way of judicial review on the usual administrative law principles (eg, failure to take into account some relevant consideration). However, in

---

45   HA 2004 s5(4).
46   HA 2004 s5(5).
47   Enforcement Guidance para [2.16].
48   HA 2004 ss8(2) and 8(3).
49   HA 2004 s8(4).

R v Southwark LBC ex p Cordwell,[50] a case under the pre-HA 2004 regime, the Court of Appeal indicated that relief by way of judicial review would only be granted in exceptional cases. It was for the local housing authority to decide on the most satisfactory course of action for the purposes of the Housing Acts. The court would not conduct a fine analysis of what was, of necessity, an inherently imprecise process of evaluation of relevant material, in order to form a different view from the local housing authority about the reasonableness of one course of action over another.

6.50   If judicial review is not an option, perhaps because the concern is with the manner in which the local housing authority went about reaching its decision rather than with the decision itself, a complaint under the local housing authority's complaints procedure – and ultimately to an ombudsman – may provide satisfaction.

Forms of action and their enforcement

Hazard awareness notice

6.51   This is simply a notice advising the recipient of the presence at the premises of a Category 1 or 2 hazard.[51] It identifies the hazard and suggests action that may be taken. Not least because it requires no action, it carries no right of appeal. Its only usefulness to a tenant may be that:

- it serves as formal notice of disrepair[52] if it identifies disrepair (or its effect) as the hazard;
- it may be presented to the local housing authority as evidence of the presence of adverse conditions justifying greater priority for the tenant on the local housing authority's waiting list for social housing;[53] or
- it may be used as evidence to satisfy the local housing authority that the tenant is homeless because the premises are no longer reasonable to continue to occupy.[54]

6.52   Most tenants and their advisers will have been expecting a firmer response than service of a hazard awareness notice if the problem

---

50   (1994) 27 HLR 594, CA.
51   HA 2004 s28 (Category 1) or s29 (Category 2).
52   On the requirement of notice as a trigger to a landlord's obligations, see paragraph 1.100.
53   See paragraph 6.11.
54   See paragraph 6.11.

at the premises is serious or urgent. For challenges to the decision to serve a hazards awareness notice rather than take stronger action, see paragraph 6.48.

Improvement notice

6.53   This form of notice requires the person on whom it is served to take the form of remedial action specified in the notice that will address the identified hazard or hazards.[55] The notice will spell out the work required, when it must start (not earlier than 28 days after service), when it must finish and what result must be achieved. It must contain statutorily prescribed information, including the rights of appeal.[56]

6.54   For most tenants, this will be the form of action they *most* seek: a clear statutory notice telling the landlord what must be done – whether by way of repair *or* improvement *or both* – to address the present state of the property and containing a timetable for action.

Prohibition order

6.55   Such an order prohibits the use of the premises for such categories of use it describes.[57] Most relevantly, it may prohibit use of the premises as a dwelling. But it is more flexible in scope than that. It may simply operate until some particular facility is installed or it may prohibit occupation only by a specified group (eg, young children). The order will describe the hazard and the action that would need to be taken before the order would be revoked. If the hazard is eliminated (whether by repair, improvement or otherwise) the order must be revoked.

6.56   Depending on the tenant's objective in invoking the local housing authority assessment procedure, this may be a preferred or less desirable outcome. In particular, the effect of the order is to enable the landlord to seek and obtain possession without the tenant being able to rely on the Rent Acts or the HA 1988.[58] Thus, for those in 'priority need' a prohibition order may serve as a passport to homelessness assistance from the local housing authority. Indeed, for even a non-priority tenant the service of a prohibition order may hold out the prospect of rehousing and compensation: see paragraph 6.74.

---

55   HA 2004 ss11 (Category 1 hazards) and 12 (Category 2 hazards).
56   HA 2004 s13.
57   HA 2004 ss20 (Category 1 hazards) and 21 (Category 2 hazards).
58   HA 2004 s33.

Demolition order

6.57　As is evident from its title, this is perhaps the most draconian form of enforcement method available to the local housing authority. The procedures for making, service and enforcement of demolition orders are set out in HA 1985 Part 9 but a complete replacement definition of 'demolition order' is inserted in s265 of that Act by HA 2004 s46 and other extensive amendments to Part 9 are made by other provisions of HA 2004. For obvious reasons, a demolition order cannot be made in respect of a listed building, however serious the hazard.

6.58　A demolition order requires the owner to demolish the premises after they have been vacated and clear the site, and gives rise to powers to demolish in default and recover expenses. A common (and obvious) response on the part of a recipient of a demolition order is to suggest that the building will cease to be used for human habitation and that a prohibition order would suffice. If not satisfied by that response, the local housing authority must take further steps, including service of any necessary notices, leading to the demolition of the property.[59]

6.59　Again, depending on the tenant's objective in invoking the local housing authority's HA 2004 assessment procedure, this may be a preferred or less desirable outcome. In particular, the effect of the order is to enable the landlord to seek and obtain possession without the tenant being able to rely on the Rent Acts or the HA 1988.[60] Thus, for those in 'priority need' a demolition order may serve as a passport to homelessness assistance from the local housing authority. Indeed, for any tenant the service of a demolition order may not be the disaster its name suggests given the rights to compensation and rehousing of occupiers that it carries: see paragraph 6.75.

Declaring a clearance area

6.60　This form of action is available where the local housing authority is satisfied that each residential building in an area (however small) contains a Category 1 hazard and that any non-residential buildings in that area are dangerous.[61] Again, this carries implications for displacement, rehousing and compensation of tenants: see paragraph 6.75.

6.61　Provisions for area clearance require separate treatment and are explored more fully in paragraph 7.2.

59　*R v Epsom and Ewell Corporation ex p RB Property Investments (Eastern)* [1964] 1 WLR 1060; [1964] 2 All ER 832; (1964) 62 LGR 498, DC.

60　HA 1985 s270.

61　HA 1985 s289 as substituted by HA 2004 s47.

Emergency action

6.62   Where the situation discovered by the local housing authority is particularly serious it may decide to take emergency action where there
is 'imminent risk of serious harm'. That action may take the form of
actually entering the premises and setting about emergency remedial works[62] (for which the costs will be recovered from the landlord)
or it may involve the local housing authority serving an emergency
prohibition order immediately preventing further occupation of the
premises.[63]

6.63   Advisers with clients presenting accounts of what are essentially
'life or limb' defects may immediately want to contact the local housing authority and press for emergency remedial action. However, in
a dangerous situation the adviser should never rely on this alone and
should consider making an interim injunction application in civil
proceedings if the defect arises from breach of the landlord's contractual or other obligations to the tenant or other occupier: see paragraph 3.96. As well as having access to the statutory provisions, the
adviser may need to refer the local housing authority's officers to the
appropriate passages in the statutory Enforcement Guidance.

Suspending action

6.64   Having resolved to serve an improvement notice or prohibition order
(as described above) the local housing authority may decide to exercise its powers to suspend the operation of the notice[64] or order.[65] In
such a case the notice or order will be endorsed to identify a specified
time after which the suspension will lapse or an event which would
cause the suspension to lapse.

6.65   While these provisions may sensibly allow time for events to un-
fold (eg, for particular tenants to move in or out), suspension may
prejudice the interests of the occupiers. For example, one appeal by
a tenant to a residential property tribunal has been concerned with

---

62 HA 2004 ss40–42.
63 HA 2004 s43. For example, on 30 July 2009, Calderdale Metropolitan Borough
    Council served an Emergency Prohibition Order, prohibiting use of a privately
    owned residential tower block on the grounds of fire safety. For further details
    see www.lacors.gov.uk/lacors/NewsArticleDetails.aspx?id=22248
64 HA 2004 s14.
65 HA 2004 s23.

the period for which (if at all) a notice should be suspended.[66] In that case, the tenant wanted the suspension lifted or limited so that she would be rendered homeless. Given the seriousness of the hazard, the tribunal agreed to limit the period of suspension.

Purchase of the property

6.66 If the local housing authority considers that it could use premises, containing a Category 1 hazard, for temporary accommodation it may purchase the property instead of making a demolition order or prohibition order.[67] Notwithstanding that the premises are, obviously, a serious hazard and that the local housing authority has earlier resolved that they are best dealt with by being emptied or demolished, the authority is entitled to carry out patch repairs to the purchased property and let it to tenants.[68] Given the state that such a property may be in, even after patch repairs, the ordinary implied covenant of fitness[69] is excluded from any temporary letting of such a property by the local housing authority.[70]

6.67 Premises retained by local housing authorities are notoriously used as 'short life' accommodation or as 'transit' lettings to homeless families, and advisers should guard against this outcome. Any attempt by the authority to retain such purchased property as a permanent part of the housing stock will be struck down by the courts.[71]

Enforcement

6.68 Tenants and their advisers will not be interested merely in the speed with which the local housing authority acts and the form of notice it serves. They will want to secure positive enforcement of the obligations which any notices or orders impose on landlords.

---

66 *Khadija Ali v Bristol CC* [2007] 15 May, Bristol RPT (ref: CH1/00HB/ HPO/2007/0005) helpfully noted with summaries of other prohibition order appeals in *Using the Housing Act 2004* (see note 3), p194.

67 HA 1985 s300(1).

68 HA 1985 s302 (as amended).

69 See paragraph 1.68.

70 HA 1985 s302 (as amended).

71 *Victoria Square Property Co v Southwark LBC* [1978] I WLR 463; [1978] 2 All ER 281, CA; and see *R v Birmingham CDC ex p Sale* (1983) 9 HLR 33; (1983) 82 LGR 69, QBD.

6.69   For example, non-compliance with either an improvement notice[72] or a prohibition order[73] is a criminal offence punishable by a fine of up to £5,000. Where a prohibition order is breached, a daily fine of £20 can be imposed for each day after conviction that the premises are occupied.

6.70   However, prosecution is at the option of the local housing authority and many are not adept at handling such prosecutions. In any event, convictions and fines bring little relief for the tenant.

6.71   What the tenant and his or her adviser need is tough enforcement action by the local housing authority in the face of landlord non-compliance. HA 2004 Schedule 3, read with the terms of the Enforcement Guidance, provides ample scope for local housing authorities to assist tenants in such circumstances – not least by undertaking the necessary works themselves and recovering the costs of doing so directly from the landlord.

Rehousing and compensation for displaced tenants

6.72   To address particularly serious defects in rented premises, the temporary or permanent departure of the tenant(s) will be necessary.

6.73   Where the tenants need to leave temporarily while work is being carried out, the local housing authority could assist with the provision or facilitation of alternative temporary accommodation and perhaps suspend the commencement date for works under an improvement notice until the tenants are temporarily relocated.

6.74   Prohibition orders will (unless suspended) raise a spectre of potentially long-term displacement. No doubt for that reason, the Enforcement Guidance advises that, when considering whether to serve a prohibition order, the local authority should also:

- have regard to the risk of exclusion of vulnerable people from the accommodation;
- ...
- consider the availability of local accommodation for rehousing any displaced occupants. Rehousing in such cases is for the authority to consider, particularly where they may have a duty to provide accommodation. It is unrealistic to expect a landlord owning a small number of properties to re-house the tenant. Landlords have no legal responsibility to re-house their tenants as a result of action by the authority, although the tenant may be able to seek redress; and

72   HA 2004 s30.
73   HA 2004 s32.

- consider whether it is appropriate to offer financial advice or assistance.[74]

6.75   Where a person is permanently displaced from residential accommodation as a result of a prohibition order, demolition notice or area clearance and suitable alternative accommodation is not available, the local housing authority is under a duty to secure that he or she will be provided with other accommodation.[75] However, the duty is for the local housing authority to 'do its best',[76] and it can offer temporary accommodation until permanent accommodation is available.[77] Any permanent accommodation need not be offered on the same terms as those on which the previous accommodation was held. But, the displaced tenant will not need to queue up on the waiting list or bid for properties under the housing allocation scheme adopted by the local housing authority under HA 1996 Part 6. That is because rehousing of such displaced tenants does not count as an allocation at all,[78] enabling displaced tenants to be dealt with by direct offers outside the usual procedures.

6.76   Such displaced occupiers will also usually be entitled to a home loss payment (currently a minimum of £4,700) and compensation for moving and redecoration costs (in the form of a disturbance payment).[79]

Council tenants

6.77   The position of private sector and housing association tenants in relation to the HA 2004 is as described above. However, where a council tenant's landlord is the local housing authority itself, that tenant does not enjoy the full benefits of HA 2004 Part 1. That is because it has been held that since a local housing authority cannot properly serve Housing Act notices upon itself, it cannot fully apply the Housing Acts in respect of its own properties.[80] The High Court has rejected

---

74 Enforcement Guidance, para [5.23].

75 Land Compensation Act 1973 s39.

76 *R v Bristol Corporation v Hendy* [1974] 1 WLR 498; [1974] 1 All ER 1047, CA.

77 *R v East Hertfordshire ex p Smith* (1990) 23 HLR 26, CA.

78 HA 1996 s160(4) and the Allocation of Housing (England) Regulations 2002 SI 3264 reg 3(2); also the Allocation of Housing (Wales) Regulations 2003 SI 239 reg 3(a).

79 Land Compensation Act 1973 Part III (as amended).

80 *R v Cardiff CC ex p Cross* (1983) 6 HLR 1, CA.

the contention that this 'discrimination' against council tenants infringes the Human Rights Act 1998.[81]

6.78   Government guidance, issued over 25 years ago, encouraged local housing authorities to make local arrangements to deal with unsatisfactory council housing.[82] It urged them to introduce and publish arrangements whereby, if a council tenant sought the help of an EHO about the condition of a property which, in the EHO's opinion was such that, if it were private property, action under the Housing Acts would be necessary, the EHO would give notice to the Director of Housing, who would ensure that necessary works were carried out within a reasonable period. It is worth exploring whether any particular local housing authority drew up and retained such quasi-statutory internal arrangements. If not, the council tenant may need to abandon the possibility of any benefit from reliance on HA 2004 and concentrate on pursuing other avenues explored in this book.

6.79   Where council property is *transferred* to a housing association, the local housing authority may invoke its HA 2004 powers and duties almost immediately post-transfer. Indeed, if it has disposed of particularly unsatisfactory housing, the local housing authority may wish to take action while its information about poor conditions is still up to date.

Conclusion

6.80   The procedures for dealing with statutorily unsatisfactory properties outlined in this chapter may sometimes constitute a double-edged sword. They may just as easily leave an owner with vacant possession or a cleared site, as provide the tenant with a repaired home. Even those tenants who would qualify for rehousing by the local housing authority may languish in defective property for substantial periods awaiting an offer of accommodation, notwithstanding the statutory priorities. It is for these reasons that advisers should be pressing local housing authorities to use their available HA 2004 powers early and creatively to tackle bad housing long before it sinks into a condition warranting the prohibition of occupation or even demolition.

---

81 *R(Erskine) v Lambeth LBC* [2003] EWHC 2479 (Admin); December 2003 *Legal Action* 9.

82 Department of the Environment Circular 21/84 para 117, Welsh Office Circular 42/84.

CHAPTER 7

Housing conditions

7.1   **Introduction**

7.2   **Area action**

7.8   Clearance areas

7.11   Renewal areas

7.15   **Asbestos**

7.20   **Asthma**

7.24   **Condensation dampness**

7.27   Express or implied terms of the tenancy

7.29   Landlord and Tenant Act 1985 s11 or Defective Premises Act 1972 s4

7.33   Environmental Protection Act 1990 s82

7.38   Housing Act 2004

7.39   Ombudsmen

7.42   **Dampness (other than condensation)**

7.47   **Dangerous buildings**

7.50   **Dilapidated buildings**

7.54   **Drains and sewers**

7.60   **Fire precautions**

7.64   **Gas safety**

continued

7.70   **Improvements**
7.71   Voluntary improvement
7.73   Compulsory improvement

7.74   **Multi-occupied property (HMOs)**

7.78   **Neighbouring property**

7.82   **Noise**

7.86   **Overcrowding**

7.90   **Refuse**

7.92   **Sanitary installations**

7.95   **Services (gas, water and electricity)**

7.97   **Vandalism**

7.99   **Vermin**

Introduction

7.1   This chapter identifies a range of housing conditions which may give rise to particular problems for tenants and other occupiers of rented housing. Most are related to disrepair and the effects of disrepair. There is no attempt here to go into detail on the wide range of topics covered. The intention is solely to give pointers to more appropriate sources from which specialised and comprehensive information can be obtained.

Area action

7.2   A tenant may find that, if the condition of their home is unsatisfactory, action taken to tackle the adverse conditions is not limited to their particular house or flat but is planned to be undertaken as part of a wider strategy to deal with an *area* containing both that home and other unsatisfactory houses. The rights and obligations of the tenant need to be carefully considered when such broader action is proposed or taken. The following paragraphs address that need.

7.3   Local authorities have long had extensive powers to address areas of unsatisfactory housing in their districts. Although the mass clearance and demolition programmes directed at 'slums' in the 20th century are no longer being adopted, local authorities have retained their powers to address areas of unsatisfactory housing. In the 21st century these are still being used to tackle small residual pockets of the worst housing and to underpin strategies for 'renewal' of particular districts. A tenant's home may be included in one of them.

7.4   The powers to tackle such areas of unsatisfactory housing are in addition to those statutory provisions enabling local authorities to deal with individual unsatisfactory houses and flats through the Housing Act (HA) 2004 (see chapter 6) and the Environmental Protection Act (EPA) 1990 (see chapter 5).

7.5   Where the most appropriate action is the clearance of the unsatisfactory housing, the authority may declare a *clearance area*. On the other hand, if housing can be renovated and rehabilitated, the appropriate action is declaration of a *renewal area*.

7.6   Tenants caught up in such area action may be relieved to see the local housing authority taking steps which may result in them being suitably rehoused and compensated for the loss of their homes. But, of necessity, there is often a long lead-time between the local housing authority deciding to use its powers and the actual work starting.

Meanwhile, the landlord will remain under any contractual obligations to repair, subject to any modification of the extent of those obligations having regard to the reduced 'life expectancy' of the premises: see paragraphs 1.12 and 1.35. The local housing authority might use its other powers described in chapters 5 and 6 of this book to achieve at least patch repairs before rehousing and demolition or renewal are put in hand.

7.7   Those tenants who would rather that a different form of action was undertaken to tackle the poor condition of their home may wish to challenge the local housing authority's decisions in the manner described in paragraph 6.48. They will also want to check carefully that the authority is operating within the strict parameters of the tight statutory conditions about how, for example, clearance areas are to be set up, organized and seen through to completion.[1]

Clearance areas

7.8   A clearance area[2] is an area which is to be cleared of all buildings.[3] A clearance area may be declared if the local housing authority is satisfied that:

- each of the residential buildings in the area contains a Category 1 hazard, and the other buildings (if any) in the area are dangerous or harmful to the health or safety of the inhabitants of the area;[4] or
- the residential buildings in the area are dangerous or harmful to the health or safety of the inhabitants of the area as a result of their bad arrangement or the narrowness or bad arrangement of the streets and the other buildings (if any) in the area are dangerous or harmful to the health or safety of the inhabitants of the area;[5] or
- each of the residential buildings in the area contains a Category 2 hazard, the other buildings (if any) in the area are dangerous or harmful to the health or safety of the inhabitants of the area, and the circumstances of the case are circumstances specified or described in an order made by the Secretary of State.[6]

---

1 Set out in HA 1985 ss298–323.
2 HA 1985 ss289–306 as extensively amended by Housing Act 2004.
3 HA 1985 s289(1).
4 HA 1985 s289(2ZA).
5 HA 1985 s289(2ZB).
6 HA 1985 s 289(2ZC).

The hazards which might constitute Category 1 or Category 2 hazards are described in chapter 6.

7.9 Declaration of a clearance area leads to a process of acquisition by compulsory purchase of the properties in that area and their subsequent demolition. The cleared site is then available to the authority for its own purposes – usually the provision of new housing.

7.10 The housing authority must:

- ensure that owners and occupiers are informed at an early stage and consulted;[7]
- ensure that it has sufficient resources to carry the scheme through and to accommodate any displaced persons who are unable to secure their own accommodation;[8] and
- pay compensation to displaced owners and some occupiers.[9]

Renewal areas

7.11 Since April 1990,[10] local authorities have had powers to take area action in respect of unsatisfactory housing through the declaration of renewal areas. The statutory arrangements are in the Local Government and Housing Act (LGHA) 1989 Part VII as since substantially modified by statutory order.[11]

7.12 A renewal area may be declared where a local housing authority is satisfied that the living conditions in an area within their district, consisting primarily of housing accommodation, are unsatisfactory, and that those conditions can most effectively be dealt with by declaring the area to be a renewal area.[12] Before making such a declaration the authority must consider a report which has reviewed:

- the living conditions in the area concerned;
- the ways in which those conditions may be improved (whether by the declaration of a renewal area or otherwise);
- the powers available to the authority (including powers available apart from the 1989 Act) if the area is declared to be a renewal area;

---

7 HA 1985 s289(2B) and (2F).
8 HA 1985 s289(4).
9 Land Compensation Acts 1961 and 1973.
10 The commencement of Local Government and Housing Act 1989 Part VII.
11 In particular, the Regulatory Reform (Housing Assistance) (England and Wales) Order 2002 SI No 1860.
12 LGHA 1989 s89(1).

- the authority's detailed proposals for the exercise of those powers during the period that the area will be a renewal area (if so declared);
- the cost of those proposals;
- the financial resources available, or likely to be available, to the authority (from whatever source) for implementing those proposals; and
- the representations (if any) made to the authority in relation to those proposals.[13]

7.13   A programme of public consultation is also required before declaration. Declaration vests the local authority with considerable additional powers over housing in the area (including the right compulsorily to acquire and repair property) and may attract additional central government and privately funded financial help to the area. The powers are to be exercised with the objects of:

- securing the improvement or repair of the premises, either by the authority or by a person to whom they propose to dispose of the premises;
- the proper and effective management and use of the housing accommodation, either by the authority or by a person to whom they propose to dispose of the premises comprising the accommodation; and
- the well-being of the persons for the time being residing in the area.[14]

7.14   **References**

- *Encyclopedia of Housing Law and Practice*, Sweet & Maxwell.
- R Burridge and D Ormandy (eds), *Unhealthy Housing: Research, Remedies and Reform*, Routledge & Chapman, 1993, chapters 14–16.

Asbestos

7.15   Asbestos, and building materials containing asbestos, have been used in the construction and modernisation of housing for decades. Asbestos and its derivatives may be found, for example, in insulation boards used for panels or in the form of sprayed-on insulation

---

13   LGHA 1989 s89(3).
14   LGHA 1989 s93(3).

coverings, as well as in some older types of textured paint. It was heavily used in system-built blocks of flats where industrialized building techniques were employed and has been extensively applied in pipe-lining.

7.16   It is now widely recognised that asbestos fibres released in air may prove prejudicial to human health. Indeed, a contractor who, ignorant of the health risk involved, carries out remedial work resulting in dangerous levels of asbestos contamination, will be held to have failed to work with reasonable skill and care.[15] It was reasonably foreseeable as early as 1925 that exposure to asbestos dust could result in pulmonary injury, including mesotheliaoma.[16]

7.17   Tenants with homes containing asbestos or suspected asbestos will be best advised initially to contact their local authority environmental health officers (EHOs): see paragraph 6.10. According to the circumstances, it may be possible to take action to cause the removal of the asbestos by the landlord. Asbestos fibres loose in air as a result of disrepair are very probably prejudicial to health and accordingly action may be taken by a local housing authority, either under the EPA 1990 (see chapter 5) or under the HA 2004 by treating the situation as a 'hazard' (see chapter 6). Additionally, where spores are being released from damaged and unrepaired parts of the premises, the tenant may have a direct remedy against the landlord under their repairing obligations (see chapters 1 and 2). Technical support and assistance may be available from the London Hazards Centre.[17]

7.18   However, the simple presence of asbestos in some part of a component in the construction of a building will not normally impose an obligation on the landlord in contract or tort unless and until it falls into disrepair.

7.19   **References**

- Asbestos Information Centre Ltd, 5a The Maltings, Stowupland Road, Stowmarket, Suffolk IP14 5AG. www.aic.org.uk.
- R Widdison, 'Asbestos in the home', October 1982 *LAG Bulletin* 114.
- *Working with Asbestos in Buildings*, Health & Safety Executive, October 2004.
- *Asbestos In The Home – Part I*, London Hazards Centre, 1997.

15 *Barclays Bank v Fairclough Building Ltd (No 2)* [1995] 44 Con LR 35; [1995] 76 BLR 1, CA and see the Control of Asbestos Regulations 2006 SI No 2739.
16 *Margereson v J W Roberts Ltd* [1996] PIQR P358; (1996) *Times* 17 April, CA.
17 London Hazards Centre, Hampstead Town Hall, 213 Haverstock Hill, London NW3 4QP. www.lhc.org.uk.

- *Asbestos removal.* A useful page on the direct gov website, enabling tenants to arrange an asbestos inspection, with links to other literature: www.direct.gov.uk/en/HomeAndCommunity/Planning/ DoingWorkYourself/DG_10022562.

Asthma

7.20   The link between asthma and poor housing conditions, particularly damp, has historically been a matter of some scientific controversy. Much of that controversy is explored in the literature mentioned in the references below. However, the link between house dust mites (which thrive in mouldy conditions) and asthma is now much more firmly established – a fact also explored in the sources referenced below.

7.21   Nevertheless, unless the landlord or other defendant admits the causal connection between disrepair or other housing conditions and the occupier's asthma, expert evidence will be required.

7.22   If liability is established, helpful guidance on the appropriate levels of compensation to be awarded where asthma has been caused or made worse are set out in the Judicial Studies Board's *Guidelines for the Assessment of General Damages in Personal Injury Cases*.[18] Illustrations of awards made by the UK courts are included in chapter 8 at paragraph 8.82. Significantly higher awards have been made to tenants by US courts.[19]

7.23   **References**

- Asthma UK, Summit House, 70 Wilson Street, London EC2A 2DB. www.asthma.org.uk.
- Stirling Howieson, *Housing and Asthma*, Taylor & Francis, 2005.
- I J Williamson, C J Martin, G McGill, R D Monie and A G Fennerty, 'Damp housing and asthma: a case-control study' and subsequent citations of that paper listed at: thorax.bmj.com/cgi/ content/abstract/52/3/229.
- D P Strachan, 'Damp housing and childhood asthma: validation of reporting of symptoms', *British Medical Journal*, 1988, 297:1223– 1226 (12 November), and subsequent citations of that paper listed at www.bmj.com/cgi/content/abstract/297/6658/1223.

---

18 9th edn, Oxford University Press, 2008.
19 *New Haverford Partnership v Stroot* [2001] 772 Atl Rep (2nd) 792 Del; November 2003 *Legal Action* 13, Supreme Court of Delaware.

- S Lau et al, 'Early exposure to house dust mite and cat allergens and development of childhood asthma, a cohort study', *The Lancet*, vol 356, pp 1392–1397, October 2000.
- D C Machado, D Horton, P T Peachell and B A Helm, 'Potential allergens stimulate the release of mediators of the allergic response from cells of mast cell lineage in the absence of sensitisation with antigen-specific IgE', *European Journal of Immunology*, 1996, 26, pp 2972–2980.
- *Mould fungal spores – their effects on health and the control, prevention and treatment of mould growth in dwellings*, Institution of Environmental Health Officers, 1985.
- D P Strachan, 'Dampness, Mould Growth and Respiratory Diseases in Children' in R Burridge and D Ormandy (eds), *Unhealthy Housing: Research, Remedies and Reform*, Routledge & Chapman, 1993.
- D Ormandy (ed), *Housing and health in Europe*, Routledge, 2009, chapter 6 'Potential sources of indoor air pollution and asthma'.

Condensation dampness

7.24   The presence of acute condensation dampness brings with it conditions of mould growth, excessive humidity and, often, insect infestation. The grave effects of these conditions on the health and well-being of tenants have now been extensively documented.

7.25   In very basic terms, condensation dampness arises when a dwelling is incapable of dealing with normal levels of water vapour due to lack of insulation, lack of ventilation, inadequate heat input, or a combination of such factors. Its presence is observed as condensed water on cooled surfaces, mould spores, damp wall coverings and plaster, infestation by house mites and destruction of soft furnishings in severe cases.

7.26   For some time tenants and their advisers have been using legal remedies among others to seek redress in such circumstances. The following short summary deals with various legal remedies and the condensation dampness problem.

Express or implied terms of the tenancy

7.27   If the landlord has agreed to keep the premises 'fit to live in' or 'in good condition', or used similar general wording, those express terms may be broken where dampness and mould growth arise from condensation and cause the premises to be in a poor condition or render them unfit to live in (see paragraph 1.15).[20]

7.28   If the premises were let furnished or provided under licence, the fact that they were 'doomed' to suffer from condensation dampness from the outset may amount to breach of the implied warranty of fitness (see paragraphs 1.38 and 1.44).

Landlord and Tenant Act 1985 s11 or Defective Premises Act 1972 s4

7.29   The more traditional contractual and common law remedies against landlords (see chapters 1 and 2) are difficult to apply in condensation cases because of the need to show that the cause of the condensation is specific disrepair to the structure or fabric of a building, rather than a design problem or inherent defect. Of course, if condensation dampness is a consequence of disrepair (eg, disrepair which has allowed the incursion of moisture or prevents ventilation) then a remedy is available in a claim for breach of the repairing obligation.[21]

7.30   In *Quick v Taff Ely BC*[22] the Court of Appeal decided that the Landlord and Tenant Act (LTA) 1985 s11 cannot provide a remedy for a tenant suffering the effects of condensation dampness unless there is actual disrepair to the structure or exterior of the dwelling. Where such disrepair *can* be shown (eg, because the condensation has corrupted woodwork or caused plaster to crumble) it will become actionable.[23] See further, paragraphs 1.18–1.23.

7.31   Because the duty in Defective Premises Act (DPA) 1972 s4 in turn springs from an obligation to repair or maintain the property, it too is of limited usefulness in the absence of actual damage to the structure or 'fabric' of the property.[24] See further, paragraphs 2.37 and 2.46.

7.32   If work to rectify condensation fails to eradicate it, a possible action may lie for breach of DPA 1972 s1 in relation to that work

---

20 *Welsh v Greenwich LBC* (2001) 33 HLR 40, CA; *Johnson v Sheffield CC* August 1994 *Legal Action* 16, Sheffield County Court; *Arnold v Greenwich LBC* [1998] May *Legal Action* 21, Woolwich County Court. See paragraph 1.15.

21 *Lloyd v Rees* [1996] CLY 3725, Pontypridd County Court.

22 [1986] QB 809

23 *Staves v Leeds CC* (1991) 23 HLR 107, CA; *Switzer v Law* [1998] 7 CL 380, Southport County Court.

24 *Abdullah v South Tyneside BC* September 1987 *Legal Action* 12, South Shields County Court.

(see paragraph 2.23). If the dwelling was negligently designed or constructed so as to generate condensation, an action may lie in negligence against the landlord or designer or builder (see paragraph 2.5).

Environmental Protection Act 1990 s82

7.33   Public health and environmental protection legislation has been long recognised as a satisfactory means of securing redress, because acute condensation dampness invariably gives rise to conditions which are 'prejudicial to health' and thus a statutory nuisance (see chapter 5). The period between 1975 and 1980 saw extensive use of Public Health Act (PHA) 1936 s99 (and now EPA s82) proceedings in condensation cases in the magistrates' courts. Indeed, by 1980/81 it had become well recognised that dampness was prejudicial to health and that condensation dampness with associated mould growth was capable of potential or actual injury to health.[25]

7.34   However, in order to establish a successful prosecution, the tenant must be able to show that (unless the problem arises from structural defects) the conditions are the responsibility of the landlord. Thus in *Dover DC v Farrar*[26] a conviction was quashed on appeal where the local authority landlord successfully established that the dwellings concerned had been constructed by it in accordance with prevailing standards and that, with sufficient use of the supplied heating system, the provision made for ventilation and insulation was adequate to avoid condensation. The fact that fuel price increases subsequent to construction meant that the tenants were unable to use the heating system was held not to be the responsibility of the landlord authority.

7.35   Regrettably, the *Dover* case has been used by local authorities and other landlords to persuade tenants, their advisers and magistrates that s82 proceedings could not successfully be founded on condensation dampness. In fact, the contrary is the case. The *Dover* decision is clear authority for the proposition that landlords can be prosecuted in relation to condensation dampness. Later cases have shown that, with the careful use of specialist written evidence and expert witnesses (especially independent EHOs), it is possible to prove in most condensation cases that the dampness does arise from the landlord's

25   *Patel v Mehtab* (1982) 5 HLR 78, QBD; *Dover DC v Farrar* (1982) 2 HLR 32, DC; and Dept. of Environment Circular 6/90 Annex 5.
26   (1982) 2 HLR 32.

failure to get the condensation equation (heat/moisture/ventilation/insulation) right.[27]

7.36   In *Tower Hamlets LBC v GLC*,[28] the Divisional Court dismissed an appeal against a conviction in relation to condensation dampness. The tenants and prosecuting authority claimed that the dwellings were insufficiently ventilated and insulated and that the inability of the flats to cope with normal moisture led to condensation for which the landlord was responsible. Considering the *Dover* case, Griffiths LJ said he did not read it as authority for the proposition that tenants should be required to use abnormal quantities of fuel to avert condensation. The court held that:

> a landlord is required to apply his mind to the necessity of ventilation and, if need be, to insulation and heating. The landlord must provide a combination of these factors to make a house habitable for the tenant.

7.37   Applying these authorities, the Divisional Court in *Birmingham DC v Kelly and Others*[29] was able to uphold convictions even though the landlord was not in breach of any contractual or other obligation to repair. Liability for the condensation dampness was established from the evidence that there was some default by the council in relation to the design of the premises which caused the condensation difficulties and thus the mould.

Housing Act 2004

7.38   Condensation dampness (or indeed any other form of dampness) may give rise to a 'hazard' for the purposes of HA 2004 Part 1. The action that may be taken in such circumstances is described in chapter 6.

Ombudsmen

7.39   The Local Government Ombudsmen[30] have regularly accepted that failures to investigate properly or to resolve complaints of condensation dampness amount to maladministration. Their reports

---

27   *Lawton v East Devon DC* (1982) unreported, noted at *Roof* July/August 1982 p28; *McGourlick v Renfrew DC* noted at [1982] *Scolag* 182 and [1986] *Scolag* 83, Paisley Sheriff Court.

28   (1983) 15 HLR 54, DC, applied in *Law v Hillingdon LBC* December 1989 *Legal Action* 16, Isleworth Crown Court.

29   (1985) 17 HLR 572, QBD.

30   See paragraphs 3.21–3.25. In Wales, the Public Services Ombudsman for Wales.

frequently contain not only strong recommendations for compensatory payments but also useful guidance on the proper approach to be adopted by councils in condensation cases. See, for example, the report on Investigation 746/1/84.[31] In a more recent complaint concerning Bristol City Council, the Local Government Ombudsman found that the council had failed, over a very long period, to carry out proper investigations in response to a tenant's complaints about her housing conditions. As a result, the family suffered damp and cold conditions for around seven years. The ombudsman said:

> The reality is that between 2001 and 2007 the only work completed by the council to mitigate the problems caused by damp/condensation was to install two extractor fans. Given the circumstances, that was wholly unacceptable.

He recommended over £8,000 compensation.[32]

7.40   The Independent Housing Ombudsman can consider similar complaints from the tenants of housing associations: see paragraph 3.21.

7.41   **References**

- T Hutton, 'Condensation' in *The Building Conservation Directory*, 2004.
- British Standards Institution BS 5250, *Code of Practice for the control of condensation in buildings*, 2002. (Examines the causes and effects of condensation in buildings. Recommendations and guidance are given for heating, ventilation and construction to control condensation.)
- Chartered Institution of Buildings Services Engineers, *IBSE Guide* section A10: 'Moisture transfer and condensation'.
- D Ormandy, *The Law of Statutory Nuisance*, Chartered Institute of Environmental Health, 1997.
- *Tackling condensation: a guide to the causes of, and remedies for, surface condensation and mould in traditional housing*, Building Research Establishment, 1991.
- D Watkinson, 'Legal remedies for condensation damp in the home', November 1985 *Legal Action* 153 and April 1986 *Legal Action* 49.
- 'Condensation', *BRE Digest* 110, 1972 edition.
- DoE, *Condensation in dwellings Part 2: Remedial measures*, HMSO, 1971.

---

31 Noted at March 1986 *Legal Action* 33.
32 *Investigation Report 06B05370*, December 2007.

■ MoPB&W, *Condensation in dwellings Part 1: Design guide*, HMSO, 1970.

■ T Markus, 'Cold, Condensation and Housing Poverty' in R Burridge and D Ormandy (eds), *Unhealthy Housing: Research, Remedies and Reform*, Routledge & Chapman, 1993.

Dampness (other than condensation)

7.42   This common problem still affects many tenants. It may take the form of penetrating dampness, construction damp, rising damp or condensation (see above).

7.43   But not all dampness in housing will be *caused* by disrepair or be the *result* of disrepair. A home may become damp by accidental flooding by occupiers or neighbours (bath and sink overflows and the like) or by the introduction and retention of too much water vapour in the home (eg, where the ventilation is obstructed by the tenant to help keep the home warm but with the effect that water vapour normally generated cannot escape). If all that a tenant can establish is that a home is 'damp' that will not necessarily fix the landlord with any liability.[33]

7.44   However, where dampness is caused by disrepair or itself causes disrepair, as has been shown in earlier chapters of this book, legal remedies for tenants are available both under contractual and common law rights (chapters 1 and 2). The enforcement of statutory obligations under the Environmental Protection and Housing Acts (see chapters 5 and 6) is not so much concerned with the reason for the presence of dampness but with the effect of it.

7.45   The parliamentary review of the dampness problem carried out 25 years ago by the Scottish Grand Committee[34] contains much information still useful today.

7.46   **References**

■ D Ormandy (ed), *Housing and health in Europe*, Routledge, 2009, chapter 7 'Damp Mould and Health'.

■ Jonathan Hetreed, *The Damp House: A Guide to the Causes and Treatment of Dampness*, Crowood Press, 2008.

■ A Oliver, *Dampness in buildings*, Blackwell Publishing, second edition, 1996.

33 *Southwark LBC v McIntosh* [2002] 08 EG 164, February 2002 *Legal Action* 22, ChD; *Ball v Plymouth CC* [2004] EWHC 134 (QB).

34 Report of the Scottish Grand Committee, House of Commons *Dampness in housing* (papers 206i and 206ii, session 1983/4).

- E G Gobert and T A Oxley, *Dampness in Buildings: Diagnosis, Treatment, Instruments*, Butterworth, second edition, 1994.
- S D Platt et al, 'Damp Housing, mould growth and symptomatic health state' *British Medical Journal*, 24 June 1989.
- S Hunt, 'Damp and Mouldy Housing: an holistic approach' in R Burridge and D Ormandy (eds), *Unhealthy Housing: Research, Remedies and Reform*, Routledge & Chapman, 1993.
- BRE, *Dampness: one week's complaints in five local authority areas*, HMSO, 1982.

Dangerous buildings

7.47 Not infrequently a property will be in such poor condition as to represent a danger not only to those within it but also to people using adjacent streets. Once notified of such a situation a local authority may either take urgent remedial action itself or may follow a procedure requiring the owner to remedy the dangerous condition or demolish the building (Building Act (BA) 1984 ss77–79, reproduced in appendix A).

7.48 No express provision is made for the removal or compensation of any tenant although rehousing may, according to the circumstances, be achieved under the HA 1996 Part 7 (Homelessness). Tenants displaced in such circumstances would have a remedy against the landlord arising from the breach of repairing obligation which led to the dangerous condition of the property.

7.49 **References**

- A Arden and M Partington, *Housing Law* (looseleaf), Sweet & Maxwell, chapter 9 'Obstructive, dangerous and dilapidated buildings'.

Dilapidated buildings

7.50 A property in very serious disrepair may fall within the statutory definition 'dilapidated', ie, one which by reason of its ruinous or dilapidated condition is seriously detrimental to the amenities of the neighbourhood (BA 1984 s79, reproduced in appendix A).

7.51 When notified of a property in such condition the local housing authority for the area may require the owner either to repair or restore the property or demolish it. In default of compliance, the local authority may itself undertake the necessary work.

7.52   Again, in addition to the tenant's ordinary remedies in contract and tort, a building in a state that requires intervention under the BA 1984 might also justify a claim for an injunction (see paragraph 3.96).

7.53   **References**

■ A Arden and M Partington *Housing Law*, Sweet & Maxwell, chapter 9.

Drains and sewers

7.54   A 'drain' means a pipeline used for the drainage of one building, while a 'sewer' means a pipeline used for the drainage of more than one building. The law does not distinguish between foul and surface water sewers. A public sewer is a sewer vested in the local water authority.[35]

7.55   Tenants may be caused serious inconvenience by the blockage, disrepair or overflow of drains as a result of landlord failure to repair or maintain them. Indeed, where the landlord is a public authority (registered social landlord or local authority) or a water authority, the tenant may have a claim in nuisance, negligence or possibly under the Human Rights Act 1998 if their home is flooded by water or sewage from drains or sewers (see paragraph 2.56). The water and housing authority might also be responsible in nuisance or negligence even if it is not the landlord.[36]

7.56   LTA 1985 s11 makes landlords responsible for keeping in repair the structure and exterior of the dwelling including 'drains': see paragraph 1.71. It seems logical to assume that the draftsman meant that a drain forms part of a dwelling up to the point it enters the public sewer.

7.57   Local authorities have extensive powers to require owners (and occupiers) to take remedial action where a drain or sewer is prejudicial to health or a nuisance (BA 1984 ss21 and 59). In default, the council may itself carry out the necessary work and recover its costs thereafter.

7.58   Similarly, a local housing authority may by notice secure the performance of small repairs if a drain or sewer is insufficiently maintained or repaired and may undertake works (PHA 1961 ss17 and 22).[37]

---

35 *Dear v Thames Water* (1994) 33 Con LR 43, QBD.
36 *Dear v Thames Water* (1994) 33 Con LR 43, QBD.
37 *Rotherham MBC v Dodds* [1986] 1 WLR 1367; [1986] 2 All ER 867, CA.

7.59 **References**

■ S H Bailey *Garner's Laws of sewers and drains*, Shaw & Sons, 2004.

Fire precautions

7.60 The powers available to tenants to require landlords to take fire precautions are poor. Although contractual and common law rights (see chapters 1 and 2) will usually require a landlord to maintain an existing fire escape or stairway retained in his or her possession, they cannot be used to compel the landlord to provide such facilities.

7.61 The tenant may therefore need to rely primarily on the willingness of the local fire authority and housing authority to intervene. The law relating to their respective responsibilities is well beyond the scope of this book. A good starting point is provided by the omnibus Regulatory Reform (Fire Safety) Order 2005.[38] That has produced some overlap between the responsibilities of fire authorities and of local housing authorities (under their HA 2004 powers discussed in chapter 6). The resulting landscape of powers and duties in relation to fire safety is well mapped out in *Housing – fire safety: Guidance on fire safety provisions for certain types of existing housing*.[39]

7.62 Note that local councils still have power to require fire precautions to be taken in certain flats and tenements of more than two storeys (BA 1984 s72).

7.63 **References**

■ BSI, *Fire Safety in Buildings*, BS 9999.
■ *Housing – fire safety: Guidance on fire safety provisions for certain types of existing housing*, LACORS, 2008.
■ *Berg v Trafford BC* (1988) 20 HLR 47, CA.
■ *Zenca and Others v Pouyiouros* September 1989 *Legal Action* 24, QBD.

Gas safety

7.64 One of the most potentially dangerous aspects of tenanted residential premises is the gas supply and the condition of facilities for using that supply (fires, boilers, cookers, etc).

38 2005 SI No 1541.
39 Local Authority Co-ordinators of Regulatory Services (LACORS), 2008.

7.65   The landlord may be under an express contractual obligation to keep that supply and the facilities in good repair and working order. If not, the provisions of LTA s11 will usually apply. They require the landlord to keep the installations for the supply of gas in repair and proper working order and also the installations for space heating and heating water (which may also depend on a gas supply). See generally chapter 1 for contractual obligations.

7.66   But legislation imposes obligations on landlords which go beyond the requirements of any contract. Under the Gas Safety (Installation and Use) Regulations 1998[40] reg 36, a landlord is responsible for making sure that any gas appliances, gas piping and flues are well maintained and safe. The obligation arises from the granting of: any periodic tenancy; any statutory tenancy; any tenancy of a fixed term less than seven years; and any licence to occupy. It requires that at least an annual safety inspection is carried out by a qualified gas servicing engineer. Until 2009 that meant a CORGI registered engineer. Since 2009 the approved registration organisation has been 'Gas Safe Register'.

7.67   Failure by the landlord to arrange an inspection is likely to result in any court dealing with a tenant's subsequent claim for damages holding that the landlord 'ought to have known' (for the purposes of DPA 1972 s4) of any defect which would have been picked up on an annual inspection: see paragraph 2.41. For an example of the application of LTA s11 and DPA 1972 in a carbon monoxide poisoning case arising from a faulty gas appliance see *Sykes v Harry and Another*.[41]

7.68   Although the regulations are enforced by the Health and Safety Executive (who may prosecute the landlord), the tenant may also want to involve the EHOs of the local housing authority, who may be satisfied that the state of any defect relating to gas is such as to render the premises a 'hazard' requiring action under HA 2004 (see chapter 6). In Autumn 2008, the Heath and Safety Executive issued a safety alert about particular gas central heating appliances (boilers) – concealed flue boiler systems – that are located on internal walls. These types of boilers may have a flue that runs through the ceiling void (the space between the ceiling and floor of the room above), within a purpose built enclosure/duct, or even through another property and may give rise to risks of gas poisoning.[42]

---

40 1998 SI No 2451.
41 [2001] EWCA Civ 167; [2001] QB 1014, CA.
42 'Safety Alert: Gas boilers – flues in voids'. HSE, 2 October 2008 and see M Hilditch, 'Hidden Danger' [2009] *Inside Housing* 13 November 2009, p21.

7.69 **References**

- *Landlords – A guide to landlords' duties: Gas Safety (Installation and Use) Regulations 1998,* Health and Safety Executive (HSE), March 2009.
- *Gas safety FAQs – tenants,* HSE, available at: www.hse.gov.uk/gas/domestic/faqtenant.htm.
- *Gas safety FAQs – landlords and letting agents,* HSE, available at: www.hse.gov.uk/gas/domestic/faqlandlord.htm.

Improvements

7.70　This book is primarily concerned with housing in need of repair rather than improvement. However, in a variety of circumstances either landlord or tenant may wish to improve property in addition to, or in place of, carrying out repairs.

Voluntary improvement

7.71　A secure tenant has a statutory right to carry out certain improvements subject to the consent of the landlord.[43] Other tenants have only such rights as are contained in their tenancy agreements.

7.72　　Where the landlord wishes to carry out improvement to occupied property the ability to do so is governed by the terms of letting or any further agreement entered into by the landlord and tenant.[44] The landlord does not otherwise have the right to enter and carry out improvements, except perhaps where they relate to health and safety work necessary to prevent injury.[45]

Compulsory improvement

7.73　Local housing authorities have long had power to secure certain works from the landlords of property in poor condition without being troubled whether the work required is of 'repair' or of 'improvement'. That is as true of the statutory schemes set out in the EPA 1990 (see chapter 5) and the HA 2004 (see chapter 6) as it was in relation to earlier similar schemes.

43　HA 1985 ss97–98.
44　*McDougall v Easington DC* [1989] 1 EGLR 93; (1989) 21 HLR 596, CA.
45　*McGreal v Wake* (1984) 13 HLR 107, CA; *McAuley v Bristol CC* [1992] QB 134, CA; *Dunn v Bradford MDC* [2002] EWCA Civ 1137; [2003] HLR 15, CA.

Multi-occupied property

7.74 Some of the worst instances of landlord neglect and disrepair are to be found in properties subject to more than one tenancy or occupancy, eg, houses converted into bedsits, hostels, hotels and houses converted into two or more flats. These are generally described as houses in multiple occupation (HMOs).[46] Although these are the most obvious types of multi-occupied property, any house or flat is in multiple occupation if it contains two or more households.

7.75 Local authorities have long had extensive powers to control the provision of facilities in such properties, the number of occupants and the means of escape from fire. In addition, the local authority has powers to intervene where there are problems of disrepair, lack of maintenance and other unsatisfactory aspects to the state of the property. In each case, a local housing authority can do the work necessary to bring the property up to standard if the manager of the HMO will not do so. Failure to comply may result in prosecution and the authority may do the necessary works in default and recoup its costs. Ultimately, the authority may compulsorily purchase the property.

7.76 The majority of these powers are now to be found in the specific provisions of the HA 2004 (relating both to standards in HMOs and to the licensing of HMOs). Tenants experiencing problems in HMOs should first ask the local housing authority whether the HMO has a licence (because if it should but does not, rent paid is recoverable and possession cannot be obtained from a shorthold tenant relying on notice given under HA 1988 s21).[47] They should at the same time invite an inspection by an EHO with a view to use of the HA 2004 powers.

7.77 **References**

- Communities and Local Government (CLG), *Licensing of Houses in Multiple Occupation in England: A guide for landlords and managers,* April 2007.
- CLG, *Licensing of Houses in Multiple Occupation in England: A guide for tenants,* April 2007.
- D Ormandy and R Burridge, *Environmental Health Standards in Housing,* 1988, chapter 6 'Houses in Multiple occupation' (for an historic account).

---

46 For the definition of HMO see HA 2004 ss254–258.
47 HA 2004 ss73–74 (rent repayment orders) and s75 notices.

Neighbouring property

7.78 The effects of disrepair are often felt beyond their immediate location. The ramifications of a structure or installation out of repair may lead to injury to health or damage to neighbouring property. Indeed, one of the most common sights in areas of high density housing is the scarring effect on a number of properties of a defective lavatory cistern overflow in an upperfloor flat.

7.79 If the neighbouring property or building in disrepair is owned by the landlord, the tenant may be able to take action under one or more of the implied covenants contained in all letting agreements including: (a) the covenant to repair common parts; (b) the covenant of quiet enjoyment; and (c) the covenant of non-derogation from grant (see chapter 1).

7.80 If the property is in other hands, the neighbouring tenant may involve the EHO of the local housing authority for the area – either on the basis that the property is a statutory nuisance (see chapter 5) or that it is dangerous or dilapidated (see paragraphs 7.47–7.53) or that it is a 'hazard' (see chapter 6).

7.81 It is possible to apply to a court for an order permitting access on to neighbouring land in order to carry out works to the dominant land which are reasonably necessary to preserve the whole or part of the dominant land and which cannot be carried out, or would be substantially more difficult to carry out, without access.[48]

Noise

7.82 Very substantial distress and inconvenience may be caused by noise nuisance. In modern-built or converted housing, this is commonly exacerbated by the lack of good insulation of party walls or between flats.

7.83 Often the tenant will be able to restrain the continuation of any *excessive or unreasonable* noise by using the procedures under the EPA 1990 Pt III (see chapter 5) or by an action in private nuisance (see chapter 2 at para 2.13). If the noise results from disrepair, eg, broken floor boards, tenants can take civil proceedings in the usual way.[49]

---

48 Access to Neighbouring Land Act 1992; *Williams v Edwards* [1997] CLY 561, Cardiff County Court.
49 *Guinan* v *Enfield LBC* June 1990 *Legal Action* 16, Westminster County Court.

7.84   If the source of noise is simply normal usage of a property, the most appropriate challenge might be thought to be one addressed to the landlord responsible for letting a dwelling insufficiently insulated against normal domestic noise. However, for the reasons explained in chapter 2 the landlord will not usually be liable in tort (see paragraph 2.3) nor will he or she be in breach of the covenant of quiet enjoyment (paragraph 1.49).[50]

7.85   There may, however, also be a remedy under the DPA 1972 s1 if the noise results from negligent building or conversion works (see chapter 2).

Overcrowding

7.86   Experience suggests a degree of correlation between properties in disrepair and those which landlords permit to become overcrowded. Statutory limits are imposed on the maximum number of persons permitted to occupy a dwelling and enforcement is the responsibility and duty of the local authority for the area (HA 1985 Part X). Furthermore, overcrowding can contribute to premises becoming a 'hazard' for the purposes of HA 2004 (see chapter 6).

7.87   Overcrowding under the HA 1985 is still measured by two standards, and failure to comply with either or both will render the overcrowding illegal. The first standard is based on the number of rooms, the number of occupants and their ages. The second is based on the size and number of rooms, the occupiers and their ages. The statutory code permits strictly limited exceptions. It is woefully inadequate as a modern standard and this has been recognized by the Government. Measures contained in HA 2004 s216 enable the Secretary of State to bring in new standards. Proposals were floated in a July 2006 consultation paper[51] (see paragraph 7.89) but no new replacement standards have yet been introduced.

7.88   Enforcement of the Part X code by local housing authorities is mandatory and may lead to the prosecution of the landlord. Overcrowding in council property is equally illegal and the code in HA 1985 Part X may be enforced by council tenants by a relator action with the fiat of the Attorney-General.[52] Illegal overcrowding may bring to an end any Rent Act security of tenure and may lead to homelessness (and possible rehousing by the local council).

---

50 *Southwark LBC v Mills* [2001] 1 AC 1, HL.
51 CLG, *Tackling Overcrowding in England: A Discussion Paper*, July 2006.
52 *DPP v Carrick* (1985) 31 *Housing Aid* 5.

7.89 **References**

- A Arden and M Partington, *Housing Law*, Sweet & Maxwell, chapter 10 'Overcrowding, multiple occupation and common lodging houses'.
- CLG, *Tackling Overcrowding in England: Self-Assessment for Local Authorities*, July 2008.
- CLG, *Tackling Overcrowding in England: Lessons from the London pilot schemes and sub-regional coordination*, June 2008.
- CLG, *Tackling overcrowding in England: An action plan*, December 2007.
- CLG, *Tackling Overcrowding in England: A Discussion Paper*, July 2006.
- D Ormandy and R Burridge, *Environmental Health Standards in Housing*, 1988, chapter 7 'Overcrowding'.

Refuse

7.90 Accumulations of rubbish may not only attract vermin (see below) but may also themselves constitute a danger to residents.[53] The former right of tenants to require a local authority to remove house refuse (PHA 1936 s72) was repealed in 1988 and a new code of refuse disposal is to be found in the Control of Pollution Act 1974 (see too the Collection and Disposal of Waste Regulations 1988[54]). This makes 'collection authorities' responsible for clearing rubbish, but local housing authority EHOs retain the power to require removal of 'accumulations' which are a public health hazard (see chapter 5).

7.91 In multi-storey blocks of flats, difficulties may be caused if the rubbish chutes and collection bins are not regularly cleared. A tenant living in a flat adjacent to a blocked chute or overspilled collection bin may have an action in private nuisance against the landlord[55] or may rely on any contractual obligation requiring the landlord to keep the area tidy or clear the rubbish.[56] In any event, there will be an implied term that landlords take reasonable steps to keep such facilities in repair.[57]

---

53 see, eg, *Dear v Newham LBC* (1988) 20 HLR 348, CA.

54 1988 SI No 819.

55 *Sillitoe v Liverpool CC* (1988) 29 November, unreported, Liverpool County Court, HHJ Stannard.

56 *Long v Southwark LBC* [2002] EWCA Civ 403; [2002] HLR 56, CA.

57 *Liverpool CC v Irwin* [1977] AC 239, HL.

Sanitary installations

7.92   Where a landlord has permitted sanitary installations to fall out of repair or out of proper working order the tenant may take action under contractual or common law repairing obligations (see chapters 1 and 2). If conditions have become prejudicial to health or a nuisance, tenants should involve the EHOs from the local housing authority to take action under the EPA 1990 (see chapter 5) or the HA 2004 (see chapter 6).

7.93   Additional powers are given to local housing authorities to deal with situations where there are insufficient sanitary conveniences in a dwelling or the existing ones require replacement. Enforcement, which is mandatory, is by notice from the council to the landlord followed, where necessary, by works in default of compliance and recovery of costs. For example, if it appears to a local authority that any water closets provided for or in connection with a building are in such a state as to be prejudicial to health or a nuisance, but that they can without reconstruction be put into a satisfactory condition, the authority must by notice require the owner or the occupier of the building to execute such works, or to take such steps by cleansing the closets or otherwise, as may be necessary for that purpose.[58]

7.94   **References**

- A Arden and M Partington, *Housing Law*, Sweet & Maxwell, para 8-61 'Sanitary accommodation'.

Services (gas, water and electricity)

7.95   Under the covenant implied in most tenancies by LTA 1985 s11, a landlord is required to keep in repair and proper working order the installations in the dwelling for the supply of gas, electricity and water (s11(1)(b)–(c)), or, in respect of certain tenancies, the installations serving the dwelling, wherever situated (see paragraph 1.69).

7.96   However, problems commonly arise where, although the installations themselves are in good order, the landlord has caused loss of supply of the services themselves, eg, by failing to pay fuel or water services bills. In these circumstances, upon receipt of a complaint from the occupiers, a local housing authority can make the necessary arrangements with the relevant boards to ensure reconnection

58   Public Heath Act 1936 s45.

of the supply. Most authorities have delegated the power to carry out this service to EHOs or tenancy relations officers. Once supply is re-established the authority can thereafter recover any necessary costs from the landlord.[59]

Vandalism

7.97 Where disrepair results from the deliberate, or negligent, act of a stranger rather than from the activities of the landlord or tenant or their visitors, responsibility for repair of the damage will lie on either or neither party according to respective repairing obligations. For example, where the landlord is liable to repair the 'exterior' this requires the replacement of glazing in a window smashed by the acts of a third party (see paragraph 1.83). Obviously, where the third party can be identified the landlord will seek redress from him or her.

7.98 In certain limited circumstances a landlord may be liable for acts of vandalism by unknown third parties which cause distress or damage to tenants. For example, the landlord of a number of adjoining properties may be liable in negligence if one property is left vacant and unsecured against vandals who destroy pipework and thereby cause flooding to the neighbouring tenanted properties, providing the damage was highly foreseeable or the case was exceptional.[60] Where damage is caused by third parties as a result of the landlord's failure to comply with repairing obligations, the damage need only be foreseeable.[61]

Vermin

7.99 One of the most unpleasant consequences of disrepair, other poor housing conditions or defective building design may be the incursion of vermin. This causes not only distress but also damage to personal possessions and in certain cases to the fabric of the property. In more modern, system-built dwellings, infestation by ants or cockroaches is not uncommon.[62]

---

59 Local Government (Miscellaneous Provisions) Act 1976 s33.
60 *Smith v Littlewoods Organisation Ltd* [1987] AC 241, HL.
61 *Morris v Liverpool CC* (1988) 20 HLR 498, CA.
62 See, eg, *Hudson v Kensington and Chelsea RLBC* December 1985 *Legal Action* 171, Bloomsbury and Marylebone County Court.

7.100   If the landlord lets premises infested by vermin those premises may be unfit for human habitation in breach of a contractual obligation (see chapter 1). If after a letting, a landlord negligently fails to deal with the vermin or the incursion is a nuisance for which the landlord is responsible, the tenant may have other remedies at common law (see paragraphs 2.8 (negligence) and 2.15 (nuisance)).

7.101   In addition, local authorities have extensive powers to take action in cases of pest infestation (Prevention of Damage by Pests Act 1949 and PHA 1936 Part II).

7.102   Premises infested with vermin are very likely to constitute a 'statutory nuisance' (see chapter 5) because they are prejudicial to health. If it can be shown that the incursion or infestation is caused by the 'act, default or sufferance' of the landlord, the tenant may rely on the processes of the EPA 1990 and, where necessary, prosecute the landlord using s82.[63]

7.103 **References**

- A Arden and M Partington, *Housing Law*, Sweet & Maxwell, para 8-93, 'Vermin'.
- M Howard, 'The effects on human health of pest infestation in houses', in R Burridge and D Ormandy (eds), *Unhealthy Housing: Research, Remedies and Reform*, Routledge & Chapman, 1993.

63 As in *White v Hackney LBC* March 1989 *Legal Action* 24, Highbury Corner Magistrates' Court.

CHAPTER 8

Damages

8.1   General principles of damages awarded in contract and tort

8.9   Damages in disrepair cases

8.11   The purpose of damages

8.13   The approach to assessment

8.14   General damages
8.15   Tenants who remain in occupation
8.33   Tenants not in occupation
8.35   Conclusion

8.36   Special damages
8.42   Aggravated and exemplary damages
8.43   Tenants' failure to mitigate loss
8.47   Contributory negligence
8.48   Interest

8.49   Using the ombudsmen

8.51   Damages cases
8.52   Court of Appeal decisions
8.61   High Court decisions
8.63   County court decisions
8.82   Awards for asthma
8.91   Awards for infestations

General principles of damages awarded in contract and tort

8.1   A detailed analysis of the principles governing the award of compensation for breach of contract or for tort is beyond the scope of this book but is given in *McGregor on Damages*, 17th edition; *Chitty on Contract* 30th edition; and *Clerk and Lindsell on Torts* 19th edition. A very brief analysis is set out below.

8.2   In a disrepair case, a tenant will be able to recover damages for loss which is caused by the landlord's breach of contract or tort and which is not too remote.

8.3   The tenant will have to prove, on the balance of probabilities, that the breach of contract or the tort was the effective or dominant cause of the loss. In contract, the voluntary intervening act of a third party will generally break the chain of causation, except where it is part of a landlord's contractual duty to protect the tenant from such acts.[1]

8.4   In *Marshall v Rubypoint*,[2] a tenant of a flat claimed damages for loss caused by a burglary which occurred when the landlord had failed to repair the communal front entrance door. The Court of Appeal held that a door which is obviously broken, and which can easily be pushed open, is an invitation to would-be burglars and that the disrepair of the door, and hence the breach of contract, was causative of the burglary. Similarly, in *Vye v English Churches Housing Group*[3] the landlord was held liable for its tenant being assaulted on the common staircase by an intruder when the front entrance door was in disrepair.

8.5   The position is slightly different in tort where a landlord will not usually be liable for the intervening act of a third party which is likely to be treated as a new independent cause. In these situations, a tenant is likely to be better off suing in contract.

8.6   Causation is most often an issue in housing disrepair cases where claims are made for damages for the effects of asthma being caused or exacerbated by damp housing conditions. Medical evidence will usually be required to prove this is the case (see paragraphs 7.20–7.21 for asthma).

8.7   A tenant will not be able to recover loss which is too remote. In contract:

> the damages ... should be such as may fairly and reasonably be considered either arising naturally, ie according to the usual course of

---

1   *See Stansbie v Troman* [1948] 2 KB 48, CA.

2   (1997) 29 HLR 850, CA.

3   November 2003 *Legal Action* 11, Lambeth County Court,

thing, from such breach of contract itself, or such as may reasonably be supposed to have been in the contemplation of the parties at the time they made the contract as the probable result of it.[4]

In tort, the test is whether damage is of such a kind as the reasonable man should have foreseen, but so long as the kind of damage is foreseeable, and occurs, the extent of the damage need not have been foreseen nor the precise manner of its incidence.

8.8   In *Mira v Aylmer Square Investments Ltd*,[5] a leaseholder who lost profits from subletting, by reason of his landlord's breach of the lease, was awarded damages because the length of the lease, its provisions relating to subletting and the common practice of subletting in that part of London meant the loss was reasonably foreseeable. By contrast, in *Berryman v Hounslow LBC*,[6] where a tenant claimed damages for a slipped disc sustained from walking up the stairs to her fifth floor flat because the lift did not work, it was held that the injury was not a foreseeable consequence of the duty to keep the lift in working order. Similarly, in *Ryan v Islington LBC*,[7] it was held that the fact that disrepair might cause a council tenant to be unable to complete the statutory purchase of her home and thus obtain a discount would not have been in the contemplation of the parties when the secure tenancy was granted; the loss was too remote to be recoverable. However, the landlord was held liable for the tenant's losses in *Marshall v Rubypoint*[8] (see paragraph 8.4). The Court of Appeal rejected the landlord's contention that the presence of a functioning internal door to the tenant's flat rendered the losses for the burglary too remote.

Damages in disrepair cases

8.9   Where a tenant has succeeded in establishing breach of the landlord's repairing obligation or a nuisance, or has shown that the landlord's negligence or breach of statutory duty has caused personal injury or damage to property, the appropriate remedy in most cases will be an award of substantial damages, ie, financial compensation. If the case has not yet come to trial but the claim for damages is clear,

---

4   *Hadley v Baxendale* (1854) 9 Exch 341.
5   (1990) 22 HLR 182, CA.
6   (1996) 30 HLR 567, CA.
7   [2009] EWCA Civ 578, CA.
8   (1997) 29 HLR 850, CA.

application may usefully be made for an award of interim damages under Civil Procedure Rules r25.6 (see paragraph 3.134).

8.10   Obviously, the landlord remains liable to compensate the tenant for damage suffered as the result of failure to repair (in breach of the express or implied terms of the contract or in tort) even if the landlord has carried out repairs before judgment or before the issue of proceedings; the tenant has an accrued cause of action as soon as the landlord's default causes loss.

The purpose of damages

8.11   The fundamental principle in awarding damages in disrepair cases is that the amount allowed should as far as possible place the tenant in the position he or she would have occupied if he or she 'had not suffered the wrong complained of, be that wrong a tort or breach of contract'.[9]

8.12   It should be noted that the purpose of awarding damages will go no further than that. The object is not 'to punish the landlords but, so far as money can, to restore the tenant to the position he would have been in had there been no breach'.[10]

The approach to assessment

8.13   Bearing in mind the principles to be applied, the courts have offered only broad guidance on the assessment of damages, although the usual rule, that both general and special damages will be available, is applied in disrepair cases. An assessment cannot be achieved by applying one set of rules to all cases regardless of the circumstances of the particular case. The facts of each case must be looked at to see what damage the tenant has suffered and how he or she may be fairly compensated by a monetary award:

> So, the true measure of damages for persons ... occupying land, whether in tort or contract, depends on the position of the plaintiffs and all the circumstances in which they have suffered loss and damage.[11]

---

9   *Dodd Properties (Kent) Ltd v Canterbury CC* [1980] 1 All ER 928, CA.
10 *Calabar Properties Ltd v Stitcher* [1983] 3 All ER 759, CA.
11 *Dodd Properties (Kent) Ltd v Canterbury CC* [1980] 1 All ER 928, CA.

General damages

8.14   In disrepair cases, the award of general damages is assessed as the 'difference in value to the tenant ... between the house in the condition in which it now is and the house in the condition in which it would be if the landlord on receipt of notice had fulfilled its obligation to repair.'[12] The calculation of this 'loss of value' to the tenant will vary according to the circumstances of the case.

Tenants who remain in occupation

8.15   If the tenant remains in residence during a period of disrepair, the general damages will be a substantial award for all the inconvenience, disappointment, discomfort, mental distress and loss of enjoyment suffered by the tenant, as well as damage for any ill health caused by the disrepair.[13] The period attracting compensation runs from the date when the landlord has had a reasonable time to carry out the repairs (in cases where knowledge is a precondition of liability) up to the date of assessment or the carrying out of the repairs.

8.16   In *Wallace v Manchester CC*[14] the Court of Appeal confirmed that the tenant's claim for loss while living in a dwelling is disrepair is for the loss of comfort and convenience. The method determining the amount needed to compensate for that loss could involve:

* a notional reduction in rent;
* a global award for discomfort and inconvenience; or
* a combination of reduced rental value *and* inconvenience.

There was, however, no requirement to assess damages separately under the two heads of reduction in rental value and inconvenience, as they were merely different methods of expressing the same concept.[15]

8.17   Historically the courts will have used all three methods for calculating damages. Advisers will need to carefully consider which approach is likely to maximise damages in any particular case.

8.18   Sometimes the court has used the rent as an indicator of the level of general damages.[16] The court looks at the rent due under the tenancy and then awards as damages a 'discount' representing the extent

---

12 *Hewitt v Rowlands* (1924) 93 LJKB 729
13 *Calabar Properties Ltd v Stitcher* [1983] 3 All ER 759, CA.
14 (1998) 30 HLR 1111, CA.
15 See 'Damages for disrepair claims: time for a rethink?' [2008] JHL 67.
16 *McCoy v Clarke* (1982) 13 HLR 89, CA.

of loss of use and enjoyment suffered by the tenant. For example, if the rent were £90 per week and the disrepair affected one third of the property, a weekly figure of £30 might provide a starting point.

8.19   This rather artificial approach can result in very high awards where high rents are charged, eg, to homeless families in temporary accommodation. But it can also result in compensation being underestimated, particularly where the rent is relatively low compared with the hardship suffered. However, nowadays the courts are concerned to ensure that tenants affected by disrepair are awarded 'substantial sums' as opposed to 'nominal or cosmetic amounts'.[17] There are, accordingly, a number of cases in which, on the facts, it has been held erroneous in law to restrict the award of general damages by reference to the rent.[18]

8.20   Certainly, the court is not obliged to 'take account of the rent as a prima facie indication of the level of any proper award' and may instead just make a single global assessment of the general damages for inconvenience and distress.[19] Thus, in *Personal Representatives of Chiodi v De Marney*[20] the Court of Appeal would not interfere with the assessment of damages under that head at £30 per week where the contractual rent for the entire premises was only £8 per week.

8.21   However, where a judge makes a global award of damages he 'would be well advised to cross-check his prospective award by reference to the rent payable for the period equivalent to the duration of the landlord's breach of covenant'.[21] The Court of Appeal has also indicated more recently that, save in exceptional cases, damages for discomfort and inconvenience should not exceed the rent payable.

> Whilst we accept that there will be cases in which the level of distress and/or inconvenience experienced by a tenant may require an award in excess of the level of rent payable ... clear reasons need to be given by the court for taking that course, and the facts of the case – notably the conduct of the landlord – must warrant such an award.[22]

8.22   In some cases, it may be fairest to seek to evaluate an award of compensation in respect of both the tenant's notional monetary loss

---

17 *Davies v Peterson* (1989) 21 HLR 63, CA.
18 *Personal Representatives of Chiodi v De Marney* (1988) 21 HLR 6, CA; *Credit Suisse v Beegas Nominees Ltd* [1994] 1 EGLR 76, ChD; *Hussein v Mehlman* [1992] 2 EGLR 87, Wood Green Trial Centre.
19 *Personal representatives of Chiodi v De Marney* (1988) 21 HLR 6, CA.
20 (1988) 21 HLR 6, CA.
21 *Wallace v Manchester CC* (1998) 30 HLR 1111, CA, per Morritt LJ.
22 *English Churches Housing Group v Shine* [2004] EWCA Civ 434; [2004] HLR 42.

(loss of rental value) and any discomfort, injury or inconvenience suffered.

8.23   For example, in *Sturolson & Co v Mauroux*,[23] the Court of Appeal did not comment adversely on the approach of a county court judge who first applied the 'discounting' method to assess the degree of loss of value to the tenant of the tenancy itself and then went on to add to it a substantial award for inconvenience, discomfort and injury to health (although the correctness of the county court judge's approach was not, in that respect, challenged).

8.24   The county court judge followed the same approach in *Brent LBC v Carmel (Murphy)*.[24] The Court of Appeal refused to interfere with the level of damages awarded, either on the ground that it was excessive or on the ground that it was calculated on a wrong basis. Other examples of county court judges adopting this approach can be found in the annual 'Repairs round-up' published in *Legal Action* magazine. However, such an approach may now be less likely given the indication from the Court of Appeal in *Wallace v Manchester CC*[25] that diminution in value is merely one method of evaluating general damages for distress and inconvenience.

8.25   It follows from this that, even where damages are awarded on the basis, in part or whole, of loss of rental value, no reduction in the damages awarded ought to be made where the rent was paid by way of housing benefit, even when the defendant landlord is also the local authority. In *Wallace v Manchester CC*[26] the Court of Appeal made it clear that the fact that a tenant is in receipt of housing benefit is irrelevant to any award of damages; the source of the money used to pay rent is irrelevant to the extent of the discomfort and inconvenience suffered by the tenant and the amount of proper compensation payable, irrespective of the court's approach to assessing general damages. Equally, given that an award of damages based on loss of rental value is simply a method of quantifying general damages, it does not attract the higher interest that special damages awards attract.

8.26   In exceptional circumstances, a very low rent, which already recognised the poor quality of the premises, can properly result in a lower award of damages.[27] However, it has been held that the fact that the rent had been registered as a fair rent, and therefore in a

23 (1988) 20 HLR 332, CA.
24 (1995) 28 HLR 203, CA.
25 (1998) 30 HLR 1111, CA.
26 (1998) 30 HLR 1111, CA.
27 *Newham LBC v Patel* (1978) 13 HLR 77, CA.

sense had been fixed with regard to the state of repair, did not affect the assessment of damages.[28]

8.27   The Court of Appeal has also approved diminution in rental value as a correct measure of damages even in cases where only a nominal rent is actually payable, for example, premises let on long leases with a ground rent. In these cases the actual rent payable is ignored and reference is made to a notional rent which would be payable if the premises were let on a short tenancy and in repair. In *Earle v Charalambous*,[29] the court decided that, for a long leaseholder, a direct analogy with global awards in relation to protected periodic tenancies was inappropriate; 'a notional judgment of the resulting reduction in rental value is likely to be the most appropriate starting point for the assessment of damages'. The Court of Appeal also rejected the view that expert valuation evidence was necessary. The judge was entitled to accept the tenant's researches about the rental values in equivalent properties.

8.28   Damages are not usually recoverable in disrepair cases for the distress and inconvenience caused by the undertaking of remedial works themselves, unless the works would not have been necessary if the landlord had performed its repairing obligations when it should have done.

8.29   If the tenant is required to move out (either temporarily while works are being undertaken or, if conditions are sufficiently serious, before remedial work even starts) any specific costs of removal or alternative accommodation can be recovered as special damages (provided they arise from the breach of contract or tort).[30] However, a separate element of general damages will be awarded for the inconvenience of having to move and live for a time in temporary accommodation. Such award will be increased if undertakings about the length of stay in temporary housing are broken by the landlord.[31]

8.30   If it can be shown that the landlord's breach of contract or duty of care caused personal injury (mental or physical) then substantial damages for that injury can be recovered.[32]

---

28 *Sturolson & Co v Mauroux* (1988) 20 HLR 332, CA; see also *Pirachia v Mavadia* December 2007 *Legal Action* 30, Lambeth County Court.

29 [2006] EWCA Civ 1090; [2007] HLR 8,

30 *Earle v Charalmbous* [2006] EWCA Civ 1090; [2007] HLR 8, CA.

31 *Lubren v Lambeth LBC* (1988) 20 HLR 165, CA.

32 *McCoy v Clark* (1982) 13 HLR 89, CA; *Attica v British Gas* [1988] QB 304, CA; *Sykes v Harry* [2001] EWCA Civ 167; [2001] QB 1014, CA; *Lips v Older* [2004] EWHC 1686 (QB).

8.31   There are few recent appellate decisions in relation to quantum of general damages, given the relatively low levels of such awards and the disproportionate costs which would be involved in appealing any such decisions.[33] However, the annual 'Repairs round-up' in *Legal Action* summarises county court cases where damages have been awarded against residential landlords. As a guide to the current 'going rate' for the assessment of general damages for disrepair, see paragraphs 8.52–8.94.

8.32   Advisers must remember to update awards made in previous cases to take account of inflation because this can make a significant difference to the amount, especially for older cases. For example, the informal tariff referred to in *Wallace v Manchester* CC of £1,000 to £2,750 per annum in 1998 would have been worth £1,320 to £3,630 per annum in January 2008. Updating is usually done by using the inflation tables in *Kemp & Kemp: The Quantum of Damages*,[34] which updates from January of one year to January of another year by using a multiplier. This is the basis of the updating set out above. However, it is possible to update to the nearest month by using the retail price index itself.

Tenants not in occupation

8.33   If the tenant has rented the property for the purpose of subletting it (or is going away temporarily and wishes to sublet) and as a result of disrepair can only sub-let for a reduced rent or cannot sublet it at all, the damages awarded will be measured by the loss of rental income from the subletting.[35]

8.34   If a long lessee is driven out of occupation by the disrepair and forced to sell the lease (or bought the lease intending to offer it for re-sale), then the damages awarded can be measured as the difference between the selling price and the price he or she would have obtained if the landlord had carried out the repairs.[36] Indeed, if it can be established that the landlord deliberately prepared the leasehold premises for sale to the present lessee in such a way as to disguise a

33 See *Vass v Pank* July 2001 *Legal Action* 25, CA.
34 Sweet & Maxwell.
35 *Calabar Properties v Stitcher* [1983] 3 All ER 759, CA; *Mira v Aylmer Square Investments Ltd* (1989) 21 HLR 284, CA; *Wallace v Manchester CC* (1998) 30 HLR 1111, CA.
36 *Calabar Properties v Stitcher* [1983] 3 All ER 759, CA; *City and Metropolitan Properties v Greycroft* [1987] 3 All ER 839, ChD, at 842–3; *Credit Suisse v Beegas Nominees Ltd* [1994] 1 EGLR 76, ChD; *Gorman and Lane v Lambeth LBC* December 2009 *Legal Action* 23.

serious repairing problem, the lessee may recover damages in deceit as well as for breach of contractual obligation.[37]

Conclusion

8.35   It will be obvious that certain of these heads represent compensation for quite specific loss. Accordingly, the courts will expect the tenant to give notice in the pleadings about the loss suffered; it will not be sufficient just to claim 'damages'.[38] The claim may also embrace the effects of the disrepair on other members of the tenant's family,[39] although family members with claims in their own right, eg, personal injury claims under the Defective Premises Act 1972 s4 have to be joined to the action as claimants.[40]

Special damages

8.36   The tenant is entitled to recover damages representing the loss in value of items of furniture and other personal belongings destroyed or damaged as a result of the landlord's failure to repair. The most common examples are carpets, furniture, curtains and clothing corrupted by dampness. Additionally, special damages may be sought for other specific loss capable of calculation in monetary terms, for example:

- cleaning costs;
- loss of earnings, eg, from time taken off work for missed appointments;
- extra heating costs (eg, for 'drying-out' dampness);
- the costs of alternative accommodation (see paragraph 8.40);
- the cost of repairs, cleaning up and redecoration (see paragraph 8.38);
- travelling and medical costs (eg, arising from personal injury);
- the cost of eating out (eg, if food storage or cooking facilities have been damaged).

---

37   *Gordon v Selico* (1986) 18 HLR 219, CA.
38   *Perestrello e Companhia Limitada v United Paint Co* [1969] 3 All ER 479, CA, at 485.
39   *Jackson v Horizon Holidays Ltd* [1975] 1 WLR 1468, CA; *Jarvis v Swan Tours* (1973) 1 QB 233, CA. The application of the principles developed in these cases involving holidays to the law of landlord and tenant was noted in *McCall v Abelesz* [1976] QB 585, CA. See too paragrah 3.45.
40   *C (a minor) v Hackney LBC* [1996] 1 All ER 973, CA.

8.37 The above list is of examples only. Those acting for the tenant should ensure that consideration is given to pleading all losses which as a matter of fact are caused by the disrepair.

8.38 If tenants themselves carry out works of repair, clearing up or redecoration, damages will be awarded to compensate for any expenses reasonably incurred.[41] Even if the works actually improve the property, no reduction is made from the damages on account of this element of betterment, if the tenant was unable to make good the damage without betterment.[42] These specific costs may be pleaded as special damages.

8.39 Courts will often make a deduction to allow for betterment in respect of special damages claims for damaged belongings. However, on the basis of the rationale set out in *Harbutt's Plasticine Ltd, v Wayne Tank and Pump Co Ltd*,[43] there should be no such deduction where it is not possible or reasonable to obtain secondhand replacements. It may, therefore, be possible to resist many arguments for deduction for betterment. The burden of proving that there should be a deduction for betterment will be on the landlord.[44]

8.40 If the disrepair renders the premises uninhabitable, the tenant may recover as damages any expenses reasonably incurred in taking alternative accommodation from the date that the premises could no longer be occupied up to the date of assessment of damages or repair.[45] Such damages will include the costs of any removals, storage of furniture, etc. Such costs should be specifically pleaded as special damages.

8.41 Each specific item for which special damages are claimed must be identified in the pleadings and at trial it will be necessary to prove the loss in respect of each item. It is therefore vital that the tenant collects and retains where possible all receipts, accounts and invoices relating to items replaced or repaired (see paragraph 3.38). Where there is likely to be a dispute over the damages claimed, the tenant would be well advised to retain (or at least photograph) any damaged item pending the trial.

---

41 *Calabar Properties v Stitcher* [1983] 3 All ER 759, CA.
42 *McGreal v Wake* (1984) 13 HLR 107, CA.
43 [1970] 1 QB 447, CA.
44 *Lagden v O'Connor* [2003] UKHL 64; [2004] 1 AC 1067 per Hope LJ at [34].
45 *Calabar Properties v Stitcher* [1983] 3 All ER 759, CA.

Aggravated and exemplary damages

8.42   Aggravated and exemplary damages are not usually recovered in disrepair claims because of the limited circumstances in which they can be awarded. Aggravated and exemplary damages can be awarded only in tort, not in contract. Aggravated damages are awarded to compensate a claimant for injury to his or her feelings of dignity and pride and for aggravation generally. Exemplary damages are punitive and are awarded to indicate the courts disapproval of the conduct in question. Exemplary damages can be awarded in a disrepair case only where there has been oppressive conduct by local government officers or where the landlord's conduct has been calculated to make a profit which may well exceed the compensation payable to the tenant.[46] Aggravated and exemplary damages are usually only awarded in unlawful eviction cases, but can be claimed in a disrepair case, where appropriate, eg where the landlord has deliberately neglected essential repairs as part of a plan to drive the tenant out.

Tenants' failure to mitigate loss

8.43   In an action for damages for breach of a *contractual* repairing obligation, it is important for tenants to show that they took whatever reasonable steps were available to mitigate or prevent loss or damage, for example, that a bucket was placed under a leak, rather than simply allowing dampness to rot the floorboards and carpets. Thus, if a tenant delayed giving notice of disrepair to the landlord (in a case where the landlord's liability was conditional on knowledge of the defect) so that the eventual damage was greater than it would otherwise have been, that tenant may see a reduction in damages on account of the failure to mitigate the loss.[47]

8.44   It is a question of fact whether the tenant has failed to mitigate loss so as to reduce any damages that would otherwise be awarded. However, there is no failure to mitigate simply because the party in breach can suggest that other measures less burdensome to the party in breach might have been taken; the claimant's conduct is not to be 'weighed in nice scales at the insistence of the party whose breach of contract has occasioned the difficulty'.[48] In particular, a claimant is not

46   *Rookes v Barnard* [1964] AC 1129, HL.

47   *Minchburn v Peck* (1988) 20 HLR 392, CA.

48   *Banco de Portugal v Waterlow and Sons Ltd* [1932] AC 452, per McMillan LJ at 506.

be to be prejudiced if he or she is financially unable to mitigate.[49]

8.45 Refusal to permit access is a common allegation and can be treated as a failure to mitigate loss or, more commonly, as an action which entirely suspends the landlord's liability.[50] Any unreasonable behaviour which results in substantial delay in the completion of remedial works or additional costs may also constitute a failure to mitigate and result in a reduction in the damages payable.[51] In *English Churches Housing Group v Shine*,[52] the tenant was held to have failed to mitigate his loss because he refused to move to alternative accommodation in breach of an undertaking and injunctions. The Court of Appeal reduced the damages awarded for the period in question and assessed the damages payable by taking the lower figure of either (1) discounting the rent by 75 per cent or (2) assessing the time in which the works would have been completed if the tenant had cooperated and awarding damages for the shorter period.

8.46 However, in cases where landlords have patently neglected to repair property, the duty to mitigate does not impose an obligation on tenants to do the work themselves.[53] Nor are tenants to be penalised for any refusal (other than an unreasonable one) to move to alternative accommodation.[54] But tenants can be expected to take reasonable measures, such as blocking up the source of draughts, moving furniture away from leaks or temporarily covering broken window glazing.

Contributory negligence

8.47 Where a tenant's action arises in *tort*, damages will be reduced if the court finds that the tenant was partly responsible for his or her losses: Law Reform (Contributory Negligence) Act 1945. In *Lips v Older*[55] where a tenant fell over the wall leading up to the front door of the premises and into the basement area below, damages were reduced by two-thirds because he was drunk and carrying a heavy load which caused him to lose his balance. Similarly, in *Sykes v Harry*[56] damages

---

49 *Dodd Properties v Canterbury CC* [1980] 1 WLR 433, CA.

50 *Granada Theatres Ltd v Freehold Investment (Leytonstone) Ltd* [1959] 1 WLR 570, CA; *Empson v Forde* [1990] 1 EGLR 131, CA.

51 *English Churches Housing Group v Shine* [2004] EWCA Civ 434; [2004] HLR 42, CA.

52 [2004] EWCA Civ 434; [2004] HLR 42, CA.

53 *Sturolson & Co v Mauroux* (1988) 20 HLR 165, CA.

54 *Lubren v Lambeth LBC* (1988) 20 HLR 162, CA; *English Churches Housing Group v Shine* [2004] EWCA Civ 434, [2004] HLR 42, CA.

55 [2004] EWHC 1686 (QB).

56 [2001] EWCA Civ 167; [2001] QB 1014, CA.

were reduced by 80 per cent because of a failure to notify the landlord of defects to the gas fire since the tenant was in the best position to execute repairs or bring them to the attention of the landlord. A similar reduction will be applied where there is a breach of contract but the contractual liability duplicates an independent tort liability. There can be no reduction for contributory negligence where there is solely a breach of contract, but the same result may be achieved by reliance on a failure to mitigate (see paragraphs 8.43–8.46) or absence of causation (see paragraph 8.3).

Interest

8.48   As it is not unknown for disrepair cases to take months or years before the stage is reached for assessment of damages, advisers should ensure than any award for a retrospective period carries with it interest assessed under County Courts Act 1984 s69.

Using the ombudsmen

8.49   As an alternative to court proceedings, tenants aggrieved by disrepair can made complaints to an ombudsman.[57]

8.50   Past investigations of repairs complaints have led to recommendations for public apologies and compensation but in recent years the compensation awarded has sometimes been less than that which might have been obtained by seeking redress in the courts. It appears that the Local Government Ombudsman uses an unofficial tariff for compensation ranging from £500 to £2,000 per annum,[58] somewhat less than the unofficial tariff of £1,000 to £2,750 per annum which the courts were applying in 1998.[59]

Damages cases

8.51   The case notes below are arranged by reference to the level of court, in chronological order. Note figures require adjusting for inflation (see paragraph 8.32).

---

57 See paragraphs 3.21–3.25.

58 Commissioners for Local Administration in England *Remedies Guidance on good practice 6*, Chapter II para 16 and *Ombudsman report relating to Canterbury CC 07/A/00415* December 2008 *Legal Action* 32.

59 *Wallace v Manchester CC* (1998) 30 HLR 1111, CA.

Court of Appeal decisions

8.52 Minchburn v Peck (1988) 20 HLR 392

A long leaseholder suffered two years of water penetration as a result of defective roof slates and three to four years of cracks to the party walls, which spoilt the decorations. There was no requirement that a tenant give notice in a long lease but there was the possiblity that the landlord would have carried out the works earlier if notice had been given. The Court of Appeal reduced the award of general damages for discomfort and dampness from £800 to £700 to make allowance for this.

8.53 Chiodi v De Marney (1988) 21 HLR 6

A flat suffered from water penetration, collapsed ceilings, rotten windows, frequent electrical problems and periods with no hot water supply. The tenant's arthritis was exacerbated and she suffered colds and flu. The tenant was awarded general damages for inconvenience and distress at the rate of £30 per week for 3½ years (£5,460) even though the rent was only £8 per week. Special damages of £4,657 and damages for injury to health of £1,500 were awarded. The Court of Appeal described the award as being 'at least at the very top of any appropriate range of any monetary awards for such a case' but declined to interfere.

8.54 Lubren v Lambeth LBC (1988) 20 HLR 165

Five years of cold and damp as a result of unspecified disrepair, which meant that the premises deteriorated from a reasonable condition at the outset to being 'appalling', resulted in an award of £4,000 to a tenant who had two adult sons. In the last two years the hot water and heating system worked intermittently and caused significant additional inconvenience. £500 was also awarded for the 14 months when the tenant was in alternative accommodation, waiting for remedial works to be completed, when the landlord had undertaken that the works would only take three months.

8.55 Davies v Peterson (1989) 21 HLR 63

One of the bedrooms and the living room in a house were uninhabitable because of damp for a period of at least 12 months. An award of £250 for discomfort, anxiety and inconvenience was appealed by the tenant. Russell LJ stated that in 1989 'the sum of £250 must ... be regarded, when awarded by way of compensation for inconvenience, anxiety and discomfort, as little more than nominal'. This was not a case in which nominal damages were appropriate and the award of general damages was increased from £250 to £1,000. 'It is plain that in this day and age the courts are prepared to award substantial sums to tenants who are the victims of defaulting landlords where disrepair occurs.'

8.56   **Brent LBC v Carmel (1995) 28 HLR 203**

From 1981 there were problems of water penetration and inadequate central heating in the winter; the tenant's teenage boy and girl had to share her bedroom as their bedroom became uninhabitable. The condition of the home became progressively worse and from 1986 onwards was appalling and intolerable. £1,000 per annum was awarded from 1981 to 1986 and thereafter £1,500 per annum. In addition, damages for loss of value of the premises assessed at 30 per cent of the rent for period 1986 to 1987 and 50 per cent from 1988 to 1993. Special damages totalling £19,320 were also awarded, with interest at 13.5 per cent from 1986 to trial. The Court of Appeal refused the council's application for leave to appeal, on the basis that the award was 'not wrong in principle or manifestly excessive'.

8.57   **Wallace v Manchester CC [1998] 30 HLR 1111**

The tenant complained that her house was in disrepair: an external wall had partially collapsed, the windows were rotten and the house suffered from a constant infestation of rats. The judge awarded £3,500 general damages on the basis of a global award to compensate the tenant for her distress and inconvenience. On the tenant's appeal it was held that 'assuming but without deciding' that there was a tariff of £1,000 to £2,750 per annum, the award of £3,500 for approximately three years of disrepair did not fall outside it. [This is assessed as a little under 50 per cent of the annualised rent in *English Churches Housing Group* v *Shine* (see paragraph 8.59) at paragraph 103.]

8.58   **Long v Southwark LBC [2002] EWCA Civ 403; [2002] HLR 56**

The tenant's flat was next to a large paladin bin into which a rubbish chute emptied. The tenant complained of noise, smells and maggot infestations around the bin from 1993 to 2001. Damages of £13,500 were awarded on the basis of £2,500 per annum for the period from 1993 to 1995 and at the rate of £1,500 for the next 5½ years.

8.59   **English Churches Housing Group v Shine [2004] EWCA Civ 434; [2004] HLR 42**

The tenant, acting in person, brought a claim for severe damp and dry rot in his basement flat, which was defended on the basis of his refusal of access. In the course of the proceedings the tenant was ordered to vacate the premises but failed to do so until February 2003 despite a number of further injunction orders against him. The remedial works to the premises were finally completed in June 2003. The trial judge awarded £19,000 for a seven-year period covering approximately May 1996 to June 2003 including £16,000 for the four years immediately before the hearing, when the tenant had refused to move to alternative accommodation.

On the landlord's appeal against the award of £16,000 for 1999 to 2003, the Court of Appeal found that the award was manifestly excessive. The judge had given no explanation of how he had arrived at it and he had failed to check it against the rent. The Court of Appeal reduced the award to £8,000, awarding 75 per cent of the rent for 1999 to 2001, when the tenant was living in very poor conditions without a bathroom and a gas supply (although this was partly because he had turned it off himself), but giving a very substantial discount for 2001 to 2003 for the tenant's failure to mitigate his loss. It assessed the damages payable for 2001 to 2003 by taking the lower figure of discounting the rent by 75 per cent and assessing the period in which the works would have been completed if Mr Shine had cooperated, which it judged to be nine months.

8.60   **Earle v Charalambous [2006] EWCA Civ 1090; [2007] HLR 8**

A long leaseholder suffered with damp and water penetration to his top floor flat from January 2000 until September 2004. By December 2002 the kitchen ceiling had partially collapsed and the tenant had to move out. The trial judge awarded damages of £20,000 from January 2000 to December 2002, when the tenant was in occupation, and £10,000 for December 2002 to September 2004, when the tenant was staying with his parents. On appeal, the Court of Appeal held that the award in respect of the first period was not supported by adequate reasoning and was excessive when viewed against the tenant's own claim. The award was reduced to £13,500 but the award in respect of the second period was upheld as it was just under half the rental value.

High Court decisions

8.61   **Sampson v Wilson (1994) 26 HLR 486**

The dwelling was in substantial disrepair. The absentee landlord and his agents carried out works of repair deliberately in such a manner as to make matters worse and drive out the tenants. Since the works were carried out without permission or exceeding any permission, there was a trespass in addition to a breach of contract, thereby permitting an award of exemplary damages to be made. The judge awarded the full amount of rent to each tenant, namely £25 and £24 per week and made an award of exemplary damages of £2,000.

8.62   **Arnold v Greenwich LBC [1998] CLY 3518; May 1998** *Legal Action* **30**

£8,750 was awarded for almost six years of modest condensation damp and mould, smells from the refuse storage area and noise from the communal rubbish chute.

County court decisions

8.63   **Walker v Lambeth LBC, September 1992** *Legal Action* **21**

For 18 months one of two lifts was out of operation and the other was subject to frequent breakdowns. The tenant had a young child and was pregnant for nine months out of the 18. She was occasionally trapped in the lift and frequently had to use the stairs to the 15th floor. Damages of £3,750 were awarded.

8.64   **Hallet v Camden LBC, August 1994** *Legal Action* **17;** *Housing Law Casebook* **para P11.62**

£300 per annum was awarded for draughty windows which were 'low in the scale of possible defects'.

8.65   **Bell v Mazehead, March 1996** *Legal Action* **14**

£15,250 was awarded for five years of water penetration through the roof and other dampness. [Over £3,000 per annum in 1996.]

8.66   **Rayson v Sanctuary Housing Association Ltd, March 1996** *Legal Action* **15**

The tenant moved into a newly completed house in 1979 and began to notice structural cracking. By 1983 the cracking was pronounced, internal door frames distorted and by 1991 the cracks 3–5 mm wide in places. £4,750 was awarded for the worst two years of severe, unsightly and worrying structural cracking.

8.67   **Pierce v Westminster CC, July 2001** *Legal Action* **27;** *Housing Law Casebook* **para P11.50**

A tenant's three-bedroomed house developed cracks owing to subsidence, with the worst being 12 mm wide. Daylight could be seen around the lounge window. The trial judge awarded general damages at annual rates of between £500 and £1,000 for a seven-year period, producing a total award of £5,450.

8.68 **Vergera v Lambeth LBC and Hyde Southbank Homes, August 2002** *Legal Action* **30;** *Housing Law Casebook* **para P11.60**

The case was described by the trial judge as the worst case of disrepair and nuisance he had ever tried. Water had penetrated various rooms of a three-bedroomed flat, windows were in disrepair, the hot water supply to the kitchen and bathroom failed on several occasions and the gas heater was not serviced. When the rest of the street was decanted, the claimant was left in occupation and the properties were allowed to fall into a state of dereliction, with rubbish accumulation, squatting and blocked drains. By 1999 there were vermin infestations, particularly by rats. The trial judge awarded £2,500 per annum for the first two years, £3,500 per annum for the next two years and £4,500 per annum for the final two years. He assessed damages for six months' inconvenience in temporary accommodation at £1,500.

8.69 **Mzae v Abigo, November 2004** *Legal Action* **29;** *Housing Law Casebook* **para P11.47**

From the commencement of the tenancy of this two-bedroom flat in March 2001 there was dampness, cracked and loose plasterwork, water penetration, overflowing drains, a mice infestation in 2003 and consistent problems with the boiler from April 2001. One bedroom was unusable because of the conditions. The trial judge accepted that the landlord was not acting deliberately or maliciously in failing to carry out repairs. Mindful of the decisions in *Wallace v Manchester CC* (paragraph 8.57) and *English Churches Housing Group v Shine* (paragraph 8.59), he made a global assessment of damages of £14,000 where the annual rent was £10,400. [Taking a 3.5 years period of liability, this sum equals approximately £4,000 per annum or 40 per cent of the annual rent.]

8.70 **Thornton v Jarrett, November 2004** *Legal Action* **27;** *Housing Law Casebook* **para P11.58**

Ms Thornton complained of severe dampness affecting her home, which she occupied with her two children aged 9 and 11, due to rising dampness, penetrating dampness from a fractured drain and condensation, from June 1998 to October 1998. She also complained that in carrying out a modernisation plan including the installation of UPVC windows, a new kitchen and bathroom from October 1998 to March 1999 the council took too long and interfered with her everyday life so as to constitute a breach of the covenant of quiet enjoyment. The premises were much improved from March 1999 but some defects remained. HHJ McKenna rejected a claim that it was reasonable to delay all repairs until the modernisation programme began in October 1998 and found that the works should have been undertaken by the end of July 1998. He accepted that the works were very noisy, dirty and disruptive with Ms Thornton confined to one bedroom for over three months. Damages of £3,000 were awarded for August 1998 to March 1999. Damages of £1,000 per annum were awarded for the period from March 1999 to trial, amounting to a total award of £7,667 plus special damages of £280. [The award for August 1998 to March 1999 amounts to an annual award of £4,500.]

8.71   **Sarmad v Okello, November 2004** *Legal Action* **29;** *Housing Law Casebook* **para P11.51**

The tenant complained of disrepair throughout the tenancy from November 1999 to November 2002. The supply of heating and hot water was intermittent for the first three years and in 2002 the heating broke down altogether. In addition, there was water penetration to the bathroom and hallway and, from April 2002, to the bedroom. From 2001, there was an infestation of rats from the take-away on the ground floor. The trial judge found conditions intolerable and awarded damages as follows:

- £2,000 pa from February 1999 to February 2002 for the intermittent heating and hot water supply;
- £1,750 pa from February 2002 to November 2002 for intermittent hot water and heating supply;
- £1,500 pa from February 1999 to February 2001 re all other defects;
- £2,000 pa February 2001–November 2002 for the rat infestation.

Total awarded £14,250.

8.72   **Cody v Philps, December 2005** *Legal Action* **28;** *Housing Law Casebook* **para P12.11**

A landlord sought to recover rent arrears from a tenant who had left the premises. The tenant accepted that the arrears were owed but counterclaimed for damages for disrepair. DJ Wright awarded damages of £1,500 for the six-month period of occupation. Although the actual disrepair was not substantial, reference had to be made to the fairly substantial rent for these premises, namely £1,473 per month.

8.73 **Shefford v Norfax Enterprises, December 2006** *Legal Action* 24; *Housing Law Casebook* **para P11.53**

The environmental health department had served notices had been served prohibiting use of two basement rooms in a flat. The landlord let the flat to three joint tenants on the basis that they would use the basement rooms as bedrooms. All the bedrooms were damp and whole flat smelled of damp. Damages of £2,750 awarded for a four-month period, based on the fact that the tenants had bargained for a three-bedroom flat and had got one bedroom and even that was in disrepair. This equated to 50 per cent of the rent of £1,300 per month.

8.74 **Sachs v Brentfield Trust, December 2006** *Legal Action* 24

A long leaseholder had water penetration to the kitchen and bathroom. The trial judge awarded 25 per cent of the rack rent of £850 per month for six years, making a total award of £15,300.

8.75 **Brongard Ltd v Sowerby, December 2007** *Legal Action* 29; *Housing Law Casebook* **para P11.26**

In a possession claim for rent arrears, a Rent Act protected tenant of a three-bedroomed house counterclaimed damages for disrepair at the property, namely high levels of dampness in the walls of the kitchen, dining room and two of the bedrooms, dislodged and missing slates to the roof, which caused water penetration to two of the bedrooms, an unstable chimney, defective and rotten windows which were in a dangerous condition, a rotten front entrance door and rotten floor joists in the kitchen and dining room. The trial judge awarded the tenant general damages of £2,700 per annum for 7.3 years (October 1999 to January 2007), totalling £19,710, and special damages of £8,319.68, which included the costs of the kitchen units which had been damaged by the damp and rotten conditions in the property.

8.76 **Pirachia v Mavadia, December 2007** *Legal Action* 30; *Housing Law Casebook* **para P11.50A**

In a possession claim for rent arrears, a Rent Act protected tenant of a three-bedroomed house counterclaimed damages for disrepair. The landlord argued that because the registered rent reflected the fact that the property was in disrepair at the time of registration, the tenant had already been compensated and his damages should be nil. HHJ Welchman, relying on *Sturolson v Mauroux* (1988) 20 HLR 332, rejected this submission but held that his global award reflected in part the fact that the registered rent was lower than it would otherwise have been because of the disrepair. The judge awarded total damages of £11,425 based on global figures per annum ranging from £300 to £2,500, but having regard to the rent payable at the date of the counterclaim of £133.50 per week:

- £2,500 per annum was awarded when the property was in a 'lamentable state of disrepair' with severe wood rot to windows, general dampness with mould growth particularly in the living room, bathroom and one of the three bedrooms, which was unusable.
- £750 per annum when works had been carried out so that the overall state of the flat had markedly improved but there were still 'substantial defects', namely some dampness to the living room and the third bedroom, water penetration to the kitchen door and cracked ceilings.
- £300 per annum when there was still some water penetration into one bedroom and through the kitchen door but in the judge's view there had been a 'sea change' at the property.

8.77   **Arabhalvaei v Rezaeipoor, December 2007** *Legal Action* **30;** *Housing Law Casebook* **para O9.12A**

In a possession claim for rent arrears, a Rent Act protected tenant of a one-bedroomed flat, which the tenant shared with his wife, counterclaimed damages for disrepair at the property and for harassment from his landlord. The disrepair included penetrating damp, cracks to various internal walls and a leaking toilet and sink. In addition the heating system was out of order at various times over the period in question, with the result that the property was without heating and hot water. Judgment was entered for the tenant in respect of a claim for 7 years 9 months. The trial judge awarded the tenant a total of £188,526.21 in damages including:

- £22,500 in respect of the disrepair, which represented 50 per cent of the rental value of £455 per calendar month over the period in question.
- Special damages of £4,926.68 in respect of works done by the tenant in default of the landlord, heating, cleaning and damages to belongings.
- Interest at 6 per cent for 3.5 years which was approximately the mid-point of the damages claim, amounting to £5,759.60 in respect of the disrepair damages.

8.78   **Murray v Kelly, December 2008** *Legal Action* **31**

The tenant counterclaimed for damages for disrepair for the following defects:

- low water pressure to the shower from August 1998 to February 2007;
- lack of heating from January to March 2000;
- leak from shower from May 2005 to February 2007;
- no hot water for three weeks in early 2005;
- leak from wash-hand basin from late 2007 to February 2007;
- leak from washing machine from early 2006 to 2007.

The tenant's rent had been £630 per month for most of the tenancy. He sought damages of £10,359 calculated as follows:

- August 1998 to February 2007 re defective shower, 8.5 years at 10 per cent of the rent = £6,426.
- January 2000 to March 2000 re lack of heating at 50 per cent of the rent = £945.
- 2005 re lack of hot water for 3 weeks, leak from wash hand basin, leak from shower at 15 per cent of the rent =£1,134.
- 2006 ongoing leak from shower, plus leak from washing machine causing leak to bedroom, kitchen and hallway at 25 per cent of the rent = £1,890.

The trial judge awarded £9,000 general damages, having found that 25 per cent diminution in value for the leaks was a bit excessive and that the damages should be lowered slightly because the landlord had attempted repairs although these had been ineffectual. She also awarded interest of £225, making a total claim award of £9,225.

8.79 **Ferguson v Jones, December 2008 *Legal Action* 32**

The tenant resided at the premises with her husband (until he passed away) and her six-year-old daughter. From the commencement of the tenancy and for a period of 17 months there was no heating or hot water throughout the property because the Emergency Gas Services had declared the heating system to be dangerous and disconnected it. The cooker was also disconnected. There was no other significant disrepair. Although the tenant had bought two heaters, these were insufficient to keep the tenant and her daughter warm. The trial judge held that the tenant was entitled to damages for inconvenience at the highest rate and, adopting a global approach, awarded damages at £2,700 per annum. An award of £4,000 was made for the total 17-month period. Special damages were awarded at £1,181.68. This included the cost of buying warm meals and two heaters.

8.80 **Aslam v Ali, December 2009 *Legal Action* 23**

The tenant of a four-bedroom house suffered from substantial disrepair from 2003. From 2003 to 2006, the central heating was inoperable to the entire house except for two rooms, and there were rotten and draughty windows, penetrating damp and defective plaster. The boiler was replaced in 2006 but the other defects remained. The judge awarded damages at 50 per cent of the rent of £60 per week from 2003 to 2006 and 33 per cent of the rent from 2006 to 2009.

8.81 **Gorman and Lane v Lambeth LBC, December 2009** *Legal Action* **23**

A long leaseholder of a one-bedroom flat suffered from cracking due to subsidence from 1994. No effective work was undertaken and eventually the flat was sold at a substantial undervalue to a developer for £85,000. A claim was issued seeking £10,000 for loss of profit on the sale of the property, £22,000 general damages, £1,500 special damages and interest of £25,000. The claim settled at the door of the court for £120,000.

Awards for asthma[60]

8.82 **Bygraves v Southwark LBC (1990)** *Kemp & Kemp* **para F2-035/2**

£5,000 to a child, who was five years old at the time of the award, for material exacerbation of very severe asthma since birth. £5,000 for future pain and suffering.

8.83 **McCaffrey v Lambeth LBC, August 1994** *Legal Action* **18;** *Kemp & Kemp* **para F2-0245/3;** *Housing Law Casebook* **para P11.43**

- £600 per annum to a young girl who suffered upper respiratory tract infections and asthma over 4½ years, including nine full-blown attacks but no hospital treatment, mainly suffering from wheezing and shortness of breath.
- £450 per annum to a young girl who suffered a large number of colds over 5½ years and developed asthma, requiring treatment from her GP on a number of occasions.
- £400 per annum to a young girl who suffered intermittently from chest problems and wheeziness sometimes requiring antibiotics.

8.84 **Stone v Redair Mersey Agencies, May 1997** *Legal Action* **18;** *Housing Law Casebook* **para P11.53**

£2000 for a six-year-old girl who had suffered four years of constant chest infections and mild asthma exacerbated by damp and draughts.

60 See 'Asthma' paragraphs 7.20–7.23.

8.85 **Alienus v Tower Hamlets LBC [1998] 1 CL 312;** *Housing Law Casebook* **para P11.22**

£11,000 to a child who contracted and suffered acute asthma for seven years.

8.86 **Conroy v Hire Token Ltd, February 2002** *Legal Action* **22;** *Housing Law Casebook* **para P11.29**

£650 each to two children aged 2 and 4, who had both suffered from coughs and colds over a six-month period as a result of severe mould growth at their home. Neither child sought medical attention, nor was there a diagnosis of asthma.

8.87 **C (a child) v Empire Estates (2002) 6 QR 13**

- £8,500 to four-year-old child who contracted asthma and suffered exacerbation of coughing. The condition was so bad that he had to take steroids daily as well as using inhalers frequently.
- £1,750 to a six-year-old child who already had asthma, which became worse after living in damp conditions for eight months. A causal link was established because there had been a clear improvement in the child's state of health when they moved to drier premises in 2002.

8.88 **Rushton and Others v Southwark LBC, December 2006** *Legal Action* **24**

- £5,500 was awarded to a child who developed breathing problems and pneumonia eight weeks after moving into the property and was admitted to hospital for two weeks. Diagnosis of asthma made. The damp conditions had exacerbated but not caused the asthma. Prognosis was good.
- £10,000 was awarded to a second child, who had worse symptoms. Admitted to hospital at eight months, followed by further asthma attacks, sometimes requiring hospital admission. Prone to respiratory infections and repeated antibiotic treatment resulted in removal of enamel from one of front teeth. Asthma had been exacerbated by the damp. Prognosis that some risk of future illness, but condition improved since leaving property.

8.89 **Smyth v Farnworth, December 2009** *Legal Action* **23**

- £5,000 was awarded to the tenant for the fact that her depression had been exacerbated by the state of the property (namely water penetration to a conservatory throughout a tenancy and a defective boiler for a five-month period) and threats (over a five-week period) which had had an effect for a period of just over two years.

- £3,500 was awarded to her son for exacerbation of asthma for a two-year period, based on the basis of the lower award in *L (a child) v Empire Estates* (see paragraph 8.87).

8.90   Reference should also be made to the Judicial Studies Board guidelines,[61] which suggests damages of up to £3,250 for mild asthma, bronchitis, colds and chest problems (usually resulting from unfit housing or similar exposure, particularly in cases of young children), treated by a GP and resolving within a few months.

Awards for infestations[62]

8.91   **Clark v Wandsworth LBC, June 1994 *Legal Action* 15; *Housing Law Casebook* para P7.19**

£3,500 per annum for a flat heavily infested with cockroaches.

8.92   **McGuigan v Southwark LBC, March 1996 *Legal Action* 14; *Housing Law Casebook* para P11.46**

Awards ranging from between £1,000 per annum to £3,500 per annum for light to very severe cockroach infestations, including £3,000 for a severe one-year ant infestation, with some cockroaches.

8.93   **Dadd v Christian Action (Enfield) Housing Association, December 1994 *Legal Action* 18**

£2,090 per annum for a rat infestation with some other disrepair.

8.94   Awards were also made for rats in *Vergera v Lambeth LBC* (see paragraph 8.68) and *Sarmad v Okello* (see paragaph 8.71).

---

61 *JSB Guidelines for the Assessment of General Damages in Personal Injury Cases* (OUP, 9th edition, 2008).
62 See 'Vermin' paragraphs 7.99–7.102.

APPENDICES

A **Legislation 229**
Defective Premises Act 1972 ss1–4   230
Building Act 1984 ss76–79   233
Landlord and Tenant Act 1985 ss8 and 11–17   240
Environmental Protection Act 1990 ss79–82   245

B **Technical information: understanding experts' reports 255**

C **Early Notification Letter (ENL) flowchart 263**

D **Precedents 265**
Introduction   266

Civil remedies (see chapter 3)
1 *Questionnaire checklist   267*
2 *Early notification letter   269*
3 *Chronology   271*
4 *List of items damaged or destroyed by disrepair   272*
5 *Particulars of claim   273*
6 *Defence and counterclaim   277*
7 *Application for injunction (form N16A)   279*
8 *Draft mandatory order   280*
9 *Tomlin order   281*

Environmental Protection Act 1990 proceedings (see chapter 5)
10 *Notice of intended proceedings   283*
11 *Initial information   284*
12 *Statement in support of information   285*
13 *Further information (enforcement)   286*
14 *Statement in support of further information   287*

Official complaint under Housing Act 2004 s4 (see chapter 6)
15 *Draft request for a complaint to be made   288*
16 *Draft official complaint   289*

E *Kemp & Kemp* **inflation table 291**

Legislation

Defective Premises Act 1972 ss1–4   230
Building Act 1984 ss76–79   225
Landlord and Tenant Act 1985 ss8 and 11–17   232
Environmental Protection Act 1990 ss79–82   237

Defective Premises Act 1972 ss1–4

Duty to build dwellings properly

1 (1) A person taking on work for or in connection with the provision of a dwelling (whether the dwelling is provided by the erection or by the conversion or enlargement of a building) owes a duty–

(a) if the dwelling is provided to the order of any person, to that person; and

(b) without prejudice to paragraph (a) above, to every person who acquires an interest (whether legal or equitable) in the dwelling;

to see that the work which he takes on is done in a workmanlike or, as the case may be, professional manner, with proper materials and so that as regards that work the dwelling will be fit for habitation when completed.

(2) A person who takes on any such work for another on terms that he is to do it in accordance with instructions given by or on behalf of that other shall, to the extent to which he does it properly in accordance with those instructions, be treated for the purposes of this section as discharging the duty imposed on him by subsection (1) above except where he owes a duty to that other to warn him of any defects in the instructions and fails to discharge that duty.

(3) A person shall not be treated for the purposes of subsection (2) above as having given instructions for the doing of work merely because he has agreed to the work being done in a specified manner, with specified materials or to a specified design.

(4) A person who–

(a) in the course of a business which consists of or includes providing or arranging for the provision of dwellings or installations in dwellings; or

(b) in the exercise of a power of making such provision or arrangements conferred by or by virtue of any enactment;

arranges for another to take on work for or in connection with the provision of a dwelling shall be treated for the purposes of this section as included among the persons who have taken on the work.

(5) Any cause of action in respect of a breach of the duty imposed by this section shall be deemed, for the purposes of the Limitation Act 1939, the Law Reform (Limitation of Actions, &c) Act 1954 and the Limitation Act 1963, to have accrued at the time when the dwelling was completed, but if after that time a person who has done work for or in connection with the provision of the dwelling does further work to rectify the work he has already done, any such cause of action in respect of that further work shall be deemed for those purposes to have accrued at the time when the further work was finished.

Cases excluded from the remedy under section 1

2 (1) Where–

(a) in connection with the provision of a dwelling or its first sale or letting for habitation any rights in respect of defects in the state of the dwelling are conferred by an approved scheme to which this section applies on a person having or acquiring an interest in the dwelling; and

(b) it is stated in a document of a type approved for the purposes of this section that the requirements as to design or construction imposed by or under the scheme have, or appear to have, been substantially complied with in relation to the dwelling;

no action shall be brought by any person having or acquiring an interest in the dwelling for breach of the duty imposed by section 1 above in relation to the dwelling.

(2) A scheme to which this section applies–

(a) may consist of any number of documents and any number of agreements or other transactions between any number of persons; but

(b) must confer, by virtue of agreements entered into with persons having or acquiring an interest in the dwellings to which the scheme applies, rights on such persons in respect of defects in the state of the dwellings.

(3) In this section 'approved' means approved by the Secretary of State, and the power of the Secretary of State to approve a scheme or document for the purposes of this section shall be exercisable by order, except that any requirements as to construction or design imposed under a scheme to which this section applies may be approved by him without making any order or, if he thinks fit, by order.

(4) The Secretary of State–

(a) may approve a scheme or document for the purposes of this section with or without limiting the duration of his approval; and

(b) may by order revoke or vary a previous order under this section or, without such an order, revoke or vary a previous approval under this section given otherwise than by order.

(5) The production of a document purporting to be a copy of an approval given by the Secretary of State otherwise than by order and certified by an officer of the Secretary of State to be a true copy of the approval shall be conclusive evidence of the approval, and without proof of the handwriting or official position of the person purporting to sign the certificate.

(6) The power to make an order under this section shall be exercisable by statutory instrument which shall be subject to annulment in pursuance of a resolution by either House of Parliament.

(7) Where an interest in a dwelling is compulsorily acquired–

(a) no action shall be brought by the acquiring authority for breach of the duty imposed by section 1 above in respect of the dwelling; and

(b) if any work for or in connection with the provision of the dwelling was done otherwise than in the course of a business by the person in occupation of the dwelling at the time of the compulsory acquisition, the acquiring authority and not that person shall be treated as the person who took on the work and accordingly as owing that duty.

Duty of care with respect to work done on premises not abated by disposal of premises

3 (1) Where work of construction, repair, maintenance or demolition or any other work is done on or in relation to premises, any duty of care owed, because of the doing of the work, to persons who might reasonably be expected to be affected by defects in the state of the premises created by the doing of the work shall not be abated by the subsequent disposal of the premises by the person who owed the duty.

(2) This section does not apply–

(a) in the case of premises which are let, where the relevant tenancy of the premises commenced, or the relevant tenancy agreement of the premises was entered into, before the commencement of this Act;

(b) in the case of premises disposed of in any other way, when the disposal of the premises was completed, or a contract for their disposal was entered into, before the commencement of this Act; or

(c) in either case, where the relevant transaction disposing of the premises is entered into in pursuance of an enforceable option by which the consideration for the disposal was fixed before the commencement of this Act.

Landlord's duty of care in virtue of obligation or right to repair premises demised

4 (1) Where premises are let under a tenancy which puts on the landlord an obligation to the tenant for the maintenance or repair of the premises, the landlord owes to all persons who might reasonably be expected to be affected by defects in the state of the premises a duty to take such care as is reasonable in all the circumstances to see that they are reasonably safe from personal injury or from damage to their property caused by a relevant defect.

(2) The said duty is owed if the landlord knows (whether as the result of being notified by the tenant or otherwise) or if he ought in all the circumstances to have known of the relevant defect.

(3) In this section 'relevant defect' means a defect in the state of the premises existing at or after the material time and arising from, or continuing because of, an act or omission by the landlord which constitutes or would if he had had notice of the defect, have constituted a failure by him to carry out his obligation to the tenant for the maintenance or repair of the premises; and for the purposes of the foregoing provision 'the material time' means–

(a) where the tenancy commenced before this Act, the commencement of this Act; and

(b) in all other cases, the earliest of the following times, that is to say–

   (i)   the time when the tenancy commences;

   (ii) the time when the tenancy agreement is entered into;

   (iii) the time when possession is taken of the premises in contemplation of the letting.

(4) Where premises are let under a tenancy which expressly or impliedly gives the landlord the right to enter the premises to carry out any description of maintenance or repair of the premises, then, as from the time when he first is, or by notice or otherwise can put himself, in a position to exercise the right and so long as he is or can put himself in that position, he shall be treated for the purposes of subsections (1) to (3) above (but for no other purpose) as if he were under an obligation to the tenant for that description of maintenance or repair of the premises; but the landlord shall not owe the tenant any duty by virtue of this subsection in respect of any defect in the state of the premises arising from, or continuing because of, a failure to carry out an obligation expressly imposed on the tenant by the tenancy.

(5) For the purposes of this section obligations imposed or rights given by any enactment in virtue of a tenancy shall be treated as imposed or given by the tenancy.

(6) This section applies to a right of occupation given by contract or any enactment and not amounting to a tenancy as if the right were a tenancy, and 'tenancy' and cognate expressions shall be construed accordingly.

Building Act 1984 ss76–79

Defective premises, demolition etc

Defective premises

76 (1) If it appears to a local authority that–

(a) any premises are in such a state (in this section referred to as a 'defective state') as to be prejudicial to health or a nuisance, and

(b) unreasonable delay in remedying the defective state would be occasioned by following the procedure prescribed by section 80 of the Environmental Protection Act 1990,

the local authority may serve on the person on whom it would have been appropriate to serve an abatement notice under the said section 80 (if the local authority had proceeded under that section) a notice stating that the local authority intend to remedy the defective state and specifying the defects that they intend to remedy.

(2) Subject to subsection (3) below, the local authority may, after the expiration of nine days after service of a notice under subsection (1) above, execute such works as may be necessary to remedy the defective state, and recover the expenses reasonably incurred in so doing from the person on whom the notice was served.

(3) If, within seven days after service of a notice under subsection (1) above, the person on whom the notice was served serves a counter-notice that he intends to remedy the defects specified in the first-mentioned notice, the local authority shall take no action in pursuance of the first-mentioned notice unless the person who served the counter-notice–

(a) fails within what seems to the local authority a reasonable time to begin to execute works to remedy the said defects, or

(b) having begun to execute such works fails to make such progress towards their completion as seems to the local authority reasonable.

(4) In proceedings to recover expenses under subsection (2) above, the court–

(a) shall inquire whether the local authority were justified in concluding that the premises were in a defective state, or that unreasonable delay in remedying the defective state would have been occasioned by following the procedure prescribed by section 80 of the Environmental Protection Act 1990, and

(b) if the defendant proves that he served a counter-notice under subsection (3) above, shall inquire whether the defendant failed to begin the works to remedy the defects within a reasonable time, or failed to make reasonable progress towards their completion,

and if the court determines that–

(i) the local authority were not justified in either of the conclusions mentioned in paragraph (a) of this subsection, or

(ii) there was no failure under paragraph (b) of this subsection,

the local authority shall not recover the expenses or any part of them.

(5) Subject to subsection (4) above, in proceedings to recover expenses under subsection (2) above, the court may–

(a) inquire whether the said expenses ought to be borne wholly or in part by some person other than the defendant in the proceedings, and

(b) make such order concerning the expenses or their apportionment as appears to the court to be just,

but the court shall not order the expenses or any part of them to be borne by a person other than the defendant in the proceedings unless the court is satisfied that that other person has had due notice of the proceedings and an opportunity of being heard.

(6) A local authority shall not serve a notice under subsection (1) above, or proceed with the execution of works in accordance with a notice so served, if the execution of the works would, to their knowledge, be in contravention of a building preservation order under section 29 of the Town and Country Planning Act 1947.

(7) The power conferred on a local authority by subsection (1) above may be exercised notwithstanding that the local authority might instead have proceeded under Part VI of the Housing Act 1985 (repair notices).

Dangerous building

77 (1) If it appears to a local authority that a building or structure, or part of a building or structure, is in such a condition, or is used to carry such loads, as to be dangerous, the authority may apply to a magistrates' court, and the court may–

(a) where danger arises from the condition of the building or structure, make an order requiring the owner thereof–

(i) to execute such work as may be necessary to obviate the danger or,

(ii) if he so elects, to demolish the building or structure, or any dangerous part of it, and remove any rubbish resulting from the demolition, or

(b) where danger arises from overloading of the building or structure, make an order restricting its use until a magistrates' court, being satisfied that any necessary works have been executed, withdraws or modifies the restriction.

(2) If the person on whom an order is made under subsection (1)(a) above fails to comply with the order within the time specified, the local authority may–

(a) execute the order in such manner as they think fit, and

(b) recover the expenses reasonably incurred by them in doing so from the person in default,

and, without prejudice to the right of the authority to exercise those powers, the person is liable on summary conviction to a fine not exceeding level 1 on the standard scale.

(3) This section has effect subject to the provisions of the Planning (Listed Buildings and Conservation Areas) Act 1990 relating to listed buildings, buildings subject to building preservation notices and buildings in conservation areas.

Dangerous building – emergency measures

78 (1) If it appears to a local authority that–

(a) a building or structure, or part of a building or structure, is in such a state, or is used to carry such loads, as to be dangerous, and

(b) immediate action should be taken to remove the danger,

they may take such steps as may be necessary for that purpose.

(2) Before exercising their powers under this section, the local authority shall, if it is reasonably practicable to do so, give notice of their intention to the owner and occupier of the building, or of the premises on which the structure is situated.

(3) Subject to this section, the local authority may recover from the owner the expenses reasonably incurred by them under this section.

(4) So far as expenses incurred by the local authority under this section consist of expenses of fencing off the building or structure, or arranging for it to be watched, the expenses shall not be recoverable in respect of any period–

(a) after the danger has been removed by other steps under this section, or

(b) after an order made under section 77(1) above for the purpose of its removal has been complied with or has been executed as mentioned in subsection (2) of that section.

(5) In proceedings to recover expenses under this section, the court shall inquire whether the local authority might reasonably have proceeded instead under section 77(1) above, and, if the court determines that the local authority might reasonably have proceeded instead under that subsection, the local authority shall not recover the expenses or any part of them.

(6) Subject to subsection (5) above, in proceedings to recover expenses under this section, the court may–

(a) inquire whether the expenses ought to be borne wholly or in part by some person other than the defendant in the proceedings, and

(b) make such order concerning the expenses or their apportionment as appears to the court to be just,

but the court shall not order the expenses or any part of them to be borne by any person other than the defendant in the proceedings unless it is satisfied that that other person has had due notice of the proceedings and an opportunity of being heard.

(7) Where in consequence of the exercise of the powers conferred by this section the owner or occupier of any premises sustains damage, but section 106(1) below does not apply because the owner or occupier has been in default–

(a) the owner or occupier may apply to a magistrates' court to determine whether the local authority were justified in exercising their powers under this section so as to occasion the damage sustained, and

(b) if the court determines that the local authority were not so justified, the owner or occupier is entitled to compensation, and section 106(2) and (3) below applies in relation to any dispute as regards compensation arising under this subsection.

(8) The proper officer of a local authority may, as an officer of the local authority, exercise the powers conferred on the local authority by subsection (1) above.

(9) This section does not apply to premises forming part of a mine or quarry within the meaning of the Mines and Quarries Act 1954.

Ruinous and dilapidated buildings and neglected sites

79 (1) If it appears to a local authority that a building or structure is by reason of its ruinous or dilapidated condition seriously detrimental to the amenities of the neighbourhood, the local authority may by notice require the owner thereof–

(a) to execute such works of repair or restoration, or

(b) if he so elects, to take such steps for demolishing the building or structure, or any part thereof, and removing any rubbish or other material resulting from or exposed by the demolition,

as may be necessary in the interests of amenity.

(2) If it appears to a local authority that–

(a) rubbish or other material resulting from, or exposed by, the demolition or collapse of a building or structure is lying on the site or on any adjoining land, and

(b) by reason thereof the site or land is in such a condition as to be seriously detrimental to the amenities of the neighbourhood,

the local authority may by notice require the owner of the site or land to take steps for removing the rubbish or material as may be necessary in the interests of amenity.

(3) Sections 99 and 102 below apply in relation to a notice given under subsection (1) or (2) above, subject to the following modifications–

(a) section 99(1) requires the notice to indicate the nature of the works of repair or restoration and that of the works of demolition and removal of rubbish or material, and

(b) section 99(2) authorises the local authority to execute, subject to that subsection, at their election either the works of repair or restoration or the works of demolition and removal of rubbish or material.

(4) This section does not apply to an advertisement as defined in section 336(1) of the Town and Country Planning Act 1990.

(5) This section has effect subject to the provisions of the Planning (Listed Buildings and Conservation Areas) Act 1990 relating to listed buildings, buildings subject to building preservation notices and buildings in conservation areas.

Landlord and Tenant Act 1985 ss8 and 11–17

Implied terms as to fitness for human habitation

8 (1) In a contract to which this section applies for the letting of a house for human habitation there is implied, notwithstanding any stipulation to the contrary–

    (a) a condition that the house is fit for human habitation at the commencement of the tenancy, and

    (b) an undertaking that the house will be kept by the landlord fit for human habitation during the tenancy.

(2) The landlord, or a person authorised by him in writing, may at reasonable times of the day, on giving 24 hours' notice in writing to the tenant or occupier, enter premises to which this section applies for the purpose of viewing their state and condition.

(3) This section applies to a contract if–

    (a) the rent does not exceed the figure applicable in accordance with the subsection (4), and

    (b) the letting is not on such terms as to the tenant's responsibility as are mentioned in subsection (5).

(4) The rent limit for the application of this section is shown by the following Table, by reference to the date of making of the contract and the situation of the premises:

TABLE

Date of making of contract	Rent limit
Before 31st July 1923.	In London: £40. Elsewhere: £26 or £16 (see Note 1).
On or after 31st July 1923 and before 6th July 1957.	In London: £40. Elsewhere: £26.
On or after 6th July 1957.	In London: £80. Elsewhere: £52.

NOTES

1. The applicable figure for contracts made before 31st July 1923 is £26 in the case of premises situated in a borough or urban district which at the date of the contract had according to the last published census a population of 50,000 or more. In the case of a house situated elsewhere, the figure is £16.

2. The references to 'London' are, in relation to contracts made before 1st April 1965, to the administrative county of London and, in relation to contracts made on or after that date, to Greater London exclusive of the outer London boroughs.

(5) This section does not apply where a house is let for a term of three years or more (the lease not being determinable at the option of either party before the expiration of three years) upon terms that the tenant puts the premises into a condition reasonably fit for human habitation.

(6) In this section 'house' includes–
   (a) a part of a house, and
   (b) any yard, garden, outhouses and appurtenances belonging to the house or usually enjoyed with it.
   ...

Repairing obligations
Repairing obligations in short leases

11 (1) In a lease to which this section applies (as to which, see sections 13 and 14) there is implied a covenant by the lessor–
   (a) to keep in repair the structure and exterior of the dwelling-house (including drains, gutters and external pipes),
   (b) to keep in repair and proper working order the installations in the dwelling-house for the supply of water, gas and electricity and for sanitation (including basins, sinks, baths and sanitary conveniences, but not other fixtures, fittings and appliances for making use of the supply of water, gas or electricity), and
   (c) to keep in repair and proper working order the installations in the dwelling-house for space heating and heating water.

(1A) If a lease to which this section applies is a lease of a dwelling-house which forms part only of a building, then, subject to subsection (1B), the covenant implied by subsection (1) shall have effect as if–
   (a) the reference in paragraph (a) of that subsection to the dwelling-house included a reference to any part of the building in which the lessor has an estate or interest; and
   (b) any reference in paragraphs (b) and (c) of that subsection to an installation in the dwelling-house included a reference to an installation which, directly or indirectly, serves the dwelling-house and which either–
      (i) forms part of any part of a building in which the lessor has an estate or interest; or
      (ii) is owned by the lessor or under his control.[1]

(1B) Nothing in subsection (1A) shall be construed as requiring the lessor to carry out any works or repairs unless the disrepair (or failure to maintain in working order) is such as to affect the lessee's enjoyment of the dwelling-house or of any common parts, as defined in section 60(1) of the Landlord and Tenant Act 1987, which the lessee, as such, is entitled to use.[2]

(2) The covenant implied by subsection (1) ('the lessor's repairing covenant') shall not be construed as requiring the lessor–
   (a) to carry out works or repairs for which the lessee is liable by virtue of his duty to use the premises in a tenant-like manner, or would be so liable but for an express covenant on his part,
   (b) to rebuild or reinstate the premises in the case of destruction or damage by fire, or by tempest, flood or other inevitable accident, or

1　Section 11(1A) added by HA 1988 s116.
2　Section 11(1B) added by HA 1988 s116.

    (c) to keep in repair or maintain anything which the lessee is entitled to remove from the dwelling-house.

(3) In determining the standard of repair required by the lessor's repairing covenant, regard shall be had to the age, character and the dwelling-house and the locality in which it is situated.

(3A) In any case where–

    (a) the lessor's repairing covenant has effect as mentioned in subsection (1A), and

    (b) in order to comply with the covenant the lessor needs to carry out works or repairs otherwise than in, or to an installation in, the dwelling-house, and

    (c) the lessor does not have a sufficient right in the part of the building or the installation concerned to enable him to carry out the required works or repairs,

then, in any proceedings relating to a failure to comply with the lessor's repairing covenant, so far as it requires the lessor to carry out the works or repairs in question, it shall be a defence for the lessor to prove that he used all reasonable endeavours to obtain, but was unable to obtain, such rights as would be adequate to enable him to carry out the works or repairs.[3]

(4) A covenant by the lessee for the repair of the premises is of no effect so far as it relates to the matters mentioned in subsection (1)(a) to (c), except so far as it imposes on the lessee any of the requirements mentioned in subsection (2)(a) or (c).

(5) The reference in subsection (4) to a covenant by the lessee for the repair of the premises includes a covenant–

    (a) to put in repair or deliver up in repair,

    (b) to paint, point or render,

    (c) to pay money in lieu of repairs by the lessee, or

    (d) to pay money on account of repairs by the lessor.

(6) In a case in which the lessor's repairing covenant is implied there is also implied a covenant by the lessee that the lessor, or any person authorised by him in writing, may at reasonable times of the day and on giving 24 hours' notice in writing to the occupier, enter the premises comprised in the lease for the purpose of viewing their condition and state of repair.

Restriction on contracting out of s11

12 (1) A covenant or agreement, whether contained in a lease to which section 11 applies or in an agreement collateral to such a lease, is void in so far as it purports–

    (a) to exclude or limit the obligations of the lessor or the immunities of the lessee under that section, or

    (b) to authorise any forfeiture or impose on the lessee any penalty, disability or obligation in the event of his enforcing or relying upon those obligations or immunities,

unless the inclusion of the provision was authorised by the county court.

(2) The county court may, by order made with the consent of the parties, authorise the inclusion in a lease, or in an agreement collateral to a lease, of provisions

---

3   Section 11(3A) added by HA 1988 s116.

excluding or modifying in relation to the lease, the provisions of section 11 with respect to the repairing obligations of the parties if it appears to the court that it is reasonable to do so, having regard to all the circumstances of the case, including the other terms and conditions of the lease.

13 Leases to which s11 applies: general rule

(1) Section 11 (repairing obligations) applies to a lease of a dwelling-house granted on or after 24th October 1961 for a term of less than seven years.

(2) In determining whether a lease is one to which section 11 applies–
  (a) any part of the term which falls before the grant shall be left out of account and the lease shall be treated as a lease for a term commencing with the grant,
  (b) a lease which is determinable at the option of the lessor before the expiration of seven years from the commencement of the term shall be treated as a lease for a term of less than seven years, and
  (c) a lease (other than a lease to which paragraph (b) applies) shall not be treated as a lease for a term of less than seven years if it confers on the lessee an option for renewal for a term which, together with the original term, amounts to seven years or more.

(3) This section has effect subject to–
  section 14 (leases to which section 11 applies: exceptions), and
  section 32(2) (provisions not applying to tenancies within Part II of the Landlord and Tenant Act 1954).

Leases to which s11 applies: exceptions

14 (1) Section 11 (repairing obligations) does not apply to a new lease granted to an existing tenant, or to a former tenant still in possession, if the previous lease was not a lease to which section 11 applied (and, in the case of a lease granted before 24th October 1961, would not have been if it had been granted on or after that date).

(2) In subsection (1)–
  'existing tenant' means a person who is when, or immediately before, the new lease is granted, the lessee under another lease of the dwelling-house;
  'former tenant still in possession' means a person who–
  (a) was the lessee under another lease of the dwelling-house which terminated at some time before the new lease was granted, and
  (b) between the termination of that other lease and the grant of the new lease was continuously in possession of the dwelling-house or of the rents and profits of the dwelling-house; and
  'the previous lease' means the other lease referred to in the above definitions.

(3) Section 11 does not apply to a lease of a dwelling-house which is a tenancy of an agricultural holding within the meaning of the Agricultural Holdings Act 1986 and in relation to which that Act applies or to a farm business tenancy within the meaning of the Agricultural Tenancies Act 1995.

(4) Section 11 does not apply to a lease granted on or after 3rd October 1980 to–
  a local authority,
  a National Park authority
  a new town corporation,
  an urban development corporation,
  the Development Board for Rural Wales,

a registered social landlord,

a co-operative housing association, or

an educational institution or other body specified, or of a class specified, by regulations under section 8 of the Rent Act 1977 or paragraph 8 of Schedule 1 to the Housing Act 1988 (bodies making student lettings)

a housing action trust established under Part III of the Housing Act 1988.

(5) Section 11 does not apply to a lease granted on or after 3rd October 1980 to–

(a) Her Majesty in right of the Crown (unless the lease is under the management of the Crown Estate Commissioners), or

(b) a government department or a person holding in trust for Her Majesty for the purposes of a government department.

Jurisdiction of county court

15 The county court has jurisdiction to make a declaration that section 11 (repairing obligations) applies, or does not apply, to a lease–

(a) whatever the net annual value of the property in question, and

(b) notwithstanding that no other relief is sought than a declaration.

Meaning of 'lease' and related expressions

16 In sections 11 to 15 (repairing obligations in short leases)–

(a) 'lease' does not include a mortgage term;

(b) 'lease of a dwelling-house' means a lease by which a building or part of a building is let wholly or mainly as a private residence, and 'dwelling-house' means that building or part of a building;

(c) 'lessee' and 'lessor' mean, respectively, the person for the time being entitled to the term of a lease and to the reversion expectant on it.

Specific performance of landlord's repairing obligations

17 (1) In proceedings in which a tenant of a dwelling alleges a breach on the part of his landlord of a repairing covenant relating to any part of the premises in which the dwelling is comprised, the court may order specific performance of the covenant whether or not the breach relates to a part of the premises let to the tenant and notwithstanding any equitable rule restricting the scope of the remedy, whether on the basis of a lack of mutuality or otherwise.

(2) In this section–

(a) 'tenant' includes a statutory tenant,

(b) in relation to a statutory tenant the reference to the premises let to him is to the premises of which he is a statutory tenant,

(c) 'landlord', in relation to a tenant, includes any person against whom the tenant has a right to enforce a repairing covenant, and

(d) 'repairing covenant' means a covenant to repair, maintain, renew, construct or replace any property.

Environmental Protection Act 1990 ss79–82

Part III: Statutory Nuisances and Clean Air

Statutory nuisances

Statutory nuisances and inspections therefor

79 (1) Subject to subsections (1ZA) to (6A) below, the following matters constitute 'statutory nuisances' for the purposes of this Part, that is to say–

(a) any premises in such a state as to be prejudicial to health or a nuisance;

(b) smoke emitted from premises so as to be prejudicial to health or a nuisance;

(c) fumes or gases emitted from premises so as to be prejudicial to health or a nuisance;

(d) any dust, steam, smell or other effluvia arising on industrial, trade or business premises and being prejudicial to health or a nuisance;

(e) any accumulation or deposit which is prejudicial to health or a nuisance;

(f) any animal kept in such a place or manner as to be prejudicial to health or a nuisance;

(fa) any insects emanating from relevant industrial, trade or business premises and being prejudicial to health or a nuisance;

(fb) artificial light emitted from premises so as to be prejudicial to health or a nuisance;

(g) noise emitted from premises so as to be prejudicial to health or a nuisance;

(ga) noise that is prejudicial to health or a nuisance and is emitted from or caused by a vehicle, machinery or equipment in a street or in Scotland, road;

(gb) smoke, fumes or gases emitted from any vehicle, machinery or equipment on a street so as to be prejudicial to health or a nuisance other than from any vehicle, machinery or equipment being used for fire brigade purposes;

(h) any other matter declared by any enactment to be a statutory nuisance;

and it shall be the duty of every local authority to cause its area to be inspected from time to time to detect any statutory nuisances which ought to be dealt with under section 80 below or sections 80 and 80A below and, where a complaint of a statutory nuisance is made to it by a person living within its area, to take such steps as are reasonably practicable to investigate the complaint.

(1A) No matter shall constitute a statutory nuisance to the extent that it consists of, or is caused by, any land being in a contaminated state.

(1B) Land is in a 'contaminated state' for the purposes of subsection (1A) above if, and only if, it is in such a condition, by reason of substances in, on or under the land, that–

(a) significant harm is being caused or there is a significant possibility of such harm being caused; or

(b) significant pollution of the water environment is being caused or there is a significant possibility of such pollution being caused;

and in this subsection 'harm', 'pollution' in relation to the water environment, 'substance' and 'the water environment' have the same meanings as in Part IIA of this Act.

(2) Subsection (1)(b), (fb), (fba) and (g) above do not apply in relation to premises (or, in respect of paragraph (fba)(ii) above, a stationary object located on premises)–

    (a) occupied on behalf of the Crown for naval, military or air force purposes or for the purposes of the department of the Secretary of State having responsibility for defence, or

    (b) occupied by or for the purposes of a visiting force;

and 'visiting force' means any such body, contingent or detachment of the forces of any country as is a visiting force for the purposes of any of the provisions of the Visiting Forces Act 1952.

(3) Subsection (1)(b) above does not apply to–

    (i) smoke emitted from a chimney of a private dwelling within a smoke control area,

    (ii) dark smoke emitted from a chimney of a building or a chimney serving the furnace of a boiler or industrial plant attached to a building or for the time being fixed to or installed on any land,

    (iii) smoke emitted from a railway locomotive steam engine, or

    (iv) dark smoke emitted otherwise than as mentioned above from industrial or trade premises.

(4) Subsection (1)(c) above does not apply in relation to premises other than private dwellings.

(5) Subsection (1)(d) above does not apply to steam emitted from a railway locomotive engine.

    (5A) Subsection (1)(fa) does not apply to insects that are wild animals included in Schedule 5 to the Wildlife and Countryside Act 1981 (animals which are protected), unless they are included in respect of section 9(5) of that Act only.

(5B) Subsection (1)(fb) does not apply to artificial light emitted from–

    (a) an airport;

    (b) harbour premises;

    (c) railway premises, not being relevant separate railway premises;

    (d) tramway premises;

    (e) a bus station and any associated facilities;

    (f) a public service vehicle operating centre;

    (g) a goods vehicle operating centre;

    (h) a lighthouse;

    (i) a prison.

(5BA) Subsection (1)(fba) above does not apply to artificial light emitted from a lighthouse (within the meaning of Part 8 of the Merchant Shipping Act 1995).

(6) Subsection (1)(g) above does not apply to noise caused by aircraft other than model aircraft.

(6A) Subsection (1)(ga) above does not apply to noise made–

    (a) by traffic,

    (b) by any naval, military or air force of the Crown or by a visiting force (as defined in subsection (2) above), or

    (c) by a political demonstration or a demonstration supporting or opposing a cause or campaign.

(7) In this Part–

'airport' has the meaning given by section 95 of the Transport Act 2000;

'appropriate person' means–

(a) in relation to England, the Secretary of State;

(b) in relation to Wales, the National Assembly for Wales;

'associated facilities', in relation to a bus station, has the meaning given by section 83 of the Transport Act 1985;

'bus station' has the meaning given by section 83 of the Transport Act 1985;

'chimney' includes structures and openings of any kind from or through which smoke may be emitted;

'dust' does not include dust emitted from a chimney as an ingredient of smoke;

'equipment' includes a musical instrument;

'fumes' means any airborne solid matter smaller than dust;

'gas' includes vapour and moisture precipitated from vapour;

'goods vehicle operating centre', in relation to vehicles used under an operator's licence, means a place which is specified in the licence as an operating centre for those vehicles, and for the purposes of this definition 'operating centre' and 'operator's licence' have the same meaning as in the Goods Vehicles (Licensing of Operators) Act 1995;

'harbour premises' means premises which form part of a harbour area and which are occupied wholly or mainly for the purposes of harbour operations, and for the purposes of this definition 'harbour area' and 'harbour operations' have the same meaning as in Part 3 of the Aviation and Maritime Security Act 1990;

'industrial, trade or business premises' means premises used for any industrial, trade or business purposes or premises not so used on which matter is burnt in connection with any industrial, trade or business process, and premises are used for industrial purposes where they are used for the purposes of any treatment or process as well as where they are used for the purposes of manufacturing;

'lighthouse' has the same meaning as in Part 8 of the Merchant Shipping Act 1995;

'local authority' means–

(a)   in Greater London, a London borough council, the Common Council of the City of London and, as respects the Temples, the Sub-Treasurer of the Inner Temple and the Under-Treasurer of the Middle Temple respectively;

(b)   in England outside Greater London, a district council;

(bb)   in Wales, a county council or county borough council;

(c)   the Council of the Isles of Scilly; and

(d)   in Scotland, a district or islands council or a council constituted under section 2 of the Local Government etc (Scotland) Act 1994;

'noise' includes vibration;

'person responsible'–

(a) in relation to a statutory nuisance, means the person to whose act, default or sufferance the nuisance is attributable;

(b) in relation to a vehicle, includes the person in whose name the vehicle is for the time being registered under the Vehicle Excise and

Registration Act 1994 and any other person who is for the time being the driver of the vehicle;

(c) in relation to machinery or equipment, includes any person who is for the time being the operator of the machinery or equipment;

'prejudicial to health' means injurious, or likely to cause injury, to health;

'premises' includes land (subject to subsection (5AB) above) and, subject to subsection (12) and, in relation to England and Wales section 81A(9) below, any vessel;

'prison' includes a young offender institution;

'private dwelling' means any building, or part of a building, used or intended to be used, as a dwelling;

'public service vehicle operating centre', in relation to public service vehicles used under a PSV operator's licence, means a place which is an operating centre of those vehicles, and for the purposes of this definition 'operating centre', 'PSV operator's licence' and 'public service vehicle' have the same meaning as in the Public Passenger Vehicles Act 1981;

'railway premises' means any premises which fall within the definition of 'light maintenance depot', 'network', 'station' or 'track' in section 83 of the Railways Act 1993;

'relevant separate railway premises' has the meaning given by subsection (7A);

'road' has the same meaning as in Part IV of the New Roads and Street Works Act 1991;

'smoke' includes soot, ash, grit and gritty particles emitted in smoke;

'street' means a highway and any other road, footway, square or court that is for the time being open to the public;

'tramway premises' means any premises which, in relation to a tramway, are the equivalent of the premises which, in relation to a railway, fall within the definition of 'light maintenance depot', 'network', 'station' or 'track' in section 83 of the Railways Act 1993;

and any expressions used in this section and in the Clean Air Act 1993 have the same meaning in this section as in that Act and section 3 of the Clean Air Act 1993 shall apply for the interpretation of the expression 'dark smoke' and the operation of this Part in relation to it.

(7A) Railway premises are relevant separate railway premises if–

(a) they are situated within–

    (i) premises used as a museum or other place of cultural, scientific or historical interest, or

    (ii) premises used for the purposes of a funfair or other entertainment, recreation or amusement, and

(b) they are not associated with any other railway premises.

(7B) For the purposes of subsection (7A)–

(a) a network situated as described in subsection (7A)(a) is associated with other railway premises if it is connected to another network (not being a network situated as described in subsection (7A)(a));

(b) track that is situated as described in subsection (7A)(a) but is not part of a network is associated with other railway premises if it is connected to track that forms part of a network (not being a network situated as described in subsection (7A)(a));

(c) a station or light maintenance depot situated as described in subsection (7A)(a) is associated with other railway premises if it is used in connection with the provision of railway services other than services provided wholly within the premises where it is situated.

In this subsection 'light maintenance depot', 'network', 'railway services', 'station' and 'track' have the same meaning as in Part 1 of the Railways Act 1993.

(7C) In this Part 'relevant industrial, trade or business premises' means premises that are industrial, trade or business premises as defined in subsection (7), but excluding–

(a) land used as arable, grazing, meadow or pasture land,

(b) land used as osier land, reed beds or woodland,

(c) land used for market gardens, nursery grounds or orchards,

(d) land forming part of an agricultural unit, not being land falling within any of paragraphs (a) to (c), where the land is of a description prescribed by regulations made by the appropriate person, and

(e) land included in a site of special scientific interest (as defined in section 52(1) of the Wildlife and Countryside Act 1981),

and excluding land covered by, and the waters of, any river or watercourse, that is neither a sewer nor a drain, or any lake or pond.

(7D) For the purposes of subsection (7C)–

'agricultural' has the same meaning as in section 109 of the Agriculture Act 1947;

'agricultural unit' means land which is occupied as a unit for agricultural purposes;

'drain' has the same meaning as in the Water Resources Act 1991;

'lake or pond' has the same meaning as in section 104 of that Act;

'sewer' has the same meaning as in that Act.

(8) Where, by an order under section 2 of the Public Health (Control of Disease) Act 1984, a port health authority has been constituted for any port health district, the port health authority shall have by virtue of this subsection, as respects its district, the functions conferred or imposed by this Part in relation to statutory nuisances other than a nuisance falling within paragraph (fb), (g) or (ga) of subsection (1) above and no such order shall be made assigning those functions; and 'local authority' and 'area' shall be construed accordingly.

(9) In this Part 'best practicable means' is to be interpreted by reference to the following provisions–

(a) 'practicable' means reasonably practicable having regard among other things to local conditions and circumstances, to the current state of technical knowledge and to the financial implications;

(b) the means to be employed include the design, installation, maintenance and manner and periods of operation of plant and machinery, and the design, construction and maintenance of buildings and structures;

(c) the test is to apply only so far as compatible with any duty imposed by law;

(d) the test is to apply only so far as compatible with safety and safe working conditions, and with the exigencies of any emergency or unforeseeable circumstances;

and, in circumstances where a code of practice under section 71 of the Control of Pollution Act 1974 (noise minimisation) is applicable, regard shall also be had to guidance given in it.

(10) A local authority shall not without the consent of the Secretary of State institute summary proceedings under this Part in respect of a nuisance falling within paragraph (b), (d), (e), (fb) or (g) and, in relation to Scotland, paragraph (ga), of subsection (1) above if proceedings in respect thereof might be instituted under regulations under section 2 of the Pollution Prevention and Control Act 1999 ...[4]

(11) The area of a local authority which includes part of the seashore shall also include for the purposes of this Part the territorial sea lying seawards from that part of the shore; and subject to subsection (12) and, in relation to England and Wales, section 81A below, this Part shall have effect, in relation to any area included in the area of a local authority by virtue of this subsection–

    (a) as if references to premises and the occupier of premises included respectively a vessel and the master of a vessel; and

    (b) with such other modifications, if any, as are prescribed in regulations made by the Secretary of State.

(12) A vessel powered by steam reciprocating machinery is not a vessel to which this Part of this Act applies.

Summary proceedings for statutory nuisances

80 (1) Subject to subsection (2A) where a local authority is satisfied that a statutory nuisance exists, or is likely to occur or recur, in the area of the authority, the local authority shall serve a notice ('an abatement notice') imposing all or any of the following requirements–

    (a) requiring the abatement of the nuisance or prohibiting or restricting its occurrence or recurrence;

    (b) requiring the execution of such works, and the taking of such other steps, as may be necessary for any of those purposes,

and the notice shall specify the time or times within which the requirements of the notice are to be complied with.

(2) Subject to section 80A(1) below, the abatement notice shall be served–

    (a) except in a case falling within paragraph (b) or (c) below, on the person responsible for the nuisance;

    (b) where the nuisance arises from any defect of a structural character, on the owner of the premises;

    (c) where the person responsible for the nuisance cannot be found or the nuisance has not yet occurred, on the owner or occupier of the premises.

(2A) Where a local authority is satisfied that a statutory nuisance falling within paragraph (g) of section 79(1) above exists, or is likely to occur or recur, in the area of the authority, the authority shall–

    (a) serve an abatement notice in respect of the nuisance in accordance with subsections (1) and (2) above; or

    (b) take such other steps as it thinks appropriate for the purpose of persuading the appropriate person to abate the nuisance or prohibit or restrict its occurrence or recurrence.

---

4   Words in EPA 1990 s79(10) to be repealed by the Pollution Prevention and Control Act 1999 from a date to be appointed.

(2B) If a local authority has taken steps under subsection (2A)(b) above and either of the conditions in subsection (2C) below is satisfied, the authority shall serve an abatement notice in respect of the nuisance.

(2C) The conditions are–

   (a) that the authority is satisfied at any time before the end of the relevant period that the steps taken will not be successful in persuading the appropriate person to abate the nuisance or prohibit or restrict its occurrence or recurrence;

   (b) that the authority is satisfied at the end of the relevant period that the nuisance continues to exist, or continues to be likely to occur or recur, in the area of the authority.

(2D) The relevant period is the period of seven days starting with the day on which the authority was first satisfied that the nuisance existed, or was likely to occur or recur.

(2E) The appropriate person is the person on whom the authority would otherwise be required under subsection (2A)(a) above to serve an abatement notice in respect of the nuisance.

(3) A person served with an abatement notice may appeal against the notice to a magistrates' court or in Scotland, the sheriff within the period of twenty-one days beginning with the date on which he was served with the notice.

(4) If a person on whom an abatement notice is served, without reasonable excuse, contravenes or fails to comply with any requirement or prohibition imposed by the notice, he shall be guilty of an offence.

(5) Except in a case falling within subsection (6) below, a person who commits an offence under subsection (4) above shall be liable on summary conviction to a fine not exceeding level 5 on the standard scale together with a further fine of an amount equal to one-tenth of that level for each day on which the offence continues after the conviction.

(6) A person who commits an offence under subsection (4) above on industrial, trade or business premises shall be liable on summary conviction to a fine not exceeding £20,000.

(7) Subject to subsection (8) below, in any proceedings for an offence under subsection (4) above in respect of a statutory nuisance it shall be a defence to prove that the best practicable means were used to prevent, or to counteract the effects of, the nuisance.

(8) The defence under subsection (7) above is not available–

   (a)   in the case of a nuisance falling within paragraph (a), (d), (e), (f), (fa) or (g) of section 79(1) above except where the nuisance arises on industrial, trade or business premises;

   (aza) in the case of a nuisance falling within paragraph (fb) of section 79(1) above except where–

      (i) the artificial light is emitted from industrial, trade or business premises, or

      (ii) the artificial light (not being light to which sub-paragraph (i) applies) is emitted by lights used for the purpose only of illuminating an outdoor relevant sports facility;

   (aa) in the case of a nuisance falling within paragraph (ga) of section 79(1) above except where the noise is emitted from or caused by a vehicle, machinery or equipment being used for industrial, trade or business purposes;

(b)   in the case of a nuisance falling within paragraph (b) of section 79(1) above except where the smoke is emitted from a chimney; and

(c)   in the case of a nuisance falling within paragraph (c) or (h) of section 79(1) above.

(8A) For the purposes of subsection (8)(aza) a relevant sports facility is an area, with or without structures, that is used when participating in a relevant sport, but does not include such an area comprised in domestic premises.

(8B) For the purposes of subsection (8A) 'relevant sport' means a sport that is designated for those purposes by order made by the Secretary of State, in relation to England, or the National Assembly for Wales, in relation to Wales. A sport may be so designated by reference to its appearing in a list maintained by a body specified in the order.

(8C) In subsection (8A) 'domestic premises' means–

(a)   premises used wholly or mainly as a private dwelling, or

(b)   land or other premises belonging to, or enjoyed with, premises so used.

(9) In proceedings for an offence under subsection (4) above in respect of a statutory nuisance falling within paragraph (g) or (ga) of section 79(1) above where the offence consists in contravening requirements imposed by virtue of subsection (1)(a) above it shall be a defence to prove–

(a)   that the alleged offence was covered by a notice served under section 60 or a consent given under section 61 or 65 of the Control of Pollution Act 1974 (construction sites, etc); or

(b)   where the alleged offence was committed at a time when the premises were subject to a notice under section 66 of that Act (noise reduction notice), that the level of noise emitted from the premises at that time was not such as to a constitute a contravention of the notice under that section; or

(c)   where the alleged offence was committed at a time when the premises were not subject to a notice under section 66 of that Act, and when a level fixed under section 67 of that Act (new buildings liable to abatement order) applied to the premises, that the level of noise emitted from the premises at that time did not exceed that level.

(10) Paragraphs (b) and (c) of subsection (9) above apply whether or not the relevant notice was subject to appeal at the time when the offence was alleged to have been committed.

Supplementary provisions

81 (1) Subject to subsection (1A) below, where more than one person is responsible for a statutory nuisance section 80 above shall apply to each of those persons whether or not what any one of them is responsible for would by itself amount to a nuisance.

(1A) In relation to a statutory nuisance within section 79(1)(ga) above for which more than one person is responsible (whether or not what any one of those persons is responsible for would by itself amount to such a nuisance), section 80(2)(a) above shall apply with the substitution of 'any one of the persons' for 'the person'.

(1B) In relation to a statutory nuisance within section 79(1)(ga) above caused by noise emitted from or caused by an unattended vehicle or unattended machinery or equipment for which more than one person is responsible, section 80A above shall apply with the substitution–

(a) in subsection (2)(a), of 'any of the persons' for 'the person' and of 'one such person' for 'that person',
(b) in subsection (2)(b), of 'such a person' for 'that person',
(c) in subsection (3), of 'any of the persons' for 'the person' and of 'one such person' for 'that person',
(d) in subsection (5), of 'any person' for 'the person', and
(e) in subsection (7), of 'a person' for 'the person' and of 'such a person' for 'that person'.

(2) Where a statutory nuisance which exists or has occurred within the area of a local authority, or which has affected any part of that area, appears to the local authority to be wholly or partly caused by some act or default committed or taking place outside the area, the local authority may act under section 80 above as if the act or default were wholly within that area, except that any appeal shall be heard by a magistrates' court or in Scotland, the sheriff having jurisdiction where the act or default is alleged to have taken place.

(3) Where an abatement notice has not been complied with, the local authority may, whether or not–
(a) proceedings have been taken for an offence under section 80(4); or
(b) a fixed penalty notice has been given under section 80(4A) in respect of that offence (regardless of whether the fixed penalty notice is accepted),
abate the nuisance and do whatever may be necessary in execution of the abatement notice.

(4) Any expenses reasonably incurred by a local authority in abating, or preventing the recurrence of, a statutory nuisance under subsection (3) above may be recovered by them from the person by whose act or default the nuisance was caused and, if that person is the owner of the premises, from any person who is for the time being the owner thereof; and the court or sheriff may apportion the expenses between persons by whose acts or defaults the nuisance is caused in such manner as the court consider or sheriff considers fair and reasonable.

(5) If a local authority is of opinion that proceedings for an offence under section 80(4) above would afford an inadequate remedy in the case of any statutory nuisance, they may, subject to subsection (6) below, take proceedings in the High Court or, in Scotland, in any court of competent jurisdiction for the purpose of securing the abatement, prohibition or restriction of the nuisance, and the proceedings shall be maintainable notwithstanding the local authority have suffered no damage from the nuisance.

(6) In any proceedings under subsection (5) above in respect of a nuisance falling within paragraph (g) or (ga) of section 79(1) above, it shall be a defence to prove that the noise was authorised by a notice under section 60 or a consent under section 61 (construction sites) of the Control of Pollution Act 1974.

(7) The further supplementary provisions in Schedule 3 to this Act shall have effect.

Expenses recoverable from owner to be a charge on premises

81A(1) Where any expenses are recoverable under section 81(4) above from a person who is the owner of the premises there mentioned and the local authority serves a notice on him under this section–
(a) the expenses shall carry interest, at such reasonable rate as the local

authority may determine, from the date of service of the notice until the whole amount is paid, and

(b) subject to the following provisions of this section, the expenses and accrued interest shall be a charge on the premises.

(2) A notice served under this section shall–

(a) specify the amount of the expenses that the local authority claims is recoverable,

(b) state the effect of subsection (1) above and the rate of interest determined by the local authority under that subsection, and

(c) state the effect of subsections (4) to (6) below.

(3) On the date on which a local authority serves a notice on a person under this section the authority shall also serve a copy of the notice on every other person who, to the knowledge of the authority, has an interest in the premises capable of being affected by the charge.

(4) Subject to any order under subsection (7)(b) or (c) below, the amount of any expenses specified in a notice under this section and the accrued interest shall be a charge on the premises–

(a) as from the end of the period of twenty-one days beginning with the date of service of the notice, or

(b) where an appeal is brought under subsection (6) below, as from the final determination of the appeal,

until the expenses and interest are recovered.

(5) For the purposes of subsection (4) above, the withdrawal of an appeal has the same effect as a final determination of the appeal.

(6) A person served with a notice or copy of a notice under this section may appeal against the notice to the county court within the period of twenty-one days beginning with the date of service.

(7) On such an appeal the court may–

(a) confirm the notice without modification,

(b) order that the notice is to have effect with the substitution of a different amount for the amount originally specified in it, or

(c) order that the notice is to be of no effect.

(8) A local authority shall, for the purpose of enforcing a charge under this section, have all the same powers and remedies under the Law of Property Act 1925, and otherwise, as if it were a mortgagee by deed having powers of sale and lease, of accepting surrenders of leases and of appointing a receiver.

(9) In this section–

'owner', in relation to any premises, means a person (other than a mortgagee not in possession) who, whether in his own right or as trustee for any other person, is entitled to receive the rack rent of the premises or, where the premises are not let at a rack rent, would be so entitled if they were so let, and

'premises' does not include a vessel.

(10) This section does not apply to Scotland.

Payment of expenses by instalments

81B(1) Where any expenses are a charge on premises under section 81A above, the local authority may by order declare the expenses to be payable with interest by instalments within the specified period, until the whole amount is paid.

(2) In subsection (1) above–

'interest' means interest at the rate determined by the authority under section 81A (1) above, and

'the specified period' means such period of thirty years or less from the date of service of the notice under section 81A above as is specified in the order.

(3) Subject to subsection (5) below, the instalments and interest, or any part of them, may be recovered from the owner or occupier for the time being of the premises.

(4) Any sums recovered from an occupier may be deducted by him from the rent of the premises.

(5) An occupier shall not be required to pay at any one time any sum greater than the aggregate of–

(a) the amount that was due from him on account of rent at the date on which he was served with a demand from the local authority together with a notice requiring him not to pay rent to his landlord without deducting the sum demanded, and

(b) the amount that has become due from him on account of rent since that date.

(6) This section does not apply to Scotland.

Summary proceedings by persons aggrieved by statutory nuisances

82 (1) A magistrates' court may act under this section on a complaint or, in Scotland, the sheriff may act under this section on a summary application, made by any person on the ground that he is aggrieved by the existence of a statutory nuisance.

(2) If the magistrates' court or, in Scotland, the sheriff is satisfied that the alleged nuisance exists, or that although abated it is likely to recur on the same premises or, in the case of a nuisance within section 79(1)(ga) above, in the same street or, in Scotland, road, the court or the sheriff shall make an order for either or both of the following purposes–

(a) requiring the defendant or, in Scotland, defender to abate the nuisance, within a time specified in the order, and to execute any works necessary for that purpose;

(b) prohibiting a recurrence of the nuisance, and requiring the defendant or defender, within a time specified in the order, to execute any works necessary to prevent the recurrence;

and, in England and Wales, may also impose on the defendant a fine not exceeding level 5 on the standard scale.

(3) If the magistrates' court or the sheriff is satisfied that the alleged nuisance exists and is such as, in the opinion of the court or of the sheriff, to render premises unfit for human habitation, an order under subsection (2) above may prohibit the use of the premises for human habitation until the premises are, to the satisfaction of the court or of the sheriff, rendered fit for that purpose.

(4) Proceedings for an order under subsection (2) above shall be brought–

(a) except in a case falling within paragraph (b), (c) or (d) below, against the person responsible for the nuisance;

(b) where the nuisance arises from any defect of a structural character, against the owner of the premises;

   (c) where the person responsible for the nuisance cannot be found, against the owner or occupier of the premises.

   (d) in the case of a statutory nuisance within section 79(1)(ga) above caused by noise emitted from or caused by an unattended vehicle or unattended machinery or equipment, against the person responsible for the vehicle, machinery or equipment.

(5) Subject to subsection (5A) below, where more than one person is responsible for a statutory nuisance, subsections (1) to (4) above shall apply to each of those persons whether or not what any one of them is responsible for would by itself amount to a nuisance.

(5A) In relation to a statutory nuisance within section 79(1)(ga) above for which more than one person is responsible (whether or not what any one of those persons is responsible for would by itself amount to such a nuisance), subsection (4)(a) above shall apply with the substitution of 'each person responsible for the nuisance who can be found' for 'the person responsible for the nuisance'.

(5B) In relation to a statutory nuisance within section 79(1)(ga) above caused by noise emitted from or caused by an unattended vehicle or unattended machinery or equipment for which more than one person is responsible, subsection (4)(d) above shall apply with the substitution of 'any person' for 'the person'.

(6) Before instituting proceedings for an order under subsection (2) above against any person, the person aggrieved by the nuisance shall give to that person such notice in writing of his intention to bring the proceedings as is applicable to proceedings in respect of a nuisance of that description and the notice shall specify the matter complained of.

(7) The notice of the bringing of proceedings in respect of a statutory nuisance required by subsection (6) above which is applicable is–

   (a) in the case of a nuisance falling within paragraph (g) or (ga) of section 79(1) above, not less than three days' notice; and

   (b) in the case of a nuisance of any other description, not less than twenty-one days' notice;

but the Secretary of State may, by order, provide that this subsection shall have effect as if such period as is specified in the order were the minimum period of notice applicable to any description of statutory nuisance specified in the order.

(8) A person who, without reasonable excuse, contravenes any requirement or prohibition imposed by an order under subsection (2) above shall be guilty of an offence and liable on summary conviction to a fine not exceeding level 5 on the standard scale together with a further fine of an amount equal to one-tenth of that level for each day on which the offence continues after the conviction.

(9) Subject to subsection (10) below, in any proceedings for an offence under subsection (8) above in respect of a statutory nuisance it shall be a defence to prove that the best practicable means were used to prevent, or to counteract the effects of, the nuisance.

(10) The defence under subsection (9) above is not available–

   (a)   in the case of a nuisance falling within paragraph (a), (d), (e), (f), (fa) or (g) of section 79(1) above except where the nuisance arises on industrial, trade or business premises;

(aa)   in the case of a nuisance falling within paragraph (ga) of section 79(1) above except where the noise is emitted from or caused by a vehicle, machinery or equipment being used for industrial, trade or business purposes;

(b)   in the case of a nuisance falling within paragraph (b) of section 79(1) above except where the smoke is emitted from a chimney;

(c)   in the case of a nuisance falling within paragraph (c) or (h) of section 79(1) above; and

(d)   in the case of a nuisance which is such as to render the premises unfit for human habitation.

(10A) For the purposes of subsection (10)(aza) 'relevant sports facility' has the same meaning as it has for the purposes of section 80(8)(aza).

(11) If a person is convicted of an offence under subsection (8) above, a magistrates' court or the sheriff may, after giving the local authority in whose area the nuisance has occurred an opportunity of being heard, direct the authority to do anything which the person convicted was required to do by the order to which the conviction relates.

(12) Where on the hearing of proceedings for an order under subsection (2) above it is proved that the alleged nuisance existed at the date of the making of the complaint or summary application, then, whether or not at the date of the hearing it still exists or is likely to recur, the court or the sheriff shall order the defendant or defender (or defendants or defenders in such proportions as appears fair and reasonable) to pay to the person bringing the proceedings such amount as the court or the sheriff considers reasonably sufficient to compensate him for any expenses properly incurred by him in the proceedings.

(13) If it appears to the magistrates' court or to the sheriff that neither the person responsible for the nuisance nor the owner or occupier of the premises or (as the case may be) the person responsible for the vehicle, machinery or equipment can be found the court or the sheriff may, after giving the local authority in whose area the nuisance has occurred an opportunity of being heard, direct the authority to do anything which the court or the sheriff would have ordered that person to do.

Technical information: understanding experts' reports

A lawyer's guide written by Mel Cairns MCIEH

Walls and brickwork

Main types of dampness

Rising damp – ground water moving up walls by capillary action into buildings

Penetrating damp – water entering the building as a result of rain or snow ingress

Condensation damp – atmospheric moisture condensing out on cold surfaces

Traumatic damp – caused by leaks/floods

Construction moisture – damp caused by building work: wet trades, plaster, mortar, paint etc

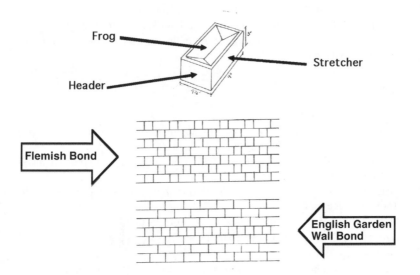

Terms used in relation to walls

Cavity wall – a wall formed of two layers of brick with a space between them, as a precaution against penetrating damp; common in buildings since the 1940s

Cold bridge – cold spot: especially at corners or concrete lintels/framing

Damp proof course – a horizontal barrier in a wall designed to prevent rising damp

Efflorescence – soluble salts collecting as white crystals on the face of bricks

Engineering bricks – dense/hard bricks (sometimes used as a damp-proof course)

Footings – foundations (in older properties sometimes formed of stepped courses of bricks)

Hygroscopic salts – salts that form on contaminated building materials which absorb or attract moisture from the air

Perpend – vertical mortar joint/end face of brick or stone

Plinth – base of the wall/column (often rendered)

Quoin – corner junction of brick walls

Render – a first layer of plaster or cement on a wall

Solid brick wall – external wall built of one layer, usually 9" thick; common in pre-1940s buildings

Sleeper wall – wall supporting floor joists (contains gaps for ventilation and so sometimes called a 'honeycomb' wall)

Stucco – render coating usually painted

Stud partition – plasterboard on timber frame

Systems building – non-traditional/prefabrication

Wall ties – metal straps linking inner and outer leaves of cavity wall

Weephole – omitting mortar joints at intervals above a damp-proof course to permit a cavity wall to drain

Roofs

Terms used in relation to roofs

Dished or settled roof – sagging of roof slope; often as a result of recovering with heavier concrete tiles without additional strengthening

Fire break wall – party wall continued up through roof space to prevent speed of fire in linked properties

Firring pieces – angled timber to support boarding and provide a self-draining slope on flat roofs

Flaunching – cement render embedding chimney pots

Nail fatigue – corrosion of slate fixings allowing slates to slip

Verge – edge of roof

Wall plate – timber along the top of a wall carrying rafters or joists

Pitched roof

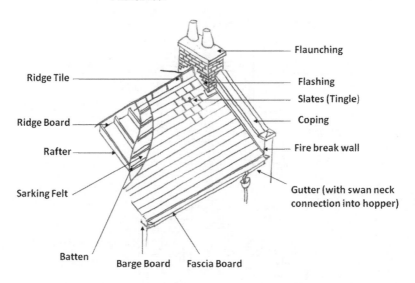

Ridge Tile

Ridge Board

Rafter

Sarking Felt

Batten

Barge Board   Fascia Board

Flaunching

Flashing

Slates (Tingle)

Coping

Fire break wall

Gutter (with swan neck connection into hopper)

Loft

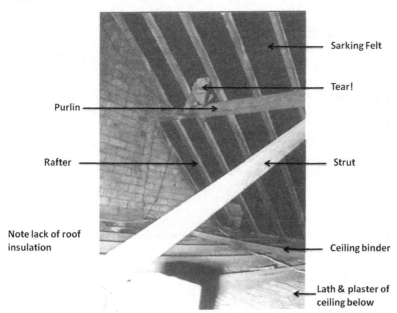

Sarking Felt

Tear!

Purlin

Rafter

Strut

Note lack of roof insulation

Ceiling binder

Lath & plaster of ceiling below

Windows

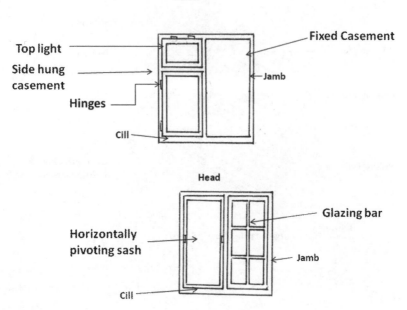

Terms used in relation to windows

Borrowed light – glazed panel in interior wall to introduce daylight from adjoining room

Crittall – steel framed windows

Espagnolette bolts – several bolts locking a door or window from a single handle/lock

Friction hinge – holds window ajar

Hopper window – small toplights or fanlight hinged on bottom edge

Spring action spiral/spring tape balances – modern versions of double hung sash replacing pulleys, cords and weights

Throating – drip details on underside edge of cills to prevent rain tracking back

Transom – horizontal rail in a window frame

Trickle vent – small adjustable vent in window head to provide background ventilation

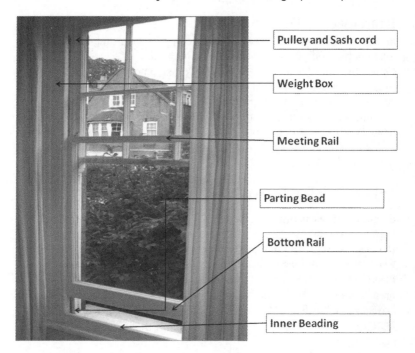

Pulley and Sash cord

Weight Box

Meeting Rail

Parting Bead

Bottom Rail

Inner Beading

Services

Terms used in relation to heating and hot water

Balanced flue – combustion gas and air supply sealed from room (ie, from/to exterior via dual flue)

Combi (combination) boiler – heats the radiators and the domestic hot water in one box; does not need a hot water tank

Cylinder stat – thermostat on hot water cylinder

Lockshield valve – valve on radiator used on installation to balance (set up) the flow of water in the system

Randall programmer – dated electro mechanical timer/programmer for central heating and hot water

Terms used in relation to electrics

Consumer unit – meter, main switch and cut-out (fuse/circuit breaker)

Junction box – covers ends of joints to conductors

Spur – socket outlet from ring main (fused/illuminated versions)

Terms used in relation to drainage:

Bolt down or double seal cover – second cover for a manhole inside a dwelling to prevent odours and flooding from back up

Cone joint – flexible joint connecting WC flush pipe to back of WC

Inspection chambers – manhole allowing access to section of drain; particularly where two or more drains meet

Rodding eye – point in pipe length where drain rods can be introduced (bolted on in cast iron pipes)

Soil stack – takes sewage to drain system; top section continues above roof to vent methane

Other technical terms

Bressemer [Breastsummer] – large heavy lintel – usually timber (older housing/shop fronts)

Dry riser – duct rising in block of flats to which the fire brigade can connect water supplies for hoses on landings

Floating floor – independent noise reducing overlay on an existing floor

French drain – shingle filled trench.

Garshey – waste disposal grinder in sink waste pipes

Half a person – child under 10 years of age in the statutory overcrowding standard

Scarf joint – angled joint in wood.

Sempatap – thin foam sheet with fibreglass on one side applied like wallpaper for insulation

Soffit – underside of stairs, arch, beam, window head etc

Splay – angle (e.g. cut brick, side wall of bay etc)

Sponge effect – potential for furnishings etc to take up water vapour temporarily

Tingle – a clip to temporarily secure loose slates

Upside down roof – Thermal insulation laid over (usually existing) flat roof

U-value – thermal transmittance co-efficient

Experts' equipment

Boroscope – allows examination of cavity walls and other voids

Carbide meter – on-site test for free moisture in walls

Current tester – detects current in wiring

Fibre optic viewer – allows examination of cavity walls and other voids

Data loggers/thermohygrometers – sample temperature and humidity data

Martindale – electric socket tester

Protimeter/damp meters – conductance/search mode/deep wall probes

Abbreviations

ABE – Association of Building Engineers

AFD – automatic fire detector

BA '84 – Building Act 1984

BBA – British Board of Agrément

BRE – Building Research Establishment

BREDEM – BRE Domestic Energy Model

BPA – British Pest Control Association

BWPDA – British Wood Preserving & Damp Proofing Association

Cat 1 – Category 1 hazard under HHSRS

Cat 2 – Category 2 hazard under HHSRS

CDM – Construction (Design & Management) Regulations

CI – cast iron

CO2 – Fire extinguisher using carbon dioxide (kitchen situations)

CIEH – Chartered Institute of Environmental Health

CIOB – Chartered Institute of Building

CIOP – Chartered Institute of Plumbing

Combi – combined heat and hot water boiler

CORGI – Council of Registered Gas Installers

COSHH – Control of Substances Hazardous to Health Regulations

CP – call point (fire alarm) or Code of Practice

CP12 – Landlords' statutory annual gas certificate under the Gas Safety (Installation & Use) Regulations

DPA – Defective Premises Act

dhs – double hung sash window

DHS – Decent Homes Standard

dpc – damp-proof course (in walls)

dpm – damp-proof membrane (in solid floors)

EDMO – Empty Dwelling Management Order

EHO – environmental health officer

EL – Emergency Lighting Unit (fire plans)

EPA – Environmental Protection Act 1990

EPO – Emergency Prohibition Order (HA 2004)

ERA – Emergency Remedial Action (HA 2004)

FED – front entrance door

FB – fire blanket (fire plans) or Fire Brigade

FMO – Final Management Order (HA 2004)

GS(I&U)R – Gas Safety (Installation and Use) Regulations

HA – Housing Act (+ date)

HAN – Hazard Awareness Notice (HA 2004 Part 1)

HASWA – Health and Safety at Work Act 1974

HD – heat detector (fire plans)

HHSRS – Housing Health and Safety Rating System (HA 2004 Part 1)
HIP – home information pack
HMO – house in multiple occupation
HSE – Health and Safety Executive
H20 – water type fire extinguisher (fire plans)
IC – inspection chamber
IEE – Institute of Electrical Engineers (now part of the IET)
IET – Institution of Engineering and Technology
IMO – Interim Management Order (HA 2004)
IN – Improvement Notice (HA 2004 Part 1)
IP – indicator panel (fire plans)
IVS – intervening ventilated space
LD (1 of 3) – grades of fire detection systems
MDHS – method for determination of hazardous substances
MO – Management Order (HA 2004)
NHER – National Home Energy Rating Scheme
OT – occupational therapist
Part P – Electrical Safety Requirements (Building Regulations)
PO – Prohibition Order (HA 2004 Part 1)
PDPA49 – Prevention of Damage by Pests Act 1949
QS – quantity surveyor
RICS – Royal Institution of Chartered Surveyors
RIDDOR – reporting of injuries, disease and dangerous occurrences
RPT – Residential Property Tribunal
RRO – Rent Repayment Order (HA 2004)
RWDP – rain-water down pipe
SA – smoke alarm (fire plans)
SAP – standard assessment procedure (energy label)
SD – smoke detector (fire plans)
S/C – self-closer
S/F – supply and fit (specifications)
Sika – tanking and waterproofing
SVP – soil vent pipe
TCRV – thermostatically controlled radiator valves
VOCs – volatile organic compounds (HHSRS)
WME – wood moisture equivalent (indicator of dampness in materials other than wood)
WWP – waste water preventer (flushing cistern)

Sources of information

Building Centre, Store Street, London W1
Dictionary of Building, 4th edn, Penguin
Tom Philbin *The Illustrated Dictionary of Building Terms*

Early Notification Letter (ENL) flowchart

CPR Pre-action Protocol for Housing Disrepair Cases, annex 5D[1]

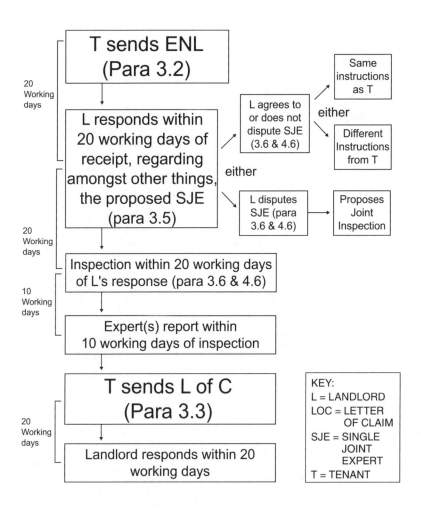

1   See chapter 3 para 3.54. This flowchart is Crown Copyright. Reproduced with the permission of the Controller of HMSO and the Queen's Printer for Scotland.

Precedents

Introduction   266

Civil remedies (see chapter 3)
1 Questionnaire checklist   267
2 Early notification letter   269
3 Chronology   271
4 List of items damaged or destroyed by disrepair   272
5 Particulars of claim   273
6 Defence and counterclaim   277
7 Application for injunction (form N16A)   279
8 Draft mandatory order   280
9 Tomlin order   281

Environmental Protection Act 1990 proceedings (see chapter 5)
10 Notice of intended proceedings   283
11 Initial information   284
12 Statement in support of information   285
13 Further information (enforcement)   286
14 Statement in support of further information   287

Official complaint under Housing Act 2004 s4 (see chapter 6)
15 Draft request for a complaint to be made   288
16 Draft official complaint   289

Introduction

This appendix contains precedent documentation for a routine disrepair case in which the tenant:

(1) brings an action for damages in the county court (see chapter 3); or

(2) brings proceedings in the magistrates' court under the Environmental Protection Act (EPA) 1990 s82 (see chapter 5); or

(3) asks for an official complaint under the Housing Act (HA) 2004.

It is assumed that, before launching the proceedings, the tenant's advisers have taken the steps recommended in this book.

The facts

Anna Tennant lives with her three-year-old son in a two-bedroom council flat on the fourth (top) floor of a council block. She has been the tenant for three years. Throughout the tenancy the premises have been damp. There are damp patches on the ceilings of the small bedroom and kitchen and rain-water penetration around the windows. The bathroom and kitchen walls are covered with black mould and the flat suffers from a cockroach infestation. There are other defects. Her rent is £95 per week and all but the water rates is paid by housing benefit.

She has complained frequently to the council's housing officer, reported the defects at the neighbourhood housing office and seen her councillor, but only limited (and largely 'botched') repair work has been undertaken.

There are alleged rent arrears of £750.

With her son in declining health, Anna turns to the Rainbow Community Law Centre for help.

Civil remedies (see chapter 3)

1 QUESTIONNAIRE CHECKLIST

INFORMATION AND DOCUMENTS NEEDED FROM YOU[1] FOR YOUR DISREPAIR CLAIM

1 Disrepair

For each item of disrepair/defect please let us know:

- The precise nature of each defect (eg, water penetration)
- Location (eg, in the lounge)
- The date when you first noticed this
- Details of any repairs done by you including the date and cost
- Any repairs done by your landlord including the date and whether these were effective

2 Complaints to your landlord

For each defect we need to know:

- When this was first reported to your landlord
- Who reported this (eg, you, member of your family, social worker etc)
- To whom you reported this (eg, housing officer, surveyor) and how this was done (eg, by telephone, letter or by visiting your housing office)
- Similar details in respect of subsequent complaints to your landlord
- Details of any visits by your landlord including the dates and person who visited

3 The effects of disrepair on you and your family

We need to know how you and your family were affected by the disrepair which will include for example:

- The nature of the inconvenience or discomfort resulting from the defect (eg, unable to use lounge for six months, ashamed to invite friends and relatives around etc)
- The effect on the physical health of you and your family
- The effect on the mental health of you and your family

4 Financial loss

You may have suffered financial loss as a result of the disrepair which may include:

Increased heating costs, in which case please let us know:

- Type of heating used
- Rooms affected
- Period of claim
- Cost in previous comparative period (eg, previous winter when there was no disrepair)
- Copies of all bills for the period of claim and previous comparative period

---

1 ie, the tenant.

Specific items damaged, eg, furniture, carpets, clothes, etc. Please fill in the attached list.[2]

Redecoration costs – please let us know:

- Which rooms were affected
- Date of redecoration costs with receipts if possible

Any other financial losses and expenses such as increased telephone bills, travel, cleaning expenses, costs of eating out of the home. Where possible please provide receipts or bills.

5　Documents

Please let me have all documents that you have in your possession relating to your case. These may include:

- Any letters or notes concerning arrangements before the tenancy commenced.
- The original signed tenancy agreement.
- Any documents handed to you with the standard terms of tenancy agreement.
- Any notices of rent increase.
- Any notices concerning housing benefit.
- Any Notices to Quit or Notices of Intention to Seek Possession.
- Old and current rent books.
- Any copy rent accounts or rent statements.
- Any repairs receipts.
- All letters and notes sent by you or received by you in connection with the tenancy since you have been a tenant.
- Correspondence with Councillors and/or MPs, if these relate to the tenancy.
- Gas, electricity bills, etc.
- Diaries and notes that you have kept of dealings with your landlord.
- Any other documents.

2　ie, the list at page 272 of this appendix.

2 EARLY NOTIFICATION LETTER

The Moors Estate Neighbourhood Housing Office
Anytown District Council
Moors Estate,
Anytown

Dear Sirs,

Anna Tennant, 17 Tower House, Moors Estate, Anytown
Moors Estate Neighbourhood Office

We are instructed by your above-named tenant. We are advising her under the Legal Help scheme. We are using the Housing Disrepair Protocol. *We enclose a copy of the Protocol for your information.*[3]

Repairs

Our client complains of the following defects at the property:

- perished wall plaster and mould growth in the kitchen;
- wet patches on the ceilings of the small bedroom and kitchen;
- mould growth on the walls of the bathroom and kitchen, caused or exacerbated by water penetration;
- rainwater penetration around the kitchen windows;
- the flat suffers from a cockroach infestation.

We enclose a schedule, which sets out the disrepair in each room.[4]

You received notice of the defects as follows:

- since March 2007 Ms Tennant has complained frequently by telephoning your housing office on numerous occasions;
- the property has been inspected by your colleagues Ms Grant in or about April 2006 and Mrs Griffiths in June 2007;
- in or about July 2008 your technical officer visited the premises and carried out an inspection;
- in about September 2008 our client reported the problems to Cllr Desmond Haines.

Please arrange to inspect the property as soon as possible. Access can be arranged directly with our client on telephone number: 0272 123456.

OR: Access will be available on the following dates and times: (list dates and times, as appropriate).

Please let us know what repairs you propose to carry out and the anticipated date for completion of the works.

---

3 Optional, but a good idea if writing to a landlord unfamiliar with housing litigation.
4 Optional, but this can be in the format used in Schedule G of the disrepair protocol.

Disclosure

Please also provide within 20 working days of receipt of this letter: all relevant records or documents including:

- a copy of tenancy agreement, including tenancy conditions;
- documents or computerised records relating to notice given, disrepair reported, inspection reports or repair works to the property;
- any other documents in the tenancy file.

We enclose a signed authority from our client for you to release this information to ourselves.

We also enclose copies of the following relevant documents from our client:

- repairs slip dated 21 August 2008;
- copy letter from Cllr Haines dated 2 October 2008.

Expert

If agreement is not reached about the carrying out of repairs within 20 working days of this letter, we propose jointly instructing a single joint expert to carry out an inspection of the property and to provide a report. We propose Ms D Expert, details below and we enclose a copy of her CV, plus a draft letter of instruction:

> Ms Denise Expert MIEH
> Expert EHC Ltd
> Robertsbridge Road
> Anytown
> Anycounty AC24 3PL

Please let us know if you agree to her appointment. If you object, please let us know your reasons within 20 working days.

If you do not object to the expert being instructed as a single joint expert, but wish to provide your own instructions, you should send those directly to her within 20 working days of this letter. Please send us a copy of your letter of instruction. If you do not agree to a single joint expert, we will instruct the above named to inspect the property in any event. In those circumstances, if you wish to instruct your expert to attend at the same time, please let us and our expert know within 20 working days of this letter.

Claim

Our client's disrepair claim requires further investigation. We will write to you as soon as possible with further details of the history of the defects and of notice relied on,[5] along with details of our client's claim for general and special damages.

Yours faithfully,

Rainbow Law Centre

---

5   Once the adviser has the tenancy documents from the landlord.

3 CHRONOLOGY[6]

Anna Tennant – 17 Towers House, Moors Estate, Anytown

Entries in ordinary font relate to documents produced by Ms Tennant.

Entries in italics relate to entries produced by Anytown DC, as part of pre-action disclosure.

Date	Event	Source and Comment
09.01.06	*Start of tenancy, Anna Tennant (AT) and Anytown DC (DC))*	*Tenancy file*
01.03.06	Approx date: AT notices dampness on ceiling in small bedroom, reports it to DC, reports gap above living room window frame	
01.04.06	Approx date: inspection by housing officer (Ms Grant)	
01.06.07	Approx date: AT complains of cockroach infestation	
01.06.07	Approx date: inspection by housing officer (Mrs Griffiths)	
01.12.07	Approx date: AT reports that dampness has spread to kitchen ceiling and mould begins to form	
22.11.08	*Arrears letter DC to AT – arrears £280.86*	*Tenancy file*
09.07.08	*Computer entry: tenant complaining of damp and insects*	*Maintenance file*
29.07.08	Technical officer from DC calls and inspects. Tells AT he suspects roof leaks.	
	etc – as per facts of case	

---

6   A chronology will not be necessary in every case.

4   LIST OF ITEMS DAMAGED OR DESTROYED BY DISREPAIR

No.	Quantity	Description	Nature of damage	Approx. date of damage	Date bought	Price paid £	Do you have the original receipt?	Cost to replace it today £	Do you have a written estimate?
1.									
2.									
3.									
4.									
5.									
6.									
7.									
8.									
9.									
10.									
11.									
12.									
13.									
14.									
etc									

5 PARTICULARS OF CLAIM

Note: the part in italics should be omitted if there is no infestation.

In the Anytown County Court   Case No: 9AT04723
BETWEEN
ANNA TENNANT   Claimant
and
ANYTOWN DISTRICT COUNCIL   Defendant

PARTICULARS OF CLAIM

1. In or about January 2006 the Claimant was granted a secure tenancy of 17 Tower House, Moors Estate, Anytown ('the premises') by the Defendant.

2. The premises consist of a two-bedroom flat on the fourth floor of a block of flats. *Surrounding the parts of the premises demised to the Plaintiff are service ducts, ducts, common parts and other parts of the structure and exterior of the block which constitute land retained by the Defendant.*

3. The premises have at all material times been occupied by the Claimant and her son Jeremy who was born on 3rd December 2005. The current rent is £95 per week.

4. The Claimant has at all material times been entitled to the benefit of:
   a) Express repairing obligations which include an obligation to repair the plaster to the premises. A copy of the relevant terms of the tenancy agreement is filed with these Particulars.
   b) A term implied by section 11 of the Landlord and Tenant Act 1985 (as amended).
   c) An implied term that the Defendant would give the Claimant quiet enjoyment of the premises.
   d) An implied term that the Defendant would ensure that the parts retained in its possession and control remain reasonably safe and do not cause damage to the Claimant or the flat (*Duke of Westminster v Guild* [1985] 1 QB 688).
   e) An implied term that the Defendant would make good and would redecorate on completing all work done further to its obligations and duties (*McGreal v Wake* (1984) 13 HLR 107).

5. Further, section 4 of the Defective Premises Act 1972 has imposed a duty on the Defendant to take such care as is reasonable in all the circumstances to ensure that the Claimant and her family should be reasonably safe from personal injury or from damage to their property due to the defective state of the premises.

6. The Defendant has throughout the period of the tenancy been in breach of the terms, duties and obligations set out above.

Particulars

i) From the outset of the tenancy there has been a half-inch gap above the window frame of the main window in the living room.

ii) From the outset of the tenancy, the pull-cord switch to the bathroom ceiling light has operated intermittently and the electrical socket provided in the hallway of the premises emits a spark when used.

iii) Some two months after the commencement of the tenancy a damp patch (approximately 2 feet in diameter) formed on the ceiling in the small bedroom. It is intermittently wet and dry and has discoloured the ceiling paper. Plaster in the area is cracked and since December 2007 rainwater has dripped from the cracks in periods of heavy rain.

iv) In March 2007 a patch similar to that described above developed on the kitchen ceiling.

v) In or about April 2007 a crack developed around the window frame of the window in the main bedroom. The plaster around that said window is loose and crumbling.

vi) The inner sills to both the aforementioned windows are rotted by reason of the accumulation of water upon them.

vii) The wallplaster to the external kitchen wall immediately below the window is cracked and since in or about November 2007 has crumbled and flaked upon contact. Black mould spots have been present on that wall since December 2007.

viii) The parapet wall to the walkway balcony immediately opposite the front door of the premises has throughout the tenancy had three of its upper row of bricks missing.

ix) The window glazing to the common stairwell providing access to the premises has been broken on two occasions. In 2007, the Defendant replaced the same after a delay of eight months. In 2008, after the glass was again broken, the Defendant replaced the same after six months.

x) In or about September 2008 a patch of damp began to develop on the wall of the premises immediately above the front door as a result of overflows from the roof guttering above.

xi) Further details of these and other defects are given in the report that is appended hereto as schedule 1, prepared by Ms Expert following an inspection on 15th January 2009.

7. *Further, since about December 2006 the premises have been infested with cockroaches, which come from parts retained by the Defendant and by reason of which the Defendant has caused a nuisance. No effective steps have been taken by the Defendant to eradicate the infestation either from the Claimant's flat or from the common parts.*

8. *The Defendant also owes the Claimant a duty of care to take reasonable steps to abate a nuisance that entered the premises from the parts retained by it and from the parts demised by it over which it had control.*

9. *Furthermore, in its treatment of the cockroaches the Defendant breached the aforesaid common law duty of care by reason of the following:*

Particulars

The Defendant:

i) *failed to carry out a survey of the block of flats in order to ascertain the full extent and origin of the infestation;*

ii) *failed to treat properly the parts retained by it;*

iii) *failed to treat properly the parts demised by it;*

iv) *failed to take any or any adequate steps to prevent/control the spread of cockroaches through the parts of the premises retained by the Defendant and from there into the demised premises;*

v) *failed to monitor after each treatment the extent of any remaining or new infestation;*

vi) *failed to treat properly or at all any remaining or new infestation after each treatment.*

10. The matters complained of in paragraph 6 and 7 above are known to the Defendant.

Particulars of knowledge

i) On occasions too numerous to particularise (but no less frequently than six times each year throughout the tenancy) the Claimant has reported the defects *and cockroaches* by telephone and in person to the Defendant at its Neighbourhood Housing Office.

ii) On occasions too numerous to particularise Housing Officers, workmen and other persons employed by the Defendant have visited the premises for the purpose of inspection.

iii) Without prejudice to the generality of the foregoing the Claimant has been visited at the premises by two successive Housing Officers (Ms Grant and Mrs Griffiths) in or about April 2006 and June 2007 respectively and both were shown the defects in the premises at the dates of their visits.

iv) In or about July 2008 a technical officer in the employ of the Defendant visited the premises and inspected the state thereof.

v) In or about September 2008 the Claimant reported the aforementioned defects *and cockroaches* to one Desmond Haines who is a councillor of the Defendant authority;

vi) On 2 February 2009 the claimant's solicitor sent a letter to the defendants notifying them of the defects. This was an 'early notification letter' as required by the CPR disrepair protocol.

11. By reason of the aforementioned breaches of terms, obligations and duties the Claimant has suffered loss, damage, distress and inconvenience.

Particulars of inconvenience and distress

i) For the duration of the tenancy the premises have been damp and unsightly and each winter have carried a pervading smell of dampness.

ii) The Claimant is forced to clean mould from the walls regularly, only to see it return within days.

iii) Decorations, carpets and soft furnishings provided at the premises by the Claimant have been ruined by dampness and/or mould growth.

iv) Clothing kept in the premises by the Claimant and her son has to be repeatedly washed and/or replaced as a result of permeation by damp odour and the effect of mould.

v) For the duration of the tenancy the Claimant has suffered stress as a result of the defects particularised above. Further stress has resulted from the failure of remedial work carried out by the Defendant in or about May 2007 and the failure of the Defendant to respond to complaints thereafter.

vi) *From the winter of 2006/07 and during each successive winter the premises have been infested with cockroaches most particularly in the kitchen area which has caused additional stress and inconvenience to the Claimant and caused her to incur additional expenditure through the cost of eating out.*

Particulars of losses and expenses

i) For six weeks in the winter of 2007/08 the Claimant was forced by conditions in the premises to leave and stay with her mother. She paid her mother £30 weekly for expenses during that stay.

ii) The Claimant has expended additional monies which she estimates at £150 per year since 2007 on heating as a result of the dampness of the premises.

iii) The Claimant has expended additional monies on eating out which she estimates at £520 per year since December 2006

12. The Claimant claims interest pursuant to the provisions of section 69 of the County Courts Act 1984 at such rate as the court may think fit.

AND THE CLAIMANT CLAIMS

i) An order for specific performance requiring the Defendant to remedy the disrepair;

ii) An injunction requiring the Defendant to take all steps necessary to discharge its statutory duty of care under section 4 of the Defective Premises Act 1972;

iii) *An injunction requiring the Defendant to take all steps necessary to eradicate the cockroach infestation from the premises and the building.*

iv) That the cost of repairs is more than £1,000;

v) Damages exceeding £5,000 but not more than £25,000;

vi) Interest on damages as provided by statute;

vii) Costs.

Dated this 27th day of April 2009

I believe that the facts stated in these Particulars of Claim are true.

Anna Tennant

Rainbow Community Law Centre
Rainbow High Street
Anytown
Solicitors for the Claimant

To: The District Judge and the Defendant

6 DEFENCE AND COUNTERCLAIM

If the Council issues possession proceedings based on the alleged rent arrears, Anna can counterclaim for damages for the disrepair. This precedent assumes that the claimants have set out their particulars of claim on the current N119 court form.

In the Anytown County Court   Case No: 9AT05106

BETWEEN

ANYTOWN DISTRICT COUNCIL   Claimant

and

ANNA TENANT   Defendant

DEFENCE AND COUNTERCLAIM

1. The Defendant denies that the Claimant has a right to possession as alleged in paragraph 1 of the Particulars of Claim but admits paragraphs 2 and 3 of the Particulars of Claim.

2. The Defendant does not admit paragraph 4 of the Particulars of Claim and requires the Claimant to prove the existence and extent of the arrears that it is claiming.

3. The Defendant claims the protection of section 84 of the Housing Act 1985 and asserts that in all the circumstances it would not be reasonable to make a possession order. The Defendant asserts that if arrears of rent have accrued, these arrears are due to the failure of the Claimant to pay and/or credit the rent account with housing benefit that is due to her.

4. In particular:
   i) The Claimant has failed to pay the Defendant her full housing benefit entitlement between February 2009 and April 2009 even though she completed a claim form in respect of the said period and has been eligible for maximum housing benefit throughout the period.
   ii) The Claimant has failed to pay any housing benefit from April 2009 to June 2009 even though the Defendant was entitled, had lodged her claim and dealt with all enquiries raised by the Claimant.

5. The Defendant cannot recall whether she received all the letters that the Claimant alleges were sent. Other than that, the Defendant admits paragraphs 5 and 6 of the Particulars of Claim.[7]

6. The Defendant relies upon the matters pleaded above and on the following facts and matters:
   i) The Defendant has been the Claimant's tenant since January 2006. She lives in the flat with her son Jeremy, who was born on 3rd December 2005. Since her son was born the Defendant has been unable to work and she is currently dependant upon income support.
   ii) If the Defendant loses her home she will have nowhere else to live.

---

7 This assumes that Anna confirms that she has received a valid notice seeking possession.

iii) The Defendant is not well. She has uterine fibroids and as a result she is severely anaemic. This makes her constantly exhausted.

7. The Defendant sets off the sums counterclaimed below to reduce or cancel out the arrears claimed by the Claimant.

COUNTERCLAIM

8. The Defendant repeats the defence set out above.

9. [From here on insert paragraphs 1–12 as per the Particulars of Claim on pages 273–276].[8]

AND THE DEFENDANT COUNTERCLAIMS FOR:

i)   An order for specific performance requiring the Claimant to remedy the disrepair;

ii) An injunction requiring the Claimant to take all steps necessary to discharge its statutory duty of care under section 4 of the Defective Premises Act 1972;

iii) An injunction requiring the Claimant to take all steps necessary to eradicate the cockroach infestation from the premises and the building.

iv) The cost of repairs, which is more than £1,000;

v)   Damages of not more than £25,000;

vi) Interest on damages as provided by statute;

vii) Costs.

Statement of truth

I ...., believe that the facts stated in this defence and counterclaim are true.[9]

Signed ....   Dated ....

Name of signatory ....

Dated the .... day of .... 20...

Rainbow Community Law Centre
Rainbow High Street
Anytown
Solicitors for the Defendant

To the District Judge and to the Claimant

---

8   But reverse 'claimant' for 'defendant' in each paragraph.
9   This wording assumes that Anna signs the statement of truth.

7 APPLICATION FOR INJUNCTION (FORM N16A)

Application for Injunction (General Form)	Name of court	Claim No.
	Anytown County Court	9AT04723
	Claimant's Name and Ref. Anna Tennant (02/1010/Ten)	
	Defendant's Name and Ref. Anytown District Council (L&D/HD/AB/23792)	

Notes on completion

Tick which boxes apply and specify the legislation where appropriate

(1) Enter the full name of the person making the application

(2) Enter the full name of the person the injunction is to be directed to

(3) Set out any proposed orders requiring acts to be done. Delete if no mandatory order is sought.

(4) Set out here the proposed terms of the injunction order (if the defendant is a limited company delete the wording in brackets and insert 'whether by its servants, agents, officers or otherwise').

(5) Set out here any further terms asked for including provision for costs

(6) Enter the names of all persons who have sworn affidavits or signed statements in support of this application

(7) Enter the names and addresses of all persons upon whom it is intended to serve this application

(8) Enter the full name and address for service and delete as required

☑ By application in pending proceedings

☐ Under Statutory provision _____

☐ This application is made under Part 8 of the Civil Procedure Rules

Seal

This application raises issues under the Human Rights Act 1998   ☐ Yes   ☒ No

The Claimant[1] Anna Tennant

applies to the court for an injunction order in the following terms:

The Defendant[2] Anytown District Council

must[3] carry out repair work as listed in the attached draft order on or before Monday 18 May 2009 at premises known as 17 Tower House, Moors Estate, Anytown,

And that[5]

The Defendant pay the costs of and incidental to this application in any event

The grounds of this application are set out in the written evidence

of[6] Anna Tennant   ~~sworn~~ (signed) on 23/4/09

This written evidence is served with this application.

This application is to be served upon[7]

The principal solicitor, Anytown District Council, Council Offices, Anytown, Anycounty

This application is filed by[8] Rainbow Community Law Centre

(the Solicitors for) the Claimant ~~(Applicant/Petitioner)~~

whose address for service is

Rainbow High Street, Anytown, Anycounty

Signed _____   Dated _____

---

* Name and address of the person application is directed to

To* of

This section to be completed by the court

This application will be heard by the (District) Judge

at

on   the   day of   20   at   o'clock

If you do not attend at the time shown the court may make an injunction order in your absence

If you do not fully understand this application you should go to a Solicitor, Legal Advice Centre or a Citizens' Advice Bureau

The court office at

is open between 10am and 4pm Mon - Fri. When corresponding with the court, please address all forms and letters to the Court Manager and quote the claim number.

N16A General form of application for injunction (04.07)   HMCS

8   DRAFT MANDATORY ORDER

This can be used for an injunction and/or specific performance.

Before His Honour Judge Right sitting at Anytown County Court on ....

UPON HEARING ....

UPON READING the Claimant's evidence dated 22nd April 2009

AND UPON the Claimant undertaking by her solicitor to abide by any order that this Court may make for the payment of damages in case this Court shall hereafter find that the Defendant has sustained any loss or damage by reason of this Order[10]

IT IS ORDERED THAT within 14 days of service of this order the Defendant shall carry out the following work at the premises known as: 17 Tower House, Moors Estate, Anytown:

a) repair the roof immediately above the premises to prevent the ingress of rainwater;

b) seal the gaps and cracks around the windows to the main bedroom of the premises;

c) provide to the solicitors for the Claimant a written report from a qualified electrical engineer setting out any work needed to the electrical system in the premises together with a proposed timescale for that work.

IT IS FURTHER ORDERED that the Defendant should pay the costs of and incidental to this hearing in any event.

PENAL NOTICE[11]

Any officer or director disobeying this order may be held to be in contempt of court and may be liable to be committed to prison.

Dated ....

Judge Right

---

10 It is hoped that the judge will not require this undertaking. See chapter 3 para 3.107.

11 But see paragraph 3.165 for the recent decision about penal notices where the defendant is a local authority.

9 TOMLIN ORDER

Order

In the	ANYTOWN COURT
Claim No.	9AT 04723
Claimant (including ref)	ANNA TENNANT (re: 02/0921/ten)
Defendant(s) (including ref)	ANYTOWN District Council (ref: LS/HD/AB/33354)
Date	6 November 2009

Before Judge ....

Upon the parties agreeing terms, and by consent

IT IS ORDERED THAT:

1. All further proceedings in this action shall be stayed upon the terms in the attached Schedule, except for the purpose of carrying such terms into effect.
2. The Claimant has permission to apply to the Court if the Defendant does not give effect to the terms set out in the Schedule.
3. The Defendant shall by 4 pm on 4 December 2009 pay to the Claimant's solicitors the sum of £10,000 on account of the Claimant's costs of the action.[12]
4. The Defendant shall pay the Claimant's costs as agreed or as assessed by the Court at a detailed assessment hearing.
5. There be a detailed assessment of the Claimant's publicly funded costs.

We hereby consent to an order in the above terms:

....
Rainbow Law Centre   The Principal Solicitor
Rainbow High Street   Anytown District Council
Anytown   Council Offices
Anycounty   Anytown
Tel:........................   Tel:........................
Fax:........................   Fax:........................
Ref: 02/0921/ten   Ref: . LS/HD/AB/33354

Solicitors for the Claimant   Solicitors for the Defendant

---

12 This is a useful way of obtaining some of the costs before a lengthy wait for a detailed assessment.

Tennant v Anytown   **Claim No.** 9AT 04723

SCHEDULE

1. The Defendant shall pay the Claimant the sum of £14,500, by 4 pm on 4 December 2009 in full and final satisfaction of all claims arising in this action.

2. In the event of late payment the Defendant will pay interest on the sum of £14,500 or any part remaining due at the applicable interest rate for unpaid County Court judgments.

3. The Defendant shall by 15 January 2010 complete the roofing works as referred to in the report dated 15 January 2009 of Ms Expert, the joint expert.

4. The said roofing work will be completed to the satisfaction of the joint expert whose reasonable further charges the Defendant shall pay.

Dated ....

Signed ....   Signed ....

Solicitor for the Claimant   Solicitors for the Defendant

Date ....   Date ....

Environmental Protection Act 1990 proceedings (see chapter 5)

10 NOTICE OF INTENDED PROCEEDINGS

The Clerk
Anytown District Council
Council Offices,
Anytown

Date: 22 January 2009

Our ref:

Your ref:

Dear Sir or Madam

Anna Tennant, 17 Tower House, Moors Estate, Anytown
Moors Estate Neighbourhood Office

We act for the above tenant.

We enclose a copy of an environmental health officer's report. You will see that the expert concludes that the state of the premises is such that they are prejudicial to the health of our client. Full particulars of the matters complained of are given in the report.

This letter is notice under section 82(6) of the Environmental Protection Act 1990 of our client's intention to bring proceedings against your authority under the provisions of the above-mentioned Act.

Unless the statutory nuisance at this dwelling is abated within 21 days of the date you have received this letter, then we are instructed to issue proceedings in the Anytown Magistrates' Court without further notice to you.

Please confirm safe receipt of this letter.

Yours faithfully,

Rainbow Law Centre

Copies to: The Borough Solicitor
The Moors Estate Neighbourhood Office

11   INITIAL INFORMATION

Note: An Information is a prescribed form under part 7 of the Criminal Procedure Rules. Currently the form can be accessed on the following link: http://www.justice.gov.uk/criminal/procrules_fin/contents/formssection/pdf/f1page1.pdf but this link may change.

INFORMATION
(Magistrates Courts Act 1980, s1)

IN THE ANYTOWN MAGISTRATES' COURT (Code)

Dated this   day of   2009

Accused: The Anytown District Council

Address: Council Offices, Anytown

Alleged offence (short particulars and statute):
That on this day a statutory nuisance as defined by section 79(1)(a) Environmental Protection Act 1990 exists at 17 Tower House, Moors Estate, Anytown and continues to exist and that the statutory nuisance (particulars of which are given in the attached statement) is the responsibility of the Anytown District Council and in so far as it results from structural defects is its responsibility as owner.

The Information of: Anna Tennant
who being a person aggrieved for the purpose of section 82 of the said Act (upon oath) states that the accused committed the offence of which particulars are given above.

Address of Informant:
c/o Rainbow Community Law Centre, Rainbow High Street, Anytown
Telephone No: 0275 125689 (ask for Ms Everett, the Informant's solicitor)

Taken (and sworn) before me this 14th day of February 2009

.... (Justice of the Peace)

.... (Justices Clerk)

12   STATEMENT IN SUPPORT OF INFORMATION

(NB: attach EHO report, submit in duplicate)

STATEMENT OF INFORMANT
(Magistrates Courts Act 1980, s1)

IN THE ANYTOWN MAGISTRATES' COURT (Code)

NAME: Anna Tennant

ADDRESS:
c/o Rainbow Community Law Centre, Rainbow High Street, Anytown

OCCUPATION: mother

I am the tenant of:
17 Tower House, Moors Estate, Anytown
('the premises')

My landlords are: The Anytown District Council, Council Offices, Anytown

The premises occupied by me are a statutory nuisance as defined by section 79(1)(a) of the Environmental Protection Act 1990 by reason of the facts set out in the attached report. I am therefore a person aggrieved for the purpose of section 82 Environmental Protection Act 1990.

The premises have been in a bad condition since March 2006; have been prejudicial to health for the whole of the last 6 months; and are prejudicial to health today. In March 2006, I informed the accused of the condition of the premises and officers employed by the accused inspected the property in April 2006 and June 2007. No effective work has been carried out within the past 6 months, or at all.

On 22nd January 2009 my solicitor, Ms Everett of the Rainbow Community Law Centre, Rainbow High Street, Anytown sent a letter giving the accused written details of the statutory nuisance and notice of my intention to bring proceedings under the Environmental Protection Act. The accused has therefore had 21 days' clear notice of my intentions and in spite of this, the defects have not been remedied.

In the circumstances, I request that the court grant me a summons against the accused.

Signed ....

Dated ....

13   FURTHER INFORMATION (ENFORCEMENT)

Note: Once again an information is a prescribed form under part 7 of the Criminal Procedure Rules. Currently the form can be accessed at http://www.justice.gov.uk/criminal/procrules_fin/contents/formssection/pdf/f1page1.pdf but this link may change.

INFORMATION
(Magistrates Courts Act 1980, s1)

IN THE ANYTOWN MAGISTRATES' COURT (Code)

Dated this 14th day of April 2009

Accused: The Anytown District Council

Address: Council Offices, Anytown

Alleged Offence: That contrary to section 82(8) of the Environmental Protection Act 1990 you have without reasonable excuse failed to comply with an order made by this court on 10th March 2009 requiring you to abate a statutory nuisance at 17 Tower House, Moors Estate, Anytown.

The Information of: Anna Tennant who being a person aggrieved for the purposes of section 82(1) of the said Act alleges that the accused committed the alleged offence and applies that the accused by summons do answer this information.

Address: Solicitor
Rainbow Community Law Centre
Rainbow High Street
Anytown

Taken before me this 14th day of April 2009

.... Justice of the Peace/Clerk to the Justices

14 STATEMENT IN SUPPORT OF FURTHER INFORMATION

STATEMENT OF INFORMANT
(Magistrates Courts Act 1980, s1)

IN THE ANYTOWN MAGISTRATES' COURT (Code)

NAME: Anna Tennant

ADDRESS:
c/o Rainbow Community Law Centre, Rainbow High Street, Anytown

OCCUPATION: mother

I am the tenant of:
17 Tower House, Moors Estate, Anytown
('the premises')

My landlords are: The Anytown District Council, Council Offices, Anytown

On 10th March 2009 a nuisance order under section 82(2) of the Environmental Protection Act 1990 was made in this court.

The accused failed to comply with the court order within the period prescribed by that order. As at 13th April 2009 no works prescribed in the court order had been started.

In the circumstances, I request the court to grant me a summons against the accused under Section 82(8) Environmental Protection Act 1990.

Signed ....

Official complaint under Housing Act 2004 s4 (see chapter 6)

15   DRAFT REQUEST FOR A COMPLAINT TO BE MADE

To: Mr John Smith, a Justice of the Peace for the Anytown Area

*Or: Ms Jenny Brown, clerk to the Anytown Parish (or Community) Council**

Our client Anna Tennant complains that the property occupied by her at 17 Tower House, Moors Estate, Anytown, being residential premises within the area of the Anytown District Council, is in such poor condition that an inspection of it should be made by the District Council so that it may determine whether the condition is a hazard and, if so, exercise its powers (and carry out any duties) given by the Housing Act 2004 Part 1.

Our client asks that you consider the documents and photographs enclosed.

She asks that if you/*your council** agree that these conditions merit a visit and inspection of the premises by an Environmental Health Officer employed by the District Council that you do cause complaint to be made to the said District Council in writing as provided by Housing Act 2004 section 4(3) requiring them to carry out an inspection of the said premises and to make such report, if any, as may be required by section 4(6). A form is supplied for your signature. We shall be pleased to submit it to the District Council if you would prefer us to do so. We also enclose, for your assistance, a copy of section 4.

Dated this 13th day of April 2010

Rainbow Community Law Centre
Rainbow High Street
Anytown
Solicitors for the Complainant

* delete as appropriate

16 DRAFT OFFICIAL COMPLAINT

To: The Proper Officer and the Senior Environmental Health Officer of the Anytown District Council, Anytown.

OFFICIAL COMPLAINT: HOUSING ACT 2004 s 4(3)

I, John Smith being an appointed Justice of the Peace for the area of Anytown

Or: I, Jenny Brown, the clerk to – and on behalf of – the Anytown Parish/ Community Council

do hereby make official complaint to you in the terms of section 4(3) Housing Act 2004 that the condition of the residential premises at 17 Tower House, Moors Estate, within the area of your District Council, calls for an inspection to be made by your Council pursuant to that section so that it may be considered whether a hazard is present and what action (if any) should be taken.

Dated this 14th day of April 2010

Signed ....

Kemp & Kemp inflation table*

In the left-hand column of this table is the year and in the right-hand column the multiplier which should be applied to the £ in January of that year to show its value in terms of the £ in January 2008.

Showing the Value of £ at Various Dates

YEAR	MULTIPLIER	YEAR	MULTIPLIER	YEAR	MULTIPLIER
1948	27.61	1969	12.27	1990	1.76
1949	26.23	1970	11.72	1991	1.61
1950	25.28	1971	10.81	1992	1.55
1951	24.40	1972	9.99	1993	1.52
1952	21.63	1972	9.28	1994	1.48
1953	20.77	1974	8.26	1995	1.44
1954	20.37	1975	6.90	1996	1.40
1955	19.61	1976	5.59	1997	1.36
1956	18.65	1977	4.80	1998	1.32
1957	17.93	1978	4.37	1999	1.28
1958	17.20	1979	4.00	2000	1.26
1959	16.92	1980	3.37	2001	1.23
1960	16.92	1981	2.98	2002	1.21
1961	16.65	1982	2.67	2003	1.18
1962	15.89	1983	2.54	2004	1.15
1963	15.43	1984	2.42	2005	1.11
1964	15.20	1985	2.30	2006	1.08
1965	14.47	1986	2.18	2007	1.04
1966	13.89	1987	2.10	2008	1.00
1967	13.36	1988	2.03		
1968	13.03	1989	1.89		

This table has been calculated from the Official Retail Prices Index, the value of the £ being taken from the figures published in January of each year, ending with January 2008.

* Reproduced from *Kemp & Kemp: Quantum of Damages* (looseleaf) with the kind permission of Thomson Reuters: www.sweetandmaxwell.co.uk. This is taken from release 109, November 2008, para INF-001.

Index

abatement notices
  appeals 5.31
  clarity 5.26
  criminal offences 5.32–5.34
  entry, right of 5.23
  environmental health officers
    (EHOs) 5.23
  failure to comply 5.32–5.34
  fines 5.33
  informal notices 5.24
  judicial review 5.44
  local authorities 5.23–5.34
  Local Government Ombudsman
    5.44
  mandatory duty 5.44
  person responsible, service on
    5.27–5.31
  recurring nuisances 5.40–5.41
  service 5.25, 5.27–5.28
  specification of works 5.26
  statutory nuisance 5.23–5.25,
    5.40–5.41, 5.44
  structural defects 5.28
  time limits 5.25
  works, recovery of costs of 5.34
access for landlord *see also* entry
  right of
  common law 1.111–1.115
  conditional fee agreements
    (CFAs) 4.79
  damages 8.45, 8.59
  entry, right of 1.111–1.117
  Housing Act 2004 6.28
  implied terms 1.111–1.117
  inspections 6.28
  protected or statutory tenancies
    1.116–1.117

  refusal 8.45, 8.59
  statute, under 1.111, 1.116–1.117
access for tenants, means of 1.45
access to neighbouring land orders
  7.81
adjoining property *see* neighbouring
  property
admissions, interim payments and
  3.134
ADR *see* alternative dispute
  resolution (ADR)
after-the-event insurance 4.88–4.90
age, character and locality 1.95
aggravated damages 3.92, 8.42
agricultural tenancies 1.98
allocation questionnaires (AQs)
  3.137–3.146
  costs estimates 3.141
  delay 3.146
  fast track claims 3.142, 3.143
  fees 3.141, 3.146
  joint experts 3.145
  mediation 3.139–3.140
  multi-track claims 3.142
  purpose 3.138
  service 3.144
  small track claims 3.142
  specimen AQ 3.142
  stay of proceedings 3.138
  time limits 3.138, 3.144
allocation to track 3.120, 4.44–
  4.46 *see also* allocation
  questionnaires (AQs)
alternative dispute resolution (ADR)
  costs 3.77
  Legal Representation 4.31
  mediation 3.139, 3.140

alternative dispute resolution
  continued
  negotiations 3.76–3.77
**ancillary property owned by
  landlord** 1.46–1.47
appeals
  abatement notices 5.31
  hazards awareness notices 6.51
  Housing Act 2004 6.48, 6.65
  improvement notices 6.48, 6.65
  legal aid 5.102
  prohibition orders 6.48, 6.65
  section 82 proceedings (EPA
    1990) 5.99, 5.102
area action 7.2–7.14
  challenging decisions 7.7
  clearance areas, declaration of
    1.68, 6.60–6.61, 6.75, 7.5,
    7.7–7.10
  local authorities 7.2–7.14
  rehousing and compensation 7.6
  renewal areas, declaration of 7.5,
    7.11–7.13
  slum clearances 7.3
asbestos
  direct remedies against landlords
    7.17
  environmental health officers
    (EHOs) 7.17
  flats 7.15
  housing conditions 7.15–7.19
  London Hazards Centre 7.17
  prejudicial to human health
    7.16–7.17
**assessments of premises under
  Housing Act 2004** 6.30–6.39
  Category 1 hazards 6.33, 6.36
  Category 2 hazards 6.33, 6.36
  dampness 6.36
  environmental health officers
    (EHOs) 6.39
  guidance 6.34, 6.39
  hazards
    definition 6.31–6.32
    identification of 6.31–6.33,
      6.36–6.37
  inspections 6.30, 6.39
  mould growth 6.36
  process, summary of 6.35

  re-assessments 6.39
assured shorthold tenancies 3.33–
  3.34
asthma
  causation 7.21, 8.6
  compensation, guidance on 7.22
  damages 8.6, 8.82–8.90
  dampness 7.20, 8.82–8.90
  dust mites 7.20
  experts 7.21
  housing conditions 7.20–7.23
attachment of earnings orders 3.173

bad housing *see* Environment
    Protection Act 1990;
    Housing Act 2004 and bad
    housing; housing conditions;
    statutory nuisance
bankruptcy 3.173
barristers *see* counsel, use of
before-the-event (BTE) insurance
    4.63–4.67
  exclusions 4.65
  notification of claims 4.65
  reporting conditions 4.67
  solicitors, freedom of choice of
    4.66
belongings, damage or loss of 8.36–
    8.37, 8.39, 8.41
betterment 8.38–8.39
blocked conduits 1.36
breach of statutory duty 2.27
builders, landlords as 2.5–2.7
bundles 3.158, 5.76
burst pipes 1.93
business efficacy 1.53

care and skill 1.56
Category 1 hazards
  assessments of premises under
    Housing Act 2004 6.33, 6.36
  clearance areas, declaring 6.60,
    7.8
  complaints 6.21, 6.23
  Environment Protection Act 1990
    5.108–5.114
  hazards awareness notices 6.51
  Housing Act 2004 6.21, 6.23,
    6.41–6.42

Category 2 hazards
assessments of premises under
Housing Act 2004 6.33, 6.36
clearance areas, declaring 7.8
complaints 6.21, 6.23
hazards awareness notices 6.51
Housing Act 2004 6.21, 6.23,
6.41–6.42
causes of action, accrual of 2.27,
3.40–3.42, 8.10
caveat emptor 1.5–1.6
CFAs *see* conditional fee agreements
(CFAs)
charging orders 3.173
children 2.18, 3.87
chimneys, cleaning 1.119
chronology 3.68–3.74
civil remedies 3.1–3.174
court proceedings 3.27–3.174
direct actions 3.3–3.26
claim forms
Courts Service website 3.88
form N1 3.88
issue of proceedings 3.88
specimen forms 3.89
claimants 3.44–3.49
damages for inconvenience and
stress caused to families
3.45, 3.47–3.48
Defective Premises Act 1972
3.46, 3.48
families 3.45, 3.47–3.48
joint tenants 3.44
occupiers' liability 3.46
third parties 3.44
clearance areas
Category 1 hazards 6.60, 7.8
Category 2 hazards 7.8
compulsory purchase 7.9
conditions 7.8
declaring clearance areas 6.60,
7.5, 7.7–7.10
fitness for human habitation 1.68
Housing Act 2004 6.60–6.61,
6.75
temporary accommodation 1.68
client care letters 4.78
common law 2.1–2.18
access for landlord 1.111–1.115

caveat emptor 1.5–1.6
express terms 1.6–1.7
implied terms 1.3, 1.37–1.38, 1.72
negligence 2.2–2.12
nuisance 2.13–2.18
common parts
express terms 1.16
immunity 2.10
implied terms 1.47, 1.98
negligence 2.10
occupiers' liability 2.21–2.22
rubbish chutes 1.16
specific performance 3.163
statutory nuisance 5.8
communal facilities 1.45
Community Legal Service (CLS) 4.3
compensation *see also* compensation
orders; damages
area action 7.6
assessment 8.50
asthma 7.22
dangerous buildings 7.48
displaced tenants 6.72–6.76
disturbance payments 6.76
Housing Act 2004 6.72–6.76
ombudsmen 8.49–8.50
Local Government Ombudsman
3.26
prohibition orders 6.56
rehousing 6.56, 7.6
Tenant Services Authority (TSA)
3.26
compensation orders
anxiety and distress 5.93–5.94
assessment 5.94
civil claims, impact on 5.97–5.98
conditional fee arrangements
5.104
costs 5.103
damages 5.97–5.98
payment, procedure for 5.106
prejudicial to health 5.93, 5.98
reasons for refusal, duty to give
5.96
section 82 proceedings (EPA
1990) 5.93–5.98
complaints *see also* ombudsmen
Category 1 or Category 2 hazards
6.21, 6.23

complaints *continued*
  delay 6.26–6.27
  disclosure 3.149
  Housing Act 2004 6.14, 6.20–
      6.25, 6.50
  Justices of the Peace, complaints
      by 6.21, 6.23–6.25
  Local Government Ombudsman
      3.22
  official complaints 6.20–6.23
  parish or community councils,
      complaints by 6.21, 6.23
  time limits 6.25
compromises *see* settlements
compulsory purchase 7.8
condensation dampness
  causes 7.25, 7.29
  Defective Premises Act 1972
      7.31–7.32
  design 7.29, 7.37
  Environmental Protection Act
      1990 7.33–7.37
  express terms 1.15, 7.27–7.28
  furnished lettings 7.28
  heating 7.36
  Housing Act 2004 7.38
  housing conditions 7.24–7.41
  implied terms 7.27–7.28
  Independent Housing
      Ombudsman 7.40
  insulation 7.36
  Landlord and Tenant Act 1985
      section 11 7.30
  licences 7.28
  Local Government Ombudsman
      7.39
  mould growth 7.24, 7.27
  ombudsmen 7.39–7.40
  repairing obligations, breach of
      7.29
  structure or exterior 1.15, 7.30–
      7.31
  ventilation 7.29, 7.36
conditional fee agreements (CFAs)
      4.68–4.99
  access for works 4.79
  challenges 4.97–4.99
  client care letters 4.78
  compensation orders 5.104
  costs 4.71, 4.74–4.76, 4.96–4.99
  counsel 4.95–4.96
  counterclaims 4.70
  damages 4.70
  disbursements 4.93
  fees 4.69
  indemnity principle 4.74
  instructions, taking initial 3.30
  legal expenses insurance 4.87–
      4.90
  Legal Representation 4.38
  model CFAs 4.77–4.79
  notice 4.91–4.92
  personal injuries 4.77
  rent arrears, clearing 4.79
  requirements 4.73–4.76
  risk assessment 4.80–4.84
  section 82 proceedings (EPA
      1990) 5.66, 5.104
  Solicitors' Code of Conduct 4.76
  success fees 4.71–4.72, 4.83–
      4.86, 4.91–4.96, 5.104
  technical challenges 4.75, 4.98
conditions *see* housing conditions
contempt, committal for 3.170
continuing obligations 1.75–1.77
contracts 1.1–1.17
  breach of contract 8.30
  causation 8.3–8.6
  damages 8.1–8.8, 8.30
  express terms 1.3–1.17
  foreseeability 8.7–8.8
  gas safety 7.65
  implied terms 1.3–1.4
  improvement notices 7.72
  inferred from circumstances 1.2
  intervening acts 8.3–8.5
  neighbouring property 7.79
  remoteness 8.7
  terms 1.3–1.17
  vermin infestations 7.100
contributory negligence 8.47
corporate landlords 3.149
correlative obligations
  business efficacy 1.53
  landlords, on 1.54
  payments by tenants 1.52
  structure and exterior by
      landlord, repair of 1.54–1.55

tenants, on 1.52–1.53
costs
  advance notice of claims 5.101
  allocation questionnaires 3.141
  alternative dispute resolution
    (ADR) 3.77
  amounts 5.100–5.101
  compensation orders 5.103
  conditional fee agreements
    (CFAs) 4.71, 4.74–4.76,
    4.96–4.99
  counterclaims 3.124
  court orders, implementation of
    3.169
  damages 3.103, 3.131, 3.137, 4.59,
    4.62
  directions 3.147
  disclosure 3.75, 3.149
  estimates 3.141, 3.155
  evidence 3.71, 3.74
  fees, waiver of 5.105
  final orders 3.169
  injunctions 3.103, 3.108
  interim applications 3.137
  judicial review 5.99
  legal aid 4.53, 4.59, 4.61–4.62
  Local Government Ombudsman
    3.25
  particulars of claim 3.94
  Pre-Action Protocol 3.52
  preparation for trial 3.155
  procedure for payment 5.106
  remedies 3.173, 3.174
  reserved costs 3.108
  schedule 3.158
  section 82 proceedings (EPA
    1990) 5.64, 5.99–5.107
  settlements 3.52, 3.125, 3.131,
    3.133
  small track claims 3.142
  statutory charge 4.59, 4.61–4.62
  wasted costs orders 5.107
counsel, use of
  conditional fee agreements
    (CFAs) 4.95–4.96, 5.66
  legal aid certificates 3.79
  letters of claim 3.83
  Listing Questionnaires (pre-trial
    checklist) 3.155

  preparation for trial 3.154
  recommendations 3.78
  section 82 proceedings (EPA
    1990) 5.66
counterclaims 3.27, 3.116–3.124
  allocation to track 3.120
  conditional fee agreements
    (CFAs) 4.70
  costs 3.124
  court fees 3.117
  damages 3.116, 3.122–3.124, 8.72,
    8.75–8.78
  legal aid certificates 3.121
  rent arrears, possession claims
    based on 3.116, 3.122–3.123
  set-off for rent 3.14–3.15, 3.118
  specimen form 3.116
  value of claim 3.120
county court 3.27, 3.95, 3.167
court proceedings 3.27–3.174
  allocation questionnaires 3.137–
    3.146
  chronology 3.68–3.74
  claim forms 3.88
  claimants 3.44–3.49
  costs 3.169
  counsel, use of 3.78–3.79
  counterclaims 3.27, 3.116–3.124
  county court 3.27, 3.95

  damages 3.169
  declarations 3.167–3.168
  disclosure 3.75, 3.149–3.150
  early notification letter (ENL)
    3.50, 3.54–3.57, 3.59
  evidence
    obtaining 3.75
    proof of evidence 3.69–3.74
  experts 3.59–3.67, 3.75, 3.145,
    3.147
  final orders 3.161–3.174
  first contact with landlord 3.55–
    3.57
  first interview, matters to
    consider after 3.40–3.48
  injunctions 3.96–3.115
  instructions, taking initial 3.30–
    3.39
  interim applications 3.134–3.137

court proceedings *continued*
  issuing proceedings 3.85–3.95
  legal aid 3.55, 3.58
  legal representation 3.28, 3.78–
      3.79
  letters of claim 3.81–3.84
  mandatory orders for works
      3.161–3.166
  mediation 3.140
  negotiations 3.76–3.77, 3.156
  particulars of claim 3.89–3.94
  Pre-Action Protocol 3.49–3.54
  preparations for trial 3.154–3.156
  proof of evidence 3.69–3.74
  remedies 3.170–3.174
  response 3.59, 3.84
  settlements 3.125–3.133
  time limits 3.40–3.43
  trials 3.157–3.160
  witness statements 3.71, 3.74,
      3.151–3.153
criminal offences *see also* section 82
      proceedings (EPA 1990)
  abatement notices 5.32–5.34
  Housing Act 2004 6.69–6.70
  improvement notices 6.69
  overcrowding 7.88
  penal notices, endorsement with
      3.115, 3.164–3.165
  prohibition orders 6.69
  statutory nuisance 5.49
Crown 1.98

damage to property
  ancillary property owned by
      landlord 1.46
  damages 8.36–8.37, 8.41
  evidence 3.72
  furniture, damage or loss of
      8.36–8.37, 8.41
  implied terms 1.37, 1.44, 1.46
  licences 1.44
  personal belongings, damage or
      loss of 8.36–8.37, 8.39, 8.41
damages 3.169, 8.1–8.94 *see also*
      compensation
  access, refusal of 8.45, 8.59
  aggravated damages 3.92, 8.42
  assessment 8.13–8.94

asthma caused by dampness 8.6,
      8.82–8.90
betterment 8.38–8.39
breach of contract 8.30
case notes 8.51–9.94
causation 8.3–8.6
causes of action, accrual of 8.10
claimants 3.45, 3.47–3.48
compensation orders 5.97–5.98
conditional fee agreements
      (CFAs) 4.70
contract 8.1–8.8
contributory negligence 8.47
costs 3.103, 3.131, 3.137, 4.59, 4.62
counterclaims 3.116, 3.122–3.124,
      8.72, 8.75–8.78
dampness
  asthma 8.82–8.90
  county court decisions 8.65,
      8.69–8.70, 8.73, 8.76–8.77,
      8.80
  Court of Appeal decisions
      8.52–8.55, 8.59–8.60
  High Court decisions 8.62
deceit 8.34
Defective Premises Act 1972 2.26
diminution in value 8.24, 8.27
displaced tenants 8.29, 8.34, 8.40,
      8.54, 8.68
disrepair cases 8.9–8.10, 8.14–
      8.32
distress and inconvenience
  case notes 8.15–8.16, 8.20–
      8.24, 8.28–8.29, 8.52–8.57
  claimants 3.45, 3.47–3.48
draughty windows 8.64, 8.80
dry rot 8.59
duty of care, breach of 8.30
economic loss 2.26
exaggerating expenses and losses
      3.38
exemplary damages 3.92, 8.42,
      8.61
expenses 3.38, 8.38, 8.40
expert evidence 8.27
fair rents 8.26
families, effect of disrepair on
      8.35
fast track claims 3.143

final orders 3.169
foreseeability 8.7–8.8
freezing injunctions 3.172
furniture, damage or loss of
    8.36–8.37, 8.41
gas safety 7.67
general damages 8.14–8.35
harassment 8.77
heating 8.54, 8.56, 8.71, 8.79–
    8.80
hot water 8.71, 8.77, 8.79
housing benefit 8.25
inflation 8.32
injunctions 3.98, 3.103, 3.109,
    3.172
instructions, taking initial 3.38
interest 8.48
interim payments 3.134, 8.9
intervening acts 8.3–8.5
legal aid 3.131, 4.42
lifts, broken 8.63
long leases 8.34, 8.52
loss of enjoyment 8.15
loss of profits 8.8
mitigation 8.43–8.46
move to alternative premises,
    refusal to 8.45–8.46
noise 8.62
nominal damages 8.55
occupation
    tenants not in occupation
        8.33–8.34
    tenants who remain in
        occupation 8.15–8.32
particulars of claim 3.92
personal belongings, damage or
    loss of 8.36–8.37, 8.39, 8.41
personal injuries 8.30, 8.35
prohibition notices 8.73
purposes of damages 8.11–8.12
refuse 8.58, 8.62, 8.68
remedial works, distress and
    inconvenience resulting fro
    8.28
remoteness 8.7
rent
    arrears 3.166, 2.122–3.124
    counterclaims 3.116, 3.122–
        3.124, 8.72, 8.75–8.78
    general damages, level of 8.18–
        8.20
    loss of rental value 8.23, 8.25–
        8.27
    reduction 8.16
    withholding rent and rent
        strikes 3.12
section 82 proceedings (EPA
    1990) 5.97–5.98
set-off against rent 3.13, 3.15–3.16
settlements 3.125–3.126, 3.128,
    3.131–3.132
special damages 8.36–8.48
statutory charge 4.59, 4.61–4.62
structural cracking 8.66–8.67,
    8.81
subsidence 8.67, 8.81
time limits 3.41
tort 8.1–8.8, 8.47
trespass 8.61
vermin infestation 8.57, 8.68,
    8.69, 8.91–8.94
water penetration 8.52–8.53,
    8.56, 8.60, 8.65, 8.68, 8.74–
    8.75
withholding rent and rent strikes
    3.12
dampness *see also* condensation
    dampness
assessments of premises under
    Housing Act 2004 6.36
asthma 7.20, 8.82–8.90
causes 7.43–7.44
damages
    asthma 8.82–8.90
    county court decisions 8.65,
        8.69–8.70, 8.73, 8.76–8.77,
        8.80
    Court of Appeal decisions
        8.52–8.55, 8.59–8.60
    High Court decisions 8.62
damp-proof courses 1.26
disproportionately extensive or
    costly work 1.26
Environmental Protection Act
    1990 7.44, 5.3
experts 3.65–3.66
flooding 7.43
Housing Acts 7.44

dampness *continued*
  housing conditions 7.42–7.46
  Human Rights Act 1998 2.54–
    2.55
  improvements 1.26
  negligence 2.3
  patch repairs 1.32, 1.34
  private and family right, right to
    respect for 2.54–2.55
  Scottish Grand Committee
    review 7.45
  water vapour 7.43
dangerous buildings 7.47–7.49
  compensation 7.48
  displaced tenants 7.48
  neighbouring property 7.80
  repairing obligations, breach of
    7.48
deceit 8.34
declarations
  clearance areas 6.60, 7.5, 7.7–7.10
  county courts 3.167
  interim declarations 3.168
  renewal areas 7.5, 7.11–7.13
decoration
  completion of works, on 1.29
  improvements, after 1.29
default judgments 3.135
Defective Premises Act 1972
  additional obligations 2.42–2.47
  application 2.25, 2.30
  breach of statutory duty 2.27
  cause of action, accrual of 2.27
  claimants 3.46, 3.48
  damages 2.26
  dampness 7.31–7.32
  design defects 2.46
  duty of care 2.24, 2.28, 2.31–2.32
  economic loss, damages for 2.26
  entry, right of 2.42–2.47
  exclusion or limitation of liability
    2.36
  families 2.28, 2.31, 2.46
  fitness for human habitation 2.23
  gas installations, inspection of
    2.41
  immunity of landlord 2.28
  improvements 2.45
  injunctions 2.47

inspection 2.39–2.41, 2.44
known of defect, where landlord
    ought to have 2.37–2.41
latent defects, inspection for
    2.39–2.40
notice to landlord 1.105
nuisance 2.46
other properties owned by same
    landlord 2.35
personal injuries 2.40, 2.43, 2.46
persons who owe duty, list of 2.24
professional or workmanlike
    manner 2.23
proper materials, use of 2.23
reversion, disposal of the 2.28
time limits 2.27, 3.42
visitors 2.28, 2.31, 2.46
defence 3.135–3.136, 5.73
definition of repair and disrepair
    1.18–1.36
  blocked conduits 1.36
  decoration 1.29
  deterioration 1.20
  disproportionately extensive or
    costly work 1.24–1.26
  guidance 1.19
  inherent defects 1.21–1.23
  patch repairs 1.31–1.35
  prevention of future damage 1.30
  renewal 1.18, 1.31–1.35
  small defects 1.26–1.28
delay
  allocation questionnaires 3.146
  complaints 6.26–6.27
  Emergency Legal Representation
    (ELR) 4.48–4.49
  Housing Act 2004 6.26–6.28
  inspections 6.26
  issue of proceedings .353
  Pre-Action Protocol 3.53
demolition
  definition 6.57
  Housing Act 2004 6.57–6.59, 6.75
  homelessness, priority need and
    6.59
  nuisance orders 5.87
  orders 6.57–6.59, 6.75
  section 82 proceedings (EPA
    1990) 5.87, 5.109

standard of repair 1.96
deposits, failure to register 6.12
derogation from grant 1.51
design defects
dampness 7.29, 7.37
Defective Premises Act 1972 2.46
Environment Protection Act 1990
5.112
deterioration 1.20, 1.28
diaries, keeping 3.37
dilapidated buildings 7.50–7.53, 7.80
diminution in value 8.24, 8.27
direct action 3.3–3.26
asbestos 7.17
Housing Ombudsman 3.21
Local Government Ombudsman
3.21–3.25
ombudsmen 3.21–3.26
receiver or manager, appointing a
3.19–3.20
reduction in rent 3.18
rent to pay for repairs, using
3.4–3.10
set-off against rent 3.13–3.17
Tenant Services Authority (TSA)
3.26
withholding rent and rent strikes
3.11–3.12
directions
compliance 3.148
costs orders 3.147
experts 3.147
preparation for trial 3.155
works to be carried out,
directions for 3.171
disbursements 4.93
disclosure 3.75, 3.149–3.150
complaints 3.149
corporate landlords 3.149
costs 3.75, 3.149
early notification letter (ENL) 3.57
experts 3.149
primary disclosure 5.72
secondary disclosure 5.73
section 82 proceedings (EPA
1990) 5.51, 5.72–5.73
tenants, by 3.150
displaced tenants *see also* rehousing
clearance areas, declaring 6.75

compensation 6.72–6.76
damages 8.29, 8.34, 8.40, 8.54,
8.68
dangerous buildings 7.48
demolition orders 6.75
Housing Act 2004 6.57–6.59,
6.72–6.76
move to alternative premises,
refusal to 8.45–8.46
prohibition orders 6.74–6.75
temporary accommodation 6.73,
6.75
**disproportionately extensive or
costly work** 1.24–1.26
**disturbance payments,
compensation for** 6.76
distress and inconvenience
claimants 3.45, 3.47–3.48
damages
case notes 8.15–8.16, 8.20–
8.24, 8.28–8.29, 8.52–8.57
claimants 3.45, 3.47–3.48
diaries, keeping 3.37
disturbance payments,
compensation for 6.76
noise 7.82
quiet enjoyment, implied term of
1.48–1.50
drains and sewers 7.54–7.59
drain, definition of 7.54
flooding 7.55
Human Rights Act 1998 2.56,
7.56
negligence 7.55
nuisance 2.56, 7.55, 7.57
prejudicial to health 7.57
remedial action 7.57
sewer, definition of 7.54
small repairs by notice, securing
7.58
structure and exterior 7.56
draughty windows 8.64, 8.80
dry rot 1.32, 1.34, 8.59
dust mites 7.20
duty of care
damages 8.30
Defective Premises Act 1972
2.24, 2.28, 2.31–2.32
negligence 2.2, 2.5–2.7, 2.19, 8.30

duty of care *continued*
  occupiers' liability 2.19
dwelling-houses
  definition 1.85–1.86
  implied terms 1.85–1.86
  installations 1.89–1.94
  structure and exterior 1.86

early notification letter (ENL) 3.50,
    3.54–3.57, 3.59
  contents 3.56
  disclosure 3.57
  legal aid 3.55
  response 3.59
  time limits 3.55
economic loss 2.11, 2.26
EHOs *see* environmental health
    officers (EHOs)
electricity 7.95–7.96
emergencies
  Emergency Legal Representation
    (ELR) 4.46–4.50
  emergency prohibition orders
    6.62
  emergency remedial orders 6.62–
    6.63
  prejudicial to health 5.36–5.39,
    5.43
  statutory nuisance 5.36–5.39, 5.43
enforcement
  gas safety 7.68
  Housing Act 2004 6.40–6.71,
    6.74
  inspections 6.16–6.17
  nuisance orders 5.88–5.90
  overcrowding 7.88
  section 82 proceedings (EPA
    1990) 5.88–5.90
  warrants of execution 3.173
enquiry, putting landlord on 1.105
entry, right of
  abatement notices 5.23
  access for landlord 1.111–1.117
  Defective Premises Act 1972
    2.42–2.47
  environmental health officers
    (EHOs) 5.23
  fitness for human habitation 1.62
  implied terms 1.74

  improvements 2.45, 7.73
  injunctions 2.47
  notice 1.74
  personal injuries 2.43, 2.46
environmental health officers
    (EHOs)
  abatement notices 5.23
  asbestos 7.17
  assessments of premises under
    Housing Act 2004 6.39
  engagement of independent
    EHOs 5.51
  entry, right of 5.23
  experts 5.53–5.55
  Housing Act 2004 6.10, 6.78
  improperly or unprofessional,
    where EHO acts 5.44
  inspections 5.43–5.44
  neighbouring property 7.80
  notice to landlord 1.103
  prejudicial to health 5.53
  reports, service of 5.54
  sanitary installations 7.92
  section 82 proceedings (EPA
    1990) 5.51, 5.53–5.55, 5.69,
    5.71
  statutory nuisance 5.42–5.45
  trial, availability for 5.69, 5.71
  visits 5.43–5.44
environmental pollution 2.51
Environment Protection Act 1990
    5.1–5.113 *see also* section 82
    proceedings (EPA 1990);
    statutory nuisance
  category 1 hazards 5.108–5.113
  dampness 5.3, 7.33–7.37, 7.44
  design defects 5.112
  Housing Acts 5.108–5.113
  noise 7.83
European Convention on Human
    Rights 2.48
evidence *see also* experts; witness
    statements
  chronology 3.69, 3.73
  contents 3.69
  costs 3.71, 3.74
  family members 3.74
  home visits 3.70
  obtaining evidence 3.75

proof of evidence 3.69–3.74
property damage 3.72
section 82 proceedings (EPA
  1990) 5.76
updating 3.73
witness statements 3.71
exclusion or limitation of liability
  2.20, 2.36, 3.8
exclusive possession 2.18
exemplary damages 3.92, 8.42, 8.61
expenses 3.38–3.39, 3.52, 3.107,
  8.38, 8.40
experts
  allocation questionnaires 3.145
  appointment 3.50
  asthma 7.21
  choice 3.64–3.67
  court proceedings 3.59–3.67, 3.75,
    3.145, 3.147
  damages 8.27
  dampness 3.65–3.66
  directions 3.147
  environmental health officers
    (EHOs) 3.66, 5.52–5.55
  Help at Court 4.23
  injunctions 3.112
  instructions 3.59–3.63
  Investigative Help 4.34
  joint experts 3.145
  joint inspections 3.61
  objections 3.63
  particulars of claim 3.91
  Pre-Action Protocol 3.50, 3.60–
    3.63
  prejudicial to health 5.53
  recommendations 3.66
  reports
    form and contents 3.67
    Help at Court 4.23
    Investigative Help 4.34
    Pre-Action Protocol 3.50
    service 5.54
    statements of truth 3.67
  section 82 proceedings (EPA
    1990) 5.53–5.55
  single joint expert 3.61–3.62
  standard of repair 1.95
express terms 1.3–1.17
  common law 1.6–1.7

common parts 1.16
condensation 1.15
coverage 1.10, 1.14
dampness 7.27–7.28
extensive repairing obligations
  1.14–1.15
fitness for human habitation
  1.38–1.43
good condition and repair 1.15
implied terms 1.73
interpretation 1.12–1.13
mould 1.15
orally, incorporated 1.3
renewal of whole property 1.12
repairing obligations 1.4
social landlords 1.16–1.17
statute 1.6–1.7
structural or external parts 1.14–
  1.15
terminology 1.12
unfair contract terms 1.8–1.9
variation 1.8, 1.11
writing 1.3
extensive or costly work,
  disproportionately 1.24–
  1.26
exterior *see* structure or exterior

fair rent 8.26
families
  children 2.18, 3.87
  claimants 3.45, 3.47–3.48
  damages 8.35
  Defective Premises Act 1972
    2.28, 2.31, 2.46
  evidence 3.74
fast track claims 3.142, 3.143, 4.45
fees *see also* conditional fee
    agreements (CFAs)
  allocation questionnaires 3.141,
    3.146
  costs 5.105
  counterclaims 3.117
  court fees 3.109, 3.117
  fixed fees 4.17
  injunctions 3.109
  section 82 proceedings (EPA
    1990) 5.105
  waiver 5.105

final orders
  costs 3.169
  damages 3.169
  declarations 3.167–3.168
  mandatory orders for works
    3.161–3.166
  remedies for breach of orders
    3.170–3.174
fines
  abatement notices 5.33
  Housing Act 2004 6.69–6.70
  improvement notices 6.69
  prohibition orders 6.69
  section 82 proceedings (EPA
    1990) 5.91–5.92
fire precautions 7.60–7.63
  fire authorities or local
    authorities, intervention
    by 7.61
  flats 7.62
  multi-occupied buildings 7.62,
    7.75
first contact with landlord 3.55–3.57
**first interview, matters to consider
  after** 3.40–3.48
fitness for human habitation 1.38–
  1.43
  clearance areas, temporary
    accommodation in 1.68
  continuing obligation 1.58, 1.60
  Defective Premises Act 1972 2.23
  entry and inspection, powers of
    1.62
  examples 1.40–1.41, 1.63–1.65
  express terms 1.42
  furnished dwellings 1.38–1.43
  guidance 1.41, 1.66
  implied terms 1.38–1.43, 1.58–
    1.68
  Law Commission proposal for
    general implied term 1.43
  maximum rent 1.59–1.60
  prohibition orders,
    accommodation subject to
    1.68
  reasonable expense 1.67
  unfair contract terms, OFT
    guidance on 1.42
  vermin infestations 7.100

flats *see also* multi-occupied
    property (HMOs)
  asbestos 7.15
  fire precautions 7.62
  noise 7.82
  receiver or manager, appointing a
    3.20
  refuse 7.91
  roofs 1.84
  statutory nuisance 5.8
  structure or exterior 1.84, 1.85
flooding 7.43, 7.55
floor joists 1.83
foreseeability 8.7–8.8
forms
  claim forms 3.88–3.89
  Emergency Legal Representation
    (ELR) 4.47
  injunctions 3.105
  Legal Representation 4.27
freezing injunctions 3.172
Full Representation 4.26, 4.31,
    4.35–4.36
funding *see* conditional fee
    agreements (CFAs); legal
    aid; legal expenses insurance
Funding Code 4.5–4.12, 4.26–4.3
  criteria 4.6, 4.9, 4.11–4.12
  Decision-Making Guidance
    (DMG) 4.6, 4.12
  Emergency Legal Representation
    (ELR) 4.46
  Legal Representation 4.29–4.31,
    4.39–4.42
  Legal Services Commission
    (LSC) Manual 4.7, 4.9–4.11
  parts and sections 4.11
  procedures 4.6, 4.9
  website 4.9
furnished lettings
  dampness 7.28
  fitness for human habitation
    1.38–1.43
  implied terms 1.38–1.43
furniture, damage or loss of 8.36–
    8.37, 8.41

gas safety 7.64–7.69 *see also* services
    (gas, electricity and water)

contractual obligations 7.65
damages 7.67
enforcement 7.68
Gas Safe Register 7.66
Health and Safety Executive 7.68
Housing Act 2004 7.68
inspections 2.41, 7.66–7.67
maintenance 7.65–7.66
proper working order 7.65
**good condition and repair, express
term on** 1.15
guilty pleas 5.67–5.68, 5.75, 5.89

harassment 8.77
hardship 3.164
hazards
assessments of premises under
Housing Act 2004 6.31–6.33,
6.36–6.37
Category 1 hazards 5.108–5.113,
6.21, 6.23, 6.33, 6.36, 6.41–
6.42, 6.51, 6.60, 7.8
Category 2 hazards 6.21, 6.23,
6.41–6.42, 6.33, 6.36, 6.51,
7.8
clearance areas, declaring 6.60,
7.8
definition 6.31–6.32
hazards awareness notices 6.51–
6.52
health *see* prejudicial to human
health
health and safety 7.68
hearing dates 3.157, 5.63, 5.71
heating
damages 8.54, 8.56, 8.71, 8.79–
8.80
dampness 7.36
Help at Court 4.2, 4.18–4.24
experts, reports of 4.23
financial eligibility 4.19
investigations 4.21–4.23
Investigative Help 4.21, 4.23
Legal Representation, boundary
with 4.21–4.24
scope 4.18, 4.24
small claims track 4.45
HMOs *see* multi-occupied property
(HMOs)

home loss payments 6.76
homelessness
demolition orders 6.59
Housing Act 2004 6.12
priority need 6.12, 6.56, 6.59
prohibition orders 6.56
hot water 8.71, 8.77, 8.79
houses in multiple occupation *see*
multi-occupied property
(HMOs)
Housing Act 2004 and bad housing
6.1–6.81
access, providing 6.28
action, selecting the appropriate
6.40–6.50
advantages of provisions 6.3
appeals 6.48, 6.65
assessment of premises 6.30–
6.39
Category 1 or Category 2 hazards
6.21, 6.23, 6.41–6.42
clearance areas, declaring 6.60–
6.61, 6.75
compensation for displaced
tenants 6.72–6.76
complaints 6.14, 6.20–6.25, 6.50
Category 1 or Category 2
hazards 6.21, 6.23
delay 6.26–6.27
Justices of the Peace,
complaints by 6.21, 6.23–
6.25
official complaints 6.20–6.23
parish or community councils,
complaints by 6.21, 6.23
time limits 6.25
council tenants 6.77–6.79
criminal offences 6.69–6.70
dampness 7.38, 7.44
delay 6.26–6.28
demolition orders 6.57–6.59, 6.75
displaced tenants, compensation
for 6.72–6.76
disturbance payments 6.76
emergency prohibition orders
6.62
emergency remedial works 6.62–
6.63
enforcement 6.40–6.71, 6.74

Housing Act 2004 and bad housing
   continued
Enforcement Guidance 6.41–
   6.44, 6.46, 6.71, 6.74
environmental health officers
   (EHOs) 6.10, 6.78
Environment Protection Act 1990
   5.108–5.111
fines 6.69–6.70
forms of action 6.51–6.71
gas safety 7.68
hazards awareness notices 6.51–
   6.52
home loss payments 6.76
homelessness 6.12
housing associations 6.79
improvement notices 6.48, 6.53–
   6.54, 6.65, 6.69
information 6.9
inspections 6.13, 6.15–6.18, 6.21
   access 6.28
   advisers, channelling requests
      through 6.18
   delay 6.26
   Enforcement Guidance 6.16–
      6.17
   further inspections 6.42
   priorities 6.17
   records 6.29
judicial review 6.26, 6.42, 6.49–
   6.50
Justices of the Peace, complaints
   by 6.21, 6.23–6.25
local housing authorities 6.1–6.81
maladministration 6.27
mobilising the local housing
   authorities 6.13–6.29
multi-occupied property (HMOs)
   7.76
overcrowding 7.86
patch repairs 6.66
possession, notice of 6.12
preparations 6.8–6.50
private sector 6.12
procedural delay 6.28
prohibition orders 6.48 6.55–
   6.56, 6.64–6.65, 6.69, 6.74–
   6.75
prosecutions 6.70

public sector tenants 6.77–6.79
purchase of property 6.66–6.67
re-housing 6.11, 6.72–6.76, 6.80
reviews of housing 6.13
suspension of action 6.64–6.65
temporary accommodation
   displaced tenants, for 6.73, 6.75
use of premises as 6.66–6.67
time limits 6.25
transparency 6.47
triggering action 6.5
vulnerable persons, displacement
   of 6.74
works undertaken by housing
   authorities 6.71
housing associations
   Housing Act 2004 6.79
   section 82 proceedings (EPA
      1990) 5.47
   statutory nuisance 5.42–5.44
housing benefit 3.9, 8.25
housing conditions
   area action 7.2–7.14
   asbestos 7.15–7.19
   asthma 7.20–7.23
   condensation dampness 7.24–7.41
   dampness other than
      condensation 7.42–7.46
   dangerous buildings 7.47–7.49
   dilapidated buildings 7.50–7.53
   drains and sewers 7.54–7.59
   fire precautions 7.60–7.63
   gas safety 7.64–7.69
   improvements 7.70–7.73
   multi-occupied property 7.74–
      7.77
   neighbouring property 7.78–7.81
   noise 7.82–7.85
   overcrowding 7.86–7.89
   refuse 7.90–7.91
   sanitary installations 7.92–7.94
   services (gas, electricity and
      water) 7.95–7.96
   standard of repair 1.95–1.96
   Tenant Services Authority (TSA)
      3.26
   vandalism 7.97–7.98
   vermin 7.99–7.103
Housing Ombudsman 3.21, 7.40

housing standards *see* Housing
Act 2004 and bad housing;
housing conditions
Human Rights Act 1998 2.48–2.56
dampness 2.54–2.55
drains and sewers 7.56
environmental pollution 2.51
European Convention on Human
Rights 2.48
nuisance 2.56
peaceful enjoyment of
possessions 2.56
private and family right, right to
respect for 2.50–2.55
public authorities 2.49, 2.53–2.54
sewage 2.56

immunity of landlord 2.3–2.4,
2.9–2.10, 2.28
implied terms 1.3–1.4
1961, tenancies before 1.99
absolute obligations 1.70
access for the landlord 1.111–
1.117
access, means of 1.45
agricultural tenancies 1.98
ancillary property owned by
landlord 1.46–1.47
care and skill 1.56
common law 1.3, 1.37–1.56, 1.72
common parts 1.47, 1.98
communal facilities 1.45
continuing obligations 1.75–1.77
correlative obligations 1.52–1.55
Crown 1.98
damage to property 1.37, 1.44,
1.46
dampness 7.27–7.28
derogation from grant 1.51
dwelling house, meaning of
1.85–1.86
entry, notice of right of 1.74
express terms, exclusion by 1.73
fitness for human habitation
1.38–1.43, 1.58–1.68
fixed-term leases 1.98
furnished dwellings 1.38–1.43
installations 1.72, 1.87–1.94
interpretation 1.75–1.94

'keep in repair' 1.76–1.77
knowledge of defects 1.98
Landlord and Tenant Act 1985
section 8 1.58–1.68
Landlord and Tenant Act 1985
section 11 1.69–1.99
landlord, for the benefit of 1.100–
1.119
licences 1.44
limitations 1.98
notice to landlord 1.100–1.110
periodic tenancies 1.98
personal injury 1.37, 1.44, 1.46
proper working order, keeping in
1.87–1.88, 1.91–1.94
quality of repair work 1.56
quiet enjoyment 1.48–1.50
repairing obligations 1.4
refuse 7.91
standard of repair 1.95–1.97
statute, by 1.3, 1.57–1.99
structure and exterior 1.72, 1.78–
1.86
tenant, for benefit of the 1.37–
1.99
use in a tenant-like manner
1.118–1.119
improvement notices
appeals 6.48, 6.65
contents 6.53
criminal offences 6.69
fines 6.69
Housing Act 2004 6.48, 6.53–
6.54, 6.64–6.65, 6.69
suspension 6.64–6.65
timetable 6.54
improvements *see also* improvement
notices
compulsory improvements 7.73
damp-proof courses 1.26
decorations 1.29
Defective Premises Act 1972 2.45
disproportionately extensive or
costly work 1.26
entry, right of 2.45, 7.72
housing conditions 7.70–7.73
letting agreements 7.72
section 82 proceedings (EPA
1990) 5.86

improvements *continued*
　voluntary improvements 7.71–
　　7.72
inconvenience and distress *see*
　distress and inconvenience
independent contractors, liability
　for 2.12
Independent Housing Ombudsman
　7.40
infestations *see* vermin infestations
inflation 8.32
inherent defects 1.21–1.23
injunctions 3.96–3.115
　costs 3.103, 3.108
　court fees 3.109
　damages 3.98, 3.103, 3.109
　Defective Premises Act 1972 2.47
　dilapidated buildings 7.52
　entry, right of 2.47
　ex parte injunctions 3.110
　expenses, undertakings to
　　reimburse 3.107
　experts at court 3.112
　form N16A 3.105
　freezing injunctions 3.172
　instructions, taking initial 3.34
　interim injunctions 3.96–3.115
　legal aid 3.106–3.107
　mandatory orders for works 3.161
　notice, on 3.110–3.111
　patch repairs 3.97
　penal notice, endorsed with 3.115
　procedure 3.104–3.115
　serious matter to be tried 3.98
　service 3.170
　social landlords 3.100
　tenant, presence of 3.112
　undertakings 3 10, 3.113–3.114
　witness statements 3.105
inspections
　access 6.28
　advisers, channelling requests
　　through 6.18
　assessments of premises under
　　Housing Act 2004 6.30, 6.39
　builders, landlords as 2.6
　Defective Premises Act 1972
　　2.39–2.41, 2.44
　delay 6.26

Enforcement Guidance 6.16–6.17
environmental health officers
　5.43–5.44
evidence 3.70
experts 3.61
fitness for human habitation 1.62
further inspections 6.42
gas installations 2.41, 7.66–7.67
Housing Act 2004 6.13, 6.15–
　6.18, 6.21, 6.28–6.29, 6.42
latent defects 2.39–2.40
multi-occupied property (HMOs)
　7.76
priorities 6.17
records 6.29
statutory nuisance 5.43–5.44
installations *see also* gas safety
　burst pipes 1.93
　dwelling houses, in 1.89–1.94
　implied terms 1.72, 1.87–1.94
　knowledge of defects 1.94
　notice 1.94
　proper working order 1.87–1.88,
　　1.91
　sanitary installations 7.92–7.94
instructions
　assured shorthold tenancies
　　3.33–3.34
　conditional fee arrangements
　　3.30
　damages 3.33, 3.38
　diary of contact with landlord,
　　keeping a 3.37
　expenses and losses, list of 3.38–
　　3.39
　experts 3.59–3.63
　identity of landlord 3.36
　inconvenience and distress, diary
　　of unnecessary 3.37
　initial, taking 3.30–3.39
　injunctions 3.34
　judicial review of refusal to grant
　　a transfer 3.32
　legal aid, eligibility for 3.30
　questionnaires for tenants 3.31
insulation 7.36, 7.82, 7.84
insurance *see* **legal expenses**
　insurance (LEI)
interest 3.125, 8.48

interim applications 3.134–3.137
    costs 3.137
    default judgments 3.135
    defence 3.135–3.136
    injunctions 3.96–3.115, 3.168
    interim payments 3.134, 8.9
    specific performance 3.135
    summary judgments 3.136
intervening acts 8.3–8.5
investigations
    CLSAPP 1 4.27
    experts, reports of 4.34
    Help at Court 4.21–4.23
    Investigative Help 4.21, 4.23,
        4.26–4.27, 4.29, 4.33–4.34
    merits test 4.33
issue of proceedings 3.85–3.95
    children 3.87
    claim forms 3.88
    costs 3.85
    county courts 3.95
    delay 3.53
    final preparations 3.85–3.87
    legal funding, notice of 3.85
    particulars of claim 3.89–3.94

joint tenants 3.44
judicial review
    abatement notices 5.44
    costs 5.99
    Housing Act 2004 6.26, 6.42,
        6.49–6.50
    instructions, taking initial 3.32
    section 82 proceedings (EPA
        1990) 5.99
Justices of the Peace, complaints by
    6.21, 6.23–6.25

'keep in repair', definition of 1.76–
    1.77
knowledge
    defect, where landlord ought to
        have known of 2.37–2.41
    Defective Premises Act 1972
        2.37–2.41
    implied terms 1.98
    installations 1.94
    notice to landlord 1.102–1.103

Landlord and Tenant Act 1985
    section 8 1.58–1.68
Landlord and Tenant Act 1985
    section 11 1.69–1.99, 7.30
latent defects
    builders, landlords as 2.6
    Defective Premises Act 1972
        2.39–2.40
    inherent defects 1.21–1.23
    inspection 2.39–2.40
legal aid 4.1–4.62
    appeals 5.102
    certificates 3.55, 3.58
        amendment 3.154, 3.174, 4.51–
            4.54
        CLSAPP 8 forms 4.52
        counsel, use of 3.79
        counterclaims 3.121
        notice of issue 4.53
        suspension 4.54
    change of circumstances,
        notification of 4.55
    Community Legal Service (CLS)
        4.3
    contributions 4.54
    costs 4.53
    counsel, use of 3.79
    counterclaims 3.121
    early notification letter (ENL)
        3.55
    Emergency Legal Representation
        (ELR) 4.46–4.50
    Funding Code 4.5–4.12
    Help at Court 4.2, 4.18–4.24, 4.45
    injunctions 3.106–3.107
    instructions, taking initial 3.30
    interim payments 3.134
    Legal Help (controlled work)
        3.30, 4.2, 4.13–4.17, 4.45,
        4.57–4.58, 5.51
    Legal Representation 4.2, 4.21–
        4.42, 4.43, 4.45, 4.58, 5.51
    Legal Services Commission
        (LSC) 4.1, 4.3–4.5, 4.53
    notice of issue of certificates 4.53
    Pre-Action Protocol 3.50
    preparation for trial 3.154
    refusal 4.43
    remedies 3.174

legal aid *continued*
responsibilities of assisted
  persons 4.54–4.55
settlements 3.131, 3.133
small claims 4.43–4.45
statutory charge 3.133, 4.56–4.62
suspension of certificates 4.54
trials 3.159
Unified Contract 4.1
legal expenses insurance (LEI)
after-the-event insurance 4.88–
  4.90
before-the-event (BTE) insurance
  4.63–4.67
conditional fee arrangements
  4.87–4.90
premiums, costs of 4.89
legal funding *see also* conditional
  fee agreements (CFAs); legal
  aid
after-the-event insurance 4.88–
  4.90
before-the-event (BTE) insurance
  4.63–4.67
issue of proceedings 3.85
legal expenses insurance 4.63–
  4.67, 4.88–4.90
Local Government Ombudsman
  3.25
notice 3.85
section 82 proceedings (EPA
  1990) 5.51, 5.102
Legal Help 4.2, 4.13–4.17
financial eligibility 3.30, 4.14
fixed fees 4.17
instructions, taking initial 3.30
online calculator 4.14
scope 4.13, 4.16
section 82 proceedings (EPA
  1990) 5.51
small claims track 4.45
statutory charge 4.57–4.58
sufficient benefit test 4.15
legal representation *see also* Legal
  Representation (legal aid)
before-the-event (BTE) insurance
  4.66
conditional fee agreements
  (CFAs) 4.76

counsel, use of 3.78–3.79, 4.95–
  4.96
court proceedings 3.28, 3.78–
  3.79
solicitors 4.66, 4.76, 5.66
Legal Representation (legal aid) 4.2,
  4.21–4.42
alternative dispute resolution 4.31
certificates, scope of 4.41
checklist 4.40
CLSAPP 1 4.27
conditional fee agreements
  (CFAs) 4.38
cost benefit ratios 4.42
damages 4.42
Emergency Legal Representation
  (ELR) 4.46–4.50
fast track claims 4.45
financial eligibility 4.27
forms 4.27
Full Representation 4.26, 4.31,
  4.35–4.36
Funding Code 4.29–4.31, 4.39–
  4.42
guidance 4.30
Help at Court 4.21–4.24
Investigative Help 4.26–4.27,
  4.29, 4.33–4.34
merits test 4.32–4.33
outgoings of tenants 4.28
personal injuries 4.39
possession proceedings 4.37
refusal 4.37–4.38, 4.43
reviews of certificates 4.41
scope 4.41
section 82 proceedings (EPA
  1990) 5.51
small claims track 4.43, 4.45
statutory charge 4.58
Legal Services Commission (LSC)
  4.1, 4.3–4.5, 4.7, 4.9–4.11,
  4.53
letters of claim 3.81–3.84
contents 3.81
counsel, papers sent to 3.83
Pre-Action Protocol 3.50
response 3.84
schedule of intended works 3.84
time limits 3.82–3.84

licences
damage to property 1.44
dampness 7.28
implied terms 1.44
multi-occupied property (HMOs)
7.76
personal injury 1.44
lifts, damages for broken 8.63
limitation of liability 2.20, 2.36, 3.8
limitation periods *see* time limits
Listing Questionnaires 3.155
litigation friends 3.87
Local Government Ombudsman
3.21–3.26
abatement notices 5.44
complaints system, completion of
landlord's 3.22
costs 3.25
dampness 7.39
maladministration 3.22, 3.24,
7.39
public funding 3.25
statutory nuisance 5.44
surveyors, appointment of 3.23
long leases
damages 8.34, 8.52
notice to landlord 1.110
loss of profits 8.8

magistrates *see* section 82
proceedings (EPA 1990)
maladministration 3.22, 3.24, 6.27,
7.39
manager or receiver, appointing a
3.19–3.20
mandatory orders for works 3.161–
3.166
hardship 3.164
injunctions 3.161
penal notices 3.164–3.165
remedies 3.170–3.171
service 3.166
specific performance 3.161–3.163
materials 2.8, 2.23
mediation 3.139, 3.140
mitigation 1.109, 8.43–8.46
mould 1.15, 6.36, 7.24, 7.27
move to alternative premises,
refusal to 8.45–8.46

multi-occupied property (HMOs)
see also flats
default, carrying out works in
7.75
fire safety 7.62, 7.75
Housing Act 2004 7.76
housing conditions 7.74–7.77
inspection 7.76
intervention, local authorities'
powers of 7.75
licences 7.76
multi-track claims 3.142

National Mediation Helpline 3.140
negligence
after letting, works carried out
2.9
before lettings, works carried out
2.8
builders, landlords as 2.5–2.7
causation 8.3–8.6
common law 2.2–2.12
common parts 2.10
contributory negligence 8.47
damages 8.1–8.8, 8.30, 8.47
dampness 2.3
defective workmanship 2.8
drains and sewers 7.55
duty of care 2.2, 2.5–2.7, 2.19,
8.30
economic loss 2.11
foreseeability 8.7–8.8
immunity of landlord 2.3–2.4,
2.9–2.10
independent contractors, liability
for 2.12
intervening acts 8.3–8.5
limits on actions 2.11–2.12
materials 2.8
noise 7.85
remoteness 8.7
vandalism 7.98
vermin infestations 7.100
negotiations 3.76–3.77, 3.156
alternative dispute resolution
(ADR) 3.76–3.77
continuing negotiation 3.156
Pre-Action Protocol 3.76
preparation for trial 3.156

negotiations *continued*
settlements 3.156
vandalism 7.98
neighbouring property
access to neighbouring land
orders 7.81
dangerous buildings 7.80
dilapidated buildings 7.80
environmental health officers
(EHOs) 7.80
housing conditions 7.78–7.81
implied covenants in letting
agreements 7.79
nuisance 2.14, 2.17
statutory nuisance 5.21, 7.80
nine-day notice procedure 5.36–
5.39, 5.43
noise
damages 8.62
distress and inconvenience 7.82
Environmental Protection Act
1990 7.83
excessive or unreasonable noise
7.83
flats 7.82
housing conditions 7.82–7.85
insulation 7.82, 7.84
negligent building or conversion
works 7.85
party walls 7.82
private nuisance 7.83
nominal damages 8.55
notice to landlord of disrepair
Defective Premises Act 1972
1.105
enquiry, putting landlord on
1.105
environmental health officers
(EHOs) 1.103
implied terms 1.100–1.110
knowledge 1.102–1.103
latent defects 1.101
list and estimates, service of
1.105
long leases 1.110
mitigation 1.109
parts of building in control of
landlord 1.108
proof of notice 1.109

reasonable time 1.106–1.107
time limits 3.41
valuers 1.104
notices *see also* notice to landlord of
disrepair
abatement notices 5.23–5.34,
5.40–5.41, 5.44
conditional fee agreements
(CFAs) 4.91–4.92
entry, right of 1.74
hazards awareness notices 6.51–
6.52
improvement notices 6.48, 6.53–
6.54, 6.64–6.65, 6.69
injunctions 3.110–3.111
installations 1.94
legal aid certificates, issue of 4.53
nine-day notice procedure 5.36–
5.39, 5.43
penal notices 3.115, 3.164–3.165
section 82 proceedings (EPA
1990) 5.56
small repairs 7.58
nuisance *see also* statutory nuisance
ancillary property owned by
landlord 2.14
another tenant's property,
affecting 2.17
before letting, defects existing
2.16
children 2.18
common law 2.13–2.18
Defective Premises Act 1972 2.36
demolition 5.87
drains and sewers 7.55, 7.57
enforcement 5.88–5.90
exclusive possession 2.18
Human Rights Act 1998 2.56
noise 7.83
orders 5.83–5.90
penalties 5.91–5.92
pest infestations 2.15
private nuisance 2.13, 2.18, 7.83,
7.91
refuse 7.91
sanitary installations 7.92–7.93
section 82 proceedings (EPA
1990) 5.83–5.90
sewage 2.56

specification of works 5.84–5.85

occupiers' liability
claimants 3.46
common parts 2.21–2.22
duty of care 2.19
exclusion or limitation of liability 2.20
visitors 2.19
Office of Fair Trading (OFT) 1.9, 1.42
ombudsmen 3.21–3.26
apologies 8.59
compensation 8.49–8.50
dampness 7.39–7.40
Housing Ombudsman 3.21, 7.40
Local Government Ombudsman 3.21–3.26, 5.44, 7.39
open sites, nuisance from 5.9
other properties owned by same landlord 2.35
overcrowding 7.86–7.89
enforcement 7.88
Housing Act 2004 7.86
prosecutions 7.88
relator actions 7.88
standards 7.87
statutory limits on number of persons 7.86–7.88

parish or community councils, complaints by 6.21, 6.23
Part 36 offers 3.125–3.132
particulars of claim 3.89–3.94
amendments 3.94
contents 3.90
costs 3.94
documents annexed or served with particulars 3.91
exemplary or aggravated damages 3.92
experts' report as annex 3.91
settlements 3.125
specimen 3.93
statements of value 3.92
partitions 1.83
parts of building
causing disrepair to other parts 1.23

notice to landlord 1.106
party walls 7.82
patch repairs 1.31–1.35
dampness 1.32, 1.34
dry rot 1.33
Housing Act 2004 6.66
injunctions 3.97
necessity or practicability 1.35
section 82 proceedings (EPA 1990) 5.86
payments into court 3.171
peaceful enjoyment of possessions 2.56
penal notices, endorsement with 3.115, 3.164–3.165
personal belongings, damage or loss of 8.36–8.37, 8.39, 8.41
personal injuries
ancillary property owned by landlord 1.46
conditional fee agreements (CFAs) 4.77
damages 8.30, 8.35
Defective Premises Act 1972 2.40, 2.43, 2.46
entry, right of 2.43, 2.46
implied terms 1.37, 1.44, 1.46
Legal Representative 4.39
licences 1.44
time limits 3.40, 3.43
pests *see* **vermin infestations**
pipes 1.93
plaster 1.80–1.81
possession
deposits, failure to register 6.12
Housing Act 2004 6.12
Legal Representation 4.37
notice 6.12
prohibition orders 6.55
section 21 notices 6.12
set-off against rent 3.17
unlicensed buildings 6.12
withholding rent and rent strikes 3.12
Pre-Action Protocol 3.49–3.54
costs and expenses of tenant, paying 3.52
delay of issue of proceedings 3.53

Pre-Action Protocol *continued*
  early notification letter (ENL)
    3.50, 3.54
  experts 3.50, 3.60–3.63
  legal aid 3.50
  letters of claim 3.50
  negotiations 3.76
  purpose 3.49
  settlements 3.50, 3.52
  time limits, extension of 3.51
  website 3.49
prejudicial to human health
  asbestos 7.16–7.17
  compensation orders 5.93, 5.98
  definition 5.12–5.13
  drains and sewers 7.57
  emergency procedure 5.36–5.39,
    5.43
  environmental health officers
    (EHOs) 5.53
  examples 5.15
  experts 5.53
  health, definition of 5.14
  nine-day notice procedure 5.36–
    5.39, 5.43
  nuisance, definition of 5.19
  rooms, arrangement of 5.11
  sanitary installations 7.92–7.93
  section 82 proceedings (EPA
    1990) 5.53, 5.93, 5.98
  statutory nuisance 5.5, 5.10–5.15,
    5.19, 5.36–5.39, 5.43
premises, definition of 5.7–5.9
preparation for trial 3.154–3.156
  cost estimates 3.155
  counsel, use of 3.154
  directions 3.155
  legal aid certificates, extension of
    3.154
  Listing Questionnaires (pre-trial
    checklist) 3.155
  negotiations, continuing with
    3.156
  section 82 proceedings (EPA
    1990) 5.71–5.77
pre-trial checklist 3.155
prevention of future damage 1.30
**private and family right, right to
    respect for** 2.49, 2.53–2.54

private nuisance 2.13, 2.18, 5.18,
    7.83, 7.91
private sector
  Housing Act 2004 6.12
  section 82 proceedings (EPA
    1990) 5.47
prohibition orders
  appeals 6.48, 6.65
  compensation 6.56
  contents 6.55
  criminal offences 6.69
  damages 8.73
  displaced tenants 6.74–6.75
  fines 6.69
  fitness for human habitation 1.68
  homelessness, priority need and
    6.56
  Housing Act 2004 6.48, 6.55–
    6.56, 6.64–6.65, 6.69, 6.74–
    6.75
  possession proceedings 6.55
  rehousing and compensation 6.56
  suspension 6.64–6.65
proper working order
  gas safety 7.65
  implied terms 1.87–1.88, 1.91–
    1.94
  installations 1.87–1.88, 1.91, 7.65,
    7.92
  sanitary installations 7.92
  services (gas, electricity and
    water) 7.95–7.96
property, damage to *see* damage to
    property
protected or statutory tenancies
    1.116–1.117, 3.18
protocol *see* Pre-Action Protocol
**public authorities, Human Rights
    Act 1998 and** 2.49, 2.53–2.54
public funding *see* conditional fee
    agreements (CFAs); legal
    aid; legal expenses insurance
public nuisance 5.18
purchase of property 6.66–6.67

quality of repair work 1.56
questionnaires 3.31 *see also*
    allocation questionnaires
    (AQs)

quiet enjoyment, implied term of 1.48–1.50

receipts for expenses and losses 3.38–3.39
receiver or manager, appointing a 3.19–3.20, 3.173
refuse
code of refuse disposal 7.90
collection authorities 7.90
damages 8.58, 8.62, 8.68
flats 7.91
housing conditions 7.90–7.91
implied terms 7.91
private nuisance 7.91
rubbish chutes 7.91
removal of accumulations by local authorities 7.90
vermin 7.90
rehousing *see also* displaced tenants
area action 7.6
compensation 6.56, 7.6
Housing Act 2004 6.11, 6.72–6.76, 6.80
prohibition orders 6.56
relator actions 7.88
remedies *see also* damages; injunctions
attachment of earnings orders 3.173
bankruptcy 3.173
charging orders 3.173
civil remedies 3.1–3.174
contempt, committal for 3.170
costs 3.173, 3.174
court proceedings 3.27–3.134, 3.170–3.174
declarations 3.167–3.168
direct actions 3.3–3.26
final orders 3.170–3.173
legal aid certificates, amendment of 3.174
mandatory orders, breach of 3.170–3.171
receivers, appointment of 3.173
specific performance 3.132, 3.135, 3.161–3.166, 3.170
statutory demands 3.173
warrants of execution 3.173

works be carried out, directions that 3.171
remoteness 8.7
renewal
definition 1.18
renewal areas, declaring 7.5, 7.11–7.13
repair and disrepair, definition of 1.31–1.35
whole property, of 1.12
renewal areas, declaring 7.5, 7.11–7.13
consultation with public 7.13
local authorities 7.11–7.13
reports 7.12
rent *see also* rent to pay for repairs, using; set-off against rent arrears
clearing 4.79
counterclaims 3.116, 3.122–3.124
possession claims 3.116, 3.122–3.124
change in condition, reduction for 3.18
conditional fee agreements (CFAs) 4.79
counterclaims 3.116, 3.122–3.124, 8.72, 8.75–8.78
damages
counterclaims 8.72, 8.75–8.78
general damages, level of 8.18–8.20
loss of rental value 8.23, 8.25–8.27
reduction 8.16
fair rent 8.26
fitness for human habitation 1.59–1.60
maximum rent 1.59–1.60
reduction 3.18, 8.26
Rent Act tenants 1.116–1.117, 3.18
set-off 3.13–3.17, 3.118
withholding rent and rent strikes 3.11–3.12
rent to pay for repairs, using 3.4–3.10
Better Deal for Tenants 3.10
exclusions in tenancy agreements 3.8

rent to pay for repairs, using
  continued
  housing benefit, tenants in
    receipt of 3.9
  reasonableness 3.5
  set-off against rent, distinguished
    from 3.6, 3.14
  statutory scheme 3.10
  unfair contract terms, exclusion
    of liability in 3.8
response
  court proceedings 3.59, 3.84
  early notification letter (ENL)
    3.59
  letters of claim 3.84
reversion, disposal of 2.28
right of entry *see* entry, right of
rooms, arrangement of 5.11
roof terraces 1.84
roofs 1.83–1.84
rubbish *see* refuse

sanitary installations 7.92–7.94
  environmental health officers
    (EHOs) 7.92
  insufficient facilities 7.93
  nuisance 7.92–7.93
  prejudicial to health 7.92–7.93
  proper working order 7.92
  replacements, need for 7.93
schedule of intended works 3.84
Scottish Grand Committee review
    7.45
section 82 proceedings (EPA 1990)
    5.45–5.107
  adjournments 5.68
  appeals 5.99, 5.102
  bundles 5.76
  clerks of local authorities, service
    of notice on 5.56
  compensation orders 5.93–5.98
    anxiety and distress 5.93–5.94
    assessment 5.94
    civil claims, impact on 5.97–
      5.98
    conditional fee arrangements
      5.104
    costs 5.103
    damages 5.97–5.98

  payment, procedure for 5.106
  prejudicial to health 5.93, 5.98
  reasons for refusal, duty to give
    5.96
conditional fee arrangements
  (CFAs) 5.66, 5.104
costs 5.64, 5.99–5.107
counsel, use of 5.66
damages 5.97–5.98
defence statements 5.73
demolition 5.87, 5.109
disclosure 5.51, 5.72–5.73
enforcement 5.88–5.90
environmental health officers
    (EHOs)
  duties 5.54
  engagement of independent
    EHO 5.51
  experts 5.53–5.55
  prejudicial to health 5.53
  reports, service of 5.54
  trial, availability for 5.69, 5.71
evidence, proof of 5.76
experts 5.53–5.55
fees, waiver of 5.105
findings 5.79
fines 5.91–5.92
first hearings 5.63–5.70
guilty pleas 5.67–5.68, 5.75, 5.89
hearing dates 5.63, 5.71
housing association tenants 5.47
improvements 5.86
information 5.57–5.62, 5.111
judicial review 5.99
legal funding 5.51, 5.102
Legal Help 5.51
Legal Representation 5.51
local authorities, against 5.45–
    5.107
magistrates, independence of
    5.77
notice of intended proceedings
    5.56
nuisance orders 5.83–5.92
occupation until work carried
    out, prohibition of 5.113
overview of procedure 5.50
patch repairs 5.86
penalties 5.91–5.92

prejudicial to health 5.53, 5.93, 5.98
preparation for trial 5.71–5.77
preparatory work 5.51
private sector tenants 5.47
procedure 5.50, 5.52–5.82
public sector tenants, action by 5.45–5.107
recurrence, orders prohibiting 5.67
schedule of items destroyed or damaged 5.51
solicitors, representation by 5.66
standard of proof 5.80, 5.111
statements 5.51, 5.60, 5.74
structural defects 5.82
summons 5.60–5.61, 5.88
time limits 5.56
trials 5.78–5.82
wasted costs orders 5.107
website 5.52
who may bring proceedings 5.48–5.49
witness statements 5.74
works schedule 5.67
works, specification of 5.84–5.85
sequestration 3.171
services (gas, electricity and water) 7.95–7.96
set-off against rent 3.13–3.17
assignment 3.16
counterclaims 3.14–3.15, 3.118
damages 3.13, 3.15–3.16
equitable set-off 3.13–3.14
possession orders 3.17
rent to pay for repairs, distinguishing using 3.6, 3.14
unfair contract terms 1.9
settlements 3.125–3.133
costs 3.52, 3.125, 3.131, 3.133
damages 3.125–3.126, 3.128, 3.131–3.132
expenses 3.52
interest 3.125
legal aid 3.131, 3.133
mediation 3.140
negotiations 3.156
Part 36 offers 3.125–3.132

particulars of claim 3.125
Pre-Action Protocol 3.50, 3.52
specific performance 3.132
specimen letters 3.125
statutory charge 3.133
Tomlin orders 3.129–3.130
sewers *see* drains and sewers
skylights 1.83
slum clearances 7.3
small claims track
allocation questionnaires 3.142
allocation to track 4.44–4.45
costs 3.142
legal aid 4.43–4.45
Help at Court 4.45
Legal Help 4.45
Legal Representation 4.43, 4.45
small defects 1.26–1.28
deterioration, meaning of 1.28
drains and sewers 7.58
solicitors
before-the-event (BTE) insurance 4.66
conditional fee agreements (CFAs) 4.76
freedom of choice of solicitor 4.66
section 82 proceedings (EPA 1990) 5.66
Solicitors' Code of Conduct 4.76
specific performance 3.135, 3.170
common parts 3.163
defence 3.135
disposal hearings 3.135
fast track claims 3.143
mandatory orders for works 3.161–3.163
settlements 3.132
standard of proof 5.80, 5.111
standard of repair
age, character and locality 1.95
demolition 1.96
expert evidence 1.95
implied terms 1.95–1.97
prospective life 1.95–1.96
standard terms 1.8
standards *see* Housing Act 2004 and bad housing; housing conditions
statements *see* witness statements

statements of truth 3.152
statutory charge 4.56–4.62
    costs 4.59, 4.61–4.62
    damages 4.59–4.60, 4.62
    Legal Help 4.57–4.58
    Legal Representation 4.58
    settlements 3.133
statutory demands 3.173
statutory nuisance 5.5–5.109 *see
        also* section 82 (EPA 1990)
        proceedings
    abatement notices 5.23–5.25,
        5.40–5.41, 5.44
    common parts 5.8
    criminal proceedings 5.49
    definition 5.5
    emergency procedures 5.36–5.39,
        5.43
    environmental health officers
        (EHOs), action by 5.42–5.45
    examples 5.15, 5.21
    flats 5.8
    High Court actions by local
        authorities 5.35
    housing association tenants,
        action by 5.42–5.44
    inspections by environmental
        health officers 5.43–5.44
    local authorities, action by 5.23–
        5.41
    Local Government Ombudsman
        5.44
    neighbouring property 5.21, 7.80
    nine-day notice procedure 5.36–
        5.39, 5.43
    nuisance, definition of 5.16–5.22
    open sites 5.9
    prejudicial to health 5.5, 5.10–5.15
        definition 5.12–5.13
        emergency procedure 5.36–
            5.39, 5.43
        examples 5.15
        health, definition of 5.14
        nine-day notice procedure
            5.36–5.39, 5.43
        nuisance, definition of 5.19
        rooms, arrangement of 5.11
    premises, definition of 5.7–5.9
    private nuisance 5.18

    public nuisance 5.17
    public sector tenants, action by
        5.45–5.49
    recurring nuisances 5.40–5.41
    remedial works, notice of
        intention to carry out 5.37–
        5.38
    state of premises 5.10–5.12
    tenants and other occupiers,
        action by 5.42–5.49
    vermin infestations 7.102
    visits by environmental health
        officers 5.43–5.44
statutory or protected tenancies
        1.116–1.117, 3.18
structure or exterior 1.14–1.15
    abatement notices 5.28
    condensation 1.15, 7.30–7.31
    correlative obligations 1.54–1.55
    cracking 8.66–8.67, 8.81
    damages 8.66–8.67, 8.81
    definition 1.78
    drains and sewers 7.56
    dwelling-houses 1.86
    examples 1.83
    express terms 1.14–1.15
    flats 1.84, 1.86
    floor joists 1.83
    implied terms 1.72, 1.78–1.86
    mould 1.15
    partitions 1.83
    plaster 1.80–1.81
    roof terraces 1.84
    roofs 1.83–1.84
    section 82 proceedings (EPA
        1990) 5.82
    skylights 1.83
    vandalism 7.97
    walls 1.83
    windows 1.83
subsidence 8.67, 8.81
success fees 4.71–4.72, 4.83–4.86,
        4.91–4.96, 5.104
summary judgments 3.136
summons 5.60–5.61, 5.88
surveyors, appointment of 3.23

temporary accommodation
    clearance areas, in 1.68

displaced tenants 6.73, 6.75
Housing Act 2004 6.66–6.67,
6.73, 6.75
Tenant Services Authority (TSA)
codes of practice 3.26
compensation 3.26
Local Government Ombudsman,
compensation awarded by
3.26
social housing 3.26
standards 3.26
terms 1.8–1.9 *see* express terms;
implied terms; unfair
contract terms
time limits 3.40–3.43
abatement notices 5.25
allocation questionnaires 3.138,
3.144
bundles, filing 3.158
cause of action, accrual of 3.40–
3.42
complaints 6.25
damages 3.41
Defective Premises Act 1972 2.27,
3.42
early notification letter (ENL)
3.55
extension 3.51
Housing Act 2004 6.25
letters of claim 3.82–3.84
notice to landlord 3.41
personal injuries 3.40, 3.43
Pre-Action Protocol 3.51
section 82 proceedings (EPA
1990) 5.56
separate actions 3.43, 3.47
Tomlin orders 3.129–3.130
tort *see also* negligence
causation 8.3–8.6
contributory negligence 8.47
damages 8.1–8.8, 8.47
foreseeability 8.7–8.8
intervening acts 8.3–8.5
remoteness 8.7
transparency 6.47
trespass 8.61
trials 3.157–3.160
bundles 3.158
costs, schedule of 3.159

environmental health officers
(EHOs), availability of 5.69,
5.71
hearing dates 3.157, 5.63, 5.71
legal aid 3.159
Listing Questionnaires (pre-trial
checklist) 3.155
preparation for trial 3.154–3.155
procedure 3.160
section 82 proceedings (EPA
1990) 578–5.82

unfair contract terms 1.8–1.9
exclusion of liability 3.8
fitness for human habitation 1.42
guidance 1.9
Office of Fair Trading 1.9, 1.42
rent to pay for repairs, using 3.8
set-off against rent, right of 1.9
standard terms 1.8
unilateral variation of terms 1.8
Unified Contract 4.1
use in a tenant-like manner
chimneys, cleaning 1.119
examples 1.118
implied terms 1.118

valuers 1.104
vandalism
distress or damage, liability for
7.98
exterior 7.97
negligence 7.98
neighbouring property 7.98
windows 7.97
variation of terms 1.8, 1.11
ventilation 7.29, 7.36
vermin infestations 7.99–7.103
breach of contract 7.100
damages 8.57, 8.68, 8.69, 8.91–
8.94
fitness for human habitation
7.100
negligence 7.100
nuisance 2.15, 7.102
refuse 7.90
visitors 2.19, 2.28, 2.31, 2.46
**visits by environmental health
officers (EHOs)** 5.43–5.44

walls 1.83, 7.82
warrants of execution 3.173
wasted costs orders 5.107
water penetration
    damages 8.52–8.53, 8.56, 8.60,
        8.65, 8.68, 8.74–8.75
    inherent defects 1.22
water services 7.95–7.96
windows 1.83, 7.97, 8.64, 8.80
withholding rent and rent strikes
    3.11–3.12
witness statements
    cooperation, lack of 3.153
    court proceedings 3.71, 3.74,
        3.151–3.153
    injunctions 3.105
    proofs of evidence 3.151
    section 82 proceedings (EPA
        1990) 5.74
    signatures 3.152

    specimen statements 3.105
    statements of truth 3.152
works
    abatement notices, doing work
        specified in 5.34
    after letting, works carried out
        2.9
    before lettings, works carried out
        2.8
    directions for works to be carried
        out 3.171
    disproportionately extensive or
        costly work 1.24–1.26
    Housing Act 2004 6.71
    mandatory orders for works
        3.161–3.166
    quality 1.56
    section 82 proceedings (EPA
        1990) 5.67, 5.84–5.85
    specification 5.84–5.85

Housing Law Casebook

Fourth edition

Nic Madge and Claire Sephton

'An essential addition to any housing practitioner's library.' *Independent Lawyer*

'An indispensable purchase.' *Adviser*

'an immensely important book for practitioners.' *Civil Justice Quarterly*

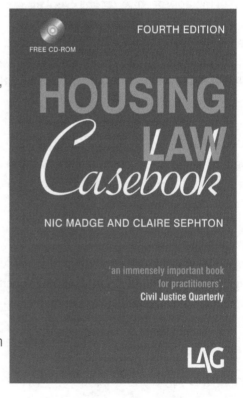

2008 Pb 978 1 903307 45 8
1192pp £55

*This edition comes with a free, fully searchable CD-Rom containing the full text of the *Housing Law Casebook*

www.lag.org.uk/books